# Representing Women

# Representing Women

*Sex, Gender, and Legislative Behavior
in Arizona and California*

*by*
Beth Reingold

The University of North Carolina Press ▾ Chapel Hill and London

Library of Congress Cataloging-in-Publication Data
Reingold, Beth.
    Representing women: sex, gender, and legislative
behavior in Arizona and California / by Beth Reingold.
        p.   cm.
    Includes bibliographical references and index.
    ISBN 0-8078-2538-7 (cloth: alk. paper)—
    ISBN 0-8078-4850-6 (pbk.: alk. paper)
    1. Women legislators—Arizona. 2. Women
legislators—California. 3. Women in politics—Arizona.
4. Women in politics—California. I. Title.
JK8278.R45 2000
328.791′092′2-dc21
                                        99-053084

Portions of Chapters 4 and 7 appeared, in somewhat
different form, in two articles previously published by
the author: "Concepts of Representation among Female
and Male State Legislators," *Legislative Studies Quarterly* 17,
no. 4 (November 1992): 509–37 (© 1992 by the Comparative
Legislative Research Center); and "Conflict and Cooperation:
Legislative Strategies and Concepts of Power among Female
and Male State Legislators," *Journal of Politics* 58, no. 2 (May
1996): 464–85 (© 1996 by the University of Texas Press).
They are reprinted here by permission of the publishers.

04   03   02   01   00     5   4   3   2   1

# Contents

# Tables

# Acknowledgments

I am an acknowledgments junkie. Rarely do I begin a scholarly book or journal article without reading the acknowledgments first. There are numerous reasons why I find these tributes so interesting and meaningful, and increasingly so. In part, I suppose this is an exercise in professional socialization—learning who should be mentioned (or not), getting a close-up and personal view of the research and writing process, preparing for that hopeful day when I will have my own acknowledgments to write. Most of all, I find acknowledgments comforting. It is reassuring to know that no one does this alone, that I am not the only one who depends upon teachers, colleagues, students, friends, and family to get through the tough times and to share in the celebration of accomplishments and good fortune. I am also reassured to see that the research we political scientists call "science" is, indeed, a community effort. We really do learn from and with each other as we give and receive critical (though not always negative) feedback. It is this sort of collaboration and constructive scrutiny that makes our work truly scientific.

With these thoughts in mind I take great pleasure in acknowledging and thanking those who have been there for me and with me. This book is the culmination of a decade's worth of work, and I am fortunate to have many people to thank. Most have fulfilled more than one role: teachers have been friends and colleagues; friends and colleagues have been family; family have been teachers. Everyone, at some point and in some way, has provided emotional support, substantive input, and practical advice without which I could not have completed this project.

First, this research would not have been possible without the generous assistance of various funding agencies at the University of California at Berkeley (UC Berkeley): the Graduate Division, the Institute for Governmental Studies, the Beatrice M. Bain Research Group, and the California Alpha Chapter of Phi Beta Kappa. I am also indebted to the legislators who so graciously agreed to participate in this study. They were the ones who taught me the most about "representing women" and legislative life in general. Despite their heavy workloads and frantic schedules, most were extremely generous with their time and wisdom. Their enthusiasm, warmth, and humor made doing the research for this book a joy. Before, during, and after my interviews with California legislators, Beth Capell provided much insight and guidance for navigating the practical and political ins and outs of the legislature. As a full-time lobbyist and political science Ph.D., Beth's "insider-outsider" perspective was invaluable. Samm MacMurdo provided similar assistance with the ins and outs of Arizona legislative politics; she was also a much-needed friendly face in a land of strangers.

Members of my dissertation committee—Jack Citrin, Nelson Polsby, and Gene Bardach of the University of California at Berkeley, and Janet Flammang of Santa Clara University—have guided and supported this research from the very beginning, and for that I am very grateful. Each offered just-right combinations of criticism and praise, skepticism and encouragement, guidance and freedom. Special thanks go to Janet, who generously gave much of her time, effort, and insight to this project—before, during, and long after the dissertation was completed. As my window to the world of women and politics and my sounding board for the world of women in academia, she has been an extremely important role model.

Jack has been so much more than a dissertation chair that it is difficult to figure out where and how to begin to acknowledge his help. He is the kind of mentor we all should aspire to be. As his student, I was and still am the beneficiary of his thoughtful intelligence, expansive knowledge, sage wisdom, curmudgeon humor, steadfast support, and generous friendship. Jack made available the quantity and quality of opportunities for professional and scholarly development that every graduate student dreams of. No one has taught me more about political science and about how to be a political scientist.

There are numerous other people who deserve a great deal of thanks for helping me get this project off the ground, from the first inklings of a dissertation prospectus, to the conduct of the research in Sacramento and Phoenix, to what in retrospect looks like an extremely rough but functional dissertation. Many friends and graduate student colleagues in the Berkeley political science department provided much-needed help and support. My dissertation study group—including Paula Consolini, Taylor Dark, John Gerring, Marissa Martino Golden, and Duane Oldfield—had a profoundly beneficial influence on the conduct and analysis of my research. Among other things, they painstakingly helped me design the interview schedule and follow-up survey, read drafts of chapters, offered constructive criticism, and held me to deadlines. Together, we shared our many frustrations, encouraged each other's progress, and learned what true collegiality is all about. I thank Marissa Martino Golden especially for her continuing support. This manuscript has benefited greatly from her input and from the opportunities she provided for additional input from others, including her colleagues and students at the University of Pennsylvania and Bryn Mawr College.

The faculty, staff, and graduate students at Berkeley's Survey Research Center (SRC) provided an extraordinarily pleasant and conducive place to work. My office mates, Don Green and later Chris Muste, were wonderful sources of knowledge, inspiration, understanding, and humor. Data archivists Ilona Einowski and Ann Gerken Green provided much expertise, especially when it came to slogging through California survey data; plus, they were instrumental in making the SRC the friendly, collegial, and productive place it was. Laura Stoker, who joined the political science and SRC faculty during my last year in residence, was tremendously helpful and generous with her time. Finally, SRC would not have been same without the other graduate students who worked (and played) there: Marty Gilens, Jim Glaser, Marissa Martino Golden, Michael Hagen, and Jon Krasno. Personally, intellectually, and professionally, I owe many thanks to these and other dear friends-and-colleagues whom I had the pleasure of meeting at Berkeley, including Michael Gorges, Deborah Norden, Mina Silberberg, and Robin Silver.

Much of the work for this project has been completed since I joined the faculty at Emory University. The Department of Political Science and the Institute for Women's Studies have provided the tangible and intangible resources necessary to complete my dissertation, continue analyzing and re-analyzing my data, write and rewrite journal articles, and write and rewrite (and rewrite!) this book manuscript. My colleagues and friends at Emory, much like their counterparts at Berkeley, have created and fostered a very collegial, stimulating, and supportive community in which to work (and play). I am deeply appreciative of all the hard work and long hours Harvey Klehr, Tom Walker, Betsy Fox-Genovese, Martine Brownley, and Robyn Fivush devoted as either chair of the Political Science Department or director of the Institute for Women's Studies; I am even more thankful for all the support and guidance they have given me over the years. Together, they made sure that I could and would want to be an active member of both faculties, without being drawn in opposite directions or simply spread too thin. My research and writing has benefited greatly from Karen O'Connor's generous, effective, and encouraging assistance. Special thanks also go to my junior (or once-junior) colleagues in political science and women's studies.

I have been blessed with a large cohort of extremely bright, interesting, and caring junior colleagues, from whom I have learned so much. At a critical juncture in the development of this manuscript, my junior cohorts in Political Science organized a forum in which I could "think out loud," reformulate many of my thoughts about the significance of this project, and construct many of the basic theoretical arguments presented here. Their feedback was most helpful and reassuring. Soon thereafter, my colleagues in Women's Studies provided another opportunity to present my work as part of our ongoing colloquium. This too was a great opportunity to clarify my arguments and receive very constructive feedback.

In addition to their scholarly and professional support, many of the faculty and staff at Emory have offered their friendship, which I consider equally important. I am especially grateful to Irene Browne, who has helped me navigate numerous twists and turns in my professional and personal lives; David Davis, whose enthusiasm about everything—from research and teaching to cooking and parenting—is infectious; and Judith Miller, whose zestful determination, indomitable will, and implacable sense of humor have helped me appreciate and treasure all that life has to offer.

Many of the students at Emory, both undergraduate and graduate, have challenged and stimulated my thoughts about sex, gender, legislative behavior, and political representation. With their help, the classroom has been an incomparable resource for knowledge and reflection. I am especially grateful to those graduate students who helped collect data, code data, transcribe interviews, edit and proofread drafts, and who carefully read and commented on those same drafts: Chris Carlson, Rebecca Davis, Heather Foust, Holly Gunning, Paige Schneider, and Liz Stiles. Their assistance and interest in this project have meant a great deal to me.

Outside the environs of UC Berkeley and Emory University, two people have been instrumental in shaping this manuscript and making its publication possible. Virginia Sapiro's extremely careful reading, detailed comments, and insightful suggestions helped transform this manuscript from a fairly tedious dissertation to a more interesting and critical text that someone outside my dissertation committee can appreciate. She challenged me to think hard, to explore new avenues, and to reexamine what I and many others had taken for granted; and she provided many valuable tools with which to accomplish such a daunting set of tasks. Lewis Bateman, my editor at the University of North Carolina Press, then guided and supported the lengthy process of rewriting and reconstructing the manuscript with the utmost of patience, understanding, and enthusiasm. Together, Virginia and Lew saw a great deal of potential in my work and devoted a considerable amount of time and effort to making sure that potential was realized; and for that I cannot thank them enough.

My final and most heartfelt thanks go to my family: my parents, Maxine and Harold Reingold; my brother and sister, Steve Reingold and Sharon Rauch; and my husband, Tom Willett. Somehow, my parents managed to instill in me a thirst for learning and a deep appreciation for all the opportunities that have been more or less available to me. I honestly don't know how they did that. Perhaps it was the combination of their confidence in my abilities and their trust in me. Perhaps it was their willingness to let me set and pursue my own goals. Perhaps it was the examples they set pursuing their own careers in education and academia. Perhaps it was their appreciation for just how long and difficult this whole process really is. (As far as I know, I am one of the very few Ph.D.'s whose parents never asked in frustration why writing a dissertation takes so long.) Most likely, it was all this and more. Certainly, my sister and brother made a difference. As older siblings often do, they helped me learn, at a very early age, how to pedal through adversity (so to speak); they taught me, usually by example, many of the most valuable lessons of life; and eventually they became two of my best friends and confidantes. Tom, the newest member of my family, has seen me through to the completion of this project. He has held my hand, held me up, and held me together. He has maintained my computers, my sanity, and my hope for the future. He has shown and taught me, in so many ways, that true love conquers all.

Over these many years, my family's support has never faltered, even when it became clear that my career would lead me far away from home or, in Tom's case, keep me away from home for too many hours in the day (and night). *Their* homes are the ones to which I want to come back when the day is done. For in the end, it is the love, pride, and joy I share with them that makes all this work worthwhile.

# Introduction

Women in Arizona and California politics made history in the 1998 elections. "It's a Woman's World" in Arizona, declared the *Los Angeles Times*, for women had just been elected to the top five statewide offices—governor, secretary of state, attorney general, treasurer, and superintendent of public instruction (Cart 1998). In California, a record number of women, ten, had been elected to the state senate, pushing the state legislature as a whole above the national average for percentage of women for the first time. "Women," a *Los Angeles Times* headline proclaimed, will "play largest role ever in [the] legislature" (Pyle 1998).

As memorable as these milestones may be, they are part and parcel of nationwide trends that began a quarter century ago. Since 1975, the percentages of women occupying elected offices at every level of American government have slowly but steadily increased: from 4 percent of members of Congress to 12 percent; from 10 percent of statewide executive officeholders (governors, lieutenant governors, secretaries of state, etc.) to 28 percent; and from 8 percent of state legislators to 22 percent.[1] Embedded within these trends lie many, many milestones and records like the ones achieved just recently in Arizona and California. As each milestone is reached, as one record is broken by another, many of the same questions arise. What exactly is so significant about the increasing presence of women in public office? What difference does it make? If women in state legislatures are playing the "largest role ever," what role is that? What does, or will, a "woman's world" look like?

This study compares the behavior of female and male members of the 1990 Arizona and California state legislatures to illuminate the broader implications and consequences of the election and integration of American women into public office. As the double entendre of the title "Representing

Women" implies, I am particularly interested in what these trends mean for the political representation of women in the United States. Are women in public office simply women who represent, or are they also women who represent women? And what about the men in public office—do they represent women? Do they represent women to the same extent their female counterparts do? Does the election of more and more women mean that women will be better represented?

I am by no means the first and only political observer to raise these questions; numerous scholars interested in the impact of women in elective office in the U.S. have been addressing such issues, directly or indirectly, for quite some time. Thus far, the bulk of this research offers a remarkably consistent set of answers: women in public office—at the national, state, and local levels—do "make a difference" and have been doing so at least since the late 1970s. The difference they make, moreover, is particularly notable on "women's issues," or "issues pertaining to the welfare of women and children" (Carroll 1991: 45).[2] As one scholar has surmised: "research evidence over the last ten years supports the belief that many women politicians are different because they see things differently, because they understand the needs of women in society in a way that men cannot, and because many, if not most of them, will try to make the nation a better place for women and their families" (Mezey 1994: 256).

To begin, research has found that the policy preferences of female officials tend to be more liberal than those of their male colleagues. Women in public office also are more feminist in their support for such issues as the Equal Rights Amendment, abortion rights, child support enforcement, harsher penalties for sexual assault and violence against women, and so forth (Barrett 1995; Burrell 1994; Diamond 1977; Dodson and Carroll 1991; Dolan 1997; Durst and Rusek 1993; Frankovic 1977; Johnson and Carroll 1978; Leader 1977; Poole and Zeigler 1985; Vega and Firestone 1995; Welch 1985).[3] Furthermore, female officeholders exhibit more concern about issues pertaining to women, children, and families. Compared to their male counterparts, they are more likely to initiate and propose such policies, more likely to express keen interest in them, and more likely to take active, leadership roles in securing their passage and implementation (Boles 1991; Burrell 1994; Dodson 1996; Dodson and Carroll 1991; Gertzog 1995; Saint-Germain 1989; Tamerius 1995; Thomas 1991, 1994; Thomas and Welch 1991).

Some evidence suggests that women in office have distinctive ways of "doing politics" (Flammang 1985: 105), which reflect dominant modes of female socialization. For example, in a 1977 survey of public officials that asked women whether they enjoyed any special advantages as a result of being women in public office, many said they were better at constituent or public relations. The women saw themselves as more approachable, more trusted, and more responsive to the needs and demands of their constituents. Some also thought that, as women, they possessed superior interpersonal skills that enabled them to be more understanding of others, more patient, and more skilled at effecting compromise. Many of the male officeholders surveyed offered the same observations about their female colleagues (Johnson and Carroll 1978: 40A–43A). Other studies have uncovered similar differences in female and male officials' attitudes toward or approaches to representational duties and activities (Beck 1991; Bers 1978; Flammang 1985; Merritt 1980; Mezey 1978b; Richardson and Freeman 1995; Thomas 1992), as well as their legislative, managerial, and leadership styles (Duerst-Lahti and Johnson 1990, 1992; Flammang 1985; Havens and Healy 1991; Jewell and Whicker 1994; Kathlene 1989, 1994; Kelly, Hale, and Burgess 1991; Rinehart 1991; Thomas 1994). Overall, this research presents female officials as more responsive to constituents and more cooperative, inclusive, and holistic in their approaches to both the substance and process of public policymaking.

As the story goes, there was a time when women in public office were so few in number and when prevailing attitudes were so much less congenial to feminism and women in power that elected women did not dare "make a difference" for women, as women (Gertzog 1995; Saint-Germain 1989; Thomas 1994; Witt, Paget, and Matthews 1994). Irwin Gertzog reported that many of these pioneers "saw their gender as a potential political liability, and they avoided identification with what were generally considered to be 'women's issues.' They believed too close association with such issues would subvert their reputation as serious, valuable legislators who were more interested in the international security and economic vitality of the country than in what were seen as the parochial and, ultimately, illegitimate concerns of women as a 'special interest' " (Gertzog 1995: 9–10; see also Gehlen 1977; Mezey 1978a, 1978b). Thus, in places where women continue to constitute a very small, very vulnerable group—including a number of state legislatures—sex differences in political behavior are few and far between; and, presumably, the representation of women and their political interests suffers. More positively, these researchers argue that the growing number of women elected and appointed to public office holds great promise for further progress on women's issues and women's political representation (see also Flammang 1987).

In reviewing this research and my own, I have come to realize that the story is not really quite so simple, nor so stark. The sex differences uncovered are differences in degree, not kind. There are almost always numerous men who behave in ways deemed representative of women, and there are almost always numerous women who do not. Usually the differences *among* women or *among* men are greater than the differences between the sexes. Differences associated with partisanship and ideology often are much greater than those related to sex or gender. The relationship between the proportion of women present in political decision-making bodies and the size and prevalence of sex differences therein is not a particularly strong one. In short, the behavior of public officials is by no means completely or even primarily a function of sex or sex ratios, even when it concerns the representation of women's policy and policymaking preferences.

The frequency and significance of sex *similarities* among public officials remains underexplored. The overlap between and the commonalities among these men and women have been relegated to "ifs, ands, or buts" that qualify the "women make a difference" conclusions. Analysis of similarity is neglected when compared to the lengthy discussions of the causes, consequences, and implications of differences (see Chapter 1).[4] When explanations for limited sex-related differentiation are provided, more often than not they center around the hegemonic force of male domination in the political world, especially that of political elites.[5] Political leaders, the vast majority of whom have always been male, interact within institutional cultures that uphold masculinity as the norm and treat as deviant anything female, feminine, or feminist (Thomas 1997: 44–47). To be successful, perhaps even to survive, female politicians must therefore act like men. It is a struggle and an achievement for women to do otherwise.

Indeed, there is no legislative body in the United States (state or national) in which women are not in the minority. And these institutions have long been viewed as men's clubs. In one of the first studies of women in public office, Jeane Kirkpatrick asserted that American state legislatures "share the *macho* culture of the locker room, the smoker, the barracks" (1974: 106, emphasis in original). All but a few of the female and male members of Congress interviewed by Gertzog (1995: 11) in the late 1970s agreed that the House could be described accurately as a "male institution." The congresswomen also were well aware of frequent "condescending, patronizing, and less often, just plain insulting treatment" from their male peers (Gertzog 1995: 68). Nearly half of all women in the aforementioned 1977 survey of public officials named problems with male chauvinism and negative stereotyping as difficulties they encountered as women in office (Johnson and Carroll 1978: 43A).

The power of such masculine norms to exact conformity is thought to be more or less severe depending upon the proportion of men and women in any given political decision-making body. According to Rosabeth Kanter's (1977) oft-cited theory and research on the effects of skewed sex ratios, women who constitute a very small "token" minority are subject to disproportionate visibility and performance pressures. They consequently are under simultaneous and potentially conflicting pressures to overachieve, or prove themselves, and to avoid making waves. As one way of coping with this situation, they may try to "cover up" or distance themselves from attributes and activities associated with femininity and/or feminism—anything that might further accentuate gender differences or create conflict and controversy. In effect, they go along in order to get along.

I have no intention, much less desire, to deny either the historical or contemporary prevalence and force of male dominance in American politics and political thought. I am reluctant, however, to grant male domination full omnipotence and omnipresence, even when women have only a "token" presence. First, I question whether *all* institutional norms and traditions in *every* political setting and situation are uniformly masculine and antithetical to women, femininity, and feminism. Second, I doubt these male norms are *so* powerful that they are capable of squelching *all* activity on behalf of women. There may be widespread agreement that women are excluded from the "inner circles of power" (Mezey 1980: 184–85; Gertzog 1995) and otherwise marginalized, but there is much less consensus on the degree to which such obstacles ultimately subvert women's political goals, constrain their behavior, or reduce their effectiveness (Gertzog 1995: 69–70, 93–94). Surely these women, who have broken formidable barriers to get where they are, are capable of resisting and overcoming at least some of these biases and constraints.[6] In sum, I question whether male domination is the only explanation for the apparent lack of differentiation between some female and male officeholders.

I am also skeptical that the power of such gender norms is solely a function of numbers, that male dominance necessarily decreases as the number or proportion of women increases (or vice versa). I can see how a "critical mass" might enable women to start thinking of themselves as a group with common interests, problems, and experiences. To paraphrase the popular feminist slogan, larger numbers may make the personal seem more political. They also may help women organize effectively, to amass coalitions large enough to effect the changes they desire (Mueller 1984). But this relationship between numbers and collective consciousness is not a logical necessity. Small numbers may reinforce solidarity by calling more attention to sex differences and by making women seem even more isolated, more unusual, more "abnormal." Such a small group also may be quite homogeneous. Increasing the number of women in this case would only increase diversity—especially if such growth were a reflection of easier access (fewer barriers) to public office—and thereby quite possibly jeopardize or reduce the degree of consensus among them (Barrett 1995: 243).[7]

I present this study of the attitudes and behavior of Arizona and California state legislators to reinforce empirically my dissatisfaction with the overemphasis on differences between female and male political elites and my doubts about explanations offered for the apparently less frequent failure or inability of women to "make a difference." Examining a variety of representational choices and activities within two very different institutional settings, my research uncovers more similarities than differences between female and male politicians. Sex, it turns out, is a poor predictor of many types of legislative behaviors, even some of those commonly deemed representative of women. In neither state did female representatives weigh the concerns, needs, or demands of their constituents more heavily than did the male representatives (Chapter 3). Nor did these women devote any less time and energy to legislative duties and the policymaking process (Chapter 3). In both state legislatures, the policy preferences and roll call votes of men and women were remarkably similar (Chapter 5). In neither institution did legislative styles, strategies, or conceptions of personal power differ according to sex (Chapter 7). There were only two facets of legislative behavior examined here in which significantly clear and consistent sex differences arose. First, female lawmakers in both states appear to have forged closer ties to their *female* constituents than did their male colleagues (Chapter 4). Second, when it came to policy priorities and leadership, both state legislatures exhibited some degree of sexual division of labor (Chapter 6). Women were more involved in "women's issues" (e.g. education, health, family law, and anything concerning women and/or children), and men were more involved in "men's issues" (e.g., regulation of business, industry, and commerce; budgeting and taxes; agriculture). As usual, however, there were plenty of men involved in "women's issues" and plenty of women leading the way on "men's issues." Additionally, there were plenty of female officials whose ties to female constituents were not particularly strong, and some male officials whose ties to women were very strong. (See Table 8.1 for a summary of these findings.)

The standard explanation for this shortage of sex-based differentiation would be that the women did not feel free to act on behalf of, or even like, women and that doing so remained a risky, costly venture in these male-dominated political institutions. The analysis of legislative status and effectiveness in Chapter 8, however, shows that engaging in activities thought to be representative of women did not exact a significant toll on legislative fortunes in either state. For this and other reasons, I consider a few other explanations.

First, I consider the fact that elected representatives, whether they are male or female, have roughly equal numbers of men and women residing in their districts. This very basic structural constraint is one primary factor that distinguishes the study of women's political representation from that of other social groups; there is no gender equivalent to a rural district or an African American district. The electoral system is simply not set up, formally speaking, for the representation of women—or men—as a distinct political group. For this reason, one could argue that male and female officials have equal incentive to serve the interests of their female constituency. One might even argue that they have equal *dis*incentives for acting on behalf of women, given that the male-dominated political recruitment and election processes would weed out most if not all candidates, male or female, who express a desire to represent women actively and explicitly. The evidence (presented in Chapter 4), however, suggests otherwise. In both states, female legislators perceived more support from their female constituents than their male colleagues did. The women in this study also were more likely than the men to see themselves as representatives of women or women's issues. Many legislators—male and female— thought their female colleagues were better able and/or more willing to take the lead on women's issues. In sum, the elected women in this study did seem more predisposed to representing women, or at least more amenable to the idea of representing women.

Thus, rather than clarify or explain the lack of sex differences in legislative behavior, this exploration makes them even more confusing. If the female legislators were more predisposed to representing women, then why were they often no more likely to actually do so? I turn to another possible explanation: that while elected officials may want to represent women or believe they are representing women, they are either unsure or in disagreement as to how one goes about doing so. They agree on the end—to represent women—but they may not see eye-to-eye on the means. At the very least, their conception of what it means to represent women may not include *all* of the types of activities and preferences examined in this and other studies of sex, gender, and legislative behavior. As I argue in Chapter 1, the discussions and expectations surrounding women in politics and the ways in which these women are supposed to "make a difference" often are deceptively uniform, uncomplicated, and unqualified. Perhaps the women and men actually in public office are less certain; or perhaps they have different ideas about what it means to represent women. Chapter 8 explores and confirms these possibilities. As the analysis reveals, the attitudes and behavior of those legislators (female and male) who seemed predisposed to the concept of representing women indicate very limited consensus on what such representation entails.

Yet another explanation for the lack of sex differences found among these Arizona and California state legislators considers the power of other institutional forces, besides district demographics, whose pressures and constraints may steer female and male legislators in similar directions. There are many norms of legislative behavior that cross gender lines, including

those of collegiality and reciprocity (Chapter 7). Political parties and ide-
ologies also exert a powerful influence over the policymaking process (see
especially Chapter 5). Although constituent service is a clearly recognized
duty of public officials, it is *legislative* skill and accomplishment that are
most highly valued and respected within the institutions (Chapter 3). And
lawmakers set their priorities accordingly. State economies and political
cultures no doubt also constrain legislative agendas, choices, and procedures (Chapter 2). These institutional forces were alive and well in the 1990
Arizona and California legislatures, affecting male and female members
alike. That does not mean that gender was irrelevant; some of these institutional structures were quite gendered, reinforcing some gender norms at
the expense of others. But this study suggests that the ways in which gender operates may not always privilege men and masculinity. The analysis of
legislative strategies and styles in Chapter 7, for example, demonstrates that
there are some very powerful institutional norms that are quite feminine,
even feminist.

The comparison of the California and Arizona legislatures also challenges the notion that sex differences, women's ability to "make a difference," and male-female power dynamics are all a straightforward function
of the proportions of women and men working within these political institutions. It is not clear that women were any better represented or that
female officials were any more unified or any more willing or able to "make a
difference" in the Arizona legislature, where they were much more numerous, than in the California legislature. Increasing the number and proportion of women in these legislatures, therefore, may not necessarily result
in greater solidarity among them and a concomitant increase in the differences between their actions and attitudes and those of their male colleagues. To the contrary, the contrasting experiences of women in the Arizona and California state legislatures suggest that as more women gain
public office—especially as more Republican and conservative women get
elected—there will be greater diversity among female politicians and less
willingness or perceived need to organize collectively (see Chapter 2).

The emphasis on sex differences in the extant research literature no
doubt is reinforced by the link between "making a difference" and the growing numbers of women in public office. "Making a difference" is a powerful
response to any who remain skeptical of or indifferent to efforts to elect
more women to public office. It is not just a matter of appearances, advocates argue; these women can make crucial, substantive, and most importantly, unique contributions to public policymaking and governance in general—especially when they have more than a "token" presence. In this light,
it is easy to see how the quest for difference can take precedence over the exploration of similarities. Common ground between women and men looks

an awful lot like conformity and the continuation of women's subordination. Differences among women seem disappointing.

I share with my colleagues a feminist-inspired interest in seeing that more and more women gain access to public office and other positions of power. I doubt I would have joined them in investigating the impact of female officeholders had I not been so motivated. Years later, my research has done little to change my initial concerns; I still believe there should be many more women actively involved in politics in leadership roles. This research, however, has led me to question whether sex differences in political behavior are the ultimate justification or vehicle for such change. At the very least, this study suggests that the "difference" strategy is a problematic one. In the final chapter, I argue that the conclusions of this study — that women oftentimes do not "make a difference" — do not mean that we should no longer care about the election or appointment of women to public office. What this study does suggest is that the *reasons* for doing so need to be reexamined and expanded.

Does the election of more women into public office mean that women will be better represented? As much as I would like to say (and sometimes do), "Of course it does," the research presented here demonstrates that the answer to this question should be a more complicated, nuanced one: it depends. It depends, first of all, on what we mean by "representation" and, more specifically, what we mean by the political representation of women (Chapters 1 and 8). What exactly does the political representation of women involve? What does it demand of elected officials? Second, it depends on what aspect of representative or legislative behavior is considered. Are we talking about roll call voting (Chapter 5) or setting the policy agenda (Chapter 6)? Or are we talking about more procedural aspects of policymaking, the ways in which policy is formulated, votes are garnered, and winning coalitions are formed (Chapter 7)? What about the more general parameters of representational life, such as the weight given to constituent service or legislative activity (Chapter 3)? How, even, do representatives define or perceive their constituencies (Chapter 4)? Finally, it may very well depend on the social context: the nature of the times; the socioeconomic, political, and cultural environment; or the institution in which or about which the question is asked (Chapter 2).

## A Methodological Note

This study of legislative behavior is based upon multiple sources of data. The primary sources were the legislators themselves. During the first six months of 1990, I interviewed eighty-one state legislators: thirty-two women and forty-nine men; fifty from Arizona and thirty-one from California. These were lengthy, face-to-face interviews that lasted anywhere from thirty minutes to almost two hours. My questions and our subsequent discussions covered just about every topic presented here: representational choices and priorities, policy goals, legislative strategies, the legislative process, the nature of power, and the status and roles of women in the legislature. At the conclusion of each interview, I handed the legislators a written questionnaire to complete and mail back to me at their leisure. This questionnaire provided some additional, more straightforward information about constituent-group support, representational priorities and policy preferences, as well as some personal background information not available from published sources. I requested interviews with all the women serving in the Arizona and California state legislatures at that time and with a representative sample of their male colleagues. Most of the lawmakers I contacted were very cooperative and generous with their time; I was granted interviews with 70 percent of the women and 59 percent of the men contacted. Most of these legislators, in turn, completed and returned the questionnaire I gave them.

The self-reported data on the preferences and priorities of state legislators were supplemented by several sources of data archived by others, including legislative histories of bills introduced, which were compiled by the state legislatures; summaries of what those bills proposed, which were written by outside observers; electoral returns collected by the secretaries of state; and biographical information published by periodicals specializing in coverage of state politics. Together, all these data provide a very detailed and very reliable portrait of the members of the 1990 Arizona and California state legislatures as well as a more general view of the political landscape of the two states. Appendix A on research design provides more detailed information about the data obtained for this study and how I obtained them.

# PART I

# Representing Women
# in Theory and in Context

## CHAPTER ONE

# Deconstructing Difference

Difference is "in." Men are from Mars; women are from Venus (J. Gray 1992). Women speak in a different voice (Gilligan 1982). Women and men just don't understand each other (Tannen 1990). Men just don't get it. " 'Difference,' " feminist essayist Katha Pollitt (1992: 799) quips, "is where the action is."

Women in politics "make a difference." "Tune in to any discussion about the increasing number of women in politics," write journalist Linda Witt, political scientist Karen Paget, and historian Glenna Matthews (1994: 265), "and you will hear" that women's presence "makes a difference." What Hege Skjeie (1991: 234) writes of Norwegian politics is easily applicable to American politics:

> A mandate of "difference" is now attached to women politicians. It has been used by women themselves to get inside the power institutions. It is recognized by party leaderships, both men and women, as a relevant political mandate. It is the basis for new expectations as presently stated from outside the power institutions.

From the woman suffrage movement, which began 150 years ago, to the 1992 "Year of the Woman" campaign season, arguments for women's full participation in politics have appealed not only to our sense of justice and equality but also to the promise of something new and different. "Either positively as the bearers of new values and perspectives, or more negatively as a silenced and thwarted majority, [women] have perceived themselves as bringing something new to the political stage. Their much-delayed entry will not only add to the dramatis personae, but of necessity alter the play" (Phillips 1991: 3).

The differences that women in public office are expected and purported to make are numerous and varied. First and foremost, female politicians are allegedly more willing and able than their male counterparts to deal with a number of public policy problems commonly referred to as "women's issues." These issues include but are not limited to those concerned strictly with equality of the sexes, women's rights, or women's health and safety. Issues often characterized as "soft" or compassionate (Shapiro and Mahajan 1986)—such as anything having to do with children, education, health, and social welfare—also are perceived as congruent with women's interests and expertise. Political candidates, activists, advocacy groups, and observers have asserted that the election of women to public office is a necessary, sometimes even sufficient condition for proper and effective action on such issues.

While the contemporary women's movement (or at least its more reform-oriented branches) has always sought to increase the number and influence of elected women (Mueller 1987a: 96–97), the defeat of the Equal Rights Amendment (ERA)—in overwhelmingly male state legislatures— provided an all-too-clear illustration of the consequences of women's absence and exclusion from positions of political power. Moreover, the support and commitment of the female legislators who did fight for the ERA held much promise for the future. Things would be different if there were more women in office—not just the Constitution, but a whole array of issues on the feminist agenda and of importance to women in general. "The lesson of the 1970s seemed clear: representation, not entitlement, was the key to gender equality" (De Hart 1995: 224–25).

In 1971, leading members of the National Organization for Women (NOW) founded the National Women's Political Caucus (NWPC) with the express purpose of opposing "racism, sexism, institutional violence and poverty through the election and appointment of women to public office, party reform and the support of women's issues and feminist candidates across party lines" (Feit 1979, quoted in Mueller 1987a: 97). The NWPC continues its efforts and in a 1993 pamphlet entitled, "Why Women, Why Politics, Why You," spells out in detail why:

Whether you're . . .
· A woman working in or outside the home,
· A single mother, a retiree or student,
· A Republican, Democrat or Independent,
· Someone who's actively involved in politics or whose only political activity is voting, . . . you deserve public officials who will make your issues a priority. As a woman, you deserve the opportunity to be equally represented by women in your government.

Today, women comprise just over 6% of the U.S. Congress and less than 20% of the state legislatures. We can't wait another 200 years for quality child care and health care, permanent protection for our reproductive freedom, affirmative action, equal pay, affordable housing . . . and the list goes on.

To win these issues, women must be on the "inside," exercising their political power. Only then will women and women's issues be given the full attention and respect they deserve.

The nomination and appointment of Clarence Thomas to the U.S. Supreme Court in 1991, despite Anita Hill's detailed account of sexual harassment under his tutelage, powerfully reinforced these lessons of women's political representation. The image of fourteen white men of the Senate Judiciary Committee sitting in judgment of an alleged case of sexual harassment involving an African American man and woman was, for many observers, prima facie evidence of the pressing need to elect more women (and racial-ethnic minorities) to public office. But it was not simply the fact that men were presiding over and evaluating a woman's testimony of sexual harassment; it was the way in which those men handled (or mishandled) the entire situation.

The senators were harshly criticized for being insensitive to and uninformed about the issue of sexual harassment. Beginning with accusations that they deliberately ignored and trivialized Anita Hill's initial, confidential statements to the FBI and ending with the popular slogan, "Men just don't get it," the all-male Senate Judiciary Committee was on trial perhaps just as much as Clarence Thomas himself. Yet, a great deal of the criticism went beyond the Senate Judiciary Committee and the single issue of sexual harassment. The entire Thomas-Hill debacle was, for many onlookers, one particularly jarring indicator of a larger, more widespread problem: the inability of mostly male elected officials to deal effectively with any number of "women's issues." "If we are ever going to make a change on any of our issues—reproductive freedom, health, violence, workplace reform—we've got to change the faces," NOW president Patricia Ireland declared. "If there was any object lesson out of [the] Clarence Thomas-Anita Hill [hearings], it was that we cannot rely on anybody else to represent us. We have to be there to represent ourselves. And it's got to be now" (Carney 1992: 1399).

Female politicians themselves have certainly been known to make very similar claims about their ability to represent women. Geraldine Ferraro, for example, sees her historic 1984 vice presidential candidacy as "a statement in and of itself. My physically being there meant we would be concerned with women's issues" (Witt, Paget, and Matthews 1994: 217). U.S. senator Nancy Kassebaum stated in a 1988 interview with *Ms.* that the increasing numbers of women in state legislatures "is where a lot of the initiative and vitality is today, trying out solutions for education and health care, malpractice legislation . . ." [*Ms.* 17(4): 58]. In her 1990 California gubernatorial race, Dianne Feinstein repeatedly emphasized that she was more trustworthy on abortion rights than her pro-choice male opponents. "The best person to safeguard a woman's right to choose," she explained, "is another woman" (Yoachum 1990, quoted in Witt, Paget, and Matthews 1994: 168). U.S. representative Darlene Hooley recently stressed the importance of women's involvement in congressional decision making, especially on issues of women's health. To illustrate, she pointed out: "It was the women that said, 'Look, mammograms should be covered'" by all health insurance policies (Hogan 1998). "When you get down to the nitty-gritty issues of dealing with children, aging, long-term care, all those are things that are a natural for women," observed veteran Washington state senator Shirley Winsley as she and her female colleagues gained a record-breaking 41 percent of the state legislative seats in the 1998 elections. "I think, generally, men like tax-type issues, they like criminal-justice issues," she added (Verhovek 1999).

Some of this rhetoric is wishful thinking, but the kinds of things these women envision are quite revealing. In 1984, former congresswoman Bella Abzug described her "possible dream" of a nation in which men and women shared political power equally:

> Never again will we have a chief executive who reports to his "fellow" Americans on the State of the Union and refers to the state of women only once in a half-sentence or not at all. Nor will we have the insulting spectacle of a President choosing, in time of crisis, a committee of Wise Men—usually the same men who got us into the crisis in the first place—to advise him and ignoring the wisdom and recommendations of women. Nor will we have an all-male Senate debating and voting on women's right to abortion. . . . Nor will we have budget planners who insist that an MX missile is more important than jobs for the unemployed, that low-priced meals for Pentagon generals are more necessary than nutrition supplements for mothers and infants, that tax breaks for multinational corporations are more desirable than cost-of-living adjustments for Social Security recipients, that nuclear power plants are more essential than protection of our soil, air, and water. (Abzug with Kelber 1984: 13)

Eight years later, in the midst of the heady "Year of the Woman" Democratic national convention, then–U.S. representative Patricia Schroeder had a similar vision: "We could finally have a friendly government in Washington. We could finally have a government that believed if you want to change the world, you change the world of a child. We could finally have a government that wouldn't try to put a gag on women's health" (Debenport 1992).

More systematic research suggests that these assertions and hopes are neither unusual nor unrepresentative of female politicians in general. For example, a study of the political advertisements of male and female candidates for the U.S. Senate between 1984 and 1986 (Kahn 1993) found significant differences in the types of issues the candidates emphasized as their particular strengths and concerns. The women spent more time talking about "social issues," such as abortion, women's rights, civil rights, gay rights, and the environment, while the men were more likely to discuss economic issues, such as taxes and the federal budget.

Members of the press have been no less reticent. In a special edition of *Time* magazine devoted to women, Margaret Carlson (1990: 17) writes: "Lots of men care about education, health care, pay equity, child care and parental leave, of course, but in a theoretical, not a life-altering, way. . . . Male politicians may not see the hundreds of Roseannes out there, or the thousands of pregnant women with no prenatal care, but female candidates do." Cokie Roberts of ABC-Television and National Public Radio had this to say to the 1990 graduating class of Bryn Mawr College:

> The women of America should basically be on their knees to the women in Congress of both political parties. . . . [For it is they who] carry the burden of the importance of issues to women and children day in and day out. They use it like Chinese water torture on their colleagues. They constantly bring those bills back to the top of the pile: child support enforcement, day care, pension reform, equal credit, domestic violence, all of these things are being brought to the floor by these women. . . . They found themselves the water carriers on women's issues because they quickly discovered that if they didn't do it, nobody else would. (Witt, Paget, and Matthews 1994: 96)

Little of this is lost on the voting public. Numerous surveys and a considerable amount of experimental research reveal a remarkably consistent tendency among both women and men to attribute different skills, traits, and issue competencies to male and female candidates, real or hypothetical. Put simply, voters tend to believe that men are better at dealing with foreign affairs, maintaining law and order, and formulating economic or fiscal policy and that women are better at handling issues of social welfare (especially on behalf of children or the "needy"), education, health, and the environment. The Louis Harris 1972 Virginia Slims Poll, which asked a national sample of women and men whether women in public office "could do a better job than men, a worse job than men, or just as good a job as men in public office" on a wide variety of issues, provides a more detailed account. On most of the issues covered, a plurality of respondents thought women and men could handle the task equally well. Large majorities, however, thought women could do a better job dealing with children and family problems and that men could do a better job directing the military. On issues such as consumer protection, welfare, health, education, world peace, and the environment, more respondents thought women would do a better job than thought men would do a better job. On the other side of the coin, men were more likely to be credited for strengthening the economy and dealing with big business, imposing law and order both at home and abroad, and balancing the federal budget.[1] More recent research demonstrates that these gender-based attributions of issue expertise are no less prevalent today than they were twenty years ago (Alexander and Andersen 1993; Brown, Heighberger and Shocket 1993; Huddy and Terkildsen 1993; Leeper 1991; McGlen and O'Connor 1995: 63–64; Rosenwasser et al. 1987; Rosenwasser and Seale 1988; Sapiro 1981–82).[2]

The "special strengths" attributed to female candidates and officials (Abzug 1984) are not limited to their commitment to and leadership on "women's issues." A more general but no less popular appeal points to various "feminine" characteristics and values traditionally associated with women that women will bring with them to public office. Adjectives such as "caring," "nurturing," "compassionate," and "cooperative" are used quite often to describe women's distinct approach to both the substance and process of public policymaking. Additionally, female politicians are seen as more honest, trustworthy, dependable, and responsive than their male counterparts. Kate Karpilow, executive director of the California Elected Women's Association for Education and Research, for example, believes that women have a "take-care" approach to politics. "The voter," she asserts, "is saying, 'Retire the back-slapping old boys. We want people who care about the people they serve'" (K. Mills 1992). When women gained a record number of nominations in the 1992 California primaries, Willie Brown, long-time Speaker of the state assembly, made a similar observation: "In this horrible election environment, women are better candidates because they have naturally better credibility. They are not normally considered corrupt. They are not normally considered crooked. They are not normally considered players. They're not normally considered gamers" (Yoachum and Gunnison 1992: A16).

This too is a common theme espoused by a diverse and numerous group of current, former, and hopeful female officials. "Tough and caring" was another of Dianne Feinstein's slogans in her 1990 gubernatorial campaign. "It is women," according to former U.S. representative Shirley Chisholm, "who can bring empathy, tolerance, insight, patience and persistence to government. . . . Our country needs women's idealism and determination"

(1970; cited in Gluck 1987: 223). "I see my role here as that of a healer," said Rose Mofford as she assumed the governorship of Arizona after the impeachment of Evan Mecham, "because women are better organized and better equipped to ask people to do things" (Dreifus 1988: 44). Making a point about the need for more women in Congress, former member Barbara Jordan stated in 1991 her belief "that women have a capacity for understanding and compassion which a man structurally does not have" (Witt, Paget, and Matthews 1994: 266). In the aftermath of settling a local labor dispute that had turned violent, Toledo mayor Donna Owens said, "I think women are capable of putting people together in ways that men can't" (Doan and Avery 1985: 77).

Advocates have been able to point to numerous polls to support these claims as well. "For years," maintains Tamar Raphael of the Fund for the Feminist Majority, "polls have shown that women politicians are considered to be more honest and to possess more integrity than men in politics" (Biemesderfer 1990: 23; see also Carlson 1990; Clift 1990; Doan and Avery 1985; Salholz 1992; Toner 1990). Indeed, both the 1972 Virginia Slims Poll and subsequent experimental research have found respondents more likely to regard "maintaining honesty and integrity in government" as a female skill than as a male skill (Leeper 1991; McGlen and O'Connor 1995; Sapiro 1981–82; Sapiro 1983). In their study of upstate New York voters, Deborah Alexander and Kristi Andersen (1993) found that voters are much more likely to associate characteristics such as "compassionate," "speaks out honestly," "works out compromises," "stands up for what they believe," and "moral" with female candidates than with male candidates.

At the most basic, general, and vague level, women in American politics are simply expected to change things for the better. "When people are frustrated and saying something needs to be done," explains Houston's first (and only) female mayor Kathy Whitmire, "they are willing to turn to somebody different" (Carlson 1990: 16). With an ironic twist, women's historic exclusion from public office becomes an asset. "By not being part of the problem, she comes across as part of the solution," says California pollster Mervin Field (Carlson 1990: 16).

This gendered version of "throw the rascals out" was presented perhaps most forcefully during the 1992 "Year of the Woman" campaign season. The spectacle of the Thomas-Hill hearings, followed by revelations of rampant, chronic check-bouncing among members of Congress, only added to the growing disillusionment with politics as usual and the usual suspects. Incestuous, corrupt, and lazy insiders had long been the pariahs of American electoral politics, but this time around women seemed poised to take advantage of the situation and ride to the rescue. Thus, upon winning her primary race for one of Pennsylvania's U.S. Senate seats, Lynn Yeakel declared: "This is a year when the voters are very angry with the political establishment and politics as usual, and women represent change. We embody change. We are the consummate outsiders" (Shepard 1992: A12). According to an October 1992 poll commissioned jointly by NBC News and the *Wall Street Journal*, many registered voters agreed; 53 percent of those polled believed that female candidates were more likely than male candidates to create political change (Biersack and Herrnson, 1994: 164).[3]

Where do these expectations come from? What is the rationale behind these expectations that women and men in public office will behave differently and in the ways outlined above? The campaign trail, the political activity that surrounds it, and the media that cover it are not known for providing detailed, in-depth analysis of any claims, much less those concerning gender differences in what politicians have to offer. And in this case, the rationale may seem rather intuitive: women will be women; men will be men. A closer look through the lenses of history, sociology, psychology, political science, and women's studies, however, reveals that there is much more to these claims than meets the eye. A vast amount of accumulated knowledge of women's lives, activities, and perspectives, both past and present, lends credence to such assertions about gender difference in the world of electoral politics.

The explanation that is most frequently offered (or simply gets the most press) points to women's shared experiences in a society that is profoundly structured by sex and gender. Female public officials, according to this "I've been there" argument, understand and appreciate what women go through in their everyday lives. As former Texas governor Ann Richards said recently, "The most sympathetic and sensitive of our men friends, no matter how hard he tries, cannot hear with a woman's ear or process information through a woman's experience" (Ezzard 1996). "If you don't walk in high heels, it's hard to appreciate what it's like," adds California state senator Jackie Speier (Pyle 1998). The experiences and values associated with motherhood and other traditional, domestic activities of women are especially salient in this discussion. "This state could use a little mothering," Dianne Feinstein told her female audiences when she was campaigning for governor in 1990 (Bonfante 1990: 24). "Our roles as caretakers, nurturers and mothers cannot help but give us a different perspective," said Geraldine Ferraro in her latest run for public office (Nagourney 1998).

Equipped with such first-hand knowledge, female policymakers are, according to this argument, not only more concerned about women's needs and interests but also more effective at addressing them. As the following profiles of newly elected women in Congress well illustrate, women's gender-specific experiences are thought to provide both insight and authority.

Lynn Woolsey, a Democratic congresswoman from California, believes she understands the plight of welfare mothers. After all, she was one herself.

"I've been there," Woolsey recalled in her Capitol Hill office. "When you've had an experience like that, it doesn't go away. It gives you a different sensitivity, a different passion, really, for what needs to be done."

. . . "It does make a difference both from how I will be listened to and my knowledge and experience of the welfare system," said Woolsey, a member of the Education and Labor Committee and the Budget Committee, panels where welfare legislation will be shaped.

"Her views will obviously carry a lot of weight in Congress. She has a very compelling personal story," said Bruce Reed, co-chairman of the White House task force on welfare reform. (Dart 1994)

Patty Murray, the new Democratic Senator from Washington who promoted herself during the campaign as a "mom in tennis shoes," said that many of her colleagues found it striking when, during the family leave discussion, she talked about having quit a secretarial job 16 years ago when she was pregnant with her first child.

"I think women do bring a personal conversation to legislation," she said.

Carrie Meek, a 66 year old new Democrat from Florida, also brought a stunningly personal angle to her testimony at a subcommittee hearing today on the subject of paying Social Security taxes for household help, offering credentials rare for that body: "I was once a domestic worker," she said. "My mother was a domestic worker. All my sisters were domestic workers." (Dowd 1993: A10)

Women's experiences also provide them unique perspectives on the policy process and the organization of legislative business. In an article on the "growing sorority in Congress," Karen Shepard, a newly elected member of the club, is said to be "appalled at the way the men have organized Congress" (Dowd 1993: A10). Committee hearings are scheduled simultaneously, which, she observes, facilitates turf-building more than meaningful participation. Women would have done things differently, Shepard asserts. "When you've done birthday parties for 20 two-year-olds all by yourself, that's actually harder than organizing Congress so that the hearings are scheduled coherently."

These testimonials reflect the current contours of gendered inequalities and divisions of labor inside and outside the home, as well as their relevance to public policy debates. No doubt much has changed in the status and roles of American women over the past few decades. Large increases in the proportions of American women (especially white, non-Hispanic women) receiving higher education, participating in the paid labor force and entering nontraditional professions have been well documented.[4] Nevertheless, current socioeconomic patterns also reveal that the experiences of women and men are still far from being equivalent.

Research on time-use patterns (Berk 1980; Coverman 1989; Coverman and Sheley 1986; DeMeis and Perkins 1996; Douthitt 1989; Galinsky and Bond 1996; Hartmann 1981; Hochschild with Machung 1989; Robinson, Yerby, Fieweger, and Somerick 1977) has found that despite the increased labor force participation of women, most women are still largely responsible for maintaining their households and raising their children. A 1992 survey of married "wage-and-salary" workers with children, for example, found women and men agreeing "that the lion's share of responsibility for maintaining the household belongs to women" (Galinsky and Bond 1996: 92–93). The typical white, middle-class, married woman is now subject to the same "double day" in the workplace and in the home that her poorer sisters have always had to deal with (Glenn 1985).

The division of labor in the home is reflected in prevailing gender divisions among the paid workforce. Occupational segregation in the labor market continues to channel women into professions and jobs that involve nurturing, caretaking, service to others, and other sorts of domestic-type duties (Hartmann 1976; Amott and Matthaei 1996). It is still a very safe bet that the elementary and secondary school teacher, the child care worker, the nurse, the secretary, the restaurant worker, the social worker and, of course, the paid housekeeper are women. On the other hand, men's professional experiences still tend to revolve around such "public" sector concerns as law, finance, business administration, commercial and industrial development, shipping, engineering, and construction. Plus, the armed forces and the defense industry are still, to a very large degree, male-dominated.[5] Thus, to the same degree that female-dominated occupations are associated with typically "feminine" traits, such as nurturance, compassion, service, and devotion, male-dominated occupations are associated with typically "masculine" traits, such as competitiveness, aggression, independence, and leadership.

Men's and women's occupational experiences in the United States continue to be not only separate but also unequal. To this day, "women's work" is devalued, in terms of both prestige and salary. Female-dominated jobs usually pay less, provide fewer benefits, and are less secure than male-dominated jobs. The result is a significant gender gap in the wages earned by female and male workers. In 1992, white women who worked full-time earned only 75 percent of what their male counterparts earned; black female workers received 88 percent of their male counterparts' earnings (Costello and Stone 1994: 309, Table 4-1). In 1991, male and female full-time, year-round workers were equally likely to receive employer- or union-provided pension plans (318, Table 4-7), and only 3 percent fewer female than male workers received health care benefits (321, Table 4-9). Nevertheless, such equity in employer-provided benefits is a very recent phenomenon. In 1987, full-time female civilian workers age 15 and older were significantly less likely than their male counterparts to receive such benefits (Ries and Stone 1992: 379, Table 7-10). Moreover, women's pensions still end up only half as large as men's because women change jobs more frequently, earn less, and take more time out of the workforce (Patterson 1996: 148–50).

Even within occupations, female full-time workers almost always earn less than male full-time workers. In 1990, female engineers received 89.5 percent of what male engineers received; female physicians received 82.9 percent of what male physicians received; female secretaries received 88.1 percent of their male colleagues' salaries; female construction workers received 82.1 percent of male earnings; female butchers and bakers received only 63.9 percent (Ries and Stone 1992: 364–65, Table 7-4). The list goes on. Nor does controlling for educational level wipe out the gender gap in wages; within each educational category, the ratio of female to male earnings is no more than 69 percent. Even more striking is the fact that the median yearly income of women with college degrees is roughly equivalent to the median yearly income of men with only high school diplomas (Ries and Stone 1992: 393, Table 8-2).

This economic vulnerability of women has been exacerbated by the increasing rates of divorce and increasing numbers of single (unwed or divorced) mothers. Women are more likely than ever before to have to— or want to—depend upon their own (relatively meager) incomes. The result has been what is commonly known as the "feminization of poverty" —women (and their children) are increasingly more likely than men to live in poverty (Abramovitz 1996; McLanahan, Sørensen, and Watson 1989; Pearce 1978; H. Scott 1984; Zinn 1989). When lawmakers discuss welfare policy they are by and large talking about a mostly female clientele, as the often derogatory term "welfare mother" implies.

While women are overrepresented among the poor, many men must also deal with the hardships and indignities of unemployment, underemployment, and poverty. There are numerous problems and political issues, however, that directly affect women only. Abortion is the most obvious example. Related issues of women's reproductive health and rights have also been the subject of political debates, public policies, and Supreme Court decisions for a long time (Gordon 1976; Rothman 1989). Victims of sexual harassment, sexual assault, and domestic violence are predominantly or almost exclusively women (Riger 1993; Warshaw 1988). Public awareness and concern about these issues may be at an all-time high, but such violence or the threat of such violence still terrorizes most women, affecting their everyday lives in ways rarely understood, much less experienced, by men (Brownmiller 1975; Gordon and Riger 1989; Russell 1975; Sheffield 1989).

The gender differences that purportedly shape women's and men's political roles, priorities, and preferences are not confined to circumstances and experiences in *adult* life. Childhood socialization and psychological development also play a significant role. Whether it be in the pages of scholarly journals (e.g., Kelly, Saint Germain, and Horn 1991), in the pages of *Time* magazine (Carlson 1990), on the campaign trail (Nagourney 1998), or on the podium at the Democratic national convention (Young 1992), the most frequently cited authority in this matter is Carol Gilligan and her 1982 book *In a Different Voice: Psychological Theory and Women's Development*. Although subject to a good deal of criticism from other scholars (e.g., Epstein 1988; Okin 1990), Gilligan's ideas and arguments still carry a great deal of weight, especially in discussions of women in politics.[6]

Gilligan, who wanted to offer women "a representation of their thought" (1982: 3), distinguishes a "male" voice that speaks in terms of separation, autonomy, and the individual self from a "female" voice that emphasizes connection, relationship, attachment, and community. These voices, according to Gilligan, are reflected in the different ways men and women, as well as boys and girls, think about, talk about, and resolve moral dilemmas. For men, morality is an issue of individual rights and fairness, exercising one's own rights without interfering with those of others. Moral problems arise from competing and conflicting rights, and their resolution requires a mode of thinking that is "formal and abstract" (19), mathematical, and impartial. The competition is resolved by arranging values and rights in a hierarchy that can then be applied in the same fashion in every situation. Women, in contrast, approach morality as an issue of responsibility and care. Moral problems arise from competing responsibilities and their resolution requires a mode of thinking that is "contextual and narrative" (19), subjective, and provisional (e.g., "it depends . . ."). For women, communication is the key; it not only resolves moral problems but also sustains a "network of connection, a web of relationships" (32) that makes morality meaningful in the first place. Thus, while men invoke an "ethic of justice" to address moral (and, presumably, political) problems, women adhere to an "ethic of care."

Although Gilligan is unclear and noncommittal about the origins of such gender differences, she relies heavily on the psychoanalytic work of Nancy Chodorow (1974, 1978) who locates similar differences in early childhood development. Chodorow's stated purpose is "to account for the reproduction within each generation of certain general and nearly universal differences that characterize masculine and feminine personality and roles" (1974: 43). The difference she refers to is that women's gender identity is defined in terms of "relation and connection to other people" (1974: 44), while men's masculinity is based on separation and differentiation from others. The explanation points to "the fact that women, universally, are largely responsible for early childhood and for (at least) later female socialization" (1974: 43). A girl's gender identity, therefore, is formulated in a context of a close, personal relationship with her gender-appropriate role model (her mother); meanwhile, a boy's gender identity is constructed in opposition to the person closest and most familiar to him (his mother) and/or in the context of a distant, abstract relationship with his father.[7] Together, the conclusions of Gilligan and Chodorow provide the foundation for assertions such as the one made by Geraldine Ferraro in her more recent campaign for the U.S. Senate:

> According to Dr. Gilligan, instead of engaging in confrontation, women are more apt to negotiate. . . . Instead of looking at short-term solutions to problems, women are more apt to think in terms of generations to come. Instead of thinking in win-lose terms, women are more apt to see the gray areas in between. (Nagourney 1998)

Gilligan's and Chodorow's propositions also form the psychological core of a large segment of feminist theory concerned with the delineation and revaluation of gender differences.[8] In constructing their own "blueprint for social change," these theorists seek "to isolate and to define those aspects of female experience that were [and still are] potential sources of strength and power for women" (H. Eisenstein 1983: xii). Central to this theoretical tradition, variously labeled "difference feminism" (Snitow 1989), "cultural feminism" (Echols 1989), "woman-centered analysis" (H. Eisenstein 1983), "social feminism" (Black 1989), "feminine feminism" (Grant 1993), or "relational feminism" (Offen 1992), is the importance of caretaking, nurturing relationships—especially, but not exclusively, those between mother and child.[9] According to these scholars, it is experience in and of such relationships that gives women a unique and valuable, if not superior, perspective on life.

Feminist political theorists—most notably Jean Bethke Elshtain, Sara Ruddick, and Kathy Ferguson—have politicized gender differences such as those discussed by Gilligan and Chodorow by applying them to the realms of political consciousness, activity, organization, and policy. Each of these scholars employs certain conceptions of women's experiences and perspectives to envision a model of political transformation. Sara Ruddick (1989) uses the work that mothers do as a model for philosophy and politics, especially peace politics. As she sees it, maternal practice and thinking center around three imperatives for raising children: preservation, growth, and social acceptance. "[T]o be a mother," says Ruddick, "is to be committed to meeting these demands by works of preservative love, nurturance, and training" (17). Ruddick is clear and forceful in her insistence that mothering naturally extends—and should extend—beyond the household to the larger community and even to global politics.

> There is nothing romantic about the extension of mothers' activity from keeping a safe home to making their neighborhoods safe. No one is surprised when mothers petition for traffic cops at school crossings or drive drug dealers off the block. If children are threatened, mothers join together, in all varieties of causes, to protect the neighborhoods they have made.
>
> Maternal care may extend as widely as the community on which growing children depend for their projects and affections. Often, for example, mothers come to feel that their children's well-being depends on the military or economic strength of their nation and its allies. (Ruddick 1989: 80)

Citing both Gilligan and Ruddick's early work, Elshtain calls for a revaluing of the private sphere, especially family life, and of women's distinctive roles within it for the purpose of transforming public, political life.

> If it is the case that women have a distinct moral language, as Carol Gilligan has argued, one which emphasizes concern for others, responsibility, care, and obligation . . . , then we must take care to preserve the sphere that makes such a morality of responsibility possible and extend its imperatives to men as well. . . . One moral and political imperative that would unite rather than divide women, that would tap what is already there but go on to redeem and transform it, would be a feminist commitment to a mode of public discourse imbedded within the values and ways of seeing that comprise what Sara Ruddick has called "maternal thinking." . . . For women to affirm the protection of fragile and vulnerable human existence as the basis of a mode of political discourse, and to create the terms for its flourishing as a worthy political activity . . . would signal a force of great reconstructive potential. (Elshtain 1993 [1981]: 335–36)

Elshtain's vision of an "ethical polity" is one informed by and imbued with "women's traditional concerns, passions, and responsibilities" (1981/93: 348); its "moral imperative," like that of motherhood, is that "the reality of a single human child be kept before the mind's eye" (1982: 59).

*The Feminist Case against Bureaucracy,* Kathy Ferguson's 1984 critique of bureaucratic organization, discourse, and practice, begins with the assumption of gender difference: "In our society, women as a group tend to experience their social worlds differently than do men as a group" (1984: 23). Ferguson's goal is to "build an alternative political discourse from the experiences of women" as "caretakers, nurturers, and providers for the needs of others" (24, 158). Relying quite heavily on Gilligan and (to a lesser extent) Chodorow, she identifies the values that arise from such experiences as "caretaking, nurturance, empathy, [and] connectedness" (25). Ferguson is quick to point out that women's experiences include both the good and the bad and that they are partly the result of systemic subordination. Yet the fact that women's experiences are rooted in oppression does not detract from their value; rather, she argues, it provides double insight: "In their role as subordinates, women's experience sheds considerable light on the nature of bureaucratic domination; in their role as caretakers, women's experience offers ground for envisioning a nonbureaucratic collective life" (26).

Historical accounts of women's political activities in the United States from the revolutionary era to the present reveal a "venerable tradition" of gender-differentiated and gender-defined politics (De Hart 1995: 239). Motherhood, women's domesticity, and female moral superiority have been the cornerstones of women's unending efforts to expand and legitimize their political and civic roles. Such uniquely female experiences and traits, which ironically are associated with the "private sphere," have also provided a foundation for women's critiques of male-dominated public life. These historical trends and continuities in women's political activities and roles are the subject of voluminous scholarship, the details and depth of which would be impossible to capture adequately here.[10] A few of the more illustrative and well-known examples, however, are worth noting.

Both Mary Beth Norton (1980) and Linda Kerber (1980) have identified what were perhaps the first attempts of middle-class, European American women to carve out an explicit political role or definition of citizenship for themselves. In the immediate aftermath of the Revolutionary War, these women combined the dictates of womanhood, republicanism, and politics into a vision of "republican motherhood," which simultaneously reinforced their identities as mothers and wives, confirmed their feminine virtue and moral influence, and established their contributions to civic life. By virtue of their own example of righteousness, integrity, and civic-mindedness, women assumed the significant task of raising their sons to become proper citizens for the new republic. Passive and indirect as this role may seem in late-twentieth-century hindsight, it proved effective in women's subsequent demands for wider access to education and greater involvement in public affairs.

The nineteenth century witnessed an unprecedented expansion of women's civic activities and public roles: from "prayer groups, missionary societies, and mother's clubs" (Evans 1989: 65) to the Women's Christian Temperance Union; from the abolition movement to the woman suffrage movement; from the Young Women's Christian Association to the settlement houses; from volunteer to professional social worker, teacher, and nurse. Within these venues and many others, middle-class women (for the most part) claimed new and expanding public spaces as their own. Once again capitalizing on their association with the private sphere, such women used the Victorian ideology of "separate spheres" to solidify women's common bonds, vindicate their public activities, and champion their reform-minded goals. Rather than deny their traditional responsibilities for children, domestic harmony, and morality, they sought simply to extend such duties beyond the immediate household.

At the dawn of the new, twentieth century, the rhetoric of the suffragists was often quite explicit in its endorsement of gender difference. As the women's social and moral reform movements grew in number and strength, and as government became more and more involved in activities historically associated with the woman's domestic "sphere" (e.g., education, sanitation, and food inspection), woman suffrage could be justified and accepted by affirming rather than challenging women's traditional roles. Women were called upon by both reformers and suffragists (many of whom were one and the same) to clean up government, to apply their housekeeping and nurturing skills to the public sphere, and to give government a good dose of morality. "Thus," writes historian Aileen Kraditor (1965: 67–68), "the statement that the home was woman's sphere was now an argument not against woman suffrage but in favor of it, for government was now 'enlarged housekeeping,' [to use Frances Willard's term] and needed the experience of the nation's housekeepers." [11]

Foreshadowing Bella Abzug's dream and Patricia Schroeder's vision, Rheta Childe Dorr anticipated in her 1910 book *What Eight Million Women Want* what urban politics would look like once "men and women divide the work of governing and administering, each according to his special capacities and natural abilities." The city, she predicted,

> will be like a great, well-ordered, comfortable, sanitary household. Everything will be as clean as in a good home. Every one, as in a family, will have enough to eat, clothes to wear, and a good bed to sleep on. There will be no slums, no sweat shops, no sad women and children toiling in tenement rooms. There will be no babies dying because of an impure milk supply. There will be no "lung blocks" poisoning human beings that landlords may pile up sordid profits. No painted girls, with hunger gnawing their empty stomachs, will walk in the shadows. All the family will be taken care of, taught to take care of them-

selves, protected in their daily tasks, sheltered in their homes. (quoted in Skocpol 1992: 332)

Women involved in the temperance movement also viewed the vote as a means to a larger, reform-oriented end. Women's votes, they reasoned, would provide the necessary majority in favor of outlawing the production and sale of alcohol. Woman suffrage was upheld not only as a way of establishing Prohibition, but also as a means by which reformers could eradicate other social and political vices, such as prostitution, child labor, and the politically corrupt alliance between big business (including but not limited to liquor) and political machines.[12] "With these arguments," Sara Evans notes, "suffrage formed a crucial strand of the Progressive movement that viewed the feminization of government as a means of reform by proposing curbs on (male) competition and corruption and new, nurturing roles for the state" (Evans 1989: 154; see also Baker 1984).

Although the passage of the Nineteenth Amendment may have "represented the endpoint of nineteenth-century womanhood and woman's political culture" (Baker 1984: 644), traditional notions of gender difference and of femininity in particular continued to define women's political roles. Women's participation in the formation and execution of the New Deal welfare state, which has only recently come to the attention of historians (Muncy 1991; Ware 1981), was in many ways an extension of the "social housekeeping" tradition of previous generations of female reformers. Even women's participation in World War II on the domestic industrial front was feminized. Government- and defense industry–sponsored ad campaigns to recruit female workers not only emphasized women's patriotic duty to support the war effort but also reassured women (and men) that their femininity would not be impaired by the rigors of the assembly line or the dangers of heavy machinery. In many instances, for example, tasks performed on the factory floor or the shipyard were compared to such everyday domestic activities as sewing and cooking (Milkman 1982, 1987; Honey 1984).[13] Expectations of gender-differentiated political participation withstood even the radical challenges to traditional arrangements of sex and gender brought forth by the women's rights and liberation movements of the 1960s and 70s. As Alice Echols (1989) documents in her history of radical and cultural feminism in the United States, and as the extensive work in feminist theory discussed earlier illustrates, the tradition of revaluing women's traditional roles as domestic and moral caretakers and offering them as antidotes to current political ills continues.

No less so than in previous eras, today's activists are calling upon women to transplant their traditional roles in the private sphere into the public sphere. Today's advocates of women's inclusion in the ranks of the governing are no less likely to promise dramatic change than were their suffragist predecessors. We are still being told that women have special skills and unique perspectives to offer, that women will change not only the face but the very heart and soul of government. As nurturing, compassionate mothers, they will be more concerned about issues of child welfare, health, and education and less willing to commit our armed forces to unnecessary or overly aggressive activities. As conscientious housekeepers, they will clean up the environment and make government more efficient.[14] As the guardians of morality and decency, they will get rid of government waste, fraud, and abuse once and for all. Being more sensitive, empathic, and sociable, female representatives will better understand their constituents' needs and be more willing to listen to their demands. At the same time, women in office are to be a progressive force with regard to women's rights and women's welfare in general, guaranteeing a future in which women and men may enjoy political, economic, and social equality.

These are the expectations—the theories and hypotheses, if you will—with which to begin this empirical examination of gender-related differences in the behavior and attitudes of female and male state legislators. But this is only a beginning. This portrait of gender difference, detailed and multifaceted as it may be, is much too simple. At best, it tells only half the story and is therefore incomplete and problematic. Underneath this canvas of clearly distinct, clearly demarcated gender boundaries are a number of unchallenged, simplifying, and misleading assumptions regarding the nature of political representation, women's political interests, and gender. "Debatable assumptions at the beginning of the century, they remain no less debatable at the end" (De Hart 1995: 239).

## Political Representation

Ultimately, the question of the impact and implications of the increasing numbers of women in public office is a question of political representation: Are women better represented now than they used to be? The answer, I argue, depends upon what is meant by 'representation' in general and the representation of women in particular. Yet all too often the different meanings and implications of 'representation' are either confused or ignored in the discussion of women in American politics. It is the purpose of this study to untangle and define these concepts of women's representation so that the empirical relationship between them may be examined.

Hanna Pitkin's (1967) work *The Concept of Representation* provides the most useful and influential framework with which to begin an analysis of the different meanings of political representation. In evaluating the nature and quality of representation, Pitkin argues, "Two directions of inquiry are open to us. We may ask what a representative does, what constitutes the activity of representing. Or we my ask what a representative is, what he must be like in order to represent" (1967: 59). Thus, Pitkin distinguishes representation as "acting for" from representation as "standing for" another. Other scholars have made similar distinctions, such as that between active and passive representation (Mosher 1968) or between the "politics of ideas" and the "politics of presence" (Phillips 1995). Anna Jónasdóttir (1988) identifies two aspects of political interest that are based on the same sort of conceptual distinction between formal presence and substantive outcomes: interest in terms of "form" refers to "the demand to 'be among', or the demand for participation in and control over society's public affairs," while interest in terms of "content" engages "the question of those substantive values that politics puts into effect and distributes" (1988: 40). Women, she argues, have an interest in both.

Complaints about the gross disparity between the percentage of women in public office and the percentage of women in the general population often reflect a general desire for our governors to resemble those they govern, to be a "representative" sample of the total population. Concerns about the percentage of women in public office may also reflect a more specific desire for women to be included amongst our leaders. Once again, Dianne Feinstein, in her 1992 race for the U.S. Senate, provided a campaign slogan that captures this sentiment perfectly: "2 percent is not enough." As Harriett Woods, president of the National Women's Political Caucus, predicted in the same year, female voters are "going to go to the voting booth and literally try to change the face of American politics" (Smolowe 1992: 35). Such admonitions focus primarily on *who our representatives are* or should be, not so much on *what they do* or should do. In this sense, a female officeholder can "represent" women by her mere presence in or occupation of that office. Without having to do anything, she "stands for" women, both descriptively and symbolically (Pitkin 1967: 113).[15] In terms of descriptive or symbolic representation, then, the answer to the question of whether women are better represented now that there are more women in public office is an easy one. Elected representatives now "look" more like the constituents they serve in terms of gender composition; although full representation of women in terms of numerical parity is still a long way away, women are symbolically present.

The value of such descriptive representation is symbolic but by no means trivial or unreal. Women's presence in such positions of power confirms and upholds cherished democratic ideals of equal and full participation of all citizens. It affirms the openness and thus the legitimacy of our democratic system by demonstrating that access to positions of power and influence in public affairs are available to all, no matter what their gender, race, class, national origin, or other attributes. To many, the election of more and more women to public office means that politics is no longer for men only, that powerful assemblies such as the Senate are no longer "the ultimate men's club[s]" (Fowler 1992). Women in public office also may provide valuable role models for other women who seek influence and power of some sort, either within the realm of politics or outside. More generally, the assimilation of a previously excluded group into the political elite could provide a powerful incentive for all group members to feel less alienated from the political process and to become more involved in public affairs. (See Chapter 9 for a more lengthy discussion of the value of greater descriptive representation of women.)

Nevertheless, there are strict limits to what descriptive representation alone can guarantee. The "breadth of characteristics and origins" included in a descriptively representative government, writes Frederick Mosher (1968: 15-16), "suggests the absence of any single ruling class from which public personnel are drawn or of any single perspective and set of motivations. But this does not necessarily mean that a public servant with given background and social characteristics will *ipso facto* represent the interests of others with like backgrounds and characteristics in his behavior and decisions." In other words, descriptive or passive representation of a group does not necessarily guarantee the substantive or active representation of the group. "Standing for" is not the same thing as "acting for."

To represent women substantively, a public official, female *or* male, must somehow act for or on behalf of women and their interests and desires. While the descriptive and symbolic representation of women depends upon the presence of women among officeholders, substantive representation depends upon the actual behavior of officeholders. "We are variously told that his [the official's] actions, or his opinions, or both must correspond to or be in accord with the wishes, or needs, or interests, of those for whom he acts, that he must put himself in their place, take their part, act as they would act" (Pitkin 1967: 114).

The point at which the distinction between the descriptive (or symbolic) and substantive representation of women becomes blurred and distorted is when one assumes that those who "stand for" women will also "act for" women. Many of us want more women in public office because we care about who our leaders are. Yet many of us, I suspect, care about who our leaders are precisely because we care about what our leaders do (or do not do). We see one type of representation as the guarantor of the other. Virginia Sapiro (1981: 710) noticed this tendency early on: "The very term, 'representation of women' is usually taken very specifically to mean increasing the number of women in political office because of the assumption that women in power would be more responsive to women's interests than men would be." Indeed, all of the previously cited arguments for electing more women to public office have this assumption in common. Sometimes, as in the case of Patricia Ireland's assertion (quoted earlier) that only women can effect change on "our issues," the argument is a very strong one: descriptive representation of women is a guarantee—and the only guarantee—of women's substantive representation. At other times, the argument is more lenient: the descriptive representation of women makes women's substantive representation significantly more likely.

How realistic are these expectations? To what degree can we rely on the election of women to public office as the answer to our current problems with "women's issues," and with government corruption, intransigence, and inaccessibility? To what degree, in other words, is the substantive representation of women's political priorities and preferences linked to the descriptive representation—the actual presence—of women themselves?

The equation of passive and active, descriptive and substantive representation is not unique to relatively recent discussions of women and politics. Much of American political history and philosophy is built upon faith in strong and tight linkages between these two modes of representation. The ideals of popular sovereignty and self-rule, for which Americans have fought ever since the Revolutionary War, are based upon the notion that government *by* the people is the most effective and legitimate method of establishing government *for* the people. James Madison and, later, John Stuart Mill extended this logic to the representation of "factions" or "classes" in American society (see also Bachrach 1967).

> We need not suppose that when power resides in an exclusive class, that class will knowingly and deliberately sacrifice the other classes to themselves: it suffices that, in the absence of its natural defenders, the interest of the excluded is always in danger of being overlooked; and when looked at, is seen with very different eyes from those of the persons whom it directly concerns. (Mill 1972 [1861], cited in Paolino 1995: 294)

A common theme links the continuous struggle to expand and enhance political participation in this country. From debates over various extensions of suffrage, to the Supreme Court's doctrine of "one man, one vote," to the Voting Rights Act of 1965, to the current concern about the number of women in public office, Americans have been deeply suspicious of the idea that it is possible for a citizen's interest, or more precisely, a group of citizens' interests to be adequately represented in government without the actual presence and direct participation of such citizens in government.

As Mary Hale and Rita Mae Kelly (1989: 3, 9) point out, "scholars concerned about making public bureaucracies more compatible with democratic principles" also have assumed that "representation based on demographic characteristics can lead to meaningful representation" in terms of both symbolic and policy benefits. "It is thought that a bureaucrat of the same background as a client will be more likely to perceive a situation similarly, respond more quickly, and resolve problems more effectively" (Hale and Kelly 1989: 3). This concept of "representative bureaucracy" (Kingsley 1944) originally reflected a concern for the class-based interests and needs of the poor in the face of a seemingly elitist civil service. More recently, the discussion has turned to issues of race, ethnicity, and gender.

In many contexts—political, theoretical, and epistemological—feminists have made similar assertions about who can, or can most effectively, speak for whom. In each case, lack of personal experience casts doubts on the willingness, effectiveness, or veracity of various spokespersons (Jones 1993). Referring, no doubt, to the experiences of women in the New Left and the civil rights movement in the 1970s, Anne Phillips (1995: 8) recognizes that "[p]art of what sustained the development of an autonomous women's movement was the arrogance of those who thought that ideas could be separated from presence." In their efforts to extend the analysis of oppression and the promise of liberation to women, female activists were ignored, patronized, or confronted with a litany of misogynist epithets from their male compatriots and leaders (Echols 1989). In more academic settings, feminists have documented a long history of male scholarship that has either distorted or more often ignored the experiences and perspectives of women. This, in turn, was a large part of what sustained (and continues to sustain) the development of feminist theory and women's studies programs in universities throughout the country.

It is, indeed, difficult to fathom the idea that "the sex of a policy maker has no relevance, and that should all administrators, legislators, and decision makers happen to be women, no difference in policy or outcome would ensue" (Hale and Kelly 1989: 11). Yet, at the same time it is difficult to swallow whole the notion that one has to be one to represent one. There is no absolute, theoretical guarantee that every single woman in public office is going to "act for" women—or that every single male official is innately incapable of doing so (Mosher 1968). In fact, there may even be cases in which the goals of descriptive and substantive representation are in direct conflict. Pitkin herself warns that "the perfection of one kind of representation . . . may preclude the perfection of other kinds in any particular case. And not every kind will even be possible in every context" (Pitkin 1967: 227)

Once again, the nomination of Clarence Thomas to the Supreme Court is instructive, only this time from the vantage point of African American representation. Groups active in the black community, such as the National Association for the Advancement of Colored People (NAACP), were torn between their desire to have at least one black justice on the Supreme Court and their fear that Thomas's conservative beliefs and past history with the Equal Employment Opportunity Commission would lead him to adopt positions on the court that were not in the best interests of the country's black citizenry. Thus, for many interested parties, the dilemma of Clarence Thomas lay in the difficulty of having to choose between descriptive and substantive representation of blacks in the American judicial system.

Carol Nechemias's analysis of the status of women in the pre-perestroika Supreme Soviet presents another case in which descriptive representation in no way guaranteed substantive representation. The Soviet electoral system, which ensured a high proportion of female deputies, "promoted the appearance, though not the substance, of substantial representation for various groups, including women" (Nechemias 1994: 3). Just as the Supreme Soviet itself "was primarily a decorative institution, designed to provide a façade but not the reality of parliamentary democracy" (1994: 5), the presence of women within the Supreme Soviet was purely symbolic. Being relatively powerless members of a relatively powerless institution, few, if any, of these women were in a position to "act for" women—or for anyone else for that matter.

Anne Phillips (1995: 25) warns against exclusive reliance on either the politics of presence or the politics of ideas for dealing with problems of political exclusion and representation. In her view, "most of the problems, indeed, arise when these two are set up as exclusionary opposites: when ideas are treated as totally separate from the people who carry them; or when the people dominate attention, with no thought given to their politics and ideas." She concludes that "it is in the relationship between ideas and presence that we can best hope to find a fairer system of representation, not in a false opposition between one or the other." The question, then, is not whether one type of representation—to the exclusion of the other—is preferable. My purpose here is not to argue that there is absolutely *no* relationship between the "who" and the "what" of political representation; nor am I interested in confirming the opposite expectation, that all women in office act for women while all men in office act for men. Rather, the assumption guiding this study is that the relationship between the descriptive and substantive modes of representation exists somewhere between these two extremes; and the question is, where?

Given the uncertain political world in which we live, this is the more relevant issue: just how well can we predict the "what" on the basis of the "who"? We, the electorate, are constantly seeking cues (or clues) to help us gauge and predict the attitudes and behavior of our elected officials. Is sex a cue we should add to the list? To what extent and/or under what conditions can we rely on sex as an indicator of behavior that represents women?

If being a woman is not a prerequisite to acting on behalf of women, does it at least increase the chances of doing so? [16]

### Women's Interests

As stated earlier, the most frequently cited rationales for why female office-holders will be more likely than their male counterparts to act for or on behalf of women rely on certain assumptions about the commonalities of women's socialization, adult experiences, and political perspectives. To even consider the possibility of women's substantive political representation—regardless of whether or not it is tied to women's actual presence in political offices—is to assume that there are certain attitudes and behaviors public officials may exhibit that correspond to the wishes, needs, experiences, and perspectives of women *in particular*. Those who argue that women should be included among the governing elite because *as women* they have unique and valuable contributions to offer are, in effect, asserting that women constitute a distinct political group whose identifiable interests need to be recognized and addressed (Mezey 1994: 258). It is this set of assumptions that receives and, perhaps, deserves the most critical scrutiny.

Virginia Sapiro was one of the first to focus such attention on this set of assumptions when she asked (in the title of her article), "When Are Interests Interesting?"

> In order to discuss representation of women we must consider whether women as a group have unique politically relevant characteristics, whether they have special interests to which a representative could or should respond. Can we argue that women as a group share particular social, economic, or political problems that do not closely match those of other groups, or that they share a particular viewpoint on the solution to political problems? If so, we can also argue that women share interests that may be represented. (Sapiro 1981: 703)

Sapiro eventually concludes that "there is a woman's interest to be represented" (1981: 705), but she and, subsequently, many other feminist scholars raise a number of challenging problems and questions surrounding this concept of women's interests. Anna Jónasdóttir (1988: 36) discusses many of these "points of conflict . . . within the discourse about the concept of interests in modern times," three of which are particularly relevant here.

One such point of conflict is the issue of whether women's interests (or any group's interests) can or should be established according to objective criteria, subjective criteria, or both. Is a statistical rundown of the differences in women's and men's socioeconomic positions in American society, such as that presented earlier in this chapter, sufficient? "Can we claim that women have certain objective interests regardless of what women themselves think?" (Jónasdóttir 1988: 36). Sapiro, for one, is confident that such empirical research on women's "objective situation" provides "evidence that women do have a distinct position and shared set of problems that characterize a special interest" (1981: 703). Yet, she cautions: "To say that women are in a different social position from that of men and therefore have interests to be represented is not the same as saying that women are conscious of these differences, that they define themselves as having special interests requiring representation, or that men and women as groups now disagree on policy issues on which women might have a special interest" (1981: 704). Furthermore, Sapiro suggests that it is the subjective—that is, women's own consciousness of their interests—that is most consequential, for "[p]olitical systems are not likely to represent previously unrepresented groups until those groups develop a sense of their own interests and place demands upon the system" (1981: 704). It is the subjective dimension of women's political interests, however, that raises the most questions and is surrounded by the most uncertainty.

One could simply assume, as the aforementioned "I've been there" argument often does, that women's subjective perspectives, preferences, and priorities are a direct and uncomplicated function of their objective experiences, social positions, or life circumstances. Commonly shared experiences, therefore, would automatically generate shared beliefs qua group interests. Many scholars who have investigated the determinants of feminist consciousness have, in fact, made such an assumption. Ethel Klein, for example, argues that women's feminist consciousness is based primarily upon direct experience with nontraditional lifestyles. By the 1970s, Klein explains, the combination of increased participation in the labor force, delayed and fewer births, and delayed and increasingly unstable marriages produced profound and widespread changes in women's lives, roles, and their very self-definitions. Women's feminist consciousness then grew out of the growing realization that their personal problems in coping with these changes were a result not of personal failure but of "unfair treatment because of one's group membership"—because as women, they were subject to systemic inequalities and injustices (Klein 1984: 2).

As I have argued elsewhere (Reingold and Foust 1998), such a view of the relationship between the personal and the political is much too simplistic. Group interest, first of all, can be independent of self-interest. Pamela Conover, for example, argues that "[w]hen a person identifies with a group, the group's interests [can] take on a symbolic value that is distinct from the individual's own self-interest; thus, ingroup influence can occur even in the absence of a sense of shared self-interest" (1988: 54). Furthermore, a considerable amount of evidence generated by researchers interested in the role of self-interest in American political behavior (see especially Sears and Funk 1990; Sears, Hensler, and Speer 1979; Sears, Lau, Tyler, and Allen 1980), including my own analysis of the determinants of feminist consciousness (Reingold and Foust 1998), suggests that an individual's life circumstances have relatively little impact on political attitudes and preferences. Policy preferences and feminist consciousness, according to this research, are primarily a function of basic, long-standing ideological predispositions and core sociocultural values, such as those dealing with equality, racism, and religiosity.

Imputing motives on the basis of objective criteria, social indicators, or life circumstances is an inferential leap of faith that is often methodologically unsound and empirically inaccurate. It also denies the possibility and confounding effects of independent thought and human agency (Mohanty 1991). As Phillips (1995: 52–53) concludes her own critique of "a politics of shared experience": "the notion that shared experience *guarantees* shared beliefs or goals has neither theoretical nor empirical plausibility . . . [in part because] it seriously underplays the capacity for reflection and transformation."[17]

If we cannot, then, assume women's collective consciousness from their objective situation, what can we say about women's subjectively defined group interests? Paraphrasing Sapiro (1981: 704), to what degree are women conscious of how their social positions differ from those of men? Do they see themselves as having special group interests requiring representation? To what degree do men and women disagree on policy issues in which women might have a particular group interest? Again, the answers are unclear and subject to much debate.

Some would argue that the emergence of large-scale feminist movements, both contemporary and historic, are "pluralist proof that many women perceive they have interests distinct from those of men" (Carroll 1994: 15), interests that are not being adequately represented in the male-dominated political system. As noted earlier, there is a long and varied historical tradition of women participating in public affairs on the basis of their perceived interests, duties, and needs as women. Yet Sapiro herself (1981: 704) noted that surveys of public opinion revealed precious few significant differences between women and men on issues concerning women's roles and status, women's rights, and feminism. If the women's movement was (in part) a concerted effort to raise women's collective consciousness, then the polls suggested that either its effect on women was more limited than many had hoped or it had just as much effect on men as on women—or both.

Then came the "gender gap." In the aftermath of the 1980 presidential election, feminist activists (most notably, Eleanor Smeal, then president of NOW), pollsters, and journalists discovered two remarkable changes in women's voting behavior. First, 1980 marked the first time that women voted at rates equal to or higher than men. And because women constitute slightly more than half the population, millions more women than men were going to the polls. Second, and even more important, women were more likely than men to vote for Democratic candidates (and less likely to vote for Republicans). According to the CBS/New York Times exit poll, only 47 percent of women supported Ronald Reagan in his bid for the presidency, compared to 56 percent of men—a gender gap of 9 percentage points (Mansbridge 1985: 165).

At last, feminists (and others) thought, politicians from both parties, political experts, and political scientists had to take women's votes seriously. No longer could they assume that the best way to a woman's vote was through her husband; nor could they discount the huge numbers of female voters. With pressure, encouragement, and aid from feminist leaders and strategists, pollsters began to routinely compare the political preferences and attitudes of women and men (Bonk 1988).

From the moment the term "gender gap" first appeared in the news media, it was thought to be surefire proof that a powerful women's voting bloc had emerged—and that it emerged as a response to widespread frustration over the stalled ratification of the Equal Rights Amendment. As Judy Mann, who was the first journalist to publicize the gender gap in her *Washington Post* column of October 16, 1981, reported:

> The National Organization for Women has put together a pamphlet entitled "Women Can Make a Difference" which could have far-reaching implications for the final campaign for the Equal Rights Amendment. For the political establishment in the six unratified states that NOW has targeted, as well as for the national political establishment, the pamphlet provides persuasive documentation that a women's vote has finally emerged. (quoted in Bonk 1988: 89–90)

Indeed, initial reports in the national press attributed Reagan's "woman problem" to his (and the Republican party's) withdrawal of support for the ERA (Bonk 1988; Mansbridge 1985). Women were mobilized, and they were mobilized around their interests as women—or so the story went.

More careful and rigorous analyses of the data, however, soon began to tell a different story (Frankovic 1982; Gilens 1988; Mansbridge 1985). Women and men, on average, did not differ in their support for the ERA. Nor were women any more likely than men to vote for the candidate who shared their position on the issue. For these reasons, neither the ERA nor the abortion issue could account for the gender gap. Instead, these scholars all agree that women were less enthusiastic about Reagan than men were primarily because they were less likely to endorse Reagan's aggressive, anti-Soviet military and foreign policy agenda.

As the analysis of the gender gap extended beyond vote choice and partisanship, researchers discovered that significant sex differences in political preferences existed on a number of issue dimensions (Clark and Clark 1996; *Public Opinion* 1982; Shapiro and Mahajan 1986; Stoper 1989). Since the beginning of polling time, women, compared to men, have taken relatively pacifist positions on international affairs. On such issues as gun control and the death penalty, women's greater aversion to the use of deadly force has extended, for quite some time, to domestic policy realms as well. New gender gaps have arisen in the 1980s and 90s: women tend to take more liberal positions than men on social welfare policies, some civil rights issues, environmental protection, and regulation of hazardous waste and nuclear power. More generally, women are more willing than men to identify themselves as liberals and to endorse expanding the scope of government and government services. Yet when it comes to issues of women's equal rights and abortion rights, the attitudes of women and men are just as similar today as they were in 1980.

Many would argue that these gender gaps in public opinion demonstrate that women's political interests *can* be identified subjectively, that is, according to women's own perceptions. "The growth of the 'gender gap' in partisanship and issue positions during the 1980s," notes one recent assessment, "has generally been taken to signify the emergence of women as a distinct constituency with an identifiable set of interests" (Clark and Clark 1996: 78). Other observers, however, are not so sanguine.

David Sears and Leonie Huddy (1990: 251), for example, argue that "from a standard interest group mobilization perspective," women have not been successfully mobilized as a political group. If they had been, reason Sears and Huddy, then "the largest differences in political attitudes between women and men [would] be on issues directly affecting women's own tangible interests," such as the ERA and reproductive rights (1990: 251; see also Seltzer, Newman, and Leighton 1997: 5–6). Instead, these are the issues on which some of the smallest differences are found. Nor, as noted above, is there much evidence to suggest that women are more likely than men to support political candidates on the basis of their support for such women's issues.

Perhaps this definition of "women's issues" is too narrow. If women are on average more economically vulnerable and therefore more likely to have to rely on the social welfare state, why should social welfare policy *not* be considered a women's issue? If women are, more often than not, primarily responsible for maintaining households and raising children, why should education and public health policy not be considered women's issues? This question of where the conceptual line between women's issues and other issues falls is addressed directly in my discussion below of the third "point of conflict" surrounding women's political interests. For now, the point I wish to make is that even if "women's issues" were defined to include any and all issues in which there was a significant gender gap in public opinion, such gaps may not be wide enough to support the notion that women constitute a political group who "share a particular viewpoint on the solution to political problems" (Sapiro 1981: 703).

Gender gaps do not voting blocs make. One recent, very thorough analysis of sex differences in public opinion and voting dismisses as "myth" the notion that the gender gap has become a "chasm," concluding, "The simple, less dramatic truth is that, despite the hype, the gender gap is not a chasm, and there is no war looming between the sexes, at least not in the political arena" (Seltzer, Newman, and Leighton 1997: 1). As shown in more detail in Chapter 5, the sex differences in opinion that characterize the gender gaps are differences in degree, not kind. Rarely are a majority of women on one side of an issue while a majority of men are on the other side. And when there are such cases, the majorities are not large ones (i.e., 45-55 vs. 55-45 splits).

The other side of this coin, or one reason why the differences in women and men's political preferences are not so great, is that differences *among* women are not insignificant; in fact, they are usually larger than the differences between women and men. This is Jónasdóttir's second "point of conflict" about women's interests: can "*all women*, across all class and race lines, . . . be said to have *certain common interests*" (1988: 38, emphasis in original)? Regardless of whether women's interests are defined objectively or subjectively, the heterogeneity of women's experiences and the multiplicity of women's identities cannot be ignored.

As feminist scholars, especially those critical of various versions of "difference feminism," have pointed out, the dangers of assuming homogeneity among women are twofold. First, such assumptions, in the extreme at least, are essentializing and sexist in and of themselves; "for one common thread that links sexism, racism, nationalism and religious bigotry is the defining of self and others by a single characteristic and being able to see nothing more" (Phillips 1991: 155). As Susan Carroll and Linda Zerilli point out, "If one is a woman, surely that is not all that one is. And those other race and class identities (to name but two) shape how one experiences being a woman and . . . how one is seen by others as a woman" (1993: 70; see also Z. Eisenstein 1988). Second, ignoring the differences among women often excludes nonwhite, poor, and/or lesbian women from the category "women" (hooks 1981, 1984; Spelman 1988). Because those with racial, class, and heterosexual privilege are usually those who have the power to define what it means to be a woman in American society, concepts of womanhood and women's interests often reflect the experiences only of those in such dominant positions.[18]

Exclusive focus on the commonalities among women also does injustice to the historical record. Historian Nancy Hewitt, for example, urges her colleagues to move "Beyond the Search for Sisterhood," arguing that "evidence from the lives of slaves, mill operatives, miners' wives, immigrants, and southern industrial workers as well as from 'true women' indicates that there was no single woman's culture or sphere." Instead, she notes, "There was a culturally dominant definition of sexual spheres promulgated by an economically, politically, and socially dominant group" (Hewitt 1985: 315). The two most notable instances of twentieth-century political movements in which women mobilized in massive numbers for a common purpose — one the woman suffrage movement, the other the drive to pass the Equal Rights Amendment — are also notable for the divisions among women they revealed. These were not simply battles of the sexes.

In the analysis of both movements, feminist historians (in particular) have stressed two related points. First, these movements were not all-inclusive. Although women from all walks of life actively supported both woman suffrage and the ERA, white, middle- to upper-class women were the recognized leaders, and it was their interests that defined movement goals, strategies, and tactics — often at the expense of their nonwhite, non-middle-class "sisters." These historians have shown, for example, how white middle- and upper-class suffrage leaders, including Elizabeth Cady Stanton herself, found that exploiting racial, ethnic, and class tensions often worked to their advantage. Enfranchising women (read: women like themselves), they argued, would counteract the votes of various "undesirable" elements of the American electorate. In the South, that was code for blacks; in the North it was code for recent immigrants, all of whom were presumed to be ignorant, illiterate, and immoral. Such arguments, of course, made meaningful coalitions with black, immigrant, and/or working-class women precarious at best (DuBois 1978; Dye 1975; Giddings 1984; Kraditor 1965; Terborg-Penn 1998).[19]

Second, both movements spawned countermovements whose leaders and followers were also women. Recall Phyllis Schlafly and her STOP-ERA troops and the many other "ladies in pink" who rallied in opposition to the ERA (Brady and Tedin 1976; Mansbridge 1986; Mathews and DeHart 1992). Moreover, feminist scholars contend, these antifeminist women, whether they organized in opposition to woman suffrage or the ERA, were not simply puppets of powerful men. They were leaders and activists in their own right who were motivated by their own very different conception of women's interests (Mansbridge 1986; Marshall 1997). Schlafly, for instance, accused "women's libbers" of "trying to make wives and mothers unhappy with their career, make them feel that they are 'second-class citizens' and 'abject slaves' " (quoted in Mansbridge 1986: 104). From this perspective, the ERA, far from uniting all women around their common interests, benefited some women at the expense of others. It was, in large part, Schlafly's ability to highlight these fundamental differences among women that, according to Jane Mansbridge (1986), made her efforts to derail ratification so successful.

In sum, Nancy Cott's assessment of American women's political activism before and after passage of the Nineteenth Amendment can apply just as well to women's political activism before and after the struggle surrounding the ERA:

> The quantity of evidence that women arrayed themselves on opposing political sides (even if they used gender-dependent justifications to do so) calls into question the very possibility of a woman bloc. Given the divisions among women and given the nature of the political system, a woman's voting bloc—or even the possibility of a lobbying bloc representing *all* women—must be considered an interpretive fiction rather than a realistic expectation, useful perhaps to some minds, but requiring a willing suspension of disbelief. (Cott 1990: 170, emphasis in original)

Such skepticism is echoed occasionally by contemporary women in politics. Upon her 1998 election to the governorship of Arizona and the simultaneous election of women to all of the other top executive offices of the state, Jane Dee Hull disputed the notion of "women's issues" altogether. "The idea that all of a sudden we are all going to go out and put forth a so-called women's agenda makes no sense at all," she said. Hull and her female cohorts, according to media reports, were "all quick to dispel any notion that they represent a monolithic 'women's' point of view" (Cart 1998). "I personally sometimes kind of bristle at the idea that there are 'women's issues' for us to carry," said Cheryl Pflug, who was recently elected to the Washington state legislature on a platform against high taxes, traffic congestion, and suburban sprawl (Verhovek 1999). Observing the 1998 U.S. Senate race between Democrat Patty Murray and Republican Linda Smith —who disagreed vehemently on many issues, including abortion—one reporter concluded: "the politics of women circa 1998 looks much more complicated and ideologically diverse than it did six years ago. Just having more women elected to office does not guarantee that any particular policies will be favored in Congress" (Verhovek 1998).

Jónasdóttir's third "point of conflict" surrounding the notion of women's interests is more normative and strategic than the other two, for it considers the long-term utility of distinguishing interests in terms of sex and gender. "In these or similar terms we are confronted with questions about whether, for instance, promoting public care for children and the elderly are to be considered women's issues, while others, such as those of economic policy or military concerns, are seen as men's issues" (Jónasdóttir 1988: 38). If, as feminist social scientists have argued, gender permeates practically every aspect of public policy—from Social Security to urban planning—so that women and men are differentially affected by each, are not *all* issues women's issues? If sex-based segregation of labor at home and in the workplace is problematic, should the solution also rely on sex-based segregation of responsibility? If so-called women's issues are not generally of concern to men, shouldn't they be? To what extent does the mere designation of certain issues as "women's issues" risk ghettoization and continued marginalization of women in politics? Women's issues, however delineated, will never be the only issues of concern to women; nor will they always be issues of concern only to women.

Emphasis on gender difference translated into sex difference is a familiar, time-tested strategy for asserting women's right to equally meaningful and effective means of political participation. From republican motherhood to social housekeeping to the gender gap, American women have offered their differences from men as a much-needed solution to contemporaneous, "man-made" social and political problems (Phillips 1991: 3; Stoper and Johnson 1977). And in so doing, they have found an effective means with which to enhance and mobilize their collective power (Offen 1992). Nonetheless, this strategy of difference has been subject to a good deal of feminist criticism and skepticism.

There is, first of all, the all-too-frequent danger of essentialism, or what Sandra Lipsitz Bem (1994: B2–3) calls "gender polarization": the "process of dichotomizing people into two sexes and of making sex matter in virtually every domain of social life." As already noted, the reification of gender differences deceptively overlooks the many characteristics that women and men share as well as the many cross-cutting cleavages, such as those related to race, class, religion, and political ideology, which divide women and divide men.

The problem with such a polarized view of the world is not simply its lack of empirical validation, however. Such reified categories may do more harm than good to the very people they are meant to describe. Those who conform must assume the risk of being locked into certain roles and activities they may not always want or need. Those who do not conform are subject to accusations of betrayal and may be viewed as problematic at best, "unnatural" at worst.[20] "Feminists are surely right to argue that people should not have to leave their sexual identities behind when they climb on to the political stage," writes Anne Phillips (1991: 156). "But neither should they have to define themselves by one criterion, in this case by gender, alone."

According to critics, gaining access to political office (and other sources of power and influence) on the basis of gender difference not only limits the access women gain; it also imposes a double standard on women seeking such access. Women should not have to prove they are extra-special in order to claim the rights and privileges to which they are justly due. This aspect of "difference feminism," writes Katha Pollitt, "is demeaning to women."

> It asks that women be admitted into public life and public discourse not because they have a right to be there but because they will improve them. . . . No one asks that other oppressed groups win their freedom by claiming to be extra-good. . . . Only for women is simple justice an insufficient argument. It is as though women don't really believe they are entitled to full citizenship unless they can make a special claim to virtue. Why isn't being human enough? (Pollitt 1992: 806–7)

(See also Deutchman 1991: 15; Stoper and Johnson 1977: 210, 216.) Ironically, then, expectations of difference can impose both a single standard and double standard on women in public office. Either way, the danger is that such standards can place serious limitations on what female officials do, how they do it, and how their behavior is viewed by others.

Reliance on stereotypes, particularly traditional gender stereotypes, assumes other risks as well. These are, after all, the very same stereotypes that have been used, time and time again, to *ex*clude women from political participation and positions of power. In Bem's words, "They are . . . categories that historically have been largely shaped by those in power, to serve as both the foundation and the rationale for their privilege" (Bem 1994: B2). Politics, according to those who have tried to prevent women from claiming their rightful political voice, is too rough, too cutthroat, too dirty for women. Politics has no place for "womanly" concerns and passions.

Stereotypes that prove advantageous at one point in time can come back to haunt us. As Deborah Rhode observes, "However feminist in inspiration, any dualistic world view is likely to be appropriated for non-feminist objectives" (Rhode 1992: 157; see also Offen 1992: 84). This boomerang effect (Stoper and Johnson 1977: 206) is no less a possibility today than it was in previous generations. It did not take long after the 1992 "Year of the Woman," for example, for male gubernatorial candidates to accuse their female opponents of being "soft on crime." While such attacks "would probably work on male opponents, pollsters say they are all the more effective on women" (Berke 1994: A8; see also Berke 1993).

I raise these "points of conflict" surrounding efforts to identify and define women's political interests not to deny unequivocally the existence of such interests, much less the possibility thereof. As with questions about the relationship between descriptive and substantive representation, simple either-or conclusions about the existence and nature of women's political interests are untenable. To rule out any possibility that women possess identifiable political interests of their own recalls the days of coverture and patriarchal assumptions that women's interests are completely subsumed by those of their fathers, husbands, and sons. To posit strictly dichotomous and oppositional sets of women's and men's interests, on the other hand, is, in its simplistic essentialism, empirically flawed and politically dangerous.

To some degree, these points of conflict can be and have been raised about the interests of other sociopolitical groups. Questions about degrees of in-group homogeneity and out-group differentiation, for example, are relevant to African Americans, labor, business, the elderly, and the poor—groups long established on the American political scene (Sapiro 1981: 703). Yet the concept of group interests continues to be widely used and accepted by political scientists and practitioners alike. Thinking about women as a political group raises a great many difficult and interesting questions that force us to think much harder about the most basic, foundational concepts of group politics. Posing such questions, as I have done in this section, is not tantamount to discarding wholesale the theoretical or empirical possibility of women's interests. Besides, it is the questions—not the answers—that are most relevant to the study at hand.

My purpose here is not to resolve the debates about women's political interests, but to focus attention upon the very uncertainty that generates such debate. This uncertainty in and of itself has important implications for the study of women's political representation in general and, more specifically, for the study of sex differences in legislative behavior. Such uncertainty provides yet another reason to look with suspicion at claims that women's descriptive representation will guarantee or foster women's substantive representation. To what degree are such expectations realistic when the very definition of women's substantive interests is so contested? Even if a female official wanted to "act for" women, how is she to determine how or what to do? As Phillips asks, "If the interests of women are varied, or not yet fully formed, how do the women elected know what the women who elected them want?" (Phillips 1995: 71). And what guarantee is there that all or even most elected women will come to the same conclusions about what women want?

## Sex and Gender

In according more weight to activities and values associated with women, care must be taken not to confuse the need for these values with the belief that only women may exercise them. . . . The trick is to bring more women into politics, and to bring more of the values traditionally associated with them into the political arena, without establishing a permanent link between the two. (Witt, Paget, and Matthews 1994: 283)

If we treat the opposition between male and female as problematic rather than known, as something contextually defined, repeatedly constructed, then we must constantly ask not only what is at stake in the proclamations or debates that invoke gender to explain or justify their positions but also how implicit understandings of gender are being invoked and reinscribed. (J. W. Scott 1986: 1074)

One of the most significant theoretical contributions of feminist scholarship is the distinction between sex and gender. At a very basic level this distinction draws a line between (presumably) straightforward biological categories of female and male and more complicated, socially constructed categories of feminine and masculine. Notions of femininity and masculinity are characteristics people tend to associate with women and men, femaleness and maleness; but the important point is that the two—sex and gender—are not necessarily or universally tied. Women can exhibit masculine traits; men can be or act feminine. Women and men can and do possess both feminine and masculine characteristics. What is considered feminine (or masculine) in one location or cultural context may not be in another. The theoretical and political point of gender as a concept distinct from sex is to allow for change and variability among both individuals and societies or cultures, to expose and eliminate stereotypes about women and men, and to allow women and men more freedom and choice in determining the contours of their lives.

Recent theorizing about gender, led by historian Joan W. Scott's (1986) explication of gender as an analytic category, explores more fully the processes and manifestations of gender's social construction, the dynamic and contextually dependent nature of gender, and gender's relationship to power. Thinking about and using the concept of gender in this way further distinguishes it from sex. First, it reinforces the notion that gender is an abstraction, or a representation of sorts, that is constructed and embodied in cultural symbols, norms, institutions and identities (J. W. Scott 1986: 1067–68). Gender in this sense is "a *cultural code of representation,* a way to categorize and control behaviors and practices that are not necessarily the result of sexual differences *in terms of sexual differences*" (Jones 1993: 220, emphasis in original).

The idea that gender is a method not only of categorization but also of control highlights another important feature or supposition of gender theory: gender is often a signifier, instrument, and/or embodiment of power relationships. It is not simply a matter of difference, but also one of asymmetries and hierarchies of value, power, and control (Duerst-Lahti and Kelly 1995a; Jones and Jónasdóttir 1988; J. W. Scott 1986). And more often than not the symbols, norms, institutions, and identities in which gender operates reflect and reinforce the dominance of what is male or masculine over whatever is female or feminine.

The third and, perhaps, most significant (for the purposes of this study) contribution of recent theorizing about gender is its emphasis on the variability and fluidity in both the meaning and salience of gender. Because womanhood and manhood are socially constructed, their meanings are dependent upon the social context in which they are constructed. The relevance of gender—the ease with which it is constructed and the force with which it is maintained—also may depend upon the social situation (Deaux and Major 1990; Epstein 1988: 79, 100–101; Thorne 1990). This social context operates, and thus varies, across multiple and interlocking levels: from the level of "Western civilization" to that of nation, state, community, workplace, or family. A social context can operate even at the level of a two-person interaction or relationship. It also exists historically and at particular points in time; thus, gender not only changes with the nature of the times but also carries certain historical meanings and force.

As Kay Deaux and Brenda Major (1990) point out, gender varies at the individual level as well. Many may think of themselves as "womanly, feminine, or feminist; [but] within any of these general categories, the beliefs and behaviors associated with the label can differ dramatically" (93). Furthermore, people may differ in the degree to which gender is a salient or relevant aspect of their lives or identities. Recognizing that "gender-related behaviors are a process of individual and social construction" assumes that "women and men make choices in their actions" (91) and, thus, allows for human agency. Such a conception of gender, then, avoids and challenges the deterministic qualities associated with the concept of sex.

Fundamental to this discussion is a rejection of "the fixed and permanent quality of the binary opposition" that all too often characterizes gender research and theory (J. W. Scott 1986: 1065). The point is that when gender is defined in terms of oppositional dichotomies of masculinity vs. femininity that are constant through time and space, much of the conceptual and analytic distinction between sex and gender is lost. Gender becomes just as reified and reifying as sex; hypotheses and expectations about gender differences become just as rigid as those of sex difference. Herein lies the reason why talk about women in politics making a difference often ends up evoking age-old sexual stereotypes: gender (the activities and values associated with women and men) gets affixed to sex (women and men in public office) as if it were "an accurate and exhaustive descriptor" of the actual be-havior and attitudes of all such women and men. But gender is never and was never intended to be "an accurate or exhaustive descriptor of the actual lives or identities of all women or all men" (Jones 1993: 222).[21]

Current discussions of women in American politics often seem oblivious to ways in which gender, in all its abstract, powerful, and variable forms, operates so differently from sex. In the same way that descriptive and sub-stantive representation are often conflated, or that women's experiences and interests are presumed to be perfectly correlated, expectations that women in public office will "make a difference" also often equate or assume direct and uncomplicated links between sex and gender. Recognition of gender difference gets translated into expectations of dichotomous, stable, and universal sex differences. It is one thing, as Witt, Paget, and Matthews assert in the quotation above, to demand greater political representation of the "activities and values associated with women" and quite another to demand greater political representation of women themselves as the only guarantee. This is not only a distinction between substantive and descrip-tive representation, but also a distinction between the representation of gender and the representation of sex.

Once again, my purpose here is to avoid taking an either/or position in debates about sex and gender; the relationship between sex and gender is too complicated to be so easily resolved. I do not care to argue or as-sume that sex and gender are either completely equivalent or completely unrelated. Instead, I proceed with the presumption that sex and gender are neither permanently nor perfectly linked and then consider the implica-tions of the uncertainty and fluidity of that relationship. Nor will I argue or assume that gender has the same meaning and the same significance to each person within each legislature, regardless of the situation. Finally, while I remain wary of the ways in which gender is embodied and exercised in power relationships, I do not assume that gender is always a matter of power hierarchy or that men are always at the top of that hierarchy.

## Conclusions

The literature reviewed here is full of warnings about the empirical, concep-tual, and normative dangers of equating descriptive and substantive rep-resentation, assuming women constitute a politically unified group with undifferentiated experiences of oppression, equating sex and gender, and forgetting that gender is a social construction and thus highly dependent upon social context (at various levels) for its meaning and significance. Yet the expectations for how women (and men) in public office will behave —expectations expressed on campaign trails, in interest group literature, the mass media, and in the empirical research—often seem to ignore these warnings. The certainty with which female officeholders are assumed to want to act for women and to be capable of doing so—and the certainty with which male officeholders are assumed to be unwilling and/or unable to do so—belie all the *un*certainty and complexity this chapter has documented.

In the following analysis of sex, gender, and legislative behavior in the 1990 Arizona and California state legislatures, all these uncertainties and complexities are placed in the foreground, up front and center. In so doing, the difficulties and thus the *un*likelihood of female legislators making a difference as women and for women are highlighted. Not only the feasibility but the value of "difference" is also reassessed. In this light, it is no longer certain that maximizing sex differences in legislative behavior will maximize women's substantive political representation and empowerment. Similarities between women and men and differences within each category become just as interesting and important as differences between women and men and the similarities within each group.

My approach is very similar to that of Deaux and Major's social-psychological model of gender. We share, first of all, a recognition that "[a]ttention to actual behavior . . . demands a model that recognizes variability and similarity—as well as stability and difference" (Deaux and Major 1990: 90). "Null" findings, those in which the attitudes and behavior of men and women are not consistently or significantly different, therefore, are not necessarily viewed as disappointing or as theoretical dead ends. This study and Deaux and Major's model also share a concern with "gender as experienced and enacted in a particular social [and/or political] context" and a belief that "it is essential to recognize evidence of changes over time and circumstance" (Deaux and Major 1990: 91). While this study of gender and legislative behavior is not designed to observe and gauge change over time, it is designed with a strong emphasis on variation in circumstance: a variety of legislative activities and priorities are examined in two very different legislative institutions. These institutions, the 1990 Arizona and California state legislatures, and the sociopolitical contexts in which they operated are the subject of the next chapter. Of particular interest are the ways in which gender and gender relations were socially and historically constructed, the degree to which gender was evident in power hierarchies, and the general salience of gender in the political life of each state institution.

## CHAPTER TWO

# Gender, Power, and Political Culture in Arizona and California

Arizona and California have a great many things in common, some more obvious than others. Both are western "frontier" states that entered the Union after significant periods of Spanish and later Mexican rule. With the exception of a small portion of what is now southern Arizona, the territory of both states was ceded to the United States in 1848 under the Treaty of Guadalupe Hildago, which ended the Mexican-American War. Western states are generally considered more liberal than others on issues of women's rights and gender equality, at least in their early stages of development. Historians have suggested several reasons, including the scarcity of women, the more democratic nature of the frontier, and the absence of English common law traditions such as coverture (Rothschild and Hronek 1987, 1992). Whatever the reason, California and Arizona were among the first states to grant women suffrage, as were most other western states.

The Progressive and Populist reform movements of the late nineteenth century found fertile ground in both territories (Berman 1992; Peirce and Hagstrom 1983; Sheridan 1986; Syer and Culver 1992). The political and economic fortunes of Arizona and California had been dominated by wealthy, centralized corporate interests, most notably the railroads and, in Arizona, mining enterprises. The response in both cases was to democratize the political process, especially through constitutional provisions for initiatives, referenda, and recalls. It was no coincidence, then, that woman suffrage was enacted in both states by ballot initiative, California's in 1911 and Arizona's in 1912. To this day, however, big business plays a large role in these neighboring states. Agricultural production in both states is still dominated by large corporations and is often referred to as "agribusiness." Business and manufacturing interest groups remain very powerful players in both political arenas (Hrebenar and Thomas 1987).

In 1990, Arizona and California faced many of the same social, economic, and political problems, most of which were related to the extraordinary population growth and economic development of the postwar era. From 1950 to 1990, Arizona's population almost quadrupled, making it the second fastest growing state in the nation (after Nevada) (Ritt 1993: 10). California was not far behind, expanding from approximately 20 million residents in 1970 to almost 30 million in 1990. In the 1980s alone, California grew by 25 percent, as compared to the national average of 10 percent (Syer and Culver 1992: 10). Most of this growth was concentrated in urban and suburban areas. In the 1980s, Phoenix was the fastest growing of the thirty largest Standard Metropolitan Statistical Areas (SMSAS) in the country (Etulain 1987: 36); growth rates for the counties surrounding Los Angeles were in the 40 to 50 percent range (Syer and Culver 1992: 10). Growth was so rapid, migration so overwhelming, that observers characterized the citizenry of both states as rootless communities of strangers (Peirce and Hagstrom 1983: 748, 800; Sheridan 1995: 319-20; Willey 1991: 43).

With this population explosion came economic growth and transformation, along with parallel shifts from rural to urban, homogeneity to heterogeneity (Mason 1987; Nash 1987; Peirce and Hagstrom 1983; Sheridan 1986). Once dominated by the "three C's"—copper, cattle, and cotton—Arizona is now primarily a manufacturing and service-oriented state with huge investments in high-tech and defense-based industries (electronics and aerospace mostly), residential and commercial real estate, health care, and tourism. Although agriculture remains an economic powerhouse, the California economy has experienced similar patterns of growth and diversification. The birth and notoriety of Silicon Valley is only one of many indicators of that state's promotion and reliance upon computer-age technological advances and the military industrial complex.

Maintaining and managing this growth defined most of the central political concerns of the two states in the 1980s (Luey and Stowe 1987; Syer and Culver 1992). Such rapid growth was not without its costs. Indeed, many of the most pressing problems the states confronted can be attributed to such growth: problems involving land use, waste disposal (toxic and nontoxic), air and water pollution, and transportation, to name a few. Water is key to any form of economic or residential development in Arizona and California, and it is in short supply. Both states, therefore, are—and always have been—dependent on vast systems of water diversion to make their deserts bloom; neither could survive, much less grow, without such monumental efforts to control and overcome nature. Water rights has long been one of the major dimensions of political conflict within and between the two states.

As the major underwriter of all the dams, aqueducts, and canals and the final arbiter of interstate conflicts over water, the federal government has been a major economic and political factor in each state. But dependence on federal largesse does not stop at the riverbanks. The burgeoning high-tech industries of both states were fueled by federal defense contracts and military expenditures. Enormous political energy, therefore, was devoted to maintaining favorable relations with the federal government and its numerous agencies in order to maintain the flow of both water and defense dollars (Hrebenar 1987; Matlack 1990; Nash 1987).

By 1990, the bright lights of economic expansion in Arizona and California were fading (Sheridan 1995; Syer and Culver 1992). The demands such growth placed on the states' resources—natural, human, administrative, and political—were becoming increasingly difficult to manage or even sustain. With the Cold War coming to an end, increasing international economic competition, and a recession gaining steam, both state governments faced serious budget crises. Protracted battles over the budget, both within the legislatures and between the legislatures and their respective governors, ensued. The 1990 Arizona legislative session wore on way past its constitutional deadline; the California legislature did not pass a budget until a month into the 1991 fiscal year.

Arizona and California voters were becoming increasingly disillusioned with their state representatives and political institutions, but the budget debacles were only one reason (Bradshaw and Bell 1987; Ritt 1993: 10; Syer and Culver 1992: 1-25, 175, 202-3). The late 1980s were witness to a number of extremely damaging and damning scandals involving very prominent political figures in both states.

(1) In 1988, Arizona governor Evan Mecham became the first governor in American history to be simultaneously impeached by the state legislature, indicted by a state grand jury, and recalled by the state voters. The crimes for which he was impeached included using $80,000 of public funds (the Governor's Protocol Fund) to aid his ailing automobile dealership, obstructing justice by impeding the state Department of Public Safety's investigation of a death threat against one of his former aides, and failing to report a $350,000 campaign loan. Before the recall election or the criminal trial could take place, the Arizona Senate voted to convict Mecham of the first two charges and remove him from office (Demoruelle and Thysell 1993; McClain 1988; Watkins 1990).

(2) Charles Keating, the man responsible for the biggest savings and loan failure in U.S. history and "one of the most recognizable symbols of one of the greediest decades in American financial history" (Sheridan 1995: 333), had strong and questionable ties to both Arizona and California politicians. U.S. senators DeConcini (D-Ariz.), McCain (R-Ariz.), and Cranston (D-Calif.)—all members of the "Keating Five"—were implicated

in the 1990 Senate Ethics Committee hearings (Syer and Culver 1992: 8; Willey 1991: 44).

(3) Meanwhile, the FBI was wrapping up a five-year undercover investigation into political corruption in the California state capitol. Posing as southern businessmen interested in exchanging money for legislative favors, the FBI agents were able to catch two California senators and several legislative aides with their hands in the proverbial cookie jar. In February 1990 (right as I began conducting interviews for this project), Senator Joseph Montoya (D-El Monte) was convicted of extortion, money laundering, and racketeering; in September of that year, former senator Paul Carpenter (D-Norwalk) was found guilty of similar crimes (Syer and Culver 1992: 4–9).

(4) Incredibly, the Arizona legislature was subject to its very own "sting" operation in 1991. The Maricopa County Organized Crime Bureau hired an FBI informer to go undercover as a Mafia-backed businessman who wanted to legalize casino gambling in Arizona. Eighteen people, including two state senators, five state representatives, and one former state representative, were eventually convicted of accepting bribes ranging from $660 to $60,250 (Sheridan 1995: 323; Willey 1991). While "Azscam" took place a year after the research for this study was conducted, it appears to be nothing other than a continuation of business as usual. As a former Arizona senator put it, "Over the last five or six years in this state, it's like you just sit around and wait for the other shoe to drop" (Willey 1991: 41). Indeed, political corruption continued plaguing Arizona citizens well past 1991. In 1997, Arizona governor Fife Symington was found guilty of defrauding lenders as a commercial real estate developer (Purdum 1997). Forced out of office, Symington was replaced by the secretary of state, Jane Dee Hull, who in 1990 was Speaker of the Arizona House of Representatives.

No doubt there were many concerns and pressures shared by Arizona and California state legislators in 1990. But it is the differences, not the similarities, between these two states that make the comparison most useful and interesting for this study of the representation of women. One of the primary questions this book addresses is whether and how context matters. Do women (or men) in public office "make a difference," do they act for women regardless of the political environment within which they work? Or is their ability, even willingness, to do so dependent, at least in part, on their surroundings? To even begin to address this issue, one must examine and compare legislative behavior in (at least) two *different* contexts. California and Arizona, the states and their legislative institutions, provide two very different contexts.

The rest of this chapter outlines the various ways in which the two states and the two legislatures differed and how those differences might be expected to affect patterns of women's political representation. The assumption, at least for now, is that actively and visibly representing women went against the grain, especially for female officials. To act for women was to effect substantive change—change in public policy, in the policy process, or even in the entire conceptualization of representative duties. This assumption is, after all, implicit in the notion that representing women is "making a *difference*." The context in which such challenges to the status quo must take place, if indeed they do take place, can be more or less conducive. Thus, each aspect of the legislators' surroundings discussed below is evaluated in these terms. To what degree might this have increased or decreased opportunities to "make a difference" for women? To what degree might this have increased or decreased pressure to conform?

Previous research, especially that available in 1990, rarely considered the possibility of contextual effects on the behavior of political elites; when it did, the focus was on numbers and, in particular, the percentage of women present in the workplace (Kanter 1977) or legislature (Saint Germain 1989; Thomas 1991). Studies of African American and Latino political representation also pointed to the power of numbers (Browning, Marshall, and Tabb 1984; Gruber 1980). As explained in the Introduction, Kanter's work provided the strongest theoretical explanation for how and why "skewed sex ratios" or being members of a very small, "token" group affects women's behavior. The smaller the minority group, the more oppressive is the environment—and the more dangerous it is for members of that group to stand out in any way. The larger the minority group, the greater the opportunities are for solidarity and coalition building—and the more freedom there is for group members (or the group as a whole) to do what they want, including standing out and standing up for their group. In this line of reasoning, numbers and percentages are, in effect, proxies for the opportunity structure and comfort level (or level of hostility) within a particular organization, from the perspective of minority group members.

In this analysis, sex ratios are but one of many indicators of the opportunities available to female legislators in California and Arizona who may have wanted to "make a difference" for women in 1990, and of the countervailing pressures to conform to standard operating procedures and norms. In 1990, women constituted 16 percent of the California legislature—close to the national average—and a full 30 percent of the Arizona legislature—one of the highest proportions of women in the country.[1] Given Kanter's reasoning, then, one would expect to find the smaller California delegation much more reluctant and much less able than the larger Arizona group to represent women in any substantive way. But once again, the story is much more complicated than that.

First, the nexus of sex, gender, and political power within any given state is bound to be more complex and multifaceted; a quick look at numbers and proportions of men and women in the state legislature cannot do it justice. Included in this chapter, therefore, is an analysis of the gender dimensions and roles of women in the political culture and history of each state. To capture fully the intricacies of women's standing within each state legislature (in 1990), I also compare the educational and occupational backgrounds, the levels of seniority and electoral security, and, most importantly, the involvement in legislative leadership of men and women within each institution. Finally, I present the legislators' own perceptions and evaluations of the status of women within their working environments.

There are numerous aspects of the sociopolitical context that are not directly or obviously related to gender hierarchies and biases but nevertheless are quite relevant to the opportunity structures the legislators faced in 1990. This is where the comparative analysis of differences between the two states begins. First, I compare the two states in terms of the scope and size of each polity and, more to the point, the professionalization of each legislature. I turn next to the political culture of each state. A notoriously ill-defined concept in political science, political culture is often used as a catch-all for anything that cannot be measured or observed directly (Wirt 1991). To clarify, but not oversimplify, the political cultures of Arizona and California, I begin with Daniel Elazar's (1972) well-known typology of political cultures in the American states. Elazar's work, however, goes only so far. Both states have experienced profound change since Elazar first presented his analysis. Furthermore, his categories do not adequately address the ideological (liberal or conservative) climate of each state. Thus, my own explication of political culture takes a more detailed look at the contours of ideological and partisan politics, past and present, in each state.

### Size and Scope (or, California: The Nation-State)

> There has never been a state even faintly resembling California.
> — Neal R. Peirce and Jerry Hagstrom, in *The Book*
> *of America: Inside Fifty States Today* (1983)

California could easily be a nation unto itself. And that in and of itself sets the state apart from all others. In terms of population, California is by far the largest state in the nation; with a 1990 population of almost 30 million, it is almost twice as large as the next biggest state (New York) and almost ten times the size of Arizona (3.6 million). With a 1985 gross state product (GSP) of $53 million, California's economy is not only much larger than that of any other American state—and again, ten times larger than Arizona's (V. Gray 1990: 23); it is also larger than the economies of most nations. Indeed, if California were a nation, its economy would be the eighth largest in the world (Syer and Culver 1992: 11). As Charles Bell wrote of California in 1984: "The point is, simply, that the state's large population, mixed economy, wealth of natural resources, and geographic situation make it a viable 'nation.' It should come as no surprise, then, that the state's politics resemble those of a nation's (for example the United States) more than most of the other 49 states" (Bell 1984: 33).

With size comes diversity as well. Ethnically, California is the most diverse state in the nation, with sizable and rapidly growing populations of Hispanics (26 percent) and Asian Americans (10 percent). Projections estimate that by the year 2003, non-Hispanic whites will be in the minority (Syer and Culver 1992: 79). Arizona also has a large Hispanic population (19 percent) and a significant number of Native Americans (6 percent), but the state's nonwhite population is smaller and less diverse than California's. California's economy is no less diverse than its citizenry. The agricultural sector alone provides a good illustration: with over 250 different commodities grown, California leads the nation in the production of no less than 48 crops (Syer and Culver 1992: 11, 68).

All this translates into a huge and unwieldy responsibility for the California state government. To deal with this incredible workload—and to compete with the executive branch and interest groups—the California legislature has become highly professionalized and institutionalized (Polsby 1968; Squire 1992). Beginning in the late 1960s, the leadership of the California legislature (most notably Jesse Unruh, Speaker of the Assembly at the time) introduced several reforms to bolster the policymaking abilities of the institution and its members (J. Mills 1987; Putnam 1992: 40–41; Squire 1992: 1029–31; Syer and Culver 1992: 197). The reforms have significantly increased the number and quality of legislative staff assigned to policy research and constituent service (and the resources available to and for them); they have raised the legislators' own salaries; and they have greatly extended the length of the legislative session. As a result, the California legislature is now one of the most professionalized and most powerful state legislatures in the country, and it is often considered a leading policy innovator (Bell 1984; Peirce and Hagstrom 1983; Squire 1992; Walker 1969).

The Arizona legislature, along with most other state legislatures, also made efforts in the 1970s to increase its policymaking capacity by expanding and improving its staff and its legislative facilities. A 1987 assessment summarized these improvements:

Many of the features of the legislature's situation have changed: offices have been provided, salaries improved, staff assistance enhanced, research capabilities increased, and tenure lengthened. Today the Arizona legislature is clearly capable of establishing its own information base for policy decisions. (Mason 1987: 31)

Nonetheless, the Arizona legislature still pales in comparison to that of its mightier neighbor; and members still take pride in its "citizen," or nonprofessional, nature. In fact, the 1990 Arizona legislature looked much like the pre-reform California legislature of the early 1960s (Squire 1992: 1029–30).

The Arizona state constitution limits the legislative session to approximately 100 days. Sessions must adjourn no later than Saturday of the week during which the 100th day of the session falls, usually late April. Beginning in 1985, Arizona legislators extended their sessions by about a month to deal with heavy workloads and unexpected crises, such as the impeachment of the governor in 1988 (R. Jones 1991: 109). The 1990 session, the longest on record, did not adjourn until late June. To Arizona legislators these sessions seemed to drag on forever, certainly longer than any of them preferred. But as lengthy as they may have seemed, they no doubt were much shorter than the unlimited sessions of the California legislators. The California legislative session continues year-round; its only limits are those of the electoral cycle. Many California legislators considered themselves full-time legislators and were even willing to publicly identify themselves as such (Squire 1992: 1034–35); very few of the Arizona legislators identified themselves as full-time legislators. Legislators' annual salaries reflected this disparity. In 1990, California legislators' salaries ($40,816) were more than twice those of their Arizona counterparts ($15,000).

Differences in the legislators' workloads are dramatically illustrated by the number of bills and the number of constituents for which they were responsible. In 1989, roughly four times as many bills were introduced in the California legislature as in the Arizona legislature (4,260 compared to 1,134, or roughly 35.5 and 12.6 per member). The California legislature also managed to enact almost five times as many bills as did the Arizona legislature (1,467 compared to 313, or roughly 12.2 and 3.5 per member). Members of the California legislature technically represented a far greater number of people than did their Arizona colleagues. With a statewide population of 3.7 million and 30 multimember legislative districts, Arizona legislators in 1990 were accountable to approximately 122,000 constituents each.[2] With a statewide population of almost 30 million residents and 80 assembly districts, California Assembly members represented approximately 372,000 constituents each—three times the number of Arizona legislators' constituents. Moreover, California senators, with only 40 districts among them, each served approximately 744,000 constituents—more than even the (then) 45 members of the California delegation to the U.S. House of Representatives.

By design, California legislators received far better staff support than did their less professionalized Arizona counterparts. In 1988, the California legislature employed a staff of almost 3,000 people, an average of about 25 per legislator (Weberg and Bazar 1988, cited in Squire 1992: 1045). Each legislator had fully staffed district and capitol offices, for which they received direct annual payments of at least $275,000 to cover expenses. At the capitol, the typical California legislator had at his or her disposal both legislative and administrative aides, including one person who did little else besides schedule appointments. In contrast, Arizona legislators had *at most* one secretary at the capitol, who handled all phone calls from constituents, all appointments, and all other administrative and secretarial duties. An Arizona representative who did not chair a standing committee shared a secretary with one other representative; senators and committee chairs in both houses each had their own secretary. Unlike their colleagues in California, Arizona legislators did not have personal legislative aides who researched and advised them on policy matters; nor did they receive any funds for maintaining district offices.[3]

All this suggests that California legislators would find it much easier to "make a difference"—for women, or anyone else—than would Arizona legislators. They simply had more resources at their disposal and more opportunities to use them, *many* more. Initially, this expectation runs counter to that based on the number or percentage of women in each legislature. In that case, the expectation was the that larger delegation of Arizona female officials would find it easier to "make a difference" for women, as women, than would the smaller delegation of California female officials. But there are a number of things about the professional nature of the California legislature to consider before concluding that it provides a conducive context for the representation of women and women's interests.

First, it is unclear how the abundant resources and opportunities of the California legislature were distributed. Those who did *not* want to "make a difference" for women—and those who actively opposed such efforts—may have had just as many resources and opportunities as those who did, perhaps even more. There also is the possibility, to be addressed shortly, that resources and opportunities were not equitably distributed between the men and women of the 1990 California legislature.

Second, there is a potential by-product of professionalization that demands greater conformity and thus reduces the chances that substantive change will take place. Professionalization often, though not necessarily, goes hand-in-hand with institutionalization, or the establishment and increased importance of custom, behavioral norms, standard operating procedures, and so on.[4] One can see how the great demands and complexity of a highly professionalized legislature would make the certainty and, perhaps, efficiency of such institutionalization attractive. Nonetheless, the strength of those institutionalized norms may prevent or discourage members from initiating the sorts of challenges and changes that are associated with the representation of women.

## Political Culture

### Elazar's Assessments

A good place to begin a discussion of political context within Arizona and California is with Daniel Elazar's *American Federalism* (1972), his influential treatise on the history and geography of political subcultures in the American states. Political culture, according to Elazar, is "the particular pattern of orientation to political action in which each political system is imbedded" and "is rooted in the cumulative historical experiences of particular groups of people" (1972: 84–85, 89). Thus, the political subcultures of the states can be traced to the various ethnic and religious groups that settled in the United States and migrated westward, bringing with them certain ideas regarding the proper roles of government, public officials, and citizens. Each of the resulting political subcultures reflects a particular combination of attitudes toward two competing notions or ideals of democratic governance: the marketplace, "in which the primary public relationships are products of bargaining among individuals and groups acting out of self-interest" (1972: 90); and the commonwealth, "in which the citizens cooperate in an effort to create and maintain the best government in order to implement certain shared moral principles" (1972: 91).

The *individualistic* subculture, with its roots among Western Europeans who came to America primarily in search of individual opportunity rather than religious freedom (and who settled in the northern states), fully embraces the marketplace paradigm. It is the embodiment of the classic liberal state. In this subculture, government exists only to mediate conflicts between competing economic actors, thereby allowing economic development to proceed as efficiently as possible. With no positive or moral agenda of its own, government's role is to be passive and minimal. It is a necessary evil "instituted for strictly utilitarian reasons, to handle those functions demanded by the people it is created to serve" (Elazar 1972: 94). In this model, politics is a messy business that requires specialization and the expertise of professionals; amateurs need not apply. Political leadership is sought as "a means of controlling the distribution of the favors and rewards of government rather than as a means of exercising governmental power for programmatic ends" (1972: 95). Not surprisingly, then, in an individualistic political subculture "a fair amount of corruption is expected in the normal course of things" (1972: 95). While political parties are generally strong and party politics competitive, parties are motivated by the same nonprogrammatic, amoral distributional concerns as their esteemed leaders.

Associated most readily with the Puritans, the *moralistic* subculture is strongly committed to the commonwealth model of democratic governance. In many respects, then, it presents the most striking contrast to the individualistic subculture. Government in the moralistic sense is good government, one that actively promotes the public welfare (economic and social), or whatever is believed to be in the public interest.[5] Political participation is a public service and duty; thus, maximum citizen involvement is expected and encouraged. Political leaders are known for their "honesty, selflessness and commitment to the public welfare" (1972: 96–97); they serve the community "even at the expense of individual loyalties and political friendships" — not to mention their own "private economic enrichment" (1972: 97). Political parties are considered useful only to the extent that they further certain principles and issues; consequently, they are easily and frequently bypassed.

The Europeans who settled in the southern states also sought economic opportunity but did so "in a plantation-centered agricultural system based on slavery and essentially anticommercial in orientation" (Elazar 1972: 112). Out of this emerged the *traditionalistic* subculture, which combines "an ambivalent attitude toward the marketplace . . . with a paternalistic and elitist conception of the commonwealth" (1972: 99). Political power — and political participation, for that matter — is limited to "a relatively small and self-perpetuating group drawn from an established elite who often inherit their 'right' to govern through family ties or social position" (1972: 99). As in the moralistic paradigm, traditionalistic government has an active role; but instead of promoting the public good, its mission is simply to maintain the existing social order — and the governing elite's position therein. As the once "solid South" illustrates, traditionalistic political systems are often characterized by one-party dominance (Key 1949). Political competition (among the elites) is based on neither partisanship nor issues, but on personalistic factions within the dominant party.

According to Elazar's analysis, California inherited two political subcultures: from the Puritans' Yankee descendants who were the first Anglo settlers, a dominant moralistic tradition; and from the opportunistic European immigrants who jumped on the Gold Rush bandwagon, a strong individualistic strain. Arizona's settlement patterns also nurtured two political subcultures, one more prevalent than the other. At the time Elazar conducted his research, the bulk of Anglo settlers in Arizona had come from the South, via Texas and New Mexico, and had brought their traditionalistic political culture with them. Indeed, Arizona and New Mexico were the only states outside the southern and border-state region in which Elazar found a dominant traditionalistic culture. Arizona also received a strong dose of the moralistic tradition from waves of Yankee and Mormon migration.

There is a lot to be said for Elazar's early assessments of the political cultures found in Arizona and California. Progressivism, a political movement that reflected much of what the moralistic culture stands for, was a significant factor in early development of both states. But while short-lived in Arizona, Progressivism has had a lasting effect on California politics (Bell 1984; Peirce and Hagstrom 1983; Putnam 1992). Perhaps the most notable legacy of the Progressive era in California is the continued, even growing, weakness of parties and partisan loyalties in electoral politics. Traditional party organizations remain practically nonexistent (Mayhew 1986). Split-ticket voting and a divided state government (Republican governors and Democratic legislative majorities) have been the norm in late-twentieth-century California politics, where voters are increasingly reluctant to declare any partisan affiliation. Party labels were no more relevant in 1990 than they were in 1946 when Earl Warren ran for governor on both the Republican and Democratic tickets (Syer 1987; Syer and Culver 1992).

In the absence of political parties there arose a strongly individualistic political culture of powerful interest groups and highly professionalized, extremely expensive, candidate-centered media campaigns. "California has its Republican and Democratic parties. . . . But in the media-dominated world of California, it is the individual candidate who matters" (Peirce and Hagstrom 1983: 752). Interest group–sponsored ballot initiatives also have become the organizational and substantive focus of much campaign activity in California. Interest groups, professional political consultants, and candidate-centered political machines perform all the traditional functions of political parties, including campaign fundraising and voter mobilization. It is no coincidence that California gave birth to the campaign management profession and leads the nation in campaign expenditures and the use of the ballot initiative (Syer and Culver 1992).[6]

By 1990, ballot initiatives had become so frequent yet so outrageously expensive and so completely dominated (and distorted) by competing special interests that they lost whatever moralistic purpose they once had. That so many of these initiatives passed—especially the 1990 proposition that imposed strict term limits on state legislators—suggested that voters were becoming increasingly cynical about the good intentions and programmatic commitments of their elected officials. In this sense, the "initiative wars" of the late 1980s and early 90s marked the ascendancy of the individualistic over the moralistic political culture of California (Barnes 1990; Putnam 1992; Schrag 1995; Syer and Culver 1992).

As Elazar predicted, Arizona has certainly seen its share of political elitism and traditionalism. "Political power in Arizona," according to one seasoned observer (Willey 1991: 43), "has always rested in the hands of a few." In the early days, the Democratic party had as much a monopoly on political power in Arizona as it did in the Deep South. But it was not the party itself that controlled government and society; it was the agricultural and mining barons—the kings of cotton, cattle, and copper—who controlled the party and ran the state (Mason 1987: 25; Peirce and Hagstrom 1983: 731–32). The Arizona Progressive movement, with its pro-union stance, was no match for Walter Douglas, president of Phelps, Dodge Corporation and chairman of the board of the Southern Pacific Railroad (Sheridan 1986: 229–30; Peirce and Hagstrom 1983: 731). After World War II, the combination of migration from the Midwest and the U.S. Supreme Court's "one-man, one-vote" decision in 1964 shifted power from rural Democrats to urban Republicans, but a small group of wealthy, paternalistic, white businessmen still held the reigns of power in Arizona (Sheridan 1995: 320; Willey 1991).

Much as Elazar's original framework helps put the political cultures of California and Arizona into perspective, it falls short of presenting a complete or completely accurate view of each political environment. Part of the problem is that the dominant political cultures of both states, as identified by Elazar in 1972, have atrophied in recent years. In case the subversion of Progressive reforms were not enough, the series of political corruption investigations, indictments, trials, and convictions that plagued both states in the late 80s and early 90s wiped out any remaining remnants of a moralistic political subculture. The embarrassing scandals that rocked Arizona can also be seen as an indication that the state's ruling elite had lost its traditionalistic grip. A "pale imitation" of its early postwar self, the Arizona business establishment left a leadership vacuum, one with plenty of room for the likes of Evan Mecham (Sheridan 1995: 318–24).

A more serious shortcoming of Elazar's typology is that it does not offer a clear view of the ideological climate of the states. Elazar himself cautioned that the political subcultures he identified "are not substitutes for the terms 'conservative' and 'liberal' and should not be taken as such" (1972: 126).[7] Arizona's brand of political conservatism, for example, is often described as individualistic, but it is nothing like the sort of individualism that characterizes California's candidate-centered and interest group–dominated campaign trails. Further complicating things are recent trends in party politics that render the moralistic weak-party model of California politics and the traditionalistic single-party model of Arizona politics obsolete. Both the ideological climate and the nature of partisan politics are important dimensions of political culture, whether or not they are incorporated in Elazar's framework; and they are particularly important in assessing the opportunities and incentives available to state legislators wanting to "make a difference" for women.

## Ideological Orientations

Arizona's reputation for being a very conservative and, since the 1950s, Republican-dominated state is in many ways well-deserved. The fact that Arizona was home of U.S. Senator (and 1964 presidential candidate) Barry Goldwater, often considered the founder of modern-day conservative Republicanism, is just one indication. It is also the only state to have voted for the Republican presidential candidate in every election from 1948 to 1992 (McClain 1988: 629; Willey 1991: 44). Since 1966, when court-ordered reapportionment took effect, Republicans have had a lock on the state legislature as well.

In 1990, 47 percent of Arizona voters registered as Republicans; 42 percent as Democrats (Ritt 1993: 12). Survey data collected between 1976 and 1988 show an even closer split in partisan identification among Arizona residents: 34.7 percent Republican; 35.4 percent Democrat; and 29.9 percent Independent (Erikson, Wright, and McIver 1993: 15). But Arizona citizens are more conservative and more Republican than these figures initially imply. First, there were only eleven states that had a higher proportion of Republican to Democratic identifiers during this time period; in this sense, then, Arizona was the twelfth-most Republican state. Second, both registration figures and self-identification measures show a significant increase in Arizona Republicanism over time. For example, between 1976 and 1988, Arizona was one of only six states outside the South that registered a Republican gain in partisan identification of over 10 percent (Erikson, Wright, and McIver 1993: 38). Third, survey research over the 1976–88 period also indicates that Arizona Republicans were some of the most conservative in the country. There were only five states (Idaho, North Dakota, Oklahoma, Texas, and Utah) in which Republicans (as a group) saw themselves as more conservative than Arizona Republicans did (Erikson, Wright, and McIver 1993: 40).

Fourth, and most important, Democrats in Arizona have always been a fairly conservative bunch—although not quite as conservative as southern Democrats (Erikson, Wright, and McIver 1993: 40; Mason 1987: 25; O'Neil 1995: 88; Ritt 1993: 11).[8] As one Arizona political scientist puts it, Arizona "is a state in which one talks about differences between the Democratic and Republican parties in terms of varying degrees of conservatism" (McClain 1988: 629). Bruce Babbitt, Arizona's Democratic governor from 1977 to 1986, provides a good illustration. Having received substantial Republican support in his election and faced with a solidly Republican state legislature, Babbitt portrayed himself as a "nonideological pragmatist" (Sheridan 1995: 322) and acted much like a Republican—a liberal Republican in Vermont or Maine, perhaps, but a Republican nonetheless (Mason 1987: 26).

> Babbitt was a social liberal but a fiscal conservative; an environmentalist who recognized the rights of ranchers, miners, and developers to make a living off the land; an advocate of business as long as business acted responsibly and within the law. He sent in the National Guard during the 1983 copper strike in Clifton-Morenci, and he appointed numerous Republicans to state commissions and boards. (Sheridan 1995: 322)

Perhaps the clearest indication of Arizona conservatism can be found in the policy choices the state has made over the years. Several studies of policy liberalism in the American states conducted in the 1980s ranked Arizona among the most conservative (Erikson, Wright, and McIver 1993; Holbrook-Provow and Poe 1987; Klingman and Lammers 1984; Rosenstone 1983). These studies examine a wide variety of public policy decisions, including such things as public education spending per pupil, average Aid to Families with Dependent Children (AFDC) payments, scope of Medicaid eligibility, when and if the Equal Rights Amendment was ratified, consumer protection efforts, antidiscrimination measures, legalization of gambling, death penalty enforcement, and tax progressivity. Among all these issue areas, Arizona appears the most conservative on social welfare policy. One study of state welfare efforts in 1985 shows Arizona falling way behind most states. On the five measures reported, Arizona ranked forty-sixth on welfare expenditure per $1,000 personal income; forty-fifth on welfare expenditure as a percentage of total state general expenditure; forty-fifth on the number of AFDC recipients per 1,000 residents; forty-first on adequacy of AFDC grants; and thirty-eighth on adequacy of AFDC grants with food stamps (Albritton 1990: 426–27). Arizona is also the only state to have refused to participate in the Medicaid program for indigent health care; and it was not until 1982 that the state set up its own alternative.

In an analysis of Arizona's public spending priorities, David Berman and Janalee Jordan-Meldrum (1993: 86) offer the following explanations for the state's relatively weak commitment to social welfare expenditures: (1) "Arizonans are unusually conservative on welfare issues;" (2) as westerners, they have an attachment "to the frontier values of individualism and self-reliance;" (3) since World War II, the state has been inundated with "relatively prosperous," conservative Republican midwesterners; and (4) "the goal of economic development has minimized [or preempted] concern with problems of poverty." As these arguments suggest, the ideological climate of Arizona is conservative, but it is a conservatism that emphasizes free enterprise—and its components, noninterference and economic growth—above all else. If Elazar's typology is at all applicable, Arizona conservatism has much more to do with individualism and the unfettered pursuit of economic opportunity than with traditionalism and the maintenance of the existing social order.

> A chief attraction of Arizona is its openness in both business and politics. Rags-to-riches stories dominate the development of the real-estate and electronics industries, just as they did in minerals and ranching in the old days. In the postwar years, Arizona's business and political culture have been governed not by a few old wealthy families trying to maintain the status quo, but by succeeding generations of entrepreneurial immigrants who see to it that the state's politicians provide a maximum amount of aid (federal water projects and pro-business state laws) and a minimum of regulation. (Peirce and Hagstrom 1983: 730)

Indeed, some would argue that Arizonans are not so much conservative as they are "fiercely independent, unafraid to buck what is a trend elsewhere and to challenge all forms of authority" (Willey 1991: 44). To one scholarly observer (O'Neil 1995: 88), "Arizona conservatism sounds more Lockean than Burkean, more libertarian than social/organic. It stresses the claims of the atomized individual against authority. It views government, especially national government, with suspicion. It demands maximal freedom and space for the individual. But it expects the individual to carry his or her weight and not become a dependent."

The saga of Arizona's battle over the Martin Luther King Jr. (MLK) holiday, one of the most controversial issues confronting state legislators and voters in 1990 (Alozie 1995: 3), provides an excellent opportunity to view the state's conservatism through these alternative lenses. In May 1990, after a protracted struggle and a very emotional debate, the state legislature, by a margin of a single vote, became one of the last to establish a state holiday honoring King. But before it could take effect, the issue was placed on the November ballot, making Arizona the only state to subject the holiday to a public vote. There were, in fact, two measures on the ballot: one would add an MLK Day to the other ten paid holidays for state workers; the other would keep the number of state-paid holidays constant by getting rid of Columbus Day before adding an MLK Day. Both proposals were defeated, the first by a narrow margin of 1.6 percent of the votes, the second by a much wider 3:1 ratio (Kastenbaum 1991: 202).

To outsiders, Arizona's refusal to honor the civil rights leader was a clear racial affront, one even the southern states had managed to avoid. Evan

Mecham had already raised racially sensitive eyebrows when, as governor, he publicly endorsed and defended a book that declared white slave owners the worst victims of slavery, deemed blacks responsible for their own oppression, and referred to black children as "pickaninnies" (Demoruelle and Thysell 1993: 44; McClain 1988: 631–32). It was Mecham, in fact, who started the whole MLK debacle during the first week of his administration by rescinding his predecessor Bruce Babbitt's executive order authorizing the holiday. The 1990 ballot initiatives and their failure to win voters' approval clinched Arizona's national reputation as a hopelessly racist state.

Yet there are other interpretations or versions of this story in which racism is only one of several potential villains. From the minute Mecham abolished the state's MLK holiday, Arizona was subject to numerous economic boycotts and cancellations of conventions, concerts, and other entertainment events—and even more threats to that effect. As the 1990 vote on the dueling ballot initiatives approached, the National Football League threatened to take the 1993 Super Bowl, scheduled to be played in Phoenix, elsewhere. According to one explanation of the defeat of the ballot initiatives, Arizona voters did not take such threats too kindly and effectively told their detractors to go to hell (Willey 1991).

There were other sources of discontent and, thus, additional explanations for opposition to the MLK holiday. Fiscal conservatives apparently protested the use of state funds for an additional state holiday. Italian Americans, and others, did not want to do away with Columbus Day. (And it was easier to vote against both propositions rather than figure out which one did which harm.) Some Mecham supporters may have voted against the holiday not because they shared his racial attitudes but because they saw another opportunity to thumb their noses at the state's business and political establishment (Willey 1991).

While many observers pooh-poohed such explanations as rhetorical window-dressing for politically incorrect racial antagonism (Alozie 1995; Kastenbaum 1991), they are in keeping with the sort of individualistic, laissez-faire, don't-tread-on-me mentality outlined above—Arizona's own brand of independent conservatism. It is also worth noting that Arizona voters reversed themselves in 1992 and approved by a wide margin (22 percent) a ballot proposition that created a state MLK holiday and consolidated Washington's and Lincoln's birthdays into a single Presidents' Day. If racial prejudice or conservatism had been the deciding factor, it is unlikely that any of these changes—the passage of time (and the national limelight) or the change in holiday-shuffling tactics or the lack of competing propositions—would have made such a difference.

In many respects, California's reputation as a bastion of liberalism is the mirror image of Arizona's reputation as a bastion of conservatism. A legendary haven for the unconventional, California is home to the student unrest of the Free Speech Movement, the hippies of Haight-Ashbury, the black nationalism of the Black Panther Party, the labor movement of Cesar Chavez and the United Farm Workers, the music of the Grateful Dead, and the hedonism of Hollywood. And while the gay rights movement got its start in New York, California can lay claim to Harvey Milk, who, as one of the first openly gay candidates to be elected to public office, represented one of the most vital and politically powerful, if not the most established, gay communities in the nation.

Yet, California is also the political birthplace of Richard Nixon, Ronald Reagan, and the tax revolts of the 1980s. Before Bill Clinton ran for president in 1992, Lyndon Johnson was the only postwar Democratic presidential candidate who could claim the support of California voters. Despite its reputation for cultural diversity and political tolerance, California cannot escape the shame of Japanese internment camps, Hollywood blacklists, the Watts race riots, or the notorious LAPD (Los Angeles Police Department).

California is just too big and too diverse for any such monolithic portrayal of its political culture. Liberalism and conservatism, Democrats and Republicans all have deep roots in California. The 1990 California congressional delegation, for example, included some of the institution's most liberal Democrats (Howard Berman, Barbara Boxer, Ron Dellums, Henry Waxman) and some of its most conservative Republicans (William Dannemeyer, Robert Dornan). Between 1958 and 1989, California voters elected two Republican and two Democratic governors for two terms each. George Deukmejian, Republican governor from 1983 to 1990, pursued a very conservative fiscal and social agenda in which tax cuts and prison building were prominently featured (Putnam 1992: 47–48; Syer and Culver 1992: 46).

Democrats could claim a plurality of California citizens, but Republicans were not that far behind. In 1990, 50 percent of California voters registered as Democrats, 39 percent as Republicans (the other 11 percent declined to list a party preference). Surveys conducted between 1976 and 1988 show 39 percent of California respondents identifying themselves as Democrats; 33 percent as Republicans; and 27 percent as Independents. In comparison to other states, California had one of the highest percentages of self-identified Democrats outside the southern and border-states region; but it also had a relatively high percentage of self-identified Republicans—only 1.4 percent less than Arizona (Erikson, Wright, and McIver 1993: 15).

The most important points about the ideological climate in 1990 California politics, however, are that the state's Democrats were very liberal, and in control. According to national surveys for 1976 to 1988, California Democrats were more liberal than Democrats in every other state except Connecticut (Erikson, Wright, and McIver 1993: 40).[9] California Independents were more liberal than those in *all* other states. Overall, then, California had the fifth highest percentage of self-identified liberals and the tenth lowest percentage of self-identified conservatives (Erikson, Wright, and McIver 1993: 16). Compared to Arizona, California had 6 percent more liberals and 6 percent fewer conservatives (and an equal percentage of moderates).

During this same time period (1970s and 80s), California had by far the most liberal set of Democratic political elites (congressional candidates, state legislators, local party chairpersons, and national convention delegates) in the country (Erikson, Wright, and McIver 1993: 103). Combine this with the fact that Democrats had maintained control of the California legislature since 1958 (with the exception of two years in the late 1960s), and you get some of nation's the most liberal public policies. Since the 1970s, California has been a national leader in environmental conservation and protection, imposing, for example, some of the toughest air and water pollution standards in the country (Peirce and Hagstrom 1983: 755; Syer and Culver 1992: 42). Compared to other states (in 1987, at least), California relied quite heavily on corporate income taxes, a fiscal policy usually favored by liberals and labor and "invariably" opposed by business interests (Hansen 1990: 342, 344). The study of state welfare efforts mentioned earlier found California and Arizona to be "at nearly opposite ends of the scale" (Albritton 1990: 429). On the same five indicators of welfare effort, California ranked, respectively, seventh, seventh, fifth, sixth, and fifteenth. And the same studies of general policy liberalism that placed Arizona in the most conservative category put California in the most liberal. For example, Robert Erikson, Gerald Wright, and John McIver's study (1993: 77) ranks California policies as the third most liberal (after New York and Massachusetts) and Arizona's as the sixth most conservative (after Arkansas, South Carolina, Mississippi, Alabama, and Indiana).

Women's policy interests, as conventionally defined (see Chapter 1), often coincide with a liberal and/or Democratic agenda. From antidiscrimination measures, to issues of reproductive rights and health, to improving the quantity and quality of child care and family leave options, to the recognition of family violence as a political issue, to combating the ever-growing problems of the feminization of poverty—all these "interests" rely upon a liberal vision of an active government and an expansive social welfare state; and they are issues that are much more likely to end up on Democratic platforms than on Republican ones. Legislators wishing to "make a difference" on these issues ostensibly would find much more support from their colleagues and constituents and many more policy precedents to draw upon in a politically liberal state than in a conservative one.

While politically diverse in many respects, the ideological climate in California in 1990 was strongly liberal in the ways that would have mattered most to state legislators looking for opportunities and approval for representing women. Such opportunities and encouragement come most directly, or most immediately, from colleagues, past and present. Dominated by very liberal Democrats and historically willing to extend the arm of the state in the name of liberal causes, the California legislature provided a most conducive ideological atmosphere for the advocacy of "women's issues"—especially in comparison to the more conservative, Republican-dominated Arizona legislature.

## Party Politics

By 1990, the "traditional" view of California as a "weak-party, strong-interest-group state" (Syer 1987: 33) was rather out-of-date and misleading in one respect. To be sure, interest groups were as strong as ever, and California political parties remained weak in terms of voter loyalties and formal electoral organization. In previous years, bipartisanship *was* the norm in the state legislature, and committee leadership positions frequently went to members of the minority party (Syer 1987: 35). Bipartisanship was especially strong in the California Senate, which had a long-standing, unwritten rule prohibiting members from helping challengers trying to unseat incumbent senators of the opposition party (Syer and Culver 1992: 195). "Senators of both parties had what amounted to a mutual nonaggression pact" (Syer 1987: 35). During the 1980s, however, partisanship within the state legislature increased dramatically. By 1990, relations between legislative Democrats and Republicans were anything but cooperative. Democrats were united under strong leadership and a mutual determination to maintain majority control. Republicans were united in their determination to wrest control from the Democrats, who, they firmly believed, had gained control unfairly and deceptively.

Ironically, it was the ascendancy of Willie Brown, the longest reigning Assembly Speaker in California history (1980–95) and the first to gain his position by putting together a coalition of Democratic and Republican votes, that marked the end of bipartisanship in the California legislature. Brown, in fact, had a knack for taking advantage of fissures and weaknesses amongst the Republicans in order to consolidate his own power and the power of the Democratic party (Richardson 1996). He also had a knack for campaign fundraising, soliciting large contributions from ever-eager corporate and labor interests and funneling them to Democrats in need, thereby assuring not only a Democratic majority in the Assembly, but also the loyalty of Democratic members (Clucas 1992). Brown also funneled a great deal of money to the state Democratic party, so much so that the distinction between his political machine and the party organization was effectively lost.

In effect, Brown was a major benefactor for the party and the party was an arm of his machine. In fact, without a Democratic governor, Willie Brown was the real leader of the party; he was the glue that held it together to keep at least one branch of the state government in Democratic hands. (Richardson 1996: 323)

"Other Assembly Speakers before Brown were adept at raising campaign funds," notes a recent biography. "But no Speaker before Brown so completely centralized the campaign apparatus or made it so completely the focus of one man's ambition" (Richardson 1996: 320). Political scientist Richard Clucas concurs, reporting that "for most of the 1980s, the Speaker was the single largest contributor to Assembly races, outspending the two major external parties and the state's largest political action committees" (Clucas 1992: 269). Willie Brown set the standard. The Democratic leadership of the state senate and the Republican leadership in both houses all tried to emulate Brown's methods and match his achievements. After a Republican senator blatantly violated the aforementioned "mutual nonaggression pact," David Roberti was elected leader of the Senate in 1980 by promising his Democratic colleagues that he would play an active role in assuring their reelection (Syer and Culver 1992: 195). Assembly Republican leader Patrick Nolan tried so hard to mirror Brown's fundraising organization that he eventually pled guilty to federal corruption charges.

The end result of all these efforts was twofold. First, they fueled the rivalry between the two parties; second, they greatly enhanced the power of the leadership within each party. As Elizabeth Capell, political scientist and California lobbyist, observes of California politics:

Centralized campaign structures deriving from each party caucus in each house mutually reinforce centralized leadership structures: as the campaign structures have grown more centralized, this has strengthened the hand of party leaders and in turn increased their obligation to assist in electing fellow partisans. (Capell 1991: 4)

There were other forces fueling party competition in the 1990 California legislature. First, the constitutional requirement of a two-thirds supermajority for passage of any measure that either raises state revenues or appropriates state funds gives a unified minority a great deal of power. Empowered by the tax revolt of 1978, Ronald Reagan's successful run for the White House in 1980, and the election of a Republican governor in 1982, conservative Republicans in the California legislature were increasingly willing and able to take advantage of this veto power. The source of the most intense interparty conflicts, however, was reapportionment.

Under the leadership of Willie Brown and Phillip Burton, the California Democratic party flexed its strongest muscles in the reapportionment battles of the early 1980s. With growing numbers of Republican voters, Republican politicians anticipated significant gains in both the state legislature and in Congress; they even harbored hopes for majority control in the former (Richardson 1996: 283). Ultimately, though, drawing the district lines was up to the Democrat-controlled state legislature and the Democratic governor, Jerry Brown. And there is no question that the lines were drawn—gerrymandered—to give the Democrats a lopsided advantage in both the state legislature and Congress. The Republicans fought back with numerous ballot propositions, but to no avail.[10] Feeling betrayed by the Speaker they had helped elect, they made no effort to hide their resentment. According to Robert Naylor, the Republican Assembly leader at the time, "That reapportionment deal poisoned the well. Just that one act dramatically altered the civility of the Assembly and the ability of parties to work together—no question about it" (Richardson 1996: 282). "There's a war going on in the Assembly over the state's future," declared Gil Ferguson, one of the Assembly's more disgruntled Republicans (Peterson 1988: 180).

At its core, then, the intense interparty rivalry of the 1980s and 1990 California legislature was not ideologically based. The Republican Party was becoming more conservative during this time period, and there is little doubt that the parties were becoming more ideologically polarized (Margolis and Zeiger 1987; Putnam 1992). But ideology was not the source of either intraparty unity or the power of party leadership, especially among the Democrats. "Democrats are held together by agreement on procedure, not philosophy," according to one caucus member. "It binds the disparate elements of the party together" (Zeiger and Block 1988: 154). Need and electability were the primary determinants of whether legislators received financial support from the leadership, not ideology or "loyal" roll call voting (Clucas 1994: 419–20).[11] Willie Brown apparently gave Assembly Democrats wide latitude to pursue their own policy goals, as long as they did not interfere with his primary goals—his own reelection as Speaker and the maintenance of the Democratic majority (Richardson 1996; Zeiger and Block 1988).

Ideology played a much larger role in Arizona. The main features of Arizona party politics in 1990 were not interparty competition and strong leadership but ideological factionalism and weak leadership within the dominant Republican party. "At various times over the past forty years, the Republican party has been divided between extreme conservative and more moderate conservative factions," notes one commentator, adding, "No one would use the term 'Liberal' Republican in Arizona" (Ritt 1993: 14). This division in the Republican Party came to a head in the late 1980s with the election and impeachment of Evan Mecham.

By his own accounts, Mecham represented the extreme right wing of the Arizona Republican Party; he made no bones about his distaste for the more moderate, business-oriented Republican establishment. Mecham's political philosophy combined the most radical version of free-enterprise, anti-government economic conservatism with the social conservatism of the increasingly powerful "Religious Right." The recision of the Martin Luther King Jr. holiday was not the only early indication of Mecham's agenda (McClain 1988: 631–33; Watkins 1990). His state budget called for the repeal of a 1 percent state sales tax, which would have reduced state revenues by $300 million, and for severe cuts in education funding, especially for the state universities. His education liaison reportedly "told a legislative committee that if parents tell their children the Earth is flat, teachers should not try to convince the child otherwise"; and his appointee to the State Board of Education stated that the women's rights movement was a creation of radical lesbians and that working women were to blame for increasing divorce rates (McClain 1988: 631). Upon learning that the organizer of the movement to recall him was gay, Mecham characterized his enemies as militant liberals, militant homosexuals, even communists; and he publicly solicited the names of homosexuals working in state government.

Meanwhile, the two factions were struggling for control over the state Republican Party. One of the major confrontations took place at the 1989 state party convention over a (Mecham-supported) resolution that declared the United States a "Christian nation" (Sheridan 1995: 323). Barry Goldwater became a prime target of the ultra-conservatives within his own party, not only for his public endorsement of Mecham's impeachment but also for his (and his first wife's) long-standing support for abortion rights and "his staunch defense of other individual matters of conscience, including the right of gays to serve in the military" (Sheridan 1995: 323).

Forced to vote on either Mecham's impeachment (in the House) or his conviction (in the Senate), Arizona legislators had to take a position on one side or the other. For the Democrats, the decision was an easy one. The Republicans, however, were deeply split. As late as the 1990 session, relations between the two Republican factions had not been mended. Mutual distrust lingered, antagonism stewed; the tension was palpable. The moderate wing had gained control of the House and Senate leadership, but the more conservative faction was contentious and restless. Party unity was very precarious; and party leadership was consequently cautious. Especially threatening—to the Republican party as whole, but especially to the ultra-conservatives—was the very real possibility that a coalition of moderate Republicans and conservative Democrats would carry the day on major legislation. Conservative Republicans were particularly concerned about being left out of the all-important budget and tax negotiations.[12]

The contrast between the interparty "procedural" conflict of the California legislature and the intraparty ideological conflict of the Arizona legislature was readily apparent in my own interviews with members of both institutions. Issues of partisanship figured prominently in the somewhat unstructured discussions I had with legislators of both states about of the nature of conflict and the sources of disagreement among their colleagues. The majority of those interviewed spoke of conflict between the two parties: 59 percent of the Arizona legislators and 70 percent of the California legislators. In describing that conflict, however, California legislators were just as likely to talk about issues as they were to talk about "pure politics" and the quest for electoral victory. A few Arizona legislators acknowledged this tactical side of partisan conflict, but most either emphasized the policy or ideological disagreements between the parties or did not explicitly recognize the distinction between policy and "politics."

Whether associated with policy debates or electoral competition, partisan conflict clearly was the dominant theme among the California legislators. Intraparty conflict was mentioned by less than a fourth of the California legislators interviewed and was viewed as a fairly unremarkable, standard characteristic of both parties. Arizona legislators, on the other hand, were just as likely to mention the factionalism within the Republican Party as they were to mention the conflicts between parties. Arizona Democrats and Republicans alike were well aware of the troubled nature of the Republican caucus and its bitter division between the ultra-conservative "Mechamites" and moderately conservative party regulars. The moderate Republicans (and some Democrats) tended to portray their more conservative rivals as uncompromising, overly partisan, and overzealous, even militant. The conservative Republicans viewed their rivals as weak willed and disloyal, liberals in sheep's clothing. The Democrats just looked on with mild amusement, anticipating opportunities to take advantage of the infighting across the aisle, yet also wary of the conservative agenda of the right wing.

As interesting and as differentiated as party politics in Arizona and California are, it is difficult to assess the implications for patterns of women's political representation across the states. Interparty competition and strong party leadership, such as that in California, could either enhance or constrain the structure of opportunities and incentives available to women and those who want to act for women, depending on who is allied with whom and on what serves the interests of those in control. Roughly the same can be said for consequences of intraparty factionalism and weak party leadership, such as that in Arizona (within the majority party at least). The effects of party politics, in essence, cannot be gauged independent of the relationships between sex, gender, and power within each state legislature.

## Sex, Gender, and Political Power

The following remarks offer a window on the world of California politics in the 1960s and early 70s:

> If you can't eat their food, drink their booze, screw their women, take their money and then vote against them, you've got no business being up here.

> Money is the mother's milk of politics.
> —Jesse "Big Daddy" Unruh, Speaker of the
> California Assembly, 1961–68 (J. Mills 1987: 1, 8)

> I like people whose balls roar when they see injustice.
> —Phillip Burton, member of the California
> Assembly, 1957–64, and the U.S. House of
> Representatives, 1964–83 (Richardson 1996: 55)

These declarations by two of the most revered California politicians masterfully encapsulate every notable aspect of California political culture in their day: the overwhelming importance of money, the desperate interdependence of lobbyists and legislators, the aggressive liberalism of leaders, and the profound absence of women in power. It was an intensely masculine culture in which women—especially beautiful young women—were sexual tokens of power, a currency of exchange, and an emblem of possession. It was a world in which one of the "social benefits of being a legislator" (regardless of marital status) was enjoying "the young women who were so freely available" (Richardson 1996: 124).

Women, as legislators, were completely absent from the California Senate until 1976, when Rose Ann Vuich, a Democrat, was elected. That year also marked the first time in California history that more than four women served in the Assembly at the same time (Syer and Culver 1992: 104). In 1976, only two women had ever been elected to a statewide executive office: Ivy Baker Priest, a Republican who served as state treasurer from 1967 to 1974; and March Fong Eu, a Democrat who, upon being elected secretary of state in 1974, became the first Asian American woman in the country to win statewide office.[13]

Change did occur. The number of female legislators increased slowly but surely. By 1980, their numbers had doubled: two in the Senate and ten in the Assembly. In 1990, five women were in the Senate, fourteen in the Assembly. Compared to other states, however, the percentage of female legislators in

California remained slightly below average; the state's ranking in the 1980s hovered between twenty-seventh and thirtieth (CAWP 1996). As governor from 1975 to 1982, Jerry Brown made a concerted effort to, in his words, "make government a mirror image of what society is" (Peirce and Hagstrom 1983: 756) by appointing unprecedented numbers of women, blacks, Latinos, and Asians to executive and judicial positions. In one of his most controversial moves, he appointed Rose Bird chief justice of the California Supreme Court, making her the first woman to occupy that position. Thirty percent of Brown's administrative appointments during his first six years in office went to women (Bayes 1989: 105). Half of his cabinet were women (Peirce and Hagstrom 1983: 755). Eu, however, remained the only woman occupying a statewide elective position in the executive branch.

In Unruh's day, the most visible symbol of masculinized power was the lunch clubs. A "decidedly male" and deeply entrenched Capitol institution, these clubs were "more than just social gatherings; they were important and discreet [sic] marketplaces of political power. Lawmakers and lobbyists mingled cutting deals, telling off-color jokes, and schmoozing well into the afternoon"—all at the expense of the lobbyists, of course (Richardson 1996: 131–32). Due in large part to new disclosure laws that prohibited lobbyists from spending more than $10 a month on a legislator, the lunch clubs had all but disappeared by 1990 (Capell 1991: 6; Richardson 1996: 320).

In 1985, the women of the California legislature declared they had had enough of their male colleagues' sexist remarks and patronizing attitudes and formed the Legislative Women's Caucus. "To provide unity in the face of disrespectful and demeaning behavior by male legislators" (Syer and Culver 1992: 104), all women, Democrats and Republicans alike, were welcomed as members of the Caucus. The Caucus quickly became an effective voice on policy matters as well, taking positions on and advancing such issues as child care, violence against women, and child support enforcement (Ellis 1991; Syer and Culver 1992: 105). Of course, there were many "women's issues," such as sex education and family planning, on which the more liberal and conservative members could not come to agreement; and on such issues, the Caucus remained silent. But there was enough consensus among the women to sustain and even strengthen the Caucus. All of the California women I interviewed expressed nothing but enthusiasm and support for the social, symbolic, and policy goals of the Caucus. The men also were quite supportive, although several expressed doubts about the group's policy effectiveness.

Much had changed. Rose Ann Vuich's bell, which she rang whenever she heard the words "gentlemen of the Senate" or some other such sexist remark on the Senate floor, was practically silent in 1990. "Women have arrived" declared one the Capitol's foremost journalists. "Women may not have yet achieved full parity with men in California politics, but the overwhelming evidence is that it's merely a matter of time, that the overt sexism that colored politics only a few years ago is rapidly disappearing" (Walters 1988: Forum 1).

Other observers were more cautious. A profile of the four women in the 1989 Senate noted that while all four "say they are proud of their legislative achievements and believe their male colleagues generally treat them as equals, . . . some say they still face a 'good old boy' network, subtle sexism and male-oriented thinking on issues such as child care" (J. Matthews 1989). Still others have argued that women are still excluded from the truly powerful positions in the California legislature. "It is one thing to be elected; it is another thing to be a power player," according to a popular textbook on California politics (Syer and Culver 1992: 104). No woman, the authors note, has ever chaired the most powerful fiscal and judiciary committees. Moreover, they add, no women were "key players in the great budget impasse of the summer of 1990."

Richard Zeiger and Sherry Bebitch Jeffe's assessment of women in California politics in 1988 sums it up: "Moving in—Yes; Moving up—Maybe." Women were not only absent from the leadership of fiscal and judiciary committees; they were also much less likely than the men to head the committees "coveted by members as fertile ground for raising campaign money" —commonly referred to as "juice" committees (Zeiger and Jeffe 1988: 8). Partly as a result, female legislators raised, on average, considerably less money than the men did and were less able to share the wealth, so to speak. "None of California's women has yet emerged as a political 'queen-maker,' able or willing to raise vast sums of money necessary to turn the course of legislative campaigns." Nor did any have enough "clout at the top of their respective caucuses" to penetrate the old boys' network that determines "who will be anointed in early party primaries" (Zeiger and Jeffe 1988: 8).[14] Not surprisingly, many female politicians believed the male-dominated leadership of both parties was more likely to "anoint" male candidates than female ones (Zeiger and Jeffe 1988: 9).

Most observers are quick to point out the more positive side of things. Effectively shut out of the high-stakes power plays, the female legislators were then free to pursue their own policy interests unconstrained by internal "politics" and untainted by "rumors of corruption and scandal" (Walters 1988: Forum 6). Thus, they earned a reputation for being independent, honest, hard-working policymakers. Not a bad reputation to have at "a time in the state's history when the electorate is increasingly alienated from its government and the state Legislature, increasingly in the grasp of special interests, finds it more and more difficult to resolve knotty political disputes" (Zeiger and Jeffe 1988: 8). Such independence also has important implications for the representation of women and women's issues in the California legislature. If, as I have argued here, party politics had little to do with ideology and being a "major player" had so little to do with public policymaking, then women's absence from "real" positions of power should in no way have inhibited either their willingness or ability to "make a difference" on women's issues. If anything, their willingness and ability to act for women was enhanced—at least, on occasion—by the solidarity and policy effectiveness of the Women's Caucus.

Arizona certainly has had its share of good old boy politics. As mentioned earlier, the state's political agenda has been controlled by small, elite groups of white businessmen since statehood, their grip having only recently slipped. A 1987 survey of Arizona state legislators uncovered convincing evidence that women faced significantly greater barriers to public office than did men (Kelly, Burgess, and Kaufmanis 1987: 52–54). As candidates, the women received less encouragement and less money from their party leaders. Overall, the average financial contribution received by women was less than half that received by men. Although the women were more likely than the men to be opposed in their primary elections, their average primary campaign expenditures were only 80 percent of that of men's. Women also were more likely to face opposition in the general election. The female legislators surveyed were well aware of gender biases in the electoral process, and much more so than their male counterparts. For example, more than three-quarters of the women, but less than 40 percent of the men agreed that not having access to the "good ole boy network" was a barrier to women's political success.[15]

At the same time, however, women have maintained a significant and widely accepted presence in Arizona politics. The contrast between Arizona and California in this respect is quite striking. Granted, both states extended suffrage to women via ballot initiatives well before the rest of the nation. Yet Arizona voters, the large majority of whom voted in favor of the initiative, supported woman suffrage much more enthusiastically than did California voters, who endorsed their initiative only by a very slight margin (Kelly 1993: 104; Rothschild and Hronek 1987: 8; Syer and Culver 1992: 103).[16] If the numbers of women in public office is any indication, Arizonans' enthusiasm toward (or, at least, comfort with) women's political participation has extended to the highest levels of political office.

"As soon as Arizona women won the franchise, they began to run for public office"—and succeed (Rothschild and Hronek 1987: 10). In 1914, Frances Munds won a seat in the state senate, Rachel Berry was elected to the state house of representatives, and five other women won county offices throughout the state (Rothschild and Hronek 1987: 10). Munds, in fact, was only the second woman in the entire country to be elected to a state senate. After

Munds, few women served in the Arizona Senate until the late 1960s; but after Berry, at least one woman served in the House of Representatives every session, except in 1925. Since 1967, the Senate has had between four and six female members (out of thirty). The number of women in the House shot up to eleven in 1953, when the overall membership was (temporarily) expanded from sixty to eighty, and has slowly increased since then (Kelly, Burgess, and Kaufmanis 1987: 42–44). Since 1979 (when CAWP started collecting such data), Arizona has been among the top ten states in terms of percentage of female legislators; since 1989, it has been among the top five.

Arizona women have maintained an impressive record of winning statewide elective offices as well. Elsie Toles became the first woman in the United States to achieve statewide office when she was elected as Arizona's state superintendent of public instruction in 1920. Elected Arizona state auditor in 1926, Ana Frohmiller became the first woman in the country to occupy such a position (Rothschild and Hronek 1987: 12–14). Frohmiller served as state auditor until 1950, when she ran for governor, won the Democratic primary, but narrowly lost the election. She was replaced by another woman, Jewel Jordan, who served until 1968. Elsie Toles was state superintendent of public instruction for only three years, but since 1965 that office has been occupied by a woman for all but five years (1970–74). Since 1981, at least one member of the state's Corporation Commission, which regulates public utilities and monitors corporations, has been female. Finally, Rose Mofford was Arizona's secretary of state for ten years before she took over the governorship in 1988 when Evan Mecham was impeached.[17]

Like his California contemporary Jerry Brown, Bruce Babbitt appointed an impressive number of women to state administrative positions: 30 percent of the 2,100 positions he filled during his nine years as governor (Hale, Kelly, Burgess, and Shapiro 1987: 69). Many of these women were appointed to positions at the highest levels, including head of the Departments of Administration, Commerce, and Water Resources. As a result, Arizona ranked fifth in the nation in the number of women appointed to cabinet-level positions between 1980 and 1985, fourth in 1986 (Hale, Kelly, Burgess, and Shapiro 1987: 71). The number and status of women in the executive branch dropped precipitously once Mecham assumed office (Hale, Kelly, Burgess, and Shapiro 1987: 81). Whereas only three states had a better record of women in cabinet-level positions than Arizona did in 1986, by 1988 only three states had a *worse* record (Kelly 1993: 105).[18] Fortunately, Mecham's purge of women was as short-lived as his administration. Upon assuming the governor's office, Rose Mofford quickly reversed course and began appointing women in far greater numbers and in the highest level positions. In 1990, women once again headed three of the ten state departments — Administration, Economic Security, and Insurance (Kelly 1993: 105).

According to Rita Mae Kelly (1987), the foremost authority on women in Arizona politics, these women present an odd mixture of conservatism and feminism. While they are feminist in their determination to participate in politics on par with men, they often are quite conservative, even antifeminist, in their policy positions and philosophical outlook. Indeed, Kelly's 1987 survey of Arizona legislators found the women as conservative as and sometimes more conservative than the men on a wide range of issues, including many feminist issues (Kelly, Burgess, and Kaufmanis 1987: 51, 56–61).[19] Kelly's profile of Donna Carlson further illustrates and typifies this synthesis of conservatism and feminism in Arizona (Kelly, Burgess, and Kaufmanis 1987: 50–51).

Having worked all her adult life to support her husband and children, Carlson first made her mark in Arizona politics in 1974, when she became the first woman elected to any political office in her Mormon-dominated district. She was elected to the state legislature and served a total of four terms. During her tenure, she became the first woman to chair the American Legislative Exchange Council, "a nonpartisan conservative issue discussion group consisting of legislators from several states" (Kelly, Burgess, and Kaufmanis 1987: 51). In 1987, she joined Evan Mecham's staff as his legislative liaison, a very high-profile position, especially for a woman in Mecham's administration. Later that year, Carlson became the primary whistle-blower and moving force behind Mecham's impeachment. She not only reported his dubious use of official funds and his undocumented campaign loans; the death threats she received as a result were the subject of the attorney general's investigation which Mecham was found guilty of obstructing (Dreifus 1988; Watkins 1990).

At the same time Carlson was pursuing such nontraditional, trailblazing public roles, she gained a reputation as the "Phyllis Schlafly of the West" (Dreifus 1988: 46). One of her first acts as state legislator was to introduce a bill "requiring women to use their husbands' names on all public documents" (Kelly, Burgess, and Kaufmanis 1987: 50). Throughout her career she was steadfast in her opposition to the Equal Rights Amendment and abortion rights. Yet, "[h]er conservatism obviously [did] not include encouraging women to stay at home, or to accept unequal treatment." Indeed, one of her primary concerns was "how legislation in general could harm professional women" (Kelly, Burgess, and Kaufmanis 1987: 51).[20] In many respects, then, her philosophical position—and that of many of her female compatriots—can be seen as a gendered version of Arizona's conservative yet individualistic and independent political culture.[21]

This is not to say that all women in the Arizona legislature thought alike or that they were unified in any organized fashion. To the contrary, Arizona lacked a formal, or even informal, legislative women's caucus. The women I interviewed offered several reasons for this. A few claimed that some of the women had once tried to organize but were ultimately unsuccessful. The primary obstacles seemed to be lack of interest and the expectation that the women would be unable to come to agreement on any significant issues. The divisions among the women reflected those of the legislature as a whole. There were the regular partisan differences, but the gulf between the moderate and conservative Republican women was just as wide as, if not wider than, that between the men of their party. Several Arizona legislators interviewed—male and female—noted that some of the worst conflicts occurred among the women. Policy disagreements among the Republican women were thought to be particularly intense and especially prone to spill over into personal grievances and grudges. If the formation of a women's caucus is any indication of the women's ability and willingness to come together both politically and socially, then the more numerous Arizona female delegation was less successful than the smaller California delegation at finding common ground.

### Status of Women in the 1990 State Legislatures

There are many sources or indicators of status, prestige, and respect operating within state legislatures, some more directly related to institutional opportunity structures than others. This section compares the men and women of the 1990 Arizona and California legislatures along three dimensions of status, beginning with those more tangentially related to institution-specific opportunities and privileges.[22] The first, *social status*, refers to the occupational and educational backgrounds the legislators bring with them. Lawmakers' prior political experience and electoral security—their political fame and fortunes, so to speak—constitute their *political status*. Most relevant to institutional power, perquisites, and opportunities are markers of a legislator's *professional status:* seniority, party (caucus) leadership, membership in prestigious or particularly powerful committees, and, of course, committee leadership.

*Social status.* Nationwide, women and men often follow different paths to political office, paths that reflect the occupational and educational sex differences found in the general population. Although these differences were greater in the 1970s than in the 1980s, as more and more women began pursuing advanced degrees and nontraditional careers, they remain significant. Female lawmakers, according to previous research, are more likely than their male colleagues to have experience in historically female-dominated occupations, especially education, and are less likely to have worked in traditionally male-dominated areas such as business and the law (Carroll and Strimling 1983; Diamond 1977; Johnson and Carroll 1978;

Stoper 1977; Thomas 1994; Werner 1966). Women in public office, like the women they are to represent, also have less accumulated experience in the paid labor force overall. Some, whose main occupation is homemaking and child rearing, have little such experience or none at all.

Status differentials are strongly associated with these occupational patterns. As mentioned in the previous chapter, female-dominated occupations tend to be concentrated in relatively low-wage and low-status areas. Among professionals, women are more likely to be found among the primary and secondary educators, for example; among wage earners, women are more likely to be found in the service sector rather than in the more lucrative and stable manufacturing and construction sectors. These status differentials in occupation are reinforced by sex differences in educational background. In the general population as well as among public officials, women are less likely than men to have pursued graduate education or to have attended professional schools in business, law, or medicine (Carroll and Strimling 1983; Diamond 1977; Johnson and Carroll 1978; Kelly, Burgess, and Kaufmanis 1987; Thomas 1994). In terms of occupation and education, then, women who obtain public office tend to enjoy less social status than do their male colleagues. Regardless of whether the skills one obtains in graduate and professional schools or in male-dominated occupations are, in fact, more relevant to political performance or legislative effectiveness than those obtained in high school, college, or female-dominated occupations, such skills are accorded a certain amount of social prestige and respect, especially in male-dominated, elite institutions (Johnson and Carroll 1978: 17A).

To some extent, these gendered patterns in occupational and educational background and status can be found among the members of the 1990 Arizona and California legislatures. The women in both state institutions were much more likely than the men to have backgrounds in female-dominated occupations. More than half (59 percent) of the Arizona female officials identified themselves as having worked as one or more of the following: social worker, homemaker, teacher (primary or secondary), health worker (but not a physician or dentist), service employee (e.g., waitress), secretary, or an employee of a nonprofit charitable organization. Most were either teachers (22 percent) or homemakers (18 percent). Only one in five (19 percent) of the Arizona male legislators fit into any of these occupational categories. Reflecting the more professional, competitive, and masculine nature of California politics, the California legislators were less likely than their Arizona counterparts to have had such occupational backgrounds. Only a third (32 percent) of the California women had experience in a female-dominated occupation, and none of them identified themselves as homemakers. Even so, that was much more experience than their male colleagues had; only 7 percent of the California men had worked in such areas.

Members of the legal profession have always had a significant, even dominant presence among political elites in the United States, especially at higher levels of office. Not so in Arizona, where the legal profession carries no particular cachet of political credentials (Hermann and Kelly 1987: 84). Hardly any of the 1990 Arizona legislators were attorneys: only 8 percent of the males and 4 percent of the females. In contrast, the 1990 California legislature had quite a few, almost all of whom were men. Over a quarter of the California male legislators were attorneys; only one (5 percent) of the nineteen California female legislators was.

What the California women may have lacked in terms of status in the legal profession, they made up for with their experience in the business world. Over half (58 percent) had a background in one or more of the following areas: accounting, banking, or financial investments; real estate investment, development, management and/or sales; insurance; small business (mostly retail, manufacturing, or service-oriented); advertising, public relations, marketing, or sales; private sector management or administration. In fact, the California women were twice as likely as the men to have had such business experience. As a group, the Arizona female legislators also had a great deal of experience in business and finance, almost as much as their male colleagues had. Almost half of these women (48 percent) had such backgrounds, as compared to 56 percent of their male colleagues.

In neither state, then, was the occupational status of female legislators consistently or uniformly inferior to that of the male legislators. While the women were more likely than the men to have backgrounds in the low-status, female-dominated "pink ghetto," they were as likely (in Arizona) or more likely (in California) to have the sorts of business experiences traditionally valued among male politicians. Sex differences in the legislators' educational status were muted and irregular as well. While the California women were less likely than the men to have law degrees, they were no less likely to have completed college or to have obtained other postgraduate degrees. The vast majority of both female and male legislators in California had college educations. In contrast, many of the Arizona legislators had not obtained college degrees, and the women were slightly less likely to have done so than the men (45 percent of the women did not have college degrees, as compared to 30 percent of the men). Yet, the Arizona women were just as likely as the men to have postgraduate degrees (usually master's degrees or MBAs). In sum, there were no clear-cut gender hierarchies in the occupational or educational backgrounds of these Arizona and California lawmakers.

*Political status.* Prior experience in elective office distinguishes the two states more than it does the two sexes in either state. Relatively few of the Arizona women and men began their legislative careers having held any other elected political position. Only five women (18 percent) and nine men (14 percent) could claim such experience. Contrary to patterns in their occupational backgrounds, however, the men's experiences were more likely to be in education than were the women's. Six of the nine men who had held previous office had served on school boards, as compared to only one of the five women. Most of the other women and men had served previously as county supervisors or city councilmembers.

Working one's way up through local office was much more common among the California legislators. One third of the male lawmakers (32 percent) had been elected to city councils, county boards of supervisors, and school boards. (A few had been mayors or trustees of community colleges.) Their female colleagues had even more experience under their collective belt: 53 percent of them had held such public offices. Contrary to their Arizona counterparts, but in congruence with their occupational backgrounds, the California women were more likely than the men to have been members of school boards (40 percent of the women who held previous office, compared to 13 percent of the men).[23]

The political status of the California women was further enhanced by their electoral security. In terms of both party registration and electoral returns, the California female legislators had somewhat safer districts than did their male colleagues. On average, the women enjoyed a 26 percent margin in the distribution of their constituents' registered party affiliations and a 46 percent margin in their last general elections; the men had on average a 20 percent margin in party registration and a 36 percent margin in their last elections. The opposite pattern is found among the Arizona legislators. With an average margin of 22 percent in their districts' party registration and an average margin of 44 percent of the votes in their last general elections, the Arizona men had considerably more electoral security than the women, whose average margins were, respectively, 15 percent and 28 percent.

These sex-related patterns in political status and their implications for the political representation of women run contrary to those suggested by comparisons of sex ratios in the two state legislatures. It is the numerically vulnerable California female delegation that had more political experience and greater electoral security than their male counterparts. Such advantageous political status can be a valuable resource for those who wish to challenge the status quo. The numerically prominent Arizona women had fewer such resources to draw upon. They had just as much political experience as the Arizona men did, but given the paucity of such experience in that "citizens" legislature, it probably did not count for much. On the other hand, it would have been difficult for the Arizona women to have ignored the relative precariousness of their electoral positions.

*Professional status.* Logic dictates that if the numbers of women in state legislatures have been increasing in recent years—if women are relative newcomers—then the women who occupy such legislative positions will, as a group, have less seniority than their male colleagues. Indeed, other studies of state lawmakers (Johnson and Carroll 1978: 28A; Kelly, Burgess, and Kaufmanis 1987: 48; Thomas 1994: 45) have found this to be the case; and the members of the 1990 Arizona and California legislatures were no different. In both states, male legislators had accumulated on average approximately three more years of service than had their female colleagues. In the California legislature, women had an average tenure of 7.6 years, men 10.4 years; in the Arizona legislature, women had served an average of 5.4 years, men 8.7 years.[24] Approximately 30 percent more California men than women had held their current office for at least eight years (81 percent compared to 53 percent). While the majority of Arizona male legislators (56 percent) had served for at least 8 years in their current positions, the majority of their female associates (61 percent) had served less than eight years.

Close observers of both legislatures, however, discount the significance of seniority. In Arizona, legislative turnover was so high—in 1990, 24 percent of the Arizona legislators were serving their first term, as compared to only 10 percent of the California legislators—that it was not unusual for leadership positions to go to those who were serving only their second or third terms (Brown 1993: 25–26). In California, committee membership and leadership positions (chairs) were held purely at the discretion of the presiding officers of each house—the Speaker of the Assembly and the president pro tempore of the Senate—and seniority had little to do with their decisions (Capell 1989). What mattered most was "party affiliation, loyalty to the leadership, ability, political philosophy, friendships," and the legislators' own policy interests and goals (Capell 1989: 11). Thus, much like his or her Arizona counterpart, a California legislator in his or her second or third term was not necessarily prohibited from chairing a standing committee.

Examining the distribution of leadership positions, then, is a much more valid and direct way to measure professional prestige in both state legislatures. At first glance, female lawmakers in both states fared quite well in this respect. They were just as likely as their male colleagues to hold leadership positions in the party caucuses and to chair standing committees. Women and men also were equally likely to serve on prestigious fiscal and judiciary committees, and on the important gatekeeping Rules Committees.[25] Plus, women in both states were just as likely as the men to be members of the majority party, having access to the additional influence and effectiveness that such majority status usually grants.

**Table 2.1    Leadership Positions in the Arizona State Legislature, 1990**

| | Legislative Chamber | |
|---|---|---|
| Leadership Category | House | Senate |
| Majority Party Leaders | ♀ Speaker<br>Speaker pro tempore<br>Majority leader<br>Majority whip | President<br>Majority leader<br>Majority whip |
| Minority Party Leaders | Minority leader<br>Assistant minority leader<br>♀ Minority whip | Minority leader<br>Assistant minority leader<br>♀ Minority whip |
| Chairs of Prestige Committees | Appropriations<br>Ways and Means<br>Judiciary<br>Rules | ♀ Appropriations<br>Finance<br>Judiciary<br>♀ Rules |
| Other Committee Chairs | ♀ Banking and Insurance<br>Commerce<br>♀ Counties and Municipalities<br>♀ Education<br>Environment<br>♀ Government Operations<br>Health<br>♀ Human Resources and Aging<br>Natural Resources and Agriculture<br>Public Institutions and Rural Development<br>Tourism, Professions, and Occupations<br>Transportation | Commerce, Labor, Insurance and Banking<br>♀ Education<br>Government<br>Health, Welfare, Aging and Environment<br>Natural Resources and Agriculture<br>Transportation |

♀ denotes position occupied by a female legislator.

A closer look at the distribution of leadership positions, however, tells a somewhat different story—one that confirms the previously mentioned suspicions that women were effectively excluded from the most powerful positions in the California legislature. Tables 2.1 and 2.2 list the legislative leadership positions and standing committees of each house of each state legislature; positions and committee chairs held by women are marked by the symbol ♀.

In California, the two women who occupied legislative leadership positions were at the bottom of the Assembly majority-party totem pole: majority whip and Democratic caucus chair (whose main responsibilities were fundraising). No woman occupied a majority leadership position in the Senate. No woman occupied a minority leadership position in either the Assembly or the Senate. None of the powerful fiscal, judiciary, or rules com-

**Table 2.2  Leadership Positions in the California State Legislature, 1990**

| Leadership Category | Legislative Chamber | |
| --- | --- | --- |
| | Assembly | Senate |
| Majority Party Leaders | Speaker<br>Speaker pro tempore<br>Assistant speaker pro tempore<br>Majority floor leader<br>♀ Majority whip<br>♀ Democratic caucus chair | President (Lt. Governor)<br>President pro tempore<br>Majority floor leader<br>Majority whip<br>Democratic caucus chair |
| Minority Party Leaders | Minority floor leader<br>Minority whip<br>Republican caucus chair | Minority leader<br>Minority whip<br>Republican caucus chair |
| Chairs of Prestige Committees | Ways and Means<br>Revenue and Taxation<br>Judiciary<br>Rules | Appropriations<br>Budget and Fiscal Review<br>Revenue and Taxation<br>Judiciary<br>Rules |
| Chairs of "Juice" Committees | Finance and Insurance<br>♀ Utilities and Commerce<br>Governmental Organization | Insurance, Claims, and<br>    Corporations<br>♀ Banking and Commerce<br>Governmental Organization |
| Other Committee Chairs | Aging and Long Term Care<br>Agriculture<br>Economic Development and<br>    New Technology<br>♀ Education<br>Elections, Reapportionment, and<br>    Constitutional Amendments<br>♀ Environmental Safety and Toxic<br>    Materials<br>♀ Government Efficiency and<br>    Consumer Protection<br>Health<br>Housing and Community<br>    Development<br>Human Services<br>Labor and Employment<br>Local Government<br>Natural Resources<br>Public Employment, Retirement<br>    and Social Security<br>Public Safety<br>Transportation<br>Water, Parks, and Wildlife | Agriculture and Water<br>    Resources<br>Bonded Indebtedness and<br>    Methods of Finance<br>Business and Professions<br>Education<br>Elections and<br>    Reapportionment<br>Constitutional<br>    Amendments<br>Energy and Public Utilities<br>♀ Health and Human Services<br>Housing and Urban Affairs<br>Industrial Relations<br>♀ Local Government<br>Natural Resources and<br>    Wildlife<br>Public Employment and<br>    Retirement<br>Toxics and Public Safety<br>    Management<br>Transportation<br>Veterans Affairs |

♀ denotes position occupied by a female legislator.

mittees were chaired by women. Women did, however, chair one of the three most lucrative "juice" committees in each chamber (Bell 1984: 52): the Utilities and Commerce Committee in the Assembly and the Banking and Commerce Committee in the Senate.

The lackluster quality of leadership positions held by California female legislators is further accentuated when compared to the positions held by their Arizona counterparts. The most powerful position in the Arizona legislature, Speaker of the House, was occupied by a woman (Jane Dee Hull). Women also served as minority whips in both the House and the Senate. In the Senate, arguably the two most powerful committees—Appropriations and Rules—were chaired by women. In terms of professional status, the Arizona women were in a much better position, individually and collectively, to effect meaningful change.

THE STATUS of women within each state and the comparisons between the two states look quite different depending on which of the three status dimensions one examines. Socially, women in both states appear well situated. Politically, the California women come out ahead of not only their male colleagues but their Arizona counterparts as well. Professionally, the Arizona women have it over the California women. Fortunately, the legislators' own perceptions of women's fortunes help put these seemingly contradictory patterns in perspective. I asked the legislators interviewed for this study whether they thought their female colleagues had any advantages or disadvantages in influencing decisions or accomplishing their goals in general. Their responses are summarized in Table 2.3.

Almost every California woman interviewed (86 percent) named at least one problem or disadvantage that she and her female colleagues confronted as women. A few noted the problem of numbers: there were just too few women around. "It's a tough burden," said one. "Women legislators have a lot to overcome," said another; we are "a minority in a man's world." About a third of the California women (36 percent) mentioned general problems with sexism and discrimination. As one legislator put it, they were "still dealing with an old boys' network," just like women in the business world. Two of these women believed it was not unusual for a female legislator's bill to be "stolen," that is, for a male legislator to get credit for legislation a woman introduced and gathered support for. A related and even more frequently cited problem was women's absence from informal social gatherings—anything from impromptu drinks at local bars to receptions organized by interest groups. Half the California women interviewed thought, or at least wondered whether, this posed a serious problem. But they were not in agreement about the source of the problem. Some felt they were excluded from such occasions by the men (legislators and/or lobbyists);

Table 2.3  Legislators' Perceptions of Women's Status

| Perceived Status of Female Legislators | Arizona Legislators | | California Legislators | |
|---|---|---|---|---|
| | Female (N = 16) (%) | Male (N = 30) (%) | Female (N = 14) (%) | Male (N = 17) (%) |
| Disadvantage(s)[a] | | | | |
| 0. none mentioned | 31 | 63 | 14 | 53 |
| 1. possibly; unsure; slight | 37 | 10 | 29 | 6 |
| 2. electoral only | 0 | 3 | 0 | 0 |
| 3. yes, at least one type | 31 | 23 | 57 | 41 |
| Type of disadvantage(s)[b] | | | | |
| 0. none mentioned | 31 | 63 | 14 | 53 |
| 1. sexism, discrimination | 56 | 17 | 36 | 23 |
| 2. lack of experience, skills | 12 | 17 | 7 | 12 |
| 3. lack of time | 6 | 3 | 0 | 6 |
| 4. do not socialize—voluntarily | 6 | 0 | 14 | 0 |
| 5. do not socialize—involuntarily | 0 | 0 | 14 | 6 |
| 6. do not socialize—both | 0 | 0 | 21 | 0 |
| 7. too few; too small minority | 0 | 0 | 21 | 6 |
| 8. electoral/financial | 12 | 3 | 7 | 6 |
| Advantage(s)[a] | (N = 15)[c] | (N = 30) | (N = 14) | (N = 16)[c] |
| 0. none mentioned | 67 | 63 | 57 | 69 |
| 1. possibly; unsure; slight | 7 | 3 | 0 | 6 |
| 2. electoral only | 13 | 7 | 7 | 0 |
| 3. yes, at least one | 13 | 27 | 36 | 25 |
| Type of advantage(s)[b] | | | | |
| 0. none mentioned | 67 | 63 | 57 | 69 |
| 1. special skills; work harder | 13 | 10 | 36 | 25 |
| 2. special treatment (general) | 7 | 10 | 0 | 6 |
| 3. special treatment from speaker | 0 | 10 | 0 | 0 |
| 4. electoral | 13 | 7 | 7 | 0 |

[a] Percentages do not add up to exactly 100 percent due to rounding (up or down) to the nearest whole number.

[b] Percentages add up to more than 100 percent because multiple responses were coded. Each figure represents the percentage of legislators who mentioned a given type of disadvantage or advantage. For example, 56 percent of all female Arizona legislators interviewed mentioned problems with sexism and discrimination.

[c] Due to time constraints, this topic was not discussed during interviews with two legislators, one Arizona woman and one California man. Thus, those legislators are excluded from this analysis.

others felt they excluded themselves because they were either uninterested or did not have the time; still others felt it was a little of both (voluntary and involuntary exclusion).

A comparison with the perceptions of the Arizona female officials is instructive. Most of the Arizona women (69 percent) were able to cite problems they thought were unique to women in their positions. The most frequently mentioned problems involved sexist double standards and stereotypes. Women, they thought, were criticized for being bitchy, while the men were admired for their aggressive determination. The women had "cat fights" while the men debated. The women were being hysterical while the men were being forceful. One Arizona legislator felt she and her female colleagues had to walk a fine line between being "bubble-heads" and "pushy broads." Like their California counterparts, they worried that because they were women they were not taken seriously, had to prove themselves, and/or had to work twice as hard as the men.

Although they shared similar types of problems, the Arizona women were more reluctant than the California women to recognize them as definite disadvantages. One Arizona woman, for example, claimed that some of her male colleagues were "still tied up in the good old boy syndrome" and would demean women on a casual basis but said that such behavior did not pose a real disadvantage. "You [an Arizona female legislator] just have to make your stand once, make your intentions clear, and you can set things straight." The Arizona female officials were just as likely to discount the seriousness of such problems as they were to believe they were real disadvantages. In contrast, the California women who perceived such problems were twice as likely to think of them as disadvantages than to consider them easily resolved or inconsequential. Moreover, the Arizona women were twice as likely as the California women to argue that they faced absolutely no problems as female legislators (31 percent compared to 14 percent). One Arizona woman, for example, thought the state legislature was "the most level playing field" she had ever seen.

It was not the case that the Arizona women worked with particularly sympathetic or understanding men. Relatively few of the Arizona male officials (37 percent) were aware of any gender-related problems their female colleagues might face, and almost half the ones who did, attributed such problems to the women's own lack of experience or skills. A couple explained that many of the women, especially the housewives, entered the legislature with very little "life experience" in such things as public affairs, paying taxes, and meeting a payroll. One pointed out that his female co-workers suffered from a "physical" problem: their voices were not as authoritative and did not carry as much weight as the men's.[26]

The Arizona men, in fact, were just as likely to argue that the women had certain advantages over the men. In most cases, they asserted that their female peers received preferential treatment or special courtesies either from other men or from the Speaker. Female members of the Arizona legislature, according to some of the male members, were often given the benefit of the doubt and were immune to criticism. Many of their male colleagues, they felt, went easy on the women; they did not deal with them as ruth-lessly as they dealt with other men. The Speaker, according to some, favored the female members. One man thought the women were more likely to get good committee assignments and better offices because of such favoritism. Another exclaimed, "the tide has turned!" and had "no doubt" that an old girls' network was in full operation.

The California men I interviewed were more cognizant of gender-related problems among their colleagues than were the Arizona men—although their level of awareness did not approach that of the California women. The California men also were more likely than the Arizona men to attribute such problems to sexism, discrimination, and exclusion rather than to the women's own inadequacies. The California male legislators were not any more or less likely than those in Arizona to cite advantages to being a female legislator, but those who did were more willing to attribute women's advan-tages to their own personal strengths rather than to preferential treatment. Some thought women had more experience with and thus more authority on "women's issues." Others cited women's ability "to stick together" or the ability of the Legislative Women's Caucus to forge bipartisan coalitions.

Interestingly, of the four groups of legislators interviewed, it was the California female lawmakers who were the most likely to sing women's praises. One believed women in public office had an advantage because they were better able than men to represent women's concerns. A couple thought the Women's Caucus gave them an advantage. Others were quite confident that women gained an advantage by simply working harder and more conscientiously. It would seem, then, that the problematic assess-ments of sex, gender, and power dynamics in the 1990 California legislature were counterbalanced somewhat by the individual determination and col-lective strength of the women—assets recognized by both female and male members. In comparison, the gender barriers facing the Arizona women appeared less numerous and less formidable—to them and to their male colleagues. What problems did exist were perceived as having fairly easy, individualistic solutions. Thus, there seemed little need for collective iden-tity or action.

## Conclusions

These configurations of sex, gender, and power were indeed much more complicated than a quick look at sex ratios within each state legislature would imply. The numerous indicators of political culture, gender bias, and the status of women examined above often seem to go in opposite direc-tions. Some suggest that the women of one or the other legislature were in a vulnerable position of gender inequality; others portray the women of one or the other legislature as fairly comfortable and even empowered within their environment. Nonetheless, there is a way a looking at all this that I believe makes sense.

The small group of California female lawmakers worked in a hostile environment, a state government notable for its historical exclusion of women and its hypermasculine culture. The inner circles of political power remained elusive, even in 1990. Well aware of the situation and determined to change it, these women were willing to confront and able to challenge their hostile surroundings as an organized and sometimes unified group. Although they lacked the power of numbers, the California women could draw strength from the collective support of the Women's Caucus, the authority of their greater political experience, the staying power of their greater electoral security, and, last but certainly not least, the policy liberalism and activist proclivities of their colleagues, past and present.

The larger Arizona female delegation enjoyed a much more established position within their state's political culture and among its power elite. They had the numbers and the positions to effect meaningful changes in public policy, in the policy process, and in political representation. The question is, did they have the will? Relatively conservative in their political outlook, yet unwilling to agree, organize, or even identify as a group, comfortable (perhaps, even, complacent) within their political environment, yet relatively vulnerable in their own districts, the Arizona women as a whole had little incentive or desire to challenge the status quo, as women.

# PART II

# Defining the Parameters of Representation

## CHAPTER THREE

# Representational Priorities

What does a representative do? Although central to an understanding of American politics, the question of what representation is or should be is one of the most difficult for political scientists to answer. Nevertheless, elected officials must somehow deal with the question, and they must do so with little concrete direction. Outside a few basic constitutional requirements (such as regular reelection), there is no formal job description, no list of duties each official must perform to keep his or her job. Bearing in mind the lessons of past experience and notions of what the political culture demands or tolerates, representatives must define and prioritize their own duties and goals.

How state legislators define and practice their job of representation is a persistent question and ongoing theme of this study. This chapter begins the analysis of sex, gender, and legislative behavior by assuming that constituents and legislation are the two primary foci of activity. As Malcolm Jewell (1982: 149) states in his definitive study of representation in state legislatures:

> Legislators have considerable freedom to choose their roles. Some become totally absorbed in the lawmaking process; some devote much of their time to their constituents; and some make a conscious effort to do both jobs well.

The question, then, is: Who chooses which role? What makes some legislators more absorbed in policymaking and some more devoted to constituents?

## Responsiveness to Constituency and Legislative Activity

To gauge legislators' commitment to their constituents, I examine their attitudes toward and activity within three of the four dimensions of responsiveness identified by Heinz Eulau and Paul Karps (1977: 242–45). Recognizing the representational significance of symbolic responsiveness, Eulau and Karps posit that there are three other components of constituent representation that are more active in nature: *service responsiveness*, which refers to "the advantages and benefits which the representative is able to obtain for particular constituents"; *allocation responsiveness*, which concerns the legislative procurement of public projects that presumably benefit constituents as a whole; and *policy responsiveness*, which characterizes the relationship between elected officials and constituents "with respect to the making of public policy."

To explore further lawmakers' policy responsiveness, I asked them to explain how they would act in a situation in which they found themselves in conflict with the majority of their district over a policy issue. Would they act on the basis of their own judgment, regardless of their constituents' preferences? Or would they subordinate their own desires to those of their constituents? This is an adaptation of the well-known typology of representational styles developed by John Wahlke, Heinz Eulau, William Buchanan, and Lorna Ferguson in 1962. According to their typology, the *delegate* is one who acts upon the mandate or instructions provided by constituents, while the *trustee* acts independently on the basis of what she or he thinks is best. The *politico* moves back and forth between both decision-making strategies, depending on the circumstances.[1] In this scheme, the delegate is the one who exhibits the greatest policy responsiveness vis-à-vis constituents. This is not to say that trustees do not consider the welfare of their constituents; rather, the delegate is simply more responsive to constituents' own assessments of their policy needs and preferences (or at least likes to think of her or himself in that way).

As explained in Chapter 1, popular stereotypes and expectations suggest that it is *women* in public office who will place more emphasis on constituency service and be more attuned to constituency needs and demands because it is women, not men, who are socialized to care for others and to value their connections and relationships with others. Indeed, constituent-related activities are often described by political scientists in such gendered terms. Alan Rosenthal (1981: 103) suggests that it is those legislators "who like and are concerned about people as individuals" who tend to be the ones who most enjoy the constituent service aspects of their job. Based on survey responses of members of Congress, John Johannes (1989: 93) describes several types of motivations for constituency service, including the "humanitarian" desire to help those in need and the perceived need to "inject personal attention into an otherwise impersonal government," to forge better connections between citizens and the bureaucracy.

Numerous studies have found that state and local officials share these gendered expectations and perspectives. Women and, sometimes, men in such positions believe that female officials are more responsive to constituents, more approachable, more trusted, and better at "human relations" (Beck 1991; Flammang 1985; Johnson and Carroll 1978: 40A–42A; Merritt 1980; Mezey 1978c). One Santa Clara County official interviewed by Janet Flammang (1985: 110) asserted, "Women are good at solving constituent problems because they are good problem solvers at home." Another of her interviewees argued that women are better representatives of their constituents than men are because women are "in touch" with "down-home realities of husbands and kids, getting the dinner and the sitter; while men leave home behind when they go to work" (111).

Not surprisingly, many female officeholders believe they receive more constituent requests and phone calls and thus do more casework than do their male colleagues (Diamond 1977: 86; Merritt 1980; Richardson and Freeman 1995). And there is good research to confirm their suspicions. One recent study (Richardson and Freeman 1995) found that female state legislators do receive, on average, more casework requests than similarly situated male legislators do. Another study found that women in local office "spend more hours in their jobs and more hours doing constituency service than men" do (Thomas 1992: 175).[2]

In defining their own roles, motivations, and objectives, female officials are, according to previous research, more likely than men to characterize themselves as particularly attentive to community relations and service. In one study of local school board members (Bers 1978: 385), women were more likely than men to state that one of their major responsibilities was to "represent [the] public"; men, on the other hand, were more likely to cite "exercise of administrative oversight." The women board members were also more likely to list "community representation," "public relations," and "commitment and caring" as their contributions to the board. The 1977 CAWP survey of public officials revealed that considerably higher proportions of women than of men "report giving major emphasis to discovering the public's views on pending issues, to educating the public about important issues and to helping constituents with their individual problems" (Johnson and Carroll 1978: 29A).

A more recent, but similar, study of city managers finds that "women did indeed show greater interest than men in serving the local community and including citizen input in their decision making" (Fox and Schuhmann 1996: 20). According to Richard Fox and Robert Schuhmann, these sex differences in representational priorities suggest that "women city managers are more likely to act as *delegates* in terms of how they represent the citizens and that male city managers are more likely to act as *trustees*" (17, emphasis in original). Other scholars have drawn similar inferences from their observations of sex differences in representational, constituent-related interests, attitudes, and roles. In her review of research on women in local government, Denise Antolini (1984: 25) concludes: "The emphasis women place on their responsibilities to the public complements the delegate model; in contrast, men in local office apparently feel greater freedom—or duty—to act independently of public sentiment." (See also Beck 1991: 108; Githens 1984: 56–57. For contrary findings and arguments, see Diamond 1977: 47–49; Githens 1977: 206–7).

If constituent-related activities are often feminized, legislative activities are masculinized. While one is "devoted" to constituent "service," another "specializes" in legislative research and "gamesmanship"—rationally analyzing "hard" facts, driving a hard bargain, strategizing, playing "hardball," winning or losing. It would be easy to assume, then, that while female officials are more responsive to their constituents, their male counterparts are more engaged in the "rough and tumble" world of policymaking. The research on actual legislative activities, roles, and interests, however, is mixed.

Many of the earlier studies found that female officeholders were quite active in the policy realm. Jeane Kirkpatrick (1974: 155) believed the political women she interviewed were policy-oriented "inventors" whose primary goals were to work out legislative solutions to public problems. Marianne Githens (1977: 207) described the female state legislators she studied as "somewhat charismatic" agitators who promoted the cause of justice for women, children, and the aged among both their colleagues and their constituents. The same CAWP survey that found women more likely than men to emphasize constituent responsibilities also showed women placing slightly more emphasis on "researching pending issues," "developing policy," and "sponsoring legislation" (Johnson and Carroll 1978: 29A). Sue Thomas and Susan Welch (1991) discovered that similarly situated female and male state legislators introduced the same number of bills and spent equivalent amounts of time with lobbyists.

Thomas (1994: 38–39) contrasts these findings with those uncovered in the 1970s by Irene Diamond (1977). In her study of "sex roles in the [Connecticut and New Hampshire] state house," Diamond discovered that female legislators were less likely to speak on the floor, less likely to interact with lobbyists, and more reluctant to engage in legislative bargaining then were their male colleagues. "What this adds up to," Thomas (1994: 39) concludes, "is that women legislators in the 1970s appeared to shrink from activities of a legislative nature and embrace those related to their backgrounds in community service and individual problem solving." The recent study of city managers mentioned earlier (Fox and Schuhmann 1996) suggests that such legislative passivity may not be entirely a thing of the past. Fox and Schuhmann report that female city managers were more reluctant than their male counterparts to describe themselves as an "entrepreneurial city manager," which was defined as "one who seeks to shape and formulate public policy" (1996: 15).

Representational duties are gendered in a great many people's minds. Constituent-related activities and concerns are routinely associated with women and feminine attributes. Lawmaking is often considered a male-dominated calling, despite research suggesting otherwise, and is frequently described in very competitive, masculine terms. In short, there are many reasons to expect male and female officials to adopt different representational priorities, ones that are gender-congruent. More often than not, however, the men and women of the 1990 Arizona and California state legislatures did not conform to such gendered expectations.

Table 3.1 presents several measures of the legislators' responsiveness to their constituencies and compares the attitudes and behavior of men and women within each state legislature. On average, female and male legislators in each state reported spending equivalent amounts of time (when in session) working on constituent casework and meeting with constituents. All four groups of representatives spent roughly 20 percent of their time on such activities.[3] Nor were there any significant sex differences in the importance lawmakers placed on each of the three dimensions of constituent responsiveness: helping people in the district who have personal problems with government (service responsiveness), making sure the district gets its fair share of government funds and projects (allocation responsiveness), and keeping in touch with the people about what the government is doing (policy responsiveness). Regardless of sex or state, legislators participating in this study were practically unanimous in saying that service responsiveness was extremely important. They also were in agreement on the importance of keeping in touch with constituents about government policy. On the third issue, allocation responsiveness, legislators differed along state lines but not along gender lines: the men and women of Arizona were equally unenthusiastic about allocation responsiveness and, most likely, what they saw as its pork-barrel aspects, while the men and women of California, on average, agreed that such activities were important.

There was only one aspect of constituent relations in which female officials appeared more responsive than their male counterparts. The Arizona women were more likely than the Arizona men to say they consulted their constituents a great deal or a fair amount when preparing and gathering

**Table 3.1 Constituent Responsiveness**

| Measure of Responsiveness | Arizona Legislators | | California Legislators | |
|---|---|---|---|---|
| | Female (N = 11) (%) | Male (N = 21) (%) | Female (N = 8) (%) | Male (N = 12) (%) |
| Time Invested: Percentage of time spent working on constituent casework and meeting with constituents | | | | |
| 0–10% | 15 | 14 | 12 | 42 |
| 11–20% | 44 | 38 | 47 | 0 |
| 21–30% | 24 | 38 | 17 | 50 |
| > 30% | 17 | 9 | 24 | 8 |
| Mean[a] | 21% | 21% | 22% | 18% |
| Service Responsiveness: Helping people in the district who have personal problems with government | | | | |
| Extremely important | 79 | 71 | 82 | 100 |
| Mean score (1–5)[b] | 4.73 | 4.57 | 4.65 | 5.00 |
| Allocation Responsiveness: Making sure the district gets its fair share of government funds and projects | | | | |
| Extremely important | 24 | 29 | 71 | 50 |
| Mean score (1–5)[b] | 3.53 | 3.38 | 4.41 | 4.33 |
| Policy Responsiveness: Keeping in touch with the people about what the government is doing | | | | |
| Extremely important | 46 | 24 | 36 | 42 |
| Mean score (1–5)[b] | 4.30 | 3.95 | 4.36 | 4.33 |
| Policy Responsiveness: Consult constituents when preparing and gathering support for legislative proposals | | | | |
| Great deal or fair amount | 54* | 25* | 59 | 58 |
| Mean score (1–5)[b] | 3.64* | 3.10* | 3.59 | 3.50 |
| Preferred Representational Style | (N = 18) | (N = 32) | (N = 14) | (N = 17) |
| Trustee | 50 | 44 | 57 | 71 |
| Politico | 33 | 25 | 21 | 12 |
| Delegate | 17 | 31 | 21 | 18 |

[a] For response options, legislators were given the following intervals: 0–5%, 6–10%, 11–20%, 21–30%, 31–50%, over 50%. The mean was calculated by taking the midpoint of each interval, with the exception of the last, which was coded as 60%.

[b] Mean score on a scale of 1 (not at all important) to 5 (extremely important).

* Sex differences for these values are statistically significant ($p \leq .05$).

support for their legislative proposals. The men and women of the California legislature were equally willing to rely on their constituents in this way when making policy.[4]

As in many other studies (Jewell 1985: 105), the trustee role was the dominant preference among these legislators, especially those from California. The women were just as enamored with this somewhat authoritative representational style as the men. The delegate role appealed to relatively few legislators, whether male or female. There was a slight sex difference among the Arizona legislators, but it was the *men* who were a bit more likely than the women to adopt the delegate role. Moreover, among those Arizona legislators who did favor the delegate role, the men were considerably more emphatic about it than the women were.

For two of the three Arizona female "delegates," the commitment to constituent opinion was limited to a willingness to listen, learn, and compromise—to alter their own positions a bit. In contrast, most of the Arizona male "delegates" had a very difficult time distinguishing their own preferences from those of their districts. A few had trouble recalling or even foreseeing any policy differences between them and their constituents because they made such a conscious effort to "stay in tune." As one of these men explained:

> I have been very active in my district, very visible. It's a poor part of town and I live there. I choose to live there and be part of the activity, part of the goals of the community. I think that's helped.

Other Arizona male "delegates" could not even fathom disagreeing with their districts because they saw themselves and their constituents as one and the same. As one man put it,

> I was born and raised in the district. I believe that on 99.9 percent of the issues I am in line with way over 51 percent of the people. I really wouldn't want to be here under any other circumstances. Not only am I representing them; I am in concert with them. . . . I am an extension of them.

Said another:

> [I'm not] so arrogant to think that I know better than they do. I feel the same as they do. . . . I feel as though I'm part of the district. I feel as though what I feel inside, what my thoughts are, I think are the thoughts of the people out there in the district. They aren't down here, but they would feel the same way. I just feel like I'm a part of them.

Turning to the legislators' attitudes toward and activity in the legislative arena (Table 3.2), the story is much the same. On most measures of com-

**Table 3.2  Legislative Activities**

| Measure of Legislative Activities | Arizona Legislators | | California Legislators | |
|---|---|---|---|---|
| | Female (N = 11) (%) | Male (N = 21) (%) | Female (N = 8) (%) | Male (N = 12) (%) |
| Importance of working on legislation | | | | |
|   Extremely important | 32 | 29 | 59 | 33 |
|   Mean score (1–5) | 4.24 | 4.19 | 4.41 | 4.17 |
| Time spent working on legislation, including committee work and time on the floor | | | | |
|   ≤ 20% | 0 | 14 | 0 | 0 |
|   21–30% | 8 | 14 | 0 | 42 |
|   31–50% | 44 | 29 | 59 | 42 |
|   > 50% | 47 | 43 | 41 | 17 |
|   Mean | 48% | 43% | 48%* | 37%* |
| Time spent meeting with lobbyists and interest groups | | | | |
|   0–5% | 7 | 14 | 12 | 0 |
|   6–10% | 15 | 48 | 12 | 17 |
|   11–20% | 53 | 29 | 64 | 83 |
|   > 20% | 25 | 10 | 12 | 0 |
|   Mean | 16% | 12% | 14% | 14% |
| Average number of bills introduced, 1989–1990 [a] | (N = 27) 47 | (N = 63) 47 | (N = 19) 67 | (N = 97) 66 |

[a] See Chapter 3, note 5 regarding calculation of these numbers.
* Sex differences for these values are statistically significant ($p \leq .05$).

mitment to and involvement in policymaking, there are no significant sex differences. And when there are sex differences, they go against popular, gendered expectations: it is the women who appear more engaged in legislation, not the men. Within each state, female and male lawmakers introduced, on average, the same number of bills.[5] Among the Arizona legislators, women and men rated working on legislation as equally important, and they devoted equivalent portions of their time to doing so. The Arizona women reported spending slightly larger portions of their time meeting with lobbyists and interest groups than did the Arizona men. The California women and men spent the same amount of time meeting with lobbyists and interest groups, but the women reported spending significantly more of their time working on legislation than did the men—approximately 10 percent more. These women also rated the importance of legislative activities slightly higher than did their male colleagues.

Overall, the women and men of the Arizona and California legislatures appear to have shared quite similar representational priorities. In only one out of six measures—and in only one state—do female legislators appear more responsive to constituents than male legislators do. And in the few instances of sex differences in legislative involvement, it is the women who appear more committed than the men. In light of popular expectations and much of the previous research discussed above, these findings are puzzling. Seen under a different light, however, I propose that the similarities between men and women revealed here can be understood.

Further analysis of the data collected for this study, plus another look at the previous research, suggest that representational priorities are associated with and influenced by (1) the culture, norms, and demands of the state and its legislature, and (2) the social, political, and professional status of the individual legislator. To the extent that female and male legislators are subject to the same institutional norms and expectations and share the same status, I argue, they will exhibit similar representational priorities.

## State-Level Institutional Context

"In the broadest sense," Jewell (1970: 465) reminds us, "the roles of legislators . . . are defined by the norms of the political culture that prevails in any society." Heinz Eulau (1994: 585) makes a similar observation about the effects of institutional norms on legislative behavior:

> [I]n legislative (and other) institutions an informal, unwritten, and to an extent, even unspoken understanding develops of what is proper and improper conduct. These normative understandings orient and channel otherwise discretionary personal and/or interpersonal behavior in a socially mandated direction and call for expressions of approval or disapproval on the part of group members.

We therefore can expect that representational roles, priorities, and choices (such as those observed in this chapter) will vary across states to the degree that the legislative norms and political cultures of the states vary. And there is evidence to suggest that such contextual factors do have an effect. When research has crossed state boundaries and state-level comparisons have been made, statewide differences are almost always revealed (Wahlke, Eulau, Buchanan, and Ferguson 1962; Jewell 1982; Freeman and Richardson 1996). Lilliard Richardson and Patricia Freeman, for example, found that "certain states [Maryland and Ohio] tend to encourage constituency service more than others [Colorado and North Carolina]" (1995: 173).

Thus, it comes as no surprise that many of the contrasts drawn between the political cultures and norms of Arizona and California in the previous chapter are reflected in the data presented in Tables 3.1 and 3.2. Members of the conservative, laissez-faire Arizona legislature were clearly less willing to endorse pork-barrel, allocative politics than were the more liberal, entrepreneurial members of the California legislature. It is easy to see how the trustee role might be more appealing and appropriate in the more professionalized California legislature and among its members who had such large, diverse constituencies. And the high volume of bills introduced is one of the distinguishing marks of a highly professionalized legislature such as California's.

Apparently, the women and men of each state legislature were equally affected by such cultural and structural pressures. Arizona female and male officials shared a common distaste for allocative politics. Male and female members of the California legislature were equally likely to opt for the trustee model over the delegate model of decision making. And the enormous policy demands of the state of California seemed to call forth just as much response (in the form of bill introduction) among female lawmakers as male lawmakers.

Some norms apparently were shared and adhered to by legislators of both states. That practically every legislator queried rated service responsiveness as extremely important suggests that constituent casework was an almost universally recognized, unquestioned duty of public office in both states. With the exception of some Arizona officials who found "bringing home the bacon" particularly distasteful, hardly any of these legislators were willing to rate any of the activities listed in Tables 3.1 and 3.2 as *un*important. What variation there was, was limited to degrees of importance. There are also a few norms of behavior, or standard operating procedures, apparent in the legislators' allocation of time. No legislator found it necessary to devote more than half his or her time to constituent casework or meetings; few even spent more than 30 percent of their time on such activities. Meanwhile, no legislator managed to spend less than 10 percent of his or her time working on legislation; all but three male Arizona legislators reported spending at least 20 percent of their time on legislation. On the other hand, it was the rare legislator (one Arizona man) who admitted to spending more than 30 percent of his time meeting with lobbyists and interest groups.

Such legislative norms, by their very (normative) nature, leave some room for individual discretion (Eulau 1994). But it is clear from the pattern of responses to questions about representational priorities that boundaries of acceptable or unacceptable, necessary or unnecessary behavior existed in the 1990 Arizona and California legislatures. More importantly, these boundaries did "orient and channel" male and female behavior alike (Eulau 1994: 585).

## Sex, Gender, Status, and Representational Priorities

There is an implicit hierarchy associated with the two types of representational activities examined in this chapter. The constituency-centered roles and activities are often considered inferior, less prestigious, and less powerful than the more policy-oriented ones. In their study of the determinants of respect in the U.S. Senate, John Hibbing and Sue Thomas, for example, found that "[t]he way to earn the respect of the congressional community is not to devote an undue amount of attention to the home fires" (1990: 140). Committee leadership and successful and specialized legislative activity, on the other hand, were associated with greater respect within the Senate (see also Caldeira and Patterson 1988; Caldeira, Clark, and Patterson 1993). Susan Abrams Beck (1991: 107–8) found in her study of local council members that the men did not respect or value the women's greater responsiveness to constituents. While these women felt that their willingness to listen made them better representatives, their male colleagues criticized them for caving in to constituent sentiment, for being too "soft-hearted," for not being "analytic enough."

As Marianne Githens points out, Wahlke and his colleagues themselves favored the trustee role, which they associated with "specialized knowledge," independent judgment, principled conviction, and rationality (Githens 1977: 203). The delegate role, they suggested, might simply reflect a "lack of political articulation and sophistication" rather than "a conscious majoritarian bias which he [the delegate] could elaborate and defend" (Wahlke, Eulau, Buchanan, and Ferguson 1962: 277; cited in Githens 1977: 204). Kirkpatrick (1974: 157) also criticizes the traditional conceptualization of trustee and delegate roles for posing a "conflict between a gross, short-sighted, self-interested majority and a wise, far-seeing public spirited representative." The idea that there is a built-in conceptual relationship between status—especially intellectual status—and representational style is reinforced by many empirical studies of representational styles. One of the most consistent findings in the extant research is that those who choose the trustee role tend to have more formal education than those who choose the delegate or politico roles (Jewell 1970, 1982, 1985).

Because the status and expertise associated with the trustee role were largely unavailable to female state legislators at the time—as were professional backgrounds in business or law—Githens (1977: 204) concluded that the women she studied were effectively discouraged from assuming such roles. Similarly, Kent Jennings and Norman Thomas (1968: 487) offered the following explanation for why male party elites in their study were much more likely than female party elites to advocate trustee-type roles:

Part of the answer may lie in the greater degree of independence and self-reliance which men enjoy in society and in politics. Men are more accustomed to making their own decisions in nonpolitical as well as political matters. Women tend to be less self-sufficient and to seek certainty and assurance in people, institutions, and concepts outside themselves. Consequently, men rely more heavily on their own judgment as a guide to decision on party matters than do their female counterparts. This sizable difference between the sexes may also be due to the larger proportion of men who were self-employed. Male occupational experiences call more for the exercise of independent judgment than do female experiences.

In sum, Antolini (1984: 26) was correct when she argued that women's greater commitment to public service and constituent participation, as reported in these earlier studies, may have been a reflection of one of two things: either their own priorities and backgrounds or their apparent lack of political, professional, and social status. Women's greater emphasis on constituency service and representation, in other words, may not have been a matter of choice; they may have lacked the status, sanction, or freedom to do otherwise. So too, their ambivalence about legislative activities (in at least two studies) may have been a reflection of social and professional constraints rather than their own preferences or desires.

The overwhelming *similarities* in women's and men's representational priorities, as revealed in this study of Arizona and California legislators, may therefore be a reflection of one of two possibilities. Either no status differential separated the constituency-related activities from the policy-oriented ones in these state legislatures, or there were few status differentials separating the male and female legislators themselves.

The first of these possibilities can be ruled out quite thoroughly, given the patterns of legislators' responses to questions about their representational priorities. Status differentials were clearly implicated. Among the Arizona and California legislators studied here, the association of status with representational priorities is particularly evident in the choice of representational style—the choice between trustee and delegate roles. As in previous research, legislators with higher levels of education were more likely to choose the trustee role; those with lower levels of education were more likely to choose the delegate role.[6] This alone suggests that the trustee role was the more prestigious, more sophisticated choice among these legislators. More telling, however, is the way the "trustees" themselves talked about, rationalized, or justified their chosen role. As did the legislators Jewell (1982) studied, many of these women and men (roughly half the trustees in each state) explained their affinity toward the trustee role in terms of their own and their constituents' confidence in their judgment. Within these conversations, the themes of knowledge and leadership figured prominently, suggesting that the legislators shared the same biases toward these representational roles as did Wahlke and his colleagues (1962).[7]

Many of these trustees, male and female alike, trusted their own judgment over their constituents' because of perceived informational disparities. In their positions as legislators, they had access to much more and much better information than did their constituents, who, in their eyes, were often either misinformed or ill-informed. One Arizona woman, for example, explained that her choice to go against her constituents on AIDS-related issues "doesn't really bother me so much because I know that I have so much more knowledge and information on the issue. Or even some of these other—you know, tax and budget issues," she continued.

> You get these people who come and tell you to just cut 5 percent across the board; men that call you and say, "I used to be the budget analyst for Gulf and Western [a prominent Arizona-based savings and loan] and I can get our budget on one page." You just know that you have so much more information. I go: "I couldn't even bring all my appropriations books to you; you would have to come down here. I'm not capable of even picking them all up." So most of those things where I was really torn I could justify it by saying that I know that they're not operating with all the knowledge I have.

A California female official offered a similar rationale for her trustee-style approach:

> There are times when, on a certain bill, people will write in and say, "Vote no for this" because they've gotten a ten-second bite on the radio. And based on that they oppose something, when the fact is they don't have all the information. I will vote the other way, feeling confident that, you know, they don't have the same information.

"Most people," lamented an Arizona male legislator, "are simply misinformed."

Many of the "politicos" also used differences in knowledge to justify their representational choices; only they were more willing than the "trustees" to admit that sometimes their constituents had more information or experience than they did. An Arizona man explained this decision-making strategy quite precisely:

> It really depends on, again, the knowledge that I have. If it's an area that I feel fairly knowledgeable with, I will go with what I think is right. As opposed to, a lot of times, what my constituents want. . . .

[But] If it's something I don't have a total handle on, then I'll usually go with what my constituents want because they, a lot of times, have more knowledge on the issue than I do.

"If you're talking about truck licensing fees," agreed a California male politico, "you're going to give more weight to people's opinions because you don't really know much about it." "If it's not a personal, moral issue," admitted a female Arizona politico, "if I'm not informed, as I have not been with a lot of issues because we have so many, I may have thought one way and with more education [from constituents] have changed my mind."

For many of the trustees, it was a matter of leadership. Their role, as they saw it, was to take charge, become informed, make good decisions, and educate others as to the merits of their decisions. A good example comes from a California man who explained how he would resolve the dilemma of having to choose between his own judgment and the demands of his constituents.

I don't change *my* position. What I do is I just work twice as hard getting the information out to the people in my district, to explain to them why I voted the way I voted. And hopefully to convince them that my vote was right. So that's what I would do. I don't believe as some do up here who would like to run an instant poll across their district every time before they decide how to vote. Some members up here like to do that. Sure, you want to be representative of your district. But there comes a time, or issues do come along where you have to exercise some leadership. And I think that is part of exercising leadership.

For some, assuming such leadership, initiative, and independence was precisely what their constituents elected them to do. Moreover, that was how the representational system was supposed to work. The following rationale from an Arizona male legislator sums up this perspective quite well:

I believe that this is a democratic republic that we live in. We don't operate via town halls, as in yesteryear in New England. People elect their legislators to go to the Capitol to look at things from a statewide and a district perspective, to make the judgment they believe is in the best interests of the state. They establish a record and they run on that record at election time. And you judge whether you want that person back in or not based on his cumulative record. I don't put my finger to the wind on each and every issue and bob back and forth. To me, that's not the kind of government that *I* want. When I was "out there," not in office, I elected somebody I thought had a brain who could get much closer to the issues than I could and would make sound decisions. And I never expected to agree with him on everything. . . . So it does not bother me that I may be voting for something that my constituents may not have wanted me to vote for.

As these two examples illustrate, this desire to lead as a trustee was often accompanied by a disdain for the more passive aspects of the delegate role. Putting one's "finger to the wind," being a slave to opinion polls was, according to these legislators, the antithesis of political leadership. At its extreme, such passivity would render them useless, unnecessary.[8] "I really don't feel that I'm here as a computer," an Arizona female trustee explained.

I'm interested in what my constituency tells me, but I don't think that I have to tally up how many yes's and how many no's and then vote that way. Because if that's what it is, then they don't need people up here.

"We could send everything to the voters and do away with this structure. But that's not the way it's set up," agreed one of her male colleagues.

It is important to note, however, that (with few exceptions) the "delegates" themselves did not perceive or describe their roles as passive, or submissive. As the examples cited above illustrate, most were classified as delegates because they were willing to negotiate a compromise with their constituents, or because they invested a great deal of effort to become a part of the community, or simply because they could not imagine ever departing from the will of the community. In no way did these legislators see themselves as mere conduits of district plebiscites. Nor were they slavishly subordinating their own will to that of others, at least in their own minds. Nonetheless, a great many of their "trustee" and "politico" colleagues did perceive, consciously or unconsciously, a status hierarchy among the different representational styles—a hierarchy that distinguished between decision-making styles that were more and less informed, assertive, and actively responsible.

Although the legislators participating in this study were not asked to explain why they chose to be more or less active in the legislative arena, there is ample evidence that such activity was associated with higher professional status in both state legislatures. In Arizona, Republicans—members of the majority party—devoted more of their time to meeting with lobbyists and interest groups and thought that working on legislation was more important than did Democrats. They also tended to introduce and sponsor more bills. Moreover, the greater legislative activity of Arizona Republicans is only partly attributable to the fact that they held a lock on committee leadership positions. Committee chairs did introduce a great many more bills than even other Republicans. Yet, Republicans on average were more active than Democrats, even if they did not chair a committee. Similar patterns were apparent among the California legislators as well. Democrats, the majority party, spent more time with lobbyists than did Republicans. Committee chairs, on average, introduced more bills.

One could argue that members of the majority party and chairs of standing committees were more involved in policymaking simply because, realistically and strategically speaking, they had better chances of success. Nonetheless, the idea that legislative activity was associated with status, prestige, respect, and leadership is more forcefully demonstrated by the legislators' responses to another set of interview questions. These questions asked the officials to discuss the meanings and sources of power within each legislative institution.[9] What, I asked, does it mean to have power around here? What are the sources of power in this legislature? The most frequent responses centered around legislative effectiveness. Almost two-thirds (63 percent) of the California legislators and over three-quarters (79 percent) of the Arizona legislators—men and women alike—thought that effective policymaking was an important source of power.[10] Power, as one California woman observed, is "the ability to pass legislation and to get the issues that concern my district resolved." An Arizona man put it quite succinctly: "Power is the ability to change the law in any manner, shape, or form." More idealistically, power is "getting through what you believe," according to an Arizona female official. "Passing something that is very important to you that you believe is right, that you've worked hard for. That's power," she added.

For some, it was the sort of controlling power a committee chair or speaker has over legislation or legislators—the power to "kill" legislation summarily or to dictate how votes are cast. For most, however, power in the form of legislative efficacy was the sort available to anyone, regardless of position. It was the sort of power associated with persuasiveness, the ability to negotiate, compromise, build consensus, establish trust, and so forth. Many, like this California female lawmaker, recognized that legislative power was available in both forms.

> I think that power is a function of several variables, one of which is position; one of which is persuasiveness, you know, ability to articulate your interests; one of which is a negotiating skill, ability to compromise, to make things happen. So even if your position is not very good, you can wield a modicum of power, a certain amount of power, by having good negotiating skills, and having the ability to compromise and make things happen. . . . If you combine all those other skills with position, you'd be very powerful.

Regardless of how hierarchical or coercive the power, though, all these legislators thought of power in terms of *legislative* accomplishments.

Hardly any lawmaker, in contrast, mentioned constituents as a source of power. And the few who did were all men, not women. Two California men and two Arizona men believed that power lay in one's ability to get things done for constituents—casework-type things, that is, not more policy-oriented things. For example, a California male legislator thought that

> One, and probably the most satisfying [type of power] is just help-ing people in the district, which may have nothing to do with legis-lation. . . . Just things . . . that you do that nobody else really hears about or knows about, but it helps.

"Ultimately," one of the Arizona men concluded, "the power . . . [comes from] the people that elected you to office." A few others (two men from California, one from Arizona) agreed that one's constituents bestow power, or are the ones who really have power, not legislators. Overall, however, constituents were only a very minor theme in these assessments of institu-tional power. Constituents and constituent service were rarely thought of as sources of power and prestige. Legislative activities—when done right—were.

Responding to constituents and making policy were, by no means, equally prestigious activities in the 1990 Arizona and California legislatures. In this way, the legislators and legislatures examined here did not differ from those of previous studies. Thus, one cannot conclude that the male legislators were just as committed to their constituents as the female legisla-tors because such behavior enjoyed some newfound importance or respect. Nor can one argue that the women in this study were just as (and some-times more) engaged in the policymaking process as their male colleagues because such activities were no longer associated with power and prestige.

The men and women of the Arizona and California legislatures had such similar representational priorities because, in many respects, they enjoyed equivalent levels of social and professional status. As revealed in Chapter 2, they possessed equal amounts of education; they were equally likely to have valued backgrounds in business or law; they were equally likely to be mem-bers of the majority party and to chair standing committees. It was not the case that constituent and legislative activities were equally prestigious. Rather, it was that the female and male legislators themselves were, by and large, equally prestigious; equally willing to assume prestigious, even elitist, roles such as the trustee; and equally determined to participate in presti-gious, power-bestowing legislative activities.

The one aspect of status that the women and men did not share equally—electoral security—can help explain one of the two exceptions to the rule of shared priorities. Recall that among Arizona legislators, the women reported relying on constituents for input on legislative matters more frequently than did the men. In large part, this can be explained by the fact that these women had more competitive districts, and those (women and men) with more competitive districts tended to consult constituents more frequently. Arizona women and men from equally competitive or equally safe districts, therefore, did not differ much at all in the degree to which they consulted constituents.

It is also interesting to note that it was the California women—the women who, as described in Chapter 2, were more determined than their Arizona counterparts to stake out their rightful place in the legislature and in state politics—who spent more time working on legislation than their male colleagues did. The gender inequalities and masculinized political culture of California, of which the female legislators were so acutely aware, did not seem to discourage or inhibit their full participation in legislative matters. If anything, they propelled the women into the legislative arena.

THE LACK of significant and consistent sex differences in Arizona and California officials' representational priorities may seem odd given previous research and the gender-stereotyped expectations about women's and men's abilities and desires. Yet I have argued that these very similarities are also quite revealing. They reveal the significance and force not of gender per se but of gender operating within a context of legislative norms, structural demands, and status hierarchies. The similarities attest to the power of such norms, demands, and hierarchies and their influence on legislative behavior. In establishing their representational priorities, the women and men in this study were guided in large part by certain assumptions about what activities were acceptable or unacceptable, required or optional, sophisticated or unsophisticated, potentially powerful or ordinarily routine.

## CHAPTER FOUR

# Women as a Constituency Group

"What does an elected representative see when he or she sees a constituency?" This is the question with which Richard Fenno (1978: xiii) began his pathbreaking research on the behavior of members of Congress while in their districts, and it is the question that guides the inquiry of this chapter. Like Fenno's work, this chapter focuses attention on the representative relationship between elected officials and their constituents. Moreover, the discussion of constituency representation presented here rests on one of Fenno's most important observations. When elected officials view their districts, they do not see singular, undifferentiated abstractions. What they each see instead is a unique, complex amalgam of constituency groups, some of whom are more prominent or more important than others.

Members of Congress, according to Fenno, distinguish between different groups, or types of constituents, in terms of the strength and intensity of the electoral support they offer. So too did the Arizona and California legislators in this study. The main concern of this study, however, is not a detailed description of all the various groups legislators see when they see their constituents. The question is not simply what do they see, but whether they "see" *women* in particular. Do they see women as a particularly supportive constituency group? Do they see women as a constituency group with particular interests or policy concerns? Taking the inquiry a step further, this chapter also examines legislators' perceptions of their own roles vis-à-vis women and the representation of women's interests. Are they, as men or women, more or less capable or willing to represent women and their policy concerns? Do they and their colleagues, as women or men, "make a difference" for women in this respect? Are they themselves willing to assume the role of women's political representative?

The answers to these questions do not (necessarily) reveal who does or does not actually "act for" women. But they do reveal who is more or less predisposed to doing so. One does not necessarily have to perceive women as a particularly supportive constituency group to take action on their behalf, but such support certainly would provide an incentive for doing so. Acting for women presumes some knowledge of what women want, at least if it is to be a conscious act. Thus, a legislator who is going to act for women should have some notion of what women's policy concerns are; at the very least, she or he should acknowledge that such "women's issues" exist. And it would help if that legislator felt capable of taking the lead on such issues. As a woman, she may feel especially capable or even responsible for doing so; as a man, he should feel no less capable or responsible. Finally, it is important to identify those legislators who see themselves as representatives of women or women's policy concerns and to look closely at what these lawmakers do (or do not do), say, and believe. As Chapter 8 reveals, it is these lawmakers who can help us understand what the representation of women means in practice as well as in theory.

There was a time when precious few elected officials thought of women as a constituency group, much less expressed a desire or even felt a need to represent them. Anne Costain (1988: 152), for example, found in her interviews with members of Congress and their staff in the mid-1970s that her questions about the existence of "a women's vote" in the district were met with "bewilderment." "Women," she concluded, "were clearly not seen as a group with electoral relevance, or with political views consistent enough to require special attention." The few women in public office at the time seemed to make an effort to avoid any association with women as a political group. Most early congresswomen, according to Irwin Gertzog (1995: 159–60), "rejected the claim that they were in Washington to represent American womanhood" and "were unprepared to represent the interests of women as a discrete group." In 1984, Marianne Githens offered the following assessment of women in state politics:

> The majority of studies focusing on female officeholders' sensitivity to women's issues and expressions of commitment to feminist concerns indicate that at the state level, at least, most women running for or holding public office scrupulously avoid any public identification with feminism or the Women's Movement. They run for public office neither as feminist nor on a platform that is predominantly concerned with women's issues. Nor once elected, do they often publicly describe their role as that of representing women's issues in particular or as that of serving as a role model to inspire other women to seek public office. (Githens 1984: 54)[1]

As the number of women in public office grew, as women in the electorate began to vote at equal or higher rates than men, and as awareness of the political and electoral significance of the "gender gap" spread, more and more elected officials—female officials especially—began to recognize, accept, and sometimes even embrace women as a political group (Gertzog 1995: 161–62). Carol Mueller (1987b: 230) reported that the vast majority of women attending CAWP's first National Forum for State Legislators in 1983 were willing and able to identity "legislation for women." "In contrast to an earlier generation of women public officials," she concluded, "women state legislators now acknowledge (1) that women are a special constituency, [and] (2) that women legislators have a special responsibility to women." By 1990, "running as a woman" was no longer thought to be a liability for female candidates (Witt, Paget, and Matthews 1994). Indeed, as the examples cited in Chapter 1 illustrate, many of the most prominent and successful members of this new generation of female politicians publicly identified themselves as advocates for women and, linking descriptive and substantive representation, emphasized their unique abilities as women to represent women.[2]

The Arizona and California legislators interviewed for this study were very much a part of this new "woman-friendly" generation. My questions about women's policy concerns were greeted with familiarity, not bewilderment. Even those who rejected the notion that women have particular policy concerns were nevertheless familiar with the concept of "women's issues" and the debates surrounding it. And regardless of their outlook, most of these politicians had clearly thought about the relationship between women's descriptive and substantive representation (if not in those terms) and could draw upon their own observations of their immediate colleagues. Perhaps most impressive is the fact that many of the legislators I interviewed identified and thought about women as a political group without being asked to do so. I cannot say that the men were any less familiar with the issues raised by my questions than the women were. It is clear from their responses to my questions, however, that the ties binding the representatives to their female constituents were much stronger among the women—especially those from California.

### The Significance of Women as a Political Group

Deeply embedded in the idea of group representation—whether it be descriptive or substantive—is the question of which groups are politically relevant enough to warrant such representation. "The history of representative government and the expansion of the suffrage," writes Hanna Pitkin, "is one long record of changing demands for representation based on changing concepts of what are politically relevant features to be represented" (1967: 87). Until very recently, for example, physical and mental disabilities were rarely considered "politically relevant features to be represented." The proposition that sex and gender are politically relevant features has an extremely long and contested history. As I hope the discussion in Chapter 1 made clear, the issue of women's political representation is intricately and necessarily tied to the issue—indeed, the question—of whether and how one considers women a political group. Recall, for example, Sapiro's assertion that "in order to discuss representation of women, we must consider whether women as a group have unique politically relevant characteristics, whether they have special interests to which a representative could or should respond" (1981: 703). In theory, at least, the recognition of women as a politically significant group with identifiable policy concerns is a prerequisite for the substantive, conscious representation of women.

This section examines the degree to which Arizona and California state legislators serving in 1990 saw women as a politically significant constituency group. Drawing on Fenno's earlier work, it begins with the presumption that legislators do make distinctions among constituency groups on the basis of electoral support and examines how legislators rated women in comparison to other constituency groups. I then explore their beliefs about the existence of so-called "women's issues," which are defined as issues about which the female electorate is particularly concerned.[3] In each case, I compare the responses of female and male lawmakers in each state.

On the follow-up written questionnaire, legislators participating in this study were asked to indicate the degree to which various (unorganized) constituency groups supported them, financially or otherwise, in their last campaign. In addition to women, the other groups listed were elderly or retired persons, ethnic minorities (specified), blue-collar workers, professionals, poor people, environmentalists, business people, and farmers. The legislators' responses are presented in Tables 4.1 and 4.2. Table 4.1 compares the group evaluations of female and male legislators of Arizona, Table 4.2 those of the women and men of the California legislature. The legislators' evaluations of support from other constituency groups besides women are included in these tables so that their evaluations of women can be put in perspective.

Although female and male legislators in Arizona reported similar levels of support from women, women stand out as the most supportive constituency group for the female officials. While 40 percent of the Arizona female legislators perceived strong support from their female constituents, no more than 25 percent perceived such high levels of support from any other constituency group listed. In contrast, the Arizona male legislators

## Table 4.1 Constituency Group Support: Arizona Legislators

| Constituency Group | Strong Opposition 1 | Moderate Opposition 2 | Little or No Opposition 3 | Moderate Support 4 | Strong Support 5 | Mean |
|---|---|---|---|---|---|---|
| **Women** | | | | | | |
| Female legislators (N = 11) | 0 | 0 | 7 | 53 | 40 | 4.34 |
| Male legislators (N = 20) | 0 | 0 | 10 | 55 | 35 | 4.25 |
| **Elderly, retired** | | | | | | |
| Female legislators (N = 11) | 0 | 0 | 32 | 43 | 25 | 3.93* |
| Male legislators (N = 21) | 0 | 0 | 5 | 33 | 62 | 4.57* |
| **Ethnic minorities** [a] | | | | | | |
| Female legislators (N = 9) | 0 | 0 | 72 | 9 | 19 | 3.47 |
| Male legislators (N = 15) | 0 | 13 | 40 | 27 | 20 | 3.53 |
| **Blue-collar workers** | | | | | | |
| Female legislators (N = 11) | 0 | 0 | 39 | 46 | 15 | 3.76 |
| Male legislators (N = 20) | 0 | 5 | 25 | 50 | 20 | 3.85 |
| **Professionals** | | | | | | |
| Female legislators (N = 11) | 0 | 0 | 15 | 68 | 17 | 4.02 |
| Male legislators (N = 21) | 0 | 0 | 19 | 29 | 52 | 4.33 |
| **Poor people** | | | | | | |
| Female legislators (N = 11) | 0 | 0 | 63 | 22 | 15 | 3.53 |
| Male legislators (N = 20) | 0 | 5 | 45 | 35 | 15 | 3.60 |
| **Environmentalists** | | | | | | |
| Female legislators (N = 11) | 0 | 0 | 64 | 14 | 22 | 3.58 |
| Male legislators (N = 20) | 0 | 0 | 40 | 45 | 15 | 3.75 |
| **Business people** | | | | | | |
| Female legislators (N = 11) | 0 | 0 | 0 | 75 | 25 | 4.25 |
| Male legislators (N = 21) | 0 | 5 | 5 | 33 | 57 | 4.43 |
| **Farmers** | | | | | | |
| Female legislators (N = 11) | 0 | 7 | 76 | 8 | 8 | 3.18* |
| Male legislators (N = 21) | 0 | 5 | 29 | 33 | 33 | 3.95* |

[a] Quite a few legislators (in Arizona and California) who completed and returned the surveys did not answer this particular item on ethnic minority group support. Part of the reason for so many cases of missing data may be that many of these legislators did not have significant numbers or percentages of such minority constituents residing in their districts. Indeed, the 1980 U.S. Census figures show that almost 60 percent of the legislators who did not answer this question had districts with no more than 16 percent minorities. It is tempting, therefore, to assume that these "missing data" legislators received little or no support from such groups and to include them in the analysis of Tables 4.1 and 4.2 as such. Doing so, however, does not change the patterns of sex differences observed here.
* Sex differences for these values are statistically significant ($p \leq .05$).

**Table 4.2   Constituency Group Support: California Legislators**

| Constituency Group | Strong Opposition 1 | Moderate Opposition 2 | Little or No Opposition 3 | Moderate Support 4 | Strong Support 5 | Mean |
|---|---|---|---|---|---|---|
| | Reported Level of Support (%) | | | | | |
| **Women** | | | | | | |
| Female legislators ($N = 8$) | 0 | 0 | 0 | 36 | 64 | 4.64* |
| Male legislators ($N = 11$) | 0 | 0 | 27 | 54 | 18 | 3.91* |
| **Elderly, retired** | | | | | | |
| Female legislators ($N = 8$) | 0 | 0 | 0 | 47 | 53 | 4.53 |
| Male legislators ($N = 12$) | 0 | 0 | 0 | 17 | 83 | 4.83 |
| **Ethnic minorities** [a] | | | | | | |
| Female legislators ($N = 4$) | 0 | 0 | 78 | 22 | 0 | 3.22* |
| Male legislators ($N = 7$) | 0 | 0 | 14 | 14 | 71 | 4.57* |
| **Blue-collar workers** | | | | | | |
| Female legislators ($N = 8$) | 0 | 0 | 36 | 52 | 12 | 3.76 |
| Male legislators ($N = 12$) | 0 | 0 | 8 | 58 | 33 | 4.25 |
| **Professionals** | | | | | | |
| Female legislators ($N = 8$) | 0 | 0 | 0 | 52 | 48 | 4.48 |
| Male legislators ($N = 12$) | 0 | 0 | 8 | 42 | 50 | 4.42 |
| **Poor people** | | | | | | |
| Female legislators ($N = 8$) | 0 | 0 | 53 | 29 | 17 | 3.64 |
| Male legislators ($N = 12$) | 0 | 8 | 33 | 33 | 25 | 3.75 |
| **Environmentalists** | | | | | | |
| Female legislators ($N = 8$) | 0 | 0 | 41 | 12 | 47 | 4.06 |
| Male legislators ($N = 11$) | 0 | 18 | 45 | 9 | 27 | 3.45 |
| **Business people** | | | | | | |
| Female legislators ($N = 8$) | 0 | 0 | 0 | 76 | 24 | 4.24 |
| Male legislators ($N = 12$) | 0 | 0 | 8 | 42 | 50 | 4.42 |
| **Farmers** | | | | | | |
| Female legislators ($N = 7$) | 0 | 0 | 40 | 13 | 47 | 4.07 |
| Male legislators ($N = 11$) | 9 | 0 | 45 | 9 | 36 | 3.64 |

[a] See note a on Table 4.1.

* Sex differences for these values are statistically significant ($p \leq .05$).

were more likely to perceive strong support from their elderly, professional, and business-oriented constituents than from their female constituents.

The patterns of sex differences in constituency support among California legislators are both very different from and very similar to those found in Arizona. On the one hand, the female California officials were much more likely to perceive strong support from women than were their male colleagues. Almost two-thirds of the California female officials claimed strong support from women, as compared to a mere 18 percent of the California male officials. In addition, the California female legislators found women more supportive than did their Arizona counterparts. But the two groups of female politicians were quite similar in that they both perceived women as their most supportive constituency group. As in Arizona, the California female officials were more likely to claim strong support from their female constituents than from any other constituency group listed. And, like their Arizona counterparts, the California male officials were more likely to perceive strong support from other constituency groups than from women. In fact, among the male California legislators, women were considered one of the least supportive groups. The only other groups that received lower average support scores from these male legislators were poor people, environmentalists, and farmers.

No doubt some of the variation in legislators' perceptions of constituent group support is tied to differences in district composition. Arizona female lawmakers, for example, reported much less support from farmers than did their male colleagues primarily because they were much less likely to hail from rural districts.[4] The important point, however, is that district demographics cannot explain why female legislators in both states rated women as their most supportive constituency group and male legislators did not. The relatively low levels of support from women reported by male representatives cannot be attributed to relatively low numbers of female constituents in their districts. Nor can district composition account for why California female officials perceived more support from women than did their Arizona female counterparts. All districts have roughly equivalent proportions of female and male constituents.

On a less obvious note, male- and female-represented districts in each state were similar with respect to constituent ideology and partisanship as well. They supported the 1988 Republican presidential candidate (George Bush) at equivalent rates and had equivalent proportions of Democratic and Republican registered voters. Thus, none of the sex differences in constituent group support, as reported in Tables 4.1 or 4.2, can be attributed to these more political aspects of district composition either. Nor were there significant partisan or, as Chapter 5 shows, ideological differences separating the female and male legislators themselves (within each state). Thus, female legislators did not perceive more support from women simply because they or their districts were more liberal or more Democratic than their male counterparts and *their* districts.

In sum, the relatively strong support these female lawmakers felt they received from women cannot be "explained away" as a coincidental reflection of district peculiarities. Women as a constituency group were, according to these data, more supportive and thus more significant to female representatives than to male representatives. Put simply, these representational ties between elected officials and female constituents were gender related.

The same cannot be said about the officeholders' attitudes regarding women's issues. Whether male or female, most believed that women as a group share particular public policy concerns. Among the Arizona officials interviewed, 76 percent of the women and 70 percent of the men believed such women's issues (as defined) did exist.[5] Among the California officials, the figures are 86 percent and 82 percent, respectively. Thus, while Arizona legislators were slightly less likely than California legislators to believe that such issues existed, there were no significant sex differences in the legislators' responses to this question.

Most legislators, like the Arizona woman quoted below, were able to identify several issues in which they thought women were particularly interested.

> Obviously, women are much more inclined to be interested in issues that affect children. They are, in my opinion, much more inclined to be concerned about issues related to the environment—particularly hazardous waste, clean air, clean water, those kind of things. Anything, again, that poses a danger to children, or their children. It becomes much more personal. Education in some respects. Women generally tend to be the ones dealing with the school system and with kids. So women tend to be more motivated by discussions about education. So it's part and parcel of women's role in society. Those are clearly not issues that motivate men.

As was the case here, most of the issues mentioned as "women's issues" address perceived needs of either women themselves or of children. Abortion, sex discrimination and economic equality, domestic violence, child care, child support, education, welfare, and public health issues were the most frequently cited. In many cases, such as the one above, women's greater interest was attributed to their socialization to and/or experience in sex-specific roles and occupations. A California male official, for example, stated that he had "read enough sociological treatises that convince me that women are much more likely to be more sensitive about human concerns." Women's concerns "are closely related to issues women have been involved in all their lives—at home, the workplace, wherever," according to one California female lawmaker. As another Arizona female official pointed out, these are the issues and problems for which women are and always have been ultimately responsible.[6] Only one legislator, a California man, explicitly associated such issues with feminism and feminist organizations.

This is not to say there was complete consensus. A notable minority of both male and female legislators (23 percent of Arizona women; 17 percent of Arizona men; 14 percent of California women; 12 percent of California men) denied the existence of such gender-related issue concerns. "I'm not sure," admitted a male Arizona legislator:

[I] think there's a perception that women *should* be concerned with some things. You know, you *should* be concerned about this or that. Some of them are really not, but they think they should be, so they try to be. . . . I don't think that the mass of them really are that concerned.

"Not here," agreed a female Arizona colleague who seemed somewhat frustrated with the situation.

We can't get women to pay attention to economic impact issues, insurance-related issues, retirement-related issues, health-related issues. There doesn't seem to be a commonality of interest on those issues. Something as simple as prenatal care, you would think, would transcend boundaries.

Another Arizona female lawmaker seemed rather pleased that there were no longer any such issues about which women were more concerned than men. At one time, she thought, women were the only ones really concerned about such issues as health care, education, child care, and the environment. But these issues that were once on the "fringe" are now "mainstream."

One California man expressed rather ambivalent feelings. Initially, he asserted that such "women's issues" were a myth.

I don't think there's such a thing, necessarily, as any group as a group. The media has a tendency to generalize—you know, that people who happen to be women all ought to have similar concerns and interests. I don't think that's necessarily true. I think, first of all, people are people. What their concerns are, are most closely tied to their own environment and condition.

But when pressed on the issue ("You don't see any issues that women simply tend to be more concerned about?"), he admitted:

I think there are some general things about women that are different than men. I think they're more sensitive on certain issues, as a species. . . . On crime issues, they're sometimes tougher because oftentimes they are more susceptible to crime. On children's issues, I think as a group, they're . . . more interested in that because oftentimes that affects them more directly. But again, I think it depends a lot on the individual condition. I think it's hard to generalize.

Finally, there were only a few legislators—three Arizona men—whose responses suggested some confusion regarding either the concept of women's issues or the nature of the question I asked. One man, for example, immediately responded by defending the abilities of his female colleagues, as if I had asked if they were less effective or inferior in some manner. Then, when I asked him if there were any issues he would consider to be "women's issues," he cited abortion, but only in the sense that he believed such decisions should be left up to women alone. Another legislator seemed to believe that women's issues were those about which *only* women were concerned. The third thought only of issues in which *opinion* rather than concern was divided along gender lines.

Regardless of whether they recognized the actual existence of women's issues (defined as issues about which women are more concerned), some legislators expressed normative objections to the concept. In this respect, the female officials—especially those in California—seemed more wary, or at least more aware, of some of the troublesome implications of such sex-segregated political interests. Six of the California women (43 percent) viewed the existence of such "women's issues" as regrettable. In their eyes, such issues should have interested men as much as they interested women. Said one: "I think there are issues that are identified as women's issues even though I think they are men's issues as well. But I think it's women that have really raised the consciousness in [such] areas." One of the California female legislators had a somewhat different objection. For her, the problem was not that *no* issues should be women's issues; rather, *all* issues should be. "I don't know of an issue that *isn't* a woman's issue," she said. "I don't care if it's the defense of this country, or law enforcement, or transportation, or whatever. We drive as many cars on the road as our male counterparts. For us to point to a specific issue and say it's a woman's issue is a mistake that we as women make. We are the majority; we are 52 percent of the population. Therefore, we need to have more say."

Four Arizona women (23 percent), but only three Arizona men (13 percent) and two California men (12 percent), expressed similar normative misgivings. Three of the Arizona women and one of their male colleagues acknowledged the existence of women's issues but either predicted or wished such issues would eventually attract men at equal rates. The other legislators (two California men, one Arizona woman, and two Arizona men) denied the existence of women's issues and pointedly objected to such generalizations, which they perceived as sex stereotyping. "There shouldn't be" issues about which women are more concerned "by virtue of the fact that they're women," asserted one of the Arizona men. "Otherwise we'd set up a formula for prejudice."

Yet, despite these objections, it is clear that the majority of female and male legislators in these two states were willing and able to see women as a constituency group with particular political interests, or policy concerns. Presumably unlike their predecessors, such recognition came easily for most of these legislators. Moreover, no one dismissed such issues as trivial or unworthy of government and political attention. To the contrary, many of the misgivings about women's issues—especially those voiced by the female officials—were based the opposite assertion, that such issues deserved *more* attention, especially from men.

### Representing Women and/or Women's Policy Concerns

Given that most of these legislators saw women as a constituency group with certain shared policy concerns, how did they perceive their own roles as female and male representatives of women? This section begins by taking a look at the legislators' own assessments of and generalizations about the role of female legislators vis-à-vis women's issues (again, defined as policy concerns shared especially by women). Do female legislators, as women, "make a difference" on these issues? Are they better able to represent women's concerns? Are they more sensitive to and thus more willing to address such concerns? Do they at least provide a unique perspective on such issues?

Because these questions presume the existence of women's issues, they were posed only to those legislators, both female and male, who were willing and able to identify certain public policy issues about which they believed women as a whole (and women as constituents in particular) were especially concerned. Specifically, these legislators were asked whether they thought (they and) their female colleagues were better able and/or more willing to represent such concerns than were (they and) their male colleagues.[7] The legislators' assessments were no doubt more impressionistic than factual, and they should be interpreted as such. As stated earlier, these interview responses are not meant to be indicators of what female and male lawmakers actually did. Rather, the responses most likely reflect, at least in part, how the legislators expected or wished they and their colleagues, as women and men, *would* behave. More importantly, they give some indication of whether the legislators, as men and women themselves, felt especially, equally, or less qualified or responsible for taking the lead on what they perceived to be women's issues.

If a female legislator believes she and her female colleagues are uniquely qualified as women to handle women's concerns, or that her male colleagues are less concerned (or unconcerned) about such issues, then she has an incentive to represent women's concerns herself. On the other hand, a male legislator has an incentive (or at least, lacks a *dis*incentive) to become personally involved in such issues if he believes exactly the opposite: that his female colleagues are no more capable or no more willing to represent women's concerns than he and his male colleagues are. Standard assumptions about the links between descriptive and substantive representation suggest, of course, that female legislators would be more likely than male legislators to have such incentives.

Many legislators—women and men of both states—did, indeed, believe that their female colleagues were more effective and hence made a difference on women's issues. Most who felt that the women they worked with were better able than the men to represent such concerns pointed to the women's personal experiences with such issues, personal experiences that the men most likely would or could never have. A female California legislator, for example, believed that she and her female colleagues were more capable in this realm

> for the simple reason that most men—even though they're fathers— aren't burdened with the responsibility for child care. On the issue of choice, women's right to have an abortion or not, most men have a different perspective because they've never physically been in a position where they actually had to make a personal choice themselves. You never know what it would feel like unless you've been there, or could possibly be there. . . . [These issues] are more paramount in their [female legislators'] minds because it might be something they've faced themselves at some point in their lives.

"We *know* what it's like to have to struggle without child care," echoed another female California official. "So from that standpoint, coming from personal experience, I think we're more effective. One of the big roles I think we have as women legislators is to sensitize our male counterparts to the importance of these issues."

A couple of women in the Arizona legislature were quite disappointed that their female colleagues were *not* more effective and active on women's issues. They *should* be, they argued. "We should be," said one,

> because we understand that the heartbeat of the family is the future of America. We *should* understand that if we make life better for our children and their families, the future of Arizona will be better—because most of us are mothers (or come from motherhood) and come from that sensitivity level.

Such sentiments did not come only from female officials. With regard to issues of domestic violence and child support, a male Arizona legislator asserted that his female colleagues can speak more directly. For a man, it's hypothetical that these poor women can't get their child support. When a woman says the same thing, it has more authority to it. Or domestic violence, where women are scared to death. A man can say that and it doesn't have the authority.

"I don't want to stereotype women in the sense that this is their only focus," began another Arizona man, "but I think that groups ought to have certain interests. Like Hispanics ought to have an interest in a Hispanic agenda, women legislators ought to have an interest in a women's agenda."

Other legislators who thought women were making a difference shied away from stating outright that female officials were (or should be) *better* on women's issues than were male officials, but they did concede that female officials were more concerned with such issues and more willing to take the lead on them. Said one Arizona man:

I'm not sure I would say they're better at it. But they seem more prepared, more ready to take them [issues such as early education, poverty, child and maternal health] up. There's a myriad of issues out there, some which get taken up and some which don't. I find that women legislators pick up these issues—generally speaking—more readily.

A few other legislators claimed that some aforementioned women's issues would not have been brought before their legislature were it not for the efforts of the female members.

A few lawmakers rejected the notion that female officials were more capable or active than male officials vis-à-vis women's concerns, but they did believe that female officials offered a unique perspective on such issues. An Arizona man, for example, did not see his female colleagues concentrating on certain issues, but he did think "women bring a different perspective to the system."

You can never put yourself in a male position and I can never put myself in a female position. I think there are different feelings. I can never experience the pain of birth. . . . It's one thing to get up, put your pants on and go to work; it's another thing to get up, get the kids out of bed, get them dressed and get them to school, make sure they have a good breakfast, and put up with them when they come home. You know, *that* kind of experience. . . . I think it adds something a little different, a different outlook on life.

On the other hand, many legislators argued that sex and gender had nothing to do with how colleagues performed on issues of concern to the female electorate. When asked whether his female colleagues were better able than his male colleagues to represent such women's issues as child care, domestic violence, and child support, one California man replied:

> Not really. I think there are very effective male legislators whose *constituents* are concerned and who can carry those issues very well. . . . There are men who carried bills to chase down fathers who [do not pay child support]. I think men and women can be equally effective; it really depends on the person. You don't need a woman to author such legislation or to carry such bills. Men can be equally effective.

Finally, there were a few legislators whose responses cannot be categorized as either clear acceptance or clear rejection of the idea that "acting for" women is (or should be) somehow related to being a woman. These legislators were quite ambivalent, shifting back and forth between acceptance and rejection of this link between "standing for" women and "acting for" women. When asked whether her female colleagues do a better job of representing the women's concerns she had just named, one female Arizona legislator initially replied, "I think the *assumption* is that we can." When asked if that assumption was true, she responded,

> Sometimes it can be an advantage; sometimes it can be a disadvantage. There's a real danger if you lean too heavily on your role as a female. You can turn some males away; it would be a disadvantage. I personally, as an individual, do not want women to run or to serve as females. I want them to serve as a legislator and to be an excellent legislator . . . based on their knowledge and capacity. The fact that they happen to be a female is another factor.

But then she went on to say:

> I'm very proud of being a woman. I have no hesitancy at all with bringing in what I consider special about being female: emotional insight, my role as a mother and as a wife. These are qualities that enhance my ability to be a good legislator.

Another example of ambivalence comes from a male California official who said that he gets "very angry when people say, 'You have to experience something to be able to represent it,'" but who also admitted that "individual experience can be a very powerful lobbying technique." Thus, he saw female legislators having certain advantages in influencing other legislators "to the extent that on some of these issues only a woman can testify with personal experience."

Although both male and female legislators fell into each of these categories—acceptance, rejection, and ambivalence—the overall pattern of re-

**Table 4.3** Do Female Legislators Make (or Should They Make) a Difference on Women's Issues?

| Response to Question | Arizona Legislators | | California Legislators | |
|---|---|---|---|---|
| | Female (N = 16) (%) | Male (N = 23) (%) | Female (N = 14) (%) | Male (N = 17) (%) |
| Yes, more effective (or should be)[a] | 50 | 39 | 86 | 18 |
| Yes, different viewpoint | 0 | 9 | 0 | 12 |
| No | 12 | 22 | 0 | 35 |
| Ambivalent | 12 | 0 | 0 | 18 |
| No women's issues identified | 25 | 30 | 14 | 18 |
| Total | 100 | 100 | 100 | 100 |

[a] Includes those who believed female legislators were (or should be) more effective and/or more willing to represent women's policy concerns.

sponses reveals rather large sex differences in perspective (see Table 4.3). The differences were most pronounced among the California officials. Every single one of the California women who acknowledged the existence of women's issues believed that she and her female colleagues were more capable of handling such issues, or at least more willing to take the lead on them.[8] Very few of their male colleagues agreed. A few of these men were willing to concede that their female colleagues could offer a unique point of view on such matters. But the largest portion of the California men flatly disagreed with the notion that the women they worked with were uniquely qualified to represent women's issue concerns.

Most of the Arizona female officials who identified women's issues also believed they and their female colleagues made a difference on such issues; but they were not as unanimous as their California counterparts. Compared to *their* California counterparts, the Arizona men were quite willing to agree that their female colleagues were especially qualified to represent women's policy concerns. Still, they were not quite so willing to embrace this idea as the Arizona women were.

What does all this say about the incentives these legislators faced with regard to representing women's concerns? To what degree might the female lawmakers have felt especially qualified or responsible for such tasks? To what degree might the male lawmakers have felt equally qualified or responsible? Clearly, the female California officials had the strongest incentives: almost all of them (86 percent) recognized that women as a constituency group had particular policy concerns; and everyone who did identify such women's issues firmly believed that they, as female lawmakers, were uniquely qualified and/or especially responsible for handling such issues. They also had the organizational resources of the Women's Caucus to back them up. Approximately half of the Arizona female officials also faced incentives to become personally involved in women's issues, for they believed, first of all, that such issues existed, and secondly, that they, as women, were more effective on such matters.

The apparent eagerness with which female officials in both states embraced the cause of women's issues did not uniformly discourage their male colleagues from doing the same. In fact, almost half of the California men (47 percent) saw themselves as (at least) equally qualified and responsible for addressing women's policy concerns, for they refused to believe that their female coworkers were better suited for the task.[9] The Arizona men seemed somewhat less secure about their role in representing women's policy concerns. Nonetheless, roughly 30 percent of the Arizona men acknowledged the existence of such women's issues *and* disputed the idea that their female colleagues had any special skills in or attachment to such matters. In sum, many of the male legislators had no excuse for bowing out of women's issues and passing the buck to their female colleagues. But within each legislature, there was reason to believe that female legislators were more likely to assume leadership roles on such issues. The women were more likely to claim expertise or responsibility for such matters—more likely, that is, than the men were to dispute such claims.

It comes as no surprise, then, that when asked (much earlier in the interviews) whether they saw themselves as representatives of any particular constituency groups or types of people, the female lawmakers were much more likely than the males to cite women, women's groups, or women's issues.[10] It is to this more direct, more individualistic measure of representative roles that I now turn.

Some of the Arizona and California legislators readily acknowledged a commitment to representing certain constituency groups while others seemed uncomfortable with the whole concept of group representation. The reluctant legislators did not want to admit they represented any particular group or groups of people other than their districts as a whole. The reasons are understandable: no one wants to play favorites; officials are elected to represent everyone, not just a select few. Several of these legislators did, however, concede a sort of unintentional group representation: they ended up representing, or were often perceived by others as representing, certain groups by virtue of the issues and issue positions they advocated or by virtue of the composition of their district. Most of the legislators who shied away from explicit recognition of group representation, however, were willing to name groups of people they found easier to represent than others. Sometimes this ease was attributed to policy agreement, sometimes to personal experiences and background, sometimes to expertise in relevant policy areas, sometimes to the reasonable manner in which the groups conduct themselves.

But whether intentional or unintentional, explicit or implicit, female legislators were much more likely than male legislators to mention representing women in this context. In fact, only three of the forty-nine men interviewed (6 percent: one in California, two in Arizona) mentioned anything about women in this part of the interview. One Arizona man, who felt he represented ideals rather than people, claimed that women's groups, along with other liberal groups ("all the good guys"), were easier to represent. They were easier for him to represent not only because their ideals were congruent with his but also because they were "reasonable in their approach to the process." In other words, they were not too dogmatic and were more willing to compromise when necessary than were other (probably conservative) groups. The other Arizona male legislator who mentioned women seemed a bit more committed to the idea of representing women: "I certainly pay attention to women's rights advocates. I've never disagreed with them on an issue of equity."

Of the three, the California man was perhaps the most committed to representing women's concerns. He felt a sort of personal identification with and special understanding of women's issues. Reflecting upon a speech he had recently given to a Business and Professional Women's chapter, he remarked:

> You know, I made some statements in there that sound sort of keyed in on the issue, but I've also practiced them. I mean, I encouraged my wife to do what *she* wanted to do. . . . I never felt it was a threat. It's not a case where people do everything else and still have a job. . . . I share in the household. I'm not a very good cook, but I try. I don't just say I'm not good. No, I try that. I virtually do every dish in the house. And I'll do housework, you know, and I make the bed every day. *Every* day. And I'll do my own laundry. So I really believe that I live what I preach about women's equality.

Reminiscent of the rationale that links women's descriptive and substantive representation on the basis of shared life experiences, this male lawmaker saw a direct link between who he was as a person (a well-intentioned, "liberated" man) and what he did as an elected official.

As with the male legislators, the level of commitment to the representation of women among female legislators varied between shallow and deep. There were, however, a good deal more female legislators who fit into this category: a full 44 percent of the women interviewed (one-third of the Arizonans and 57 percent of the Californians) spontaneously mentioned women, women's groups, or women's issues in their discussion of group representation.[11] The weakly or reluctantly committed included the California woman who said, "I don't see myself as representing necessarily any particular group or anything like that," but then went on to say that she worked a lot with women's groups and found them easier to represent than other groups. Another California female official explained that she had a general representational duty to represent everyone, but "beyond that there are representational roles that you find yourself taking on because of the issues you've been involved with." She believed she was perceived by others to be a strong advocate for women "by virtue of being a woman [who takes] on issues that are perceived (regrettably) to be 'women's issues,'" such as family law, children's issues, and health care policy.

Several of the female legislators who seemed more committed to the idea of representing women pointed to personal experience as an important factor that made them particularly good representatives of women. "Because I've been there," explained a California woman. "Women's issues come easy to me," claimed an Arizona female official, "because I'm a woman. I might have lived through it once or twice." Finally, another Arizona woman felt she represented Republican women not only because she "support[s] the same things" but also, as she put it, "[because] I have been through so many different phases of life that I have a special feeling for [their problems and concerns]." One experience she considered particularly helpful in giving her a better understanding of such things was being a single mother. All three of these female officials (plus one other) clearly acknowledged a direct relationship between who they were and what they did, between being a woman and being a representative of women.

## Conclusions

Much of the evidence presented here suggests that women as a constituency group were more significant, more important to female lawmakers than to male lawmakers. Although the men were just as likely as the women to acknowledge the existence of women's issues, they were less likely to perceive women as one of their most supportive constituency groups; they were less confident of their ability or responsibility to advocate women's issues; and they were much less likely to see themselves as representatives of women, women's groups, or women's issues. In other words, the female officials were more likely to accept the link between descriptive and substantive representation of women—the link between being a woman and actively representing women and their concerns—than their male colleagues were to reject such a link.

There also were notably significant differences between legislators of the two states. First, the California female lawmakers were more likely than their Arizona counterparts to perceive strong support from their female constituents. At the same time, the California men were less likely than the Arizona men to perceive strong support from female constituents. Second, California legislators, female and male, were slightly more likely than the Arizona legislators to acknowledge the existence of women's issues, issues they thought concerned women more than men. Third, the women of the Arizona legislature were less likely than the California women to believe they made (or should make) a difference on women's issues, that they were more capable of, more willing to, or more responsible for representing women's concerns than were their male colleagues. Meanwhile, the men of the Arizona legislature were more likely than the California men to believe that their female colleagues were more effective representatives on women's issues. Finally, the California female officials were more likely than those of Arizona to see themselves as representatives of women or women's issues, to acknowledge their own role in the active representation of women.

Overall, there is a fairly consistent pattern in which the Arizona lawmakers appear rather centrist on these matters while the California women and men are often located at opposite extremes. What all this suggests is that the entire issue of women's political representation was more salient, more controversial, and more polarizing within the California legislature. I offer two explanations for, or two forces behind, these state-level differences.

First, the more liberal and Democratic nature of California politics may have made state politicians more attuned to women's political representation. Nationally, the Democratic party has been the main beneficiary of the increasing rates of women's political participation (at all levels, from the voting booth to national elective office) and the increasing frequency and significance of "gender gaps" in public opinion and voting behavior. From both an ideological and a vote-maximizing, rational-actor point of view, then, Democratic elected officials have greater incentive than their Republican colleagues to recognize women as a constituency group and to address women's political concerns. Indeed, the Democratic legislators in this study were somewhat more likely than the Republicans to perceive female constituents as strongly supportive, to acknowledge the existence of women's issues, and to believe that female lawmakers were especially qualified or responsible for representing women's policy concerns. Democrats in both states also were much more likely than Republicans to identify themselves as representatives of women or women's issues.

Thus, the fact that the California legislators were more Democratic than those of Arizona (61 percent compared to 44 percent) sheds some light on why they were more likely to recognize women's issues. It also provides some explanation for why the California female lawmakers seemed to embrace the cause of women's representation more enthusiastically than did their Arizona counterparts. But ideology and partisan politics cannot tell us why the men of the California legislature—who were more Democratic and liberal than the men of the Arizona legislature—were so wary of their female constituents and so defensive about their ability and willingness to represent women's concerns.

The California Legislative Women's Caucus, I believe, provides another clue to this puzzle. One of the purposes of the Caucus was to inform or educate members of the legislature about the concerns of women, both within and outside the Capitol. The evidence presented in this chapter suggests that the Caucus was quite successful in this respect. Another function of the Caucus was to provide opportunities for female legislators to organize as women, for women—to enable women to represent women. One of its primary goals, in other words, was to forge links between the descriptive and substantive representation of women. Given the enthusiasm with which the California women supported the Caucus (see Chapter 2), it is not surprising that they were so much more willing than their Arizona counterparts to acknowledge and accept their roles in and responsibility for representing women.[12]

What is surprising, or at least intriguing, is that the Legislative Women's Caucus seems to have had the opposite effect among the California male legislators. Perhaps feeling threatened by the mobilization and solidarity of their female colleagues, these men were very uncomfortable with the idea that female officials are better, or at least more willing, representatives of women's concerns. Compared to their counterparts in Arizona, the California men had more opportunities and more reason to confront this issue and to realize the negative implication: if female legislators do a better job of representing women's concerns, then, logic dictates, male legislators do a worse job. While most California male legislators rejected this idea, they nevertheless may have worried that their female constituents accepted it. This, in turn, could explain why so few of these California male officials perceived strong support from their female constituents. Such insecurities also help explain why, when asked whether they saw themselves as representatives of certain constituency groups, only one California man mentioned women.

There is some indication that the California women also thought long and hard about the implications of such gendered politics. Recall they were the ones most likely to voice normative objections to the concept of women's issues per se and to argue that men should be just as concerned about such issues as women. In short, these issues of women's political representation seemed not only more salient but also more complicated to the California legislators.

This is not what one would expect, given the much larger (and longer) numerical presence of women in the Arizona legislature. Previous research on sex, gender, and legislative behavior (e.g., Gertzog 1995; Saint-Germain 1989; Thomas 1994) has argued that women in public office are more willing and able to "make a difference" for women, as women, as their numbers increase. This chapter, however, raises the possibility that the exact opposite may occur. As I argued in Chapter 2, the Arizona female officials were too numerous, too secure, and too diverse to consider themselves a cohesive group and organize as such. Being a woman in the state legislature seemed less remarkable to them than it did to their California counterparts. The relatively unremarkable, unrecognized nature of gender politics within the Arizona legislature seems to have spilled over into the members' beliefs and attitudes about the significance of women as a constituency group. Having many other female colleagues may in theory make it easier for women in state legislatures to organize and *act* for women; but this chapter suggests that having so many other women around may also make it less likely that the female politicians will *want* to or feel the *need* to act for women themselves.

# PART III

# Policymaking

## CHAPTER FIVE

# Policy Preferences

In the study of sex, gender, and legislative behavior, policymaking inevitably assumes center stage. It is, after all, what distinguishes legislators from all other political officeholders—executives, administrators, bureaucrats, and judges included. More importantly, the ways in which women in public office are expected to "make a difference" for women, as women, often point to such policy-related activities (see Chapter 1). This chapter begins the exploration of women's impact on public policy by comparing the policy preferences of the women and men of the 1990 Arizona and California state legislatures. Both attitudes, measured by survey responses, and behavior, recorded in roll call votes, are examined across a wide range of political issues. Thus, the analysis provides an estimate of the female legislators' potential and actual impact on the direction and content of public policy in each state. At issue in this analysis is not only who is more or less likely to support what, but also whether female officials are more likely than their male colleagues to support women and their (alleged) policy interests.

Political scientists have long been intrigued by the possibility of sex differences in legislators' policy attitudes and roll call voting behavior. Our interest no doubt reflects in part the dominant concerns of those who study legislative behavior and representation (in the American context) in general. Additionally, our inquiries have been motivated by certain questions and expectations about sex, gender, and representation. Although some scholars do not present such questions and expectations explicitly, and many address more than one set of concerns, three fairly distinct patterns emerge.

Some researchers have been interested in simply determining whether or not the policy preferences of men and women in public office differ. In doing so, they address the most general, overarching question about women in politics: "what difference does their presence in office make?" (Dodson and Carroll 1991: 1). These concerns usually lead to an examination of sex differences in traditional measures of legislative voting behavior, which focus on either degrees of partisan support (e.g., party support scores), on general political ideology (e.g., Conservative Coalition support scores, general interest group ratings), or simply on attitudes toward a wide variety of controversial issues (e.g., Gehlen 1977; Johnson and Carroll 1978; Thomas 1989).

A second set of questions focuses on the policy responsiveness of public officials to trends in public opinion, particularly those related to sex and gender. The main question here is whether women and men in public office act like women and men in the electorate. More specifically, researchers often take note of "gender gaps" in public opinion surveys, which show women significantly more likely than men to take liberal stances on issues of government-sanctioned (or -controlled) force and violence (e.g., military aggression, defense spending, gun control, death penalty), social welfare, and government regulation in the interest of environmental protection and public health and safety. Are these gender gaps, researchers wonder, reflected among the political elite? In one of the most influential studies, Susan Welch (1985: 126) presents the research question as "whether the greater liberalism of the 'woman in the street' compared to the 'man in the street' is reflected in public officials" (see also Burrell 1994; Poole and Zeigler 1985; Rapoport, Stone, and Abramowitz 1990). Because gender gaps among the electorate have been observed on such a wide range of issues, these researchers also tend to focus on composite measures of general policy liberalism among elected officials.

The third type of inquiry adopts a feminist perspective, either explicitly or implicitly, to pose more specific questions about legislators' willingness to act for women by supporting feminist positions on certain "women's issues," or "issues of special concern to women" (Burrell 1994: 158; see also Leader 1977, Dolan 1997). The assumption, or hypothesis, here is twofold: that female officials are most likely to make their mark on women's issues, and that that mark will be a feminist one. In her review of this literature, Susan Gluck Mezey, for example, notes:

While Senator [Nancy] Kassebaum [R-Kansas] would dispute the assertion that women officeholders must adopt feminist positions in order to "act for" women in society, most feminists (including myself) would argue that women in office "act for" women to the extent that they support feminist positions on questions such as family leave, child care, or reproductive rights. (Mezey 1994: 268)

Researchers adopting this approach compare female and male officials' attitudes toward and votes on such issues as the Equal Rights Amendment, abortion, child care, parental leave, domestic violence, and comparable worth. In identifying women's issues and feminist positions therein, researchers often rely on the legislative monitoring efforts of feminist-oriented interest groups such as the National Women's Political Caucus (Burrell 1994), the National Federation of Business and Professional Women's Clubs (Durst and Rusek 1993), and the National Organization for Women (Thomas 1989). A recent study of congressional roll call voting patterns relies on the Congressional Caucus for Women's Issues to identify "legislative initiatives considered important to women and the family" (Dolan 1997: 84).

Despite such variations in theoretical motivations and expectations, in the types of policy issues examined, and in the measures of policy preferences employed, the conclusions of these various investigations are remarkably similar.[1] In Congress and in state legislatures, there is ample evidence that from the late 1970s to the present, women have tended to be more liberal and more feminist than men. Moreover, these policy differences between female and male officials have been only partly attributable to differences in partisanship and constituencies. It is often the case that women in public office are more likely than men to be Democrats and/or to serve relatively liberal (more urban and/or minority) districts. Yet, compared to men of the same party and with similar districts, women in these studies are still more liberal and feminist. Even among those who identify themselves as liberal or feminist, female officials (in at least one study) are still more likely than their male counterparts to take liberal, feminist policy positions (Dodson and Carroll 1991).

Against this backdrop, the policy preferences of the men and women of the 1990 Arizona and California legislatures appear oddly congruent. Relatively few significant sex differences arise in the following analysis of both the attitudes and voting behavior of the legislators. The next section of this chapter examines those attitudes and voting patterns in detail. Like the previous research, I explore policy preferences in three areas, going from the most general to the most specific: overall policy liberalism, support for women's (usually liberal) positions on gender gap issues, and support for feminist positions on issues of women's rights, status, and well-being. Next, the findings of this study are assessed in light of previous research on gender gaps in elite and mass policy preferences. I propose several reasons why the dearth of sex differences revealed here may not be so surprising or out of the ordinary. Finally, this chapter concludes by considering the argument that policy preferences and roll call votes in particular are the least important aspects of policymaking and the least likely place in which to find women making a difference.

## Measures of Policy Preferences

The legislators in this study were asked in the written questionnaire to state their preferences on a number of gender gap issues, ones on which men and women in the general public tend to differ, as well as on a few readily identifiable feminist, or women's rights, issues.[2] Specifically, the legislators indicated whether they felt government should do more, is doing enough, should do less, or should not get involved at all in the following areas: controlling air and water pollution, improving the availability and quality of medical care, protecting the consumer against poor services or products and unreasonable prices, improving the quality of public education, assuring full employment, assuring equal rights for minorities, assuring equal rights for women, and providing child care services for parents.[3] In each case, those who advocated a more active government role are considered both more liberal and (for the time being) more supportive of women and women's interests than those who wanted to maintain or reduce the scope of government involvement. Legislators also were asked to state their opinions on the death penalty and on the legal status of abortion.[4] Those who opposed the death penalty and legal restrictions on abortion are considered more liberal, more supportive of women, and more feminist. Table 5.1 compares the responses of female and male lawmakers within each state.

In terms of their personal policy preferences, these men and women agreed more than they disagreed. Female and male legislators of both states were in full agreement on several gender gap issues: pollution control, public education, employment, and the death penalty. On other gender gap issues, health care and minority rights, there were only very small and inconsistent sex differences. Contrary to expectations, female lawmakers in both states took slightly more *conservative* positions on health care than their male colleagues did. And while the Arizona women were a bit more liberal than the Arizona men on minority rights, the opposite was true among the California officials: the men were a bit more liberal than the women.

The only gender gap issue that elicited significantly and consistently different responses from female and male officeholders was consumer protection. Female legislators in both states took more liberal positions than did their male colleagues. While most of the Arizona women (58 percent) favored expanding government efforts in this policy realm, most of the Arizona men (62 percent) chose the status quo. Most of the California women (65 percent) also chose to maintain current levels of government activity,

## Table 5.1  Legislators' Opinions on Gender Gap and Women's Rights Issues

| Issue | Opinion on Proper Scope of Government Activity Needed (%) | | | | Mean Score |
|---|---|---|---|---|---|
| | More Government (4) | Same Amount (3) | Less Government (2) | No Government (1) | |
| **Controlling air and water pollution** | | | | | |
| Arizona legislators | | | | | |
| Men | 67 | 33 | 0 | 0 | 3.67 |
| Women | 68 | 24 | 8 | 0 | 3.59 |
| California legislators | | | | | |
| Men | 50 | 50 | 0 | 0 | 3.50 |
| Women | 59 | 41 | 0 | 0 | 3.59 |
| **Improving the availability and quality of medical care** | | | | | |
| Arizona legislators | | | | | |
| Men | 62 | 38 | 0 | 0 | 3.62 |
| Women | 59 | 24 | 8 | 8 | 3.34 |
| California legislators | | | | | |
| Men | 83 | 17 | 0 | 0 | 3.83 |
| Women | 59 | 41 | 0 | 0 | 3.59 |
| **Protecting the consumer** | | | | | |
| Arizona legislators | | | | | |
| Men | 24 | 62 | 14 | 0 | 3.09 |
| Women | 58 | 25 | 8 | 8 | 3.23 |
| California legislators | | | | | |
| Men | 33 | 33 | 17 | 17 | 2.83 |
| Women | 35 | 65 | 0 | 0 | 3.35 |
| **Improving the quality of public education** | | | | | |
| Arizona legislators | | | | | |
| Men | 76 | 19 | 5 | 0 | 3.71 |
| Women | 83 | 17 | 0 | 0 | 3.83 |
| California legislators | | | | | |
| Men | 92 | 0 | 8 | 0 | 3.83 |
| Women | 71 | 29 | 0 | 0 | 3.71 |
| **Assuring full employment** | | | | | |
| Arizona legislators | | | | | |
| Men | 14 | 76 | 5 | 5 | 3.00 |
| Women | 37 | 46 | 17 | 0 | 3.21 |
| California legislators | | | | | |
| Men | 33 | 25 | 25 | 17 | 2.75 |
| Women | 0 | 71 | 29 | 0 | 2.71 |
| **Assuring equal rights for minorities** | | | | | |
| Arizona legislators | | | | | |
| Men | 33 | 48 | 19 | 0 | 3.14 |
| Women | 59 | 24 | 8 | 8 | 3.34 |

Table 5.1 (*continued*)

| Issue | More Government (4) | Same Amount (3) | Less Government (2) | No Government (1) | Mean Score |
|---|---|---|---|---|---|
| | Opinion on Proper Scope of Government Activity Needed (%) | | | | |
| California legislators | | | | | |
| Men | 50 | 42 | 8 | 0 | 3.42 |
| Women | 47 | 24 | 29 | 0 | 3.17 |
| **Assuring equal rights for women** | | | | | |
| Arizona legislators | | | | | |
| Men | 29 | 67 | 5 | 0 | 3.24 |
| Women | 51 | 32 | 8 | 8 | 3.26 |
| California legislators | | | | | |
| Men | 50 | 42 | 8 | 0 | 3.42 |
| Women | 47 | 36 | 17 | 0 | 3.29 |
| **Providing child care services for parents** | | | | | |
| Arizona legislators | | | | | |
| Men | 19 | 52 | 24 | 5 | 2.86 |
| Women | 68 | 7 | 8 | 17 | 3.26 |
| California legislators | | | | | |
| Men | 54 | 9 | 18 | 18 | 3.00 |
| Women | 59 | 41 | 0 | 0 | 3.59 |

| | Agree Strongly (1) | Agree Somewhat (2) | Disagree Somewhat (3) | Disagree Strongly (4) | Mean Score |
|---|---|---|---|---|---|
| | Opinion Regarding Issue (%) | | | | |
| **Death Penalty** | | | | | |
| Arizona legislators | | | | | |
| Men | 67 | 24 | 5 | 5 | 1.48 |
| Women | 73 | 7 | 14 | 7 | 1.55 |
| California legislators | | | | | |
| Men | 67 | 17 | 8 | 8 | 1.58 |
| Women | 65 | 35 | 0 | 0 | 1.35 |

**Table 5.1** (*continued*)

| Issue | Should Never Be Permitted (1) | Mother's Life at Risk, Rape, or Incest Only Permissible Conditions (2) | Up to Woman and Doctor (3) | Should Always Be Permitted (4) | Mean Score |
|---|---|---|---|---|---|
| | | Opinion Regarding Issue (%) | | | |
| **Abortion** | | | | | |
| Arizona legislators | | | | | |
| Men | 5 | 25 | 55 | 15 | 2.80 |
| Women | 0 | 34 | 36 | 30 | 2.97 |
| California legislators | | | | | |
| Men | 0 | 17 | 58 | 25 | 3.08 |
| Women | 0 | 41 | 24 | 35 | 2.94 |

NOTE: A total of 52 legislators responded to these survey questions: 21 Arizona men, 11 Arizona women, 12 California men, and 8 California women. One Arizona man neglected to answer the question on abortion and is therefore excluded from the analysis of that issue.

but none of them wanted such efforts curtailed. California male legislators, on the other hand, were evenly distributed along the spectrum; one-third favored expansion, one-third favored maintenance, one-third favored reduction.

With respect to sex differences, the legislators' responses to women's rights issues were mixed. On the one hand, male lawmakers of both states were on average no less (or more) liberal than their female colleagues on issues of equal rights for women and abortion.[5] On the other hand, the largest of gender gaps among the legislators occurred on the issue of child care. Among Arizona legislators, women were much more likely than men to favor increasing government efforts to provide such services. While two-thirds of the women wanted to increase the state's role in providing child care, half the men wanted to maintain the status quo and almost a third wanted to *reduce* government activity. Men and women of the California legislature were equally likely to favor expanding government efforts to provide child care to parents. But while a substantial percentage (36 percent) of California male legislators believed that such efforts should be reduced, not a single one of their female colleagues agreed. All of the California female officials who did not advocate more government involvement chose to maintain current levels of activity instead.

To get an idea of legislators' general policy liberalism across all these issues, I combined their responses to all ten questions listed in Table 5.1. This index of policy liberalism was created by adding the numbers (1–4) associated with each response option for each legislator. Index scores thus have a possible range from 10, being extremely conservative, to 40, being extremely liberal.[6] Despite the few sex differences in legislative opinions noted above, the average index scores of Arizona female and male legislators and California female and male legislators are practically identical. All four groups have an average score of approximately 31. There was, then, no general tendency in either state for female officials to take more liberal positions than their male colleagues on either gender gap or women's rights issues.

Analysis of the legislators' voting behavior lends further support to this conclusion. Moreover, because the roll call voting data allow one to examine *all* legislators' positions on a much wider range of issues (not just those of my sample of legislators), such analysis can contribute to a more nuanced understanding of policy preferences. Over 100 roll call votes were recorded: 23 in the Arizona House, 26 in the Arizona Senate, 35 in the California Assembly, and 28 in the California Senate.[7] The bills and motions upon which the Arizona and California legislators voted cover the most hotly debated issues of the sessions: gender gap issues of social welfare, environmental protection, public health and safety, and gun control; women's rights issues of reproductive health, child care, family leave, and pay equity; and other ideologically charged issues such as privatization, taxes, auto insurance, labor relations, flag desecration, and animal rights. (Appendix B provides a full list of all roll call votes recorded and analyzed for this study and short descriptions of each proposed bill and motion.)

Table 5.2 compares the frequency with which male and female legislators of each state cast liberal (and/or pro-women) votes on three sets of issues: (1) all issues included in the roll call vote data; (2) gender gap issues only; and (3) women's rights issues only.[8] These frequencies, or indices of policy liberalism, were calculated separately for each legislative chamber since each voted on a different set of bills and motions.[9] In addition to comparing female and male voting behavior within each legislative chamber, Table 5.2 also compares the voting patterns of men and women within each chamber's party caucus (Democrat and Republican).

On women's rights issues, on gender gap issues, and on all issues combined, the level of agreement between men and women of each legislative chamber is remarkably high. Rarely is there more than a 10 percentage-point difference in the proportion of liberal votes cast by women and men. For the most part, Democrats cast mostly liberal votes and Republicans cast mostly conservative votes, regardless of sex. California Assembly Democrats and Republicans were somewhat more polarized than partisans of the

**Table 5.2  Roll Call Voting: Percentage of Liberal Votes Cast**

| Roll Call Vote | Arizona Legislators | | California Legislators | |
|---|---|---|---|---|
| | Men<br>% (N) | Women<br>% (N) | Men<br>% (N) | Women<br>% (N) |
| **All votes recorded** | | | | |
| House/Assembly | 51 (38) | 54 (22) | 61 (64) | 55 (14) |
| Senate | 54 (25) | 58 (5) | 67 (33) | 74 (5) |
| House/Assembly | | | | |
|   Democrats | 79 (17) | 84 (9) | 95 (38) | 96 (7) |
|   Republicans | 28 (21) | 33 (13) | 12 (26) | 14 (7) |
| Senate | | | | |
|   Democrats | 87 (11) | 98 (2) | 89 (21) | 86 (3) |
|   Republicans | 28 (14) | 32 (3) | 27 (11) | 56 (2) |
| **Gender gap issues**[a] | | | | |
| House/Assembly | 51 | 62[b] | 63 | 58 |
| Senate | 58 | 60 | 67 | 76 |
| House/Assembly | | | | |
|   Democrats | 70 | 83 | 96 | 97 |
|   Republicans | 36 | 48 | 15 | 20 |
| Senate | | | | |
|   Democrats | 91 | 100 | 85 | 86 |
|   Republicans | 32 | 33 | 31 | 62 |
| **Women's rights issues**[a] | | | | |
| House/Assembly | 56 | 64[c] | 60 | 51 |
| Senate | 58 | 70 | 71 | 68 |
| House/Assembly | | | | |
|   Democrats | 65 | 65 | 97 | 100 |
|   Republicans | 48 | 63 | 6 | 3 |
| Senate | | | | |
|   Democrats | 86 | 100 | 96 | 92 |
|   Republicans | 36 | 50 | 22 | 33 |

[a] The numbers of legislators voting on gender gap issues and on women's rights issues are the same as those reported for all votes recorded.

[b] Two of the 14 votes recorded as liberal are in fact conservative yet pro-women, in the sense that women (in public opinion polls) are more likely than men to take the conservative position: H2354, regarding sex shops (conservative vote is antipornography); and H2433, regarding drunk driving (conservative vote increases the amount of time after arrest in which suspects' blood alcohol level can be tested).

[c] One of the three votes recorded as liberal (or feminist) can be considered conservative: H2354, regarding sex shops (antipornography).

California Senate or the two Arizona houses, but the Assembly women were just as polarized as the Assembly men.

The level and durability of consensus between the men and women of the California Assembly are particularly noteworthy. Of the thirty-five Assembly votes recorded, twenty-seven elicited sex differences of 10 percent or less. The other eight votes saw sex differences of between 11 and 25 percentage points. More interestingly, Assembly women voted more *conservatively* than the men on all but two of these eight bills. The women took more conservative positions on the regulation of hazardous waste facilities, air quality management, auto insurance regulation, solid waste management, recycling, and the federal Civil Rights Act of 1990; they were more liberal on a bill guaranteeing mental health insurance coverage and, in an apparently contradictory fashion, on another bill on solid waste reduction and recycling.

Outside the California Assembly, some significant gender gaps in roll call voting did arise and are worth examining closely. Women in the Arizona House, Democrats and Republicans alike, were slightly more likely than their male colleagues to cast liberal or pro-women votes on gender gap issues. A variety of such issues elicited the greatest sex differences in support among these lawmakers. Arizona female representatives were especially more likely (between 14 and 19 percentage points more likely) to support the following: the establishment of a statewide Martin Luther King holiday; the imposition of various taxes on potential polluters to fund the state's water quality Superfund; a ban on the use of tropical hardwood in state buildings; a mandate that public schools offer AIDS education at all grade levels; and allowing DUI (driving under the influence) suspects to undergo blood-alcohol testing up to two hours after arrest. They also were considerably less likely than the men to support a bill allowing residents to carry concealed weapons. On the other hand, there were a good number of gender gap issues on which these men and women basically agreed: a state university tuition freeze; a Superfund tax on household products, water use, and landfills; civil penalties for violations of air pollution regulations; health insurance breaks for small businesses; pool fences; automobile seat belts; and compassionate leave for prison inmates. Moreover, the sex differences that did occur were not all that consequential. In only two of the fourteen votes cast on gender gap issues in the Arizona House did women's votes make a difference in the final outcome: women provided the winning margin on the Superfund tax on potential polluters bill and on the AIDS education bill. While two-thirds of the women supported these two bills, only 45 percent and 50 percent of the men supported them, respectively.

On women's rights issues, the female and male Democrats of the Arizona House were in perfect agreement. Among the House Republicans, however, women's rights issues tended to gain somewhat more support from women than from men. In particular, these Republican women were more likely to support increased restrictions on "sex shops" (16 percent more likely than Republican men) and medical malpractice subsidies for obstetricians serving poor communities (20 percent more likely). Neither of these bills would have passed were it not for these women's votes, although it is important to note, again, that approximately half the men (47 percent and 50 percent, respectively) did support these bills, just not a majority. It is also worth noting that equal percentages of the House Republican (and Democratic) men and women supported a bill adding nonabortion family planning services to Arizona's version of Medicaid.

The five women of the Arizona Senate also were more likely than their male colleagues to support two of the four women's rights bills considered here: tax credits for employers providing day care, and the licensing and regulation of midwives. Bare majorities of the male senators voted for these measures, compared to all but one of the female senators (80 percent). On the other hand, the Senate women were no more (or less) likely than the men to support the other two women's rights measures: the aforementioned medical malpractice subsidy and a state-sponsored child care resource and referral system.

The largest gender gap in legislators' roll call voting patterns reported in Table 5.2 is between the two women and eleven men of the California Senate Republican caucus. These two women, known for their moderate stances, cast significantly more liberal votes than did their male counterparts. They were especially prone to take liberal positions on gender gap issues such as reducing air pollution, preserving coastal resources, supporting AIDS education, mandating control of hazardous waste and "acutely" hazardous materials, and banning assault weapons. Both women supported each of these bills, in stark contrast to the Republican men of the Senate. Together with two of their three Democratic female colleagues, they provided the winning margin for one of these bills, the one on coastal resources—which, once again, exactly half the Senate men supported.

The Republican women of the California Senate were not much more liberal than their male counterparts, however, on women's rights issues. They seemed quite reluctant to support such measures, in fact. They split their votes on the issue of family leave; one voted in favor of requiring child care facilities in public buildings while the other abstained; both abstained on a resolution supporting the then-proposed federal Civil Rights Act of 1990; and both voted against establishing a commission on pay equity.

Several conclusions are clear from this analysis of both personal policy preferences and roll call voting behavior. First, truly significant sex differences, or gender gaps, among Arizona and California state legislators were few and far between. Among *some* subdivisions of the Arizona legislators, *some*, but not all, proposals dealing with gender gap and women's rights issues gained more support from women than from men. In the California legislature, *some* of these types of proposals gained more support from women than from men, but only among the thirteen Republicans in the

Senate (only two of whom were women). Clearly, the magnitude or even existence of sex differences in legislators' policy preferences depended on fairly specific variations in who and what was involved. Furthermore, in the few instances in which women's support did make the difference between a bill's final passage and failure, the men were not overwhelmingly opposed to the bill; they were shy of a winning majority by just one or two votes.

Second, policy preferences, especially those expressed via votes on the floors of the legislative chambers, were profoundly influenced by political party affiliation. This was especially the case in the California legislature, where members of each party were clearly and uniformly loyal and steadfast to whatever ideological or partisan interests were at stake. The California Senate Republicans seem to have been the only ones even partly immune to such intense partisanship. Even in the Arizona legislature, where the majority (Republican) party was racked by internal factionalism, partisan divisions ran deep—just not quite as deep as in California.

The third conclusion is a direct result of the second, and the flip side of the first: differences among female legislators were much greater and much more frequent than differences between female and male legislators. On controversial issues such as those examined here, consensus among female lawmakers was just as rare as consensus among male lawmakers (see Table 5.1). With few exceptions (the Arizona House on women's rights issues and the California Senate overall), the voting patterns of Democratic and Republican women were just as polarized as those of Democratic and Republican men (see Table 5.2).

### Are Arizona and California Exceptions to the Rule?

At first glance, the dearth of sex differences among these Arizona and California state legislators stands in contrast to the findings of other studies of policy attitudes and voting behavior of American public officials. Perhaps this is simply because the women and men of these two legislatures were exceptional. For example, unlike the women who have served in Congress (and the women of many other state legislatures), these women were not predominantly Democratic (Gertzog 1995).[10] The California female lawmakers were almost evenly divided between Democrats and Republicans; approximately three-fifths of the Arizona female lawmakers were Republican, as were three-fifths of their male colleagues. But other studies of elected officials have found sex differences *within* party delegations, especially among Republicans. Thus, the somewhat unusual number of Republican women in the Arizona and California legislatures would not necessarily diminish the overall "gap" between female and male legislators.

Another possibility is that the male and female *constituents* of Arizona and California were exceptional. As the classic studies of legislative voting behavior suggest, constituency characteristics and political party are the two best predictors of what policy proposals lawmakers tend to support or oppose (Collie 1985; Hamm, Hedlund, and Anderson 1994; Jewell and Patterson 1986; Uslaner 1986). And, as mentioned earlier, one of the primary rationales for expecting gender gaps among elected officials is the idea that female and male representatives represent female and male constituents respectively. Perhaps, then, there were so few gender gaps among Arizona and California state legislators because there were few gender gaps among their constituents. While there are no available polls of constituents within each state legislative district nor any of Arizona residents as a whole, there is a wealth of surveys of California residents conducted by the Field Institute in the late 1980s with which to investigate this possibility.[11]

Table 5.3 displays the results of numerous California Polls conducted between 1988 and 1990. Women's and men's opinions are compared along a range of issues similar to those used to gauge the policy preferences of legislators: general attitudes about the scope of government activity and more specific responses to issues such as the death penalty, domestic violence, gun control, government aid to the poor, environmental protection against oil and gas drilling, the safety of nuclear power plants, occupational health and safety, AIDS, cigarette taxes for health care programs, abortion, and affirmative action.

Clearly, California women were more liberal than California men on most of these issues, and they were no less so than women in nationwide polls.[12] In several polls, for example, at least 10 percent more women than men preferred a larger government providing more services to a smaller one providing fewer services. California women tended to be less enthusiastic about the death penalty, more willing to make domestic violence (against spouses and children) punishable by law, and more supportive of various gun control measures than were the men. With respect to social welfare, women were more willing to grant government aid for the hungry and homeless and to improve the economic status of minority groups. Women were more likely to push for increased restrictions and regulations on oil and gas exploration and drilling, as well as on nuclear power plants; they also were likely to want the governor to restore funding for the state's Occupational Safety and Health Agency.

There is, in short, little reason to believe that the policy preferences of the women and men of the California legislature were so similar because the female and male citizens of California were exceptionally undifferentiated. Gender gaps, while conspicuously absent in the California legislature,

**Table 5.3  Gender Gaps in Policy Preferences of California Residents, 1988–1990**

| Policy Preferences | Percentage of Respondents[a] | | Gender Gap (W – M) |
| | Women (W) | Men (M) | |
| --- | --- | --- | --- |
| **General Political Predispositions** | | | |
| Prefers a larger government providing more services to a smaller government providing fewer services. | | | |
|     February 1988 | 52 | 42 | 10* |
|     October 1988 | 50 | 40 | 10* |
|     January 1989 | 54 | 37 | 17* |
| The next president should *not* continue along the same path of Ronald Reagan's policies. (October 1988) | 54 | 47 | 7* |
|     Average gender gap (general political) | | | 11 |
| **Death Penalty, Violence, Gun Control** | | | |
| Somewhat or strongly opposed to the death penalty. (December 1989)[b] | 22 | 16 | 6* |
| Favors doing away with the death sentence as a punishment for serious crimes. (December 1989) | 14 | 15 | –1 |
| Would prefer life in prison without the possibility of parole and requiring prisoners to work in prison and give part of their earnings to the families of victims rather than the death penalty. (December 1989) | 80 | 64 | 16* |
| Hitting one's spouse hard enough to leave a big, painful bruise should be punishable by law. (December 1989) | 86 | 77 | 9* |
| Hitting one's child hard enough to leave a big, painful bruise should be punishable by law. (December 1989) | 83 | 72 | 11* |
| Yelling, screaming, or verbally threatening one's child should be punishable by law. (December 1989) | 28 | 19 | 9* |
| Yelling, screaming, or threatening a child can be as serious as or more serious than physically beating a child. (December 1989) | 79 | 70 | 9* |
| Favors strongly or somewhat extending the state's 15-day waiting period and background check of persons seeking to acquire a handgun to include purchasers of all firearms. (January 1990) | 88 | 76 | 12* |
| Persons who have committed violent misdemeanors should *not* be allowed to purchase a firearm in California. (January 1990) | 93 | 86 | 7* |
| Persons on probation should *not* be allowed to purchase a firearm in California. (January 1990) | 91 | 83 | 8* |
|     Average gender gap (death penalty, violence, gun control) | | | 8.6 |

Table 5.3 (*continued*)

| Policy Preferences | Percentage of Respondents[a] | | Gender Gap (W − M) |
|---|---|---|---|
| | Women (W) | Men (M) | |
| **Social Welfare** | | | |
| Favors ballot proposition that would provide state government funds to assist hungry and homeless people.[c] | | | |
| July 1988 | 86 | 71 | 15* |
| September 1988 | 75 | 67 | 8* |
| October 1988 | 71 | 65 | 6 |
| November 1988 | 65 | 59 | 6* |
| Believes government should make every effort to improve the economic status of minority groups. (July 1989) | 47 | 38 | 9* |
| Average gender gap (social welfare) | | | 8.8 |
| **Environmental Protection and Regulation; Health and Public Safety** | | | |
| Would like to see less or no gas and oil exploration and mining in the California desert. (September 1988) | 54 | 42 | 12* |
| Current government restrictions prohibiting drilling of oil and gas wells on government park lands and forest reserves should *not* be relaxed. (July 89) | 72 | 72 | 0 |
| Oil companies should *not* be allowed to drill more oil and gas wells in state tidelands along the California seacoast. (July 1989) | 81 | 74 | 7* |
| Building of more nuclear power plants should *not* be allowed in California. (July 1989) | 78 | 60 | 18* |
| Does not believe that nuclear power plants operating in California are safe enough to continue operating at present levels. (July 1989) | 59 | 40 | 19* |
| Favors ballot proposition that would require the governor to restore funding for the state Occupational Safety and Health Agency.[c] | | | |
| July 1988[d] | 78 | 63 | 15* |
| September 1988[d] | 78 | 65 | 13* |
| October 1988[d] | 73 | 66 | 7* |
| November 1988[d] | 70 | 64 | 6* |
| Favors ballot proposition that would require AIDS and communicable disease testing of persons charged with sex and assault crimes.[c] | | | |
| July 1988 | 89 | 81 | 8* |
| September 1988 | 85 | 82 | 3 |
| October 1988 | 85 | 76 | 9* |
| November 1988 | 79 | 75 | 4 |

Table 5.3 (*continued*)

| Policy Preferences | Percentage of Respondents[a] | | Gender Gap (W – M) |
|---|---|---|---|
| | Women (W) | Men (M) | |
| Favors ballot proposition that would require the reporting of persons exposed to AIDS to health officers and notifying others.[c] | | | |
| July 1988 | 81 | 70 | 11* |
| September 1988 | 65 | 62 | 3 |
| October 1988 | 64 | 65 | –1 |
| November 1988 | 59 | 55 | 4 |
| Favors ballot proposition that would impose additional cigarette and tobacco tax to provide state funding of medical care, health education, and other programs.[c] | | | |
| July 1988 | 76 | 73 | 3 |
| September 1988 | 61 | 63 | –2 |
| October 1988 | 63 | 62 | 1 |
| November 1988 | 54 | 62 | –8* |
| Average gender gap (environmental protection, health and safety) | | | 6.8 |

**Abortion, Women's Rights**

| Policy Preferences | Women (W) | Men (M) | Gender Gap (W – M) |
|---|---|---|---|
| Approve second- or third-trimester abortion. | | | |
| January 1989 | 34 | 33 | 1 |
| July 1989 | 29 | 38 | –9* |
| State should continue paying for abortions for women who can't afford to pay for them themselves. | | | |
| January 1989 | 59 | 59 | 0 |
| July 1989 | 60 | 64 | –4 |
| Opposes a proposed amendment to the U.S. Constitution that would make it illegal for any woman to have an abortion unless her life was in danger. | | | |
| January 1989 (strongly opposes) | 66 | 58 | 8* |
| July 1989 (opposes) | 71 | 76 | –5* |
| Opposes a law that would require teenage girls to receive their parents' approval before they can get an abortion. (July 1989) | 38 | 35 | 3 |
| Favors either new laws in California that would make it easier to get an abortion, or making no changes in existing abortion laws. (July 1989) | 66 | 71 | –5 |

Table 5.3 (*continued*)

| Policy Preferences | Percentage of Respondents[a] | | Gender Gap (W – M) |
|---|---|---|---|
| | Women (W) | Men (M) | |
| Favors giving members of the following groups special preference in hiring and promotion. (February 1988) | | | |
|   Blacks | 26 | 20 | 6* |
|   Women | 32 | 28 | 4 |
|   Hispanics | 24 | 18 | 6* |
|   Asians | 17 | 12 | 5* |
| Favors reserving openings in colleges and universities for members of the following groups of students. (February 1988) | | | |
|   Blacks | 29 | 25 | 4 |
|   Women | 28 | 26 | 2 |
|   Hispanics | 27 | 26 | 1 |
|   Asians | 23 | 20 | 3 |
|     Average gender gap (abortion, women's rights) | | | 1.2 |
|     Average gender gap (abortion only) | | | −1.4 |
| **All Issues** | | | |
|   Average gender gap (all questions) | | | 5.8 |
|   Average gender gap (all questions except abortion and women's rights) | | | 7.6 |

SOURCE: California Polls, 1988–1990.

[a] Entries are percentages of poll respondents who expressed an opinion on the issue. Respondents who indicated that they either did not know what their opinion was or had not thought much about the issue were excluded from this analysis.

[b] Respondents were asked either this question or the next, not both.

[c] Asked of registered voters only.

[d] Female respondents were significantly more likely than male respondents to refrain from expressing an opinion on the issue because they either did not know or had not thought much about the issue.

* These gender gaps are statistically significant ($p \leq .05$).

were alive and well among the California electorate. Nonetheless, a closer look at Table 5.3 does reveal some similarities between California citizens and their state representatives.

First, California men and women did not always differ. Few significant gender gaps arose on issues of abortion and affirmative action, for example. What little disagreement on abortion-related issues there was often found the women slightly more *conservative* than the men. Gender gaps on affirmative action never rose above 6 percentage points. There was no significant disagreement between the sexes on affirmative action in university admissions for anyone—women, blacks, Hispanics, or Asians. On affirmative action in hiring and promotion, male and female respondents were more likely to agree when the target group was women than when the beneficiaries were racial and ethnic minorities.

Agreement between the sexes was not limited to women's rights issues. In three separate polls preceding the November 1988 general election, California women and men were equally likely to support a ballot proposition raising cigarette and tobacco taxes to pay for medical care and public health education programs. But on the eve of the election, women's support dropped by almost 10 percentage points, leaving them 8 percentage points *less* supportive than men. Respondents were queried about four other ballot initiatives in the months preceding the 1988 election. On one—the one requiring AIDS testing of persons charged with sex and assault crimes—women were more supportive than men in the July and October polls, but in agreement with men in the September and November polls. On another, which required the reporting and notification of persons exposed to AIDS, women were more supportive than men in July, but equally supportive in September, October, and November. On the third and fourth propositions, which provided state funds to assist hungry and homeless people and required the governor to restore funding for occupational safety and health, women started out in July much more supportive than men (a 15 percentage point gap) but ended up in November only slightly more supportive (a 6 percentage point gap).

In each of these cases, the existence, size, and direction of gender gaps depended on when the question was posed and to whom (the sample of respondents). As the campaigns for and against these ballot propositions progressed, voters may have received additional information and been exposed to arguments they had not previously considered. For example, the tobacco industry waged a major campaign against the cigarette tax proposition, arguing that if levied only in California, such taxes would lead to an interstate black market in cigarettes and thus an increase in crime. Those polled later in the campaign, therefore, might have responded to a different set of concerns than those who were polled earlier—concerns that might have turned more women than men against the proposals. Thus, the fluctuating gender gaps may also have been the result of changes in the ways the issues were framed and the problems were defined.

In some cases, gender gaps depended on precisely *how* the question was asked. In the December 1989 poll, for example, half the respondents were asked whether they favored or opposed (strongly or somewhat) the death penalty, and the other half were asked whether they favored "doing away with the death sentence" or felt that "the death sentence should be kept as a punishment for serious crime, as it is now." On the first question, 6 percent more women than men said they opposed the death penalty. On the second question, 1 percent fewer women than men said they wanted to do away with the death sentence. Later, in the same survey, everyone was asked whether they preferred a combination of life in prison and victim restitution over the death penalty. In this instance, 16 percent more women than men favored the alternative to the death penalty. (For another example of question-wording-induced fluctuations, see the pair of questions about oil and gas drilling asked in the July 1989 poll.) It is certainly possible that gender gaps in the California (and Arizona) legislature came and went—oftentimes within the same issue area—for similar reasons: the timing of each vote and the specific provisions of each bill may have introduced various cross-pressures and additional considerations that, depending on the individual legislator, may have overridden whatever sex-specific or gender-related concerns they may have had.

The most important observation about the gender gaps in Table 5.3 is that they are not all that large. The average gender gap for all items listed in the table is a mere 5.8 percentage points. Excluding the questions about abortion and women's rights, which usually do not elicit gender gaps in national polls, raises the average gender gap to 7.6 percentage points. The largest single gender gap was 19 percentage points; most of the statistically significant gender gaps (twenty-two out of thirty-five) were less than 10 percentage points.

Now, in a close election, a gender gap of 7.6 percentage points can make a huge difference, the difference between victory and defeat. Yet, as Cynthia Fuchs Epstein (1988: 183) argues, the focus on gender gaps tends to obscure the fact that "the overlaps in voting patterns of women and men far exceed the differences." In only six instances out of the fifty-six survey items listed in Table 5.3 were majorities of women and men on opposite sides of an issue—and three of those instances were in response to the same question. On three separate surveys, a majority of women opted for a larger government providing more services while a majority of men favored a smaller government providing fewer services. Similarly, while most men polled in October 1988 thought the next president should follow in Ronald Reagan's footsteps, most women did not. The other two instances of opposing majorities occurred in response to questions about gas and oil exploration in the California desert and the safety of nuclear power plants operating in the state.

The fact that majorities of men and women are on the same side on most issues has profound consequences for their representatives. Take the example of a female legislator who is committed to giving her female constituents a voice in public policymaking by carefully voting according to how the majority of women in her district (or in the state) would vote. In almost all cases, according to this analysis, the majority of women in her district would vote for or against the same bills as the majority of men in her district would. It would not matter if the women's majority were larger than the men's, for the legislator has only two options: yea or nay. She cannot express the stronger majority voice of the women by voting "yea strongly." In the end, those legislators who try to represent what women in public opinion polls say they want end up voting just like any other legislator.[13]

THE LARGE NUMBER but small magnitude of gender gaps in California public opinion provides not only a rationale for the limited frequency and size of gender gaps among California and Arizona public officials but also evidence that there is nothing extraordinary about these two states. Further evidence of the unexceptional nature of gender politics in Arizona and California can be found, once again, through a closer look at the previous research on public officials—one that pays as much attention to gender *overlaps* (Epstein 1988) as to gender gaps. Although the research of others has revealed many more gender gaps than is evident here among Arizona and California legislators, many of these studies also reveal that gender gaps in legislators' policy preferences are neither universal nor very large, especially in comparison to partisan differences.

To begin, studies that examine elite opinion on specific issues (as opposed to summary measures) show that while women are more liberal than men on most issues, they are not more liberal on all issues. *Gender gaps do not occur on all issues.* The two CAWP studies in 1977 and 1988 are particularly instructive. In the 1977 study, the authors (Johnson and Carroll 1978) point out that while the female officials surveyed were more liberal on four "women's issues" (the ERA, abortion, homemaker social security, and government child care), as well as on three other issues (busing, criminal penalties, and mandatory retirement), they were no more liberal than the male officials on issues regarding the defense budget and federal revenue for cities. Similarly, the 1988 CAWP study of state legislators (Dodson and Carroll 1991) finds significant sex differences in opinion on six issues (privatization, death penalty, nuclear power, legalization of abortion, parental consent for minors' abortion, and the ERA) but not on two others (government provision of child care and increasing taxes for social services).

The fact that the 1977 CAWP study found a gender gap on child care but the 1988 study did not points to another important conclusion one can draw from previous research: *gender gaps do not occur all the time.* In her 1985 study of congressional voting behavior, Welch notes that "gender differences have decreased over time. . . . primarily because of the reduction in the liberalism of female members" (1985: 131). Picking up where Welch left off, Arturo Vega and Juanita Firestone (1995) examined congressional voting behavior from 1981 to 1992. In the twelve years studied, they found significant sex differences in only three (1982, 1991, and 1992) and an average gender gap of only 11 points (on a 0–100 scale). Comparing their findings to Welch's report of a 20-point average gender gap, they confirm her predictions: "This difference suggests converging rather than diverging voting patterns" (Vega and Firestone 1995: 215). In one of the most recent studies of sex differences in congressional voting behavior, Julie Dolan (1997) warns that with the Republican takeover in 1994 and, more significantly, the increasing number of *conservative* Republican women and the decreasing number of Democratic women in Congress, we might see fewer and fewer gender gaps in the future.

The third observation one can draw from previous research is that *gender gaps do not occur among all legislators.* Numerous studies find significant gender gaps only or primarily among Republicans (Burrell 1994; Dolan 1997; Thomas 1989; Vega and Firestone 1995; Welch 1985). Female and male Democrats, especially those outside the southern states, tend to be equally liberal or feminist. Sue Thomas, for a particularly relevant example, finds that Republican women of the 1983–84 California Assembly were "much more supportive of women's rights issues than Republican men" but that Democratic men were almost as supportive as Democratic women (1989: 43). Citing Welch's (1985) study, she offers the following explanation: "The difference between the two parties can possibly be accounted for by the hypothesis that the Democrats are already so supportive of women's rights legislation, little residual effect is possible, just as in Congress the northern Democrats were so liberal that little gender difference was found" (Thomas 1989: 49).

Another important point to note is that in this research on public officials *the gender gaps that are uncovered are not always wide chasms.* The gender gaps uncovered in the 1977 CAWP study of sex differences in elite policy positions range from a 7 point gap on government-provided child care to a 19 point gap on the ERA (Johnson and Carroll 1978: 35A). Similarly, the gender gaps reported in the 1988 CAWP study of state legislators' policy attitudes range from a 12 point gap on privatization to an 18 point gap on the ERA (Dodson and Carroll 1991: 15). In some of the earliest studies, researchers note only slight differences between the sexes. Irene Diamond (1977: 49) reports in her study of state legislators that "women had slightly more 'liberal' policy views on all the issue areas that were examined" (day care, using force vs. social welfare to discourage riots, whether state labor laws benefit women, abortion). Reviewing her own research, Mezey (1994: 262, 268) recalls uncovering "slight differences between the sexes" in her study of support for women's rights policy among local politicians (Mezey 1978a) and a "positive but weak relationship between sex and feminist policy positions" in another study of Hawaiian public officials (Mezey 1978b).

Sex differences often appear just as restricted in studies of roll call voting behavior. Barbara Burrell's 1994 study of congressional voting behavior is indicative. Burrell uses a number of summary measures of voting patterns to gauge the impact of sex on legislative behavior: the Conservative Coalition Support Scores (1987–92), the *National Journal*'s liberalism rating (1992), the National Women's Political Caucus (NWPC) voting scores on women's rights issues (1987–90), and her own analysis of votes on five bills affecting women, which were included in the 1992 *Women's Voting Guide* (published by the Women's Political Action Group). On all four scales, which range from 0 to 100, Democratic men and women differ by no more than 9 points. On the first two scores of general ideology, Republican women are more liberal than Republican men by 14 and 13 points, respectively. Sex differences among Republicans are greater on the measures of support for women's rights: on average, Republican women score 37 points higher than their male counterparts on the NWPC index, and support 45 percent more of the women's issues identified in the *Women's Voting Guide*.

While Republican women are often slightly and sometimes considerably more liberal than GOP men in this and other studies, they are by no means more liberal than Democratic men or women. As almost every study makes clear, *sex differences pale in comparison to party differences.* Among political elites, party affiliation is a much stronger predictor of policy preferences than is sex, especially when it comes to roll call votes. "It is important to remember," Keith Poole and Harmon Zeigler (1985: 173) caution in their study of the U.S. House of Representatives, "that on core issues, such as jobs programs, the differences *between* the two parties are far more significant politically. They form the backdrop against which our discussion of gender differences takes place. The ideological gulf between women Democrats and women Republicans is as wide as that between the men. . . . Women as a group are as different from each other in party terms as men."

In sum, the women and men of the 1990 Arizona and California state legislatures had a lot in common with other lawmakers in other studies. Sometimes they agreed, sometimes they disagreed; rarely did they find themselves completely divided on opposite ends of the spectrum. Policy preferences are reflections of numerous potential factors, only a few of which are gender related. Gender may very well have entered into their decision-making process, but so too did many other considerations, not the least of which was partisanship and the ideological lenses and coalitional obligations that go with it.

## Conclusions: Looking in the Wrong Place?

In the very first CAWP study of women in political office, Jeane Kirkpatrick (1974: 166–67) observed: "Beyond agreement on some few, very basic beliefs about women's rights and women's place, these women see issues as Republicans and Democrats, liberals and conservatives, easterners or westerners. They did not all agree with the proposition . . . that *as women* they should support a particular child care bill, or health program, or welfare scheme" (emphasis in original). Over two decades and many more studies later, this assessment still has a lot of truth to it.

The overwhelming influence of partisanship is the primary explanation offered here for high levels of policy agreement between female and male lawmakers. The fact that gender gaps among constituents are rarely large enough to pit a majority of one sex against another is another factor considered here as an explanation for why roll call votes are not well differentiated by sex. Karin Tamerius (1995) offers another interesting explanation for the findings reported here: policy preferences, especially in the form of roll call votes, are a poor measurement tool for gauging sex differences in legislative behavior and the potential impact of women on policymaking.

Roll call votes are faulty measures for two related reasons, according to Tamerius. First, they reflect the majoritarian and, thus, male biases of the policymaking process.

> Developed largely by men to answer questions of interest to men about the political behavior of men, many existing tools contain an inherent male bias. In the study of legislative behavior, for example, the traditional emphasis on roll-call voting, which assumes that enactment is the most important stage in the legislative process, privileges majority and, therefore, male interests. . . . From the perspective of women and other legislative minorities, however, critical stages of the legislative process are more properly identified as agenda setting and policy formulation, since the vast majority of policies of interest to underrepresented groups, including feminist bills, never receive consideration on the floor. (Tamerius 1995: 96)

In other words, it is next to impossible for women—especially feminists— to have a significant impact on this very late stage of the game. Second, Tamerius argues that roll call voting is a relatively costless activity. With respect to the issues at stake, casting votes does not require particularly high levels of support (or opposition), commitment (to the issue or of personal resources), awareness, or expertise (1995: 103–4). It does not take much for a legislator to vote in support of women and their political interests, when given the opportunity. The votes of relatively uninterested male legislators, therefore, can look just like those of strongly committed female legislators.

In her early study of sex differences in congressional behavior, Shelah Leader (1977: 284) also commented that "voting is only one kind of political activity and possibly not the most important." Both Leader and Tamerius

point to policy *leadership* as the kind of activity that is not only more consequential, but also more likely to elicit significant sex differences. Sympathy
is one thing, they argue; proposing and introducing legislation of concern
to women, mobilizing support for such initiatives, and seeing them through
the process are another. If the substantive representation of women is something more than mere sympathy, if it takes a considerable amount of support, commitment, awareness, and expertise, then it is in the realm of policy
leadership and priorities where truly significant sex differences may lie. Investigation of this proposition is the topic of the next chapter.

## CHAPTER SIX

# Policy Priorities

In examining the policy priorities of the women and men of the 1990 Arizona and California legislatures, this chapter addresses the question of whether there was a sexual "division of labor in political attention" (Sapiro 1981: 703). What types of issues captured the attention of female and male lawmakers? Who was more or less likely to take the lead on what? Were female officials more apt to take the lead on so-called women's issues? The analysis presented in this chapter, like that of the preceding chapters, focuses on both attitudes and behavior: what issues legislators say they care about the most and what issues legislators actually address when they introduce and sponsor legislation.

The issue of who does what legislatively is crucial for several reasons. First, from the perspective of the individual legislator, the formulation, introduction, and sponsorship of legislation are the most meaningful and oftentimes the most time-consuming activities. "For legislators who sponsor 20, 30, 40, or more bills, responding to an agenda determined by others [i.e., roll call voting] may be an important part of their job, but it is not the part they relish most," according to one of the classic texts on state legislatures (Rosenthal 1981: 64). "What they relish most," it reports, "is the law-making agenda they themselves set forth, by sponsoring bills and working for their enactment." A legislator's policy priorities and accomplishments are the main components of her or his reputation and identity, both within and outside the legislative chamber. As one legislative assistant in the U.S. Senate put it: "it is very important what they [senators] do legislatively. Bills generate themes of the senator's overall services . . . legislation defines the senator" (Schiller 1995: 187). Recall, also, that the source of institutional power and prestige most frequently cited by officials interviewed for this study was legislative leadership and, more specifically, the ability to get one's legislation passed (see Chapter 3). Legislators "pride themselves on their personal legislative triumphs and feel that enactments represent the most valuable contributions they can make" (Rosenthal 1981: 70).

The importance of legislative leadership is not simply its credit-claiming potential. Getting issues on the agenda is key to policy representation and responsiveness. Despite all the attention it gets from scholars and interested observers alike, roll call voting is only one stage of the policy process, only one aspect of representation, *and*, one could argue, not the most crucial. Most bills of any substance never get far enough along in the process to be voted on; and by the time they do come up for a vote, most of the important decisions, negotiations, amendments and so forth have already been made, usually in the standing committees.

> The floor stage is the culmination of a very complex process that favors the nonpassage of legislation. Before feminist [or any] issues are voted on, they must be drafted, promoted, and shepherded through the committee system. Members of the legislature must define their legislative agenda and the issues they will emphasize. It is the purposive activity of representatives involving sponsorship and direction of legislation that is crucial to policy representation. (Burrell 1994: 161)

Moreover, attention to *how* issues get decided (yea or nay) neglects the very important question of *what* issues get decided. The study of political power and political representation cannot be limited only to questions about what passes and what fails; it must also include questions about what is even considered and what is not (Bachrach and Baratz 1962; Cobb and Elder 1983; Gaventa 1980). Getting issues on the political agenda is all that more important to groups, such as women, who historically have been un- or underrepresented and marginalized, for it is their concerns that will most likely be left out (Cobb and Elder 1983: 9–13; Schattschneider 1960).

It follows, then, that agenda-setting, or policy leadership, is the realm where female officials are most often expected to "make a difference." Barbara Burrell, for example, in her study of women in the U.S. House of Representatives, concludes: "The purposive activity of women within a legislative body on behalf of women's interests in the polity through the initiation of legislation to achieve equality is the single most significant aspect of women's presence as political leaders" (1994: 151–52). As I outlined in Chapter 1, citizens, activists, political leaders, political candidates, public officials, and political scientists alike expect (or promise) that women in public office will be more aware of, more knowledgeable of, more committed to, and more actively involved in "women's issues" than their male counterparts are. This expectation and the degree to which it was met in the 1990 Arizona and California state legislatures is the focus of this chapter.

## Gauging Policy Priorities

To examine sex differences in legislators' policy priorities—or, the sexual division of policy activity and leadership—I rely on three different sources of information. First are the legislators' own statements of their primary policy goals and priorities, obtained at the beginning of each interview.[1] Second, I classify the subject matter of the bills introduced in 1990 by the legislators, as primary sponsors.[2] This information is then supplemented by data on the legislators' committee assignments.[3]

Each of these measures of policy priorities has its own limitations, for which I attempt to compensate. The first indicator of policy commitment, like any subjective assessment of an individual's own behavior, is subject to bias. What legislators say they do and what they actually do may not be the same. Self-reports of legislative activity may be biased toward whatever is thought socially desirable, prestigious, or important. Wanting to present themselves in the best possible light, these lawmakers, intentionally or unintentionally, may also have placed more emphasis on successful policy initiatives than on failed ones.

Examination of legislators' actual policy proposals provides a good reality check, but it too is subject to error. Not every bill is equally important. Nor does every bill require the same amount of the sponsor's time and effort. Some bills are introduced merely for the symbolic sake of entering them onto the record. "They are for show only: to identify a sponsor with a position, not with an actual law; to satisfy groups making a request that does not seem justifiable even to the sponsor; and simply to please constituents" (Rosenthal 1981: 69). For these reasons, the introduction of one or two bills on a particular subject matter carries little weight in the following analysis. Instead, I determine whether a significant proportion of legislators' bills lie within a particular subject, or issue area.

Legislators in both Arizona and California were able to request their committee assignments; yet, if previous research is any indication, not everyone's requests were granted, and women's requests may have been refused more often than men's (Carroll and Taylor 1989).[4] Thus, committee assignments do not always reflect policy interests or expertise. Furthermore, membership on legislative committees can serve other goals that are not policy related. In addition to—or instead of—making policy, committee work can help legislators gain influence, power, and prestige among their colleagues, or it can help them better serve the interests of their constituents and, thus, get reelected (Fenno 1973; Jewell and Patterson 1986). For these reasons, committee assignments too are an imprecise measure of policy goals and activity. Nonetheless, when put in the context of the first two measures (legislators' stated goals and priorities and the substantive profile of the bills they introduce), committee assignments do indicate whether or not a legislator is in a particularly good position to act upon his or her policy priorities.

### "Women's Issues" and "Men's Issues"

Just as there are various ways of gauging legislators' policy priorities, there also are various ways of delineating the sorts of "women's issues" that female legislators are most often expected to prioritize. In distinguishing "women's issues" from other issues, researchers, as well as women and men "on the street," tend to rely (implicitly or explicitly) on traditional gender roles and stereotypes, or conceptions of feminism, or both as guidelines. The 1988 CAWP study of state legislators' policy priorities, for example, distinguishes "women's traditional areas of interest" from "women's rights" bills; in turn, both types of legislation are included in their category of "women's distinctive concerns" (Dodson and Carroll 1991; Mandel and Dodson 1992).

Defined in terms of traditional notions of gender, women's issues span a wide range of concerns related to women's domestic and public roles as caregivers and nurturers: anything having to do with children, families, education, health care, the welfare of the poor and needy, and the environment. In every published study of gender-stereotyped beliefs about political candidates and officials, involvement and competency in these issue areas are much more likely to be attributed to women than to men (Alexander and Andersen 1993; Brown, Heighberger, and Shocket 1993; Huddy and Terkildsen 1993; Leeper 1991; Rosenwasser and Seale 1988; Sapiro 1981–82, 1983). Environmental issues is the only area in which the research findings are mixed. In some studies, people do tend to believe that women are more capable of handling environmental problems (Alexander and Andersen 1993; Sapiro 1983); in others, women are not thought to be any more capable than men when it comes to dealing with the environment (Rosenwasser and Seale 1988; Sapiro 1981–82).

Most of these gendered expectations about women's "traditional" areas of concern have been confirmed by studies of public officials' policy priorities (Boles 1991; Diamond 1977; Dodson and Carroll 1991; Kirkpatrick 1974; Mandel and Dodson 1992; Saint-Germain 1989; Thomas 1994; Thomas and Welch 1991; Welch and Thomas 1991) and committee assignments (Carroll and Taylor 1989; Diamond 1977; Thomas and Welch 1991). With few exceptions, these studies report that female politicians are more likely than their male counterparts to take the lead on issues involving children, families, education, health, and welfare.[5] The few studies that examine activity in environmental issues, however, do not find women to be more active than men (Mezey 1978a, 1978b; Thomas 1994).

Of course, when political issues get defined in terms of traditional gender roles and stereotypes, people tend to associate certain issues with *men's* traditional interests and activities as well. Yet, compared to the wide range of issues presumed to be of women's traditional interest, and the consistency with which such assumptions are made (and confirmed), the range and frequency of assumptions and stereotypes about "men's issues" are rather limited. The relative infrequency of male stereotyping in this respect no doubt reflects the general nature of stereotyping, namely the tendency to stereotype subordinate groups more frequently than dominant groups (Conover 1981, cited in Leeper 1991; Sapiro 1993).

Public opinion research does show that people almost invariably assume that men are better able than women to deal with foreign affairs, especially when they involve the military (Alexander and Andersen 1993; Gallup Report 1984; Huddy and Terkildsen 1993; Rosenwasser and Seale 1988; Sapiro 1981–82, 1983). Such issues, however, have little relevance for state legislators, male or female, who have practically no authority over the conduct of foreign and military affairs. Some, but not all, studies have found three other issue areas in which men are often thought to be more competent than women: business and economic development (Alexander and Andersen 1993; Brown, Heighberger, and Shocket 1993; Gallup Report 1984); state budget and taxes (Alexander and Andersen 1993; Sapiro 1983), and agriculture (Alexander and Andersen 1993; Sapiro 1981–82). The findings are fairly mixed, however, even within the same study. Deborah Alexander and Kristi Andersen (1993: 534–35), for example, found that voters tend to believe that male candidates will do a better job with foreign trade, taxes, and agriculture. Yet, they also found, unexpectedly, that voters thought *women* would do a better job handling government spending and the federal deficit. Virginia Sapiro's (1983) analysis of the 1972 Virginia Slims Poll shows that while men are often thought to be more capable of dealing with "big business," they are not seen as any more able than women to strengthen the economy. Respondents also were only slightly more willing to believe that men were better than women at balancing the federal budget.

Research on legislators' policy priorities does not have as much to say about "men's issues," or stereotypically masculine bailiwicks, as they do about "women's issues." There is some evidence, however, that male lawmakers are more likely to prioritize business and economic issues (Kahn 1993; Thomas and Welch 1991; Welch and Thomas 1991) and state fiscal policy (Diamond 1977; Dodson and Carroll 1991; but see Fox and Schuhmann 1996; Thomas 1994). There are no available reports on whether or not male legislators pay more attention to agricultural issues than do their female colleagues.

In addition to gender roles and stereotypes, feminism generates certain assumptions about the meaning of "women's issues" and those who champion them. The contemporary feminist movement in the U.S. has, at least since the late 1960s, focused attention on a number of previously ignored or dismissed women's issues, including sex discrimination in education, employment, wages, benefits, and credit; the sexual division of domestic labor and family responsibilities; violence against women; women's health care; women's reproductive rights and health; and the feminization of poverty (Githens 1994). These are just some of the most prominent issues on feminist agendas, certainly the ones that have received the most attention from policymakers in recent years. But because these problems were ignored and/or exacerbated by male policymakers for so long, feminists have focused their hopes and expectations for solving these problems on the rapidly growing number of women in public office.

This prototypical feminist definition of women's issues is, in two respects, more narrow in scope than the one based on traditional gender roles. First, it focuses on women's self- or group interest rather than on women's traditionally altruistic interest in helping others. For example, Susan Carroll's oft-cited definition of women's issues identifies such issues as those "where policy consequences are likely to have a more immediate and direct impact on significantly larger numbers of women than of men" (1994: 15). The feminist women's issues listed above and as defined by Carroll are about women first and foremost; they are only secondarily about children, families, education, health, welfare, and poverty. Indeed, many of these women's issues also involve interests that are traditionally male-dominated, such as business and labor, but only secondarily. Second, feminist-defined women's issues do not simply address the status and material well-being of women; they *promote* the status and material well-being of women in ways that feminists advocate. A bill that restricts access to legal abortions, for example, addresses the status and material well-being of women most immediately and directly. But from a (mainstream, Western) feminist perspective, it does not promote women's status or well-being; it seriously harms women.

A feminist definition of women's issues, therefore, delineates not only the primary subject matter of the questions or problems at hand (women), but also general (feminist) directions for answering the questions and solving the problems (Saint-Germain 1989: 957). Thus, researchers such as Susan Gluck Mezey use Carroll's definition to identify such women's issues as "*advocacy of* federally funded childcare, concern about rape and domestic violence, a desire to *improve* women's employment opportunities *through pay equity and affirmative action policies* and *enforcement* of sex discrimination and sexual harassment laws, and *support for* reproductive rights" (Mezey 1994: 259, emphasis added). The 1988 CAWP study defines women's rights bills as "those that dealt specifically with issues of direct concern to women generally (e.g., legislation concerning rape, teen pregnancy or women's health) or in terms of their special concerns as wage earners (e.g., pay equity), mothers balancing home and work (e.g., maternity leave, day care) or marital partners (e.g., domestic violence, spousal retirement benefits, division of property in divorce)." Moreover, any bills that seemed antifeminist in intent were excluded from this category (Dodson and Carroll 1991: 38).

Every study of sex differences in legislative behavior that has examined activity on this narrowly defined set of feminist or women's rights issues has found that female lawmakers are more likely than their male counterparts to sponsor, cosponsor, or simply work on such bills (Dodson and Carroll 1991; Saint-Germain 1989; Tamerius 1995). Sue Thomas (Thomas 1994; Thomas and Welch 1991) also found that female state legislators were more likely to list among their top five priority bills at least one that deals with women specifically. Thomas, however, did not distinguish feminist from nonfeminist bills; both are included in her category of women's issues. Nonetheless, all of these studies confirm feminists' expectations and hopes that women in public office would make a difference on issues addressing women's own interests and needs.

Indeed, no matter how broadly or narrowly "women's issues" are defined, the research on legislative activity is quite consistent: female legislators place a high priority on these issues more often than male legislators do. For the purposes of my own analysis of the policy priorities of Arizona and California state legislators, however, I maintain the various distinctions between "women's issues" defined according to traditional gender roles, those defined by the degree to which they affect women in particular, and those defined according to feminist principles.

I begin by examining levels of commitment to and leadership activity on two types of women's issues in the 1990 Arizona and California legislatures: (1) issues that, in an immediate and direct way, are about women exclusively (e.g., abortion, sex discrimination) or almost exclusively (e.g., domestic violence, breast cancer); and (2) issues that reflect women's traditional areas of concern, including children, families, education, health, poverty, and the environment. From here on, I refer to this first set of issues as "women" issues. The other issue areas will be labeled "children and family," "education," "public health and safety," "poverty," and "environment." Together, all these issues are presumed to be "women's issues." This chapter also investigates sex differences in leadership and activity on certain "men's issues": (1) business, finance, and commerce (labeled "commerce"), (2) state budget and taxes (labeled "fiscal"), and (3) agriculture (labeled "agriculture").

These issue categories reflect only the subject matter of legislators' self-reported policy goals and concerns, bills introduced, and committee assignments—not their ideological direction or approach (liberal vs. conservative, feminist vs. antifeminist). Each policy goal and bill introduced was assigned between one and four very specific subject codes, which are listed in Appendix C, Table C.1. Because of the specificity of these codes, most goals and bills received more than one subject code. For example, the issue of children's mental health would receive one code for mental health, another for children. A bill proposing criminal sanctions to keep drugs and gangs away from school grounds would be given four codes: one for drugs, one for gangs, one for children (including juveniles), another for K–12 education.

Each of the six categories of women's issues and three types of men's issue areas listed above is, in effect, an aggregation of a number of more specific subject codes. For example "women" issues and bills include all those that received one or more of the following subject codes: (045) for abortion; (210) for women; (215) for women and infants or pregnant women; and (342) for sex offenses or domestic violence. Being classified as a women issue does not prevent a policy goal or bill from also being included in another issue area. For example, a bill mandating insurance coverage for mammographies would be included not only in the women category, but also in the health and public safety and the commerce categories. Table C.2 in Appendix C lists the subject codes aggregated for each of the nine issue areas examined in this chapter.

In a similar fashion, standing committees in both legislatures often had jurisdiction over multiple issue areas. The Arizona Senate Committee on Health, Welfare, Aging, and the Environment is one of the most extreme examples. Furthermore, legislative proposals within each issue category could be addressed by more than one committee. For example, many women issues, such as abortion, were addressed in the judiciary committees of each chamber. Other women issues, such as prenatal care, were addressed in the various health-related committees. Thus, there are often multiple and overlapping standing committees that are relevant to each issue area. Table C.3 of Appendix C lists the relevant standing committees for each issue area, in each legislative chamber.[6]

In this chapter, I also estimate the extent to which activity and leadership in any of these issue areas could be characterized as feminist and whether women's activity was more feminist than men's. In doing so, however, I adhere to the notion that in order to be feminist, policy goals and proposals must not only "have a more immediate and direct impact on significantly larger numbers of women than of men" (Carroll 1994: 15) but must also be "aimed at gaining equality for or improving the status of women" (Saint-Germain 1989: 960) *from a feminist perspective.* In other words, to determine whether or not a policy goal or proposal is feminist, I examine both its subject matter and the ideological intent behind it. To determine whether or not the legislative activists in a particular policy area were heading in a feminist direction—and whether female activists were more likely than male activists to do so—I examine the intersections of legislators' policy priorities and policy preferences.

First, I identify subsamples of legislators who were active in each of the nine issue areas: women, children and families, health and public safety, poverty, the environment, commerce, fiscal policy, and agriculture.[7] Second, for each issue area, I estimate the percentage of female and male legislative activists who may also be considered feminist activists. Feminist activists are those who meet two criteria (in addition to being active in a particular policy area). First, their stated policy goals and/or legislative initiatives (bills introduced) *also* deal specifically, immediately, directly, or primarily with women.[8] For example, feminist activists in health policy are those who either cited women (or women-specific issues such as abortion or domestic violence) as a policy priority (in addition to health issues), or introduced at least one bill that dealt with both women and health (e.g., insurance coverage for mammographies).[9] Second, feminist activists must have cast more liberal than conservative votes on women's rights legislation (see Chapter 5).

## Policy Activity and Leadership

As is so often expected (and found elsewhere), policy activity and leadership were, to varying degrees, sex segregated in the 1990 Arizona and California legislatures. Sex differences in policy priorities and activities were especially notable in the Arizona legislature; similar, though muted, patterns of sex differences were present in the California legislature as well. Table 6.1 shows the degree to which female and male members of each legislature were active in each of the nine issue areas delineated above: women, children and families, education, health and public safety, poverty, environment, commerce, fiscal matters, and agriculture. Within each issue area, "active" legislators are those who cited the issue area as a personal policy priority *or* who devoted a relatively high proportion (greater than the state median) of the bills they introduced in 1990 to such issue concerns, or both.

Table 6.1  Policy Activism and Leadership

| | Arizona Legislators | | California Legislators | |
|---|---|---|---|---|
| | Men (N = 32) (%) | Women (N = 18) (%) | Men (N = 17) (%) | Women (N = 14) (%) |
| Issue Area | | | | |
| **"Women's Issues"** | | | | |
| Women | | | | |
|   Active | 31* | 78* | 35 | 64 |
|   Leader | 0 | 11 | 0* | 29* |
| Children and Families | | | | |
|   Active | 44* | 72* | 59 | 57 |
|   Leader | 6* | 33* | 12 | 36 |
| Education | | | | |
|   Active | 59 | 78 | 59 | 64 |
|   Leader | 9* | 56* | 23 | 36 |
| Health and Public Safety | | | | |
|   Active | 59 | 67 | 59 | 64 |
|   Leader | 19 | 39 | 23 | 43 |
| Poverty | | | | |
|   Active | 56 | 67 | 47 | 50 |
|   Leader | 3 | 17 | 6 | 14 |
| Environment | | | | |
|   Active | 56 | 50 | 59 | 64 |
|   Leader | 16 | 28 | 23 | 29 |
| **"Men's Issues"** | | | | |
| Commerce | | | | |
|   Active | 66* | 39* | 65 | 43 |
|   Leader | 22 | 11 | 23 | 14 |
| Fiscal | | | | |
|   Active | 84* | 39* | 53 | 50 |
|   Leader | 37* | 11* | 12 | 0 |
| Agriculture | | | | |
|   Active | 62* | 28* | 35 | 36 |
|   Leader | 9 | 6 | 12 | 7 |

NOTE: *Active* legislators are those who either mentioned the issue area as a policy priority, or devoted a relatively high proportion of their bills (greater than the state median) to the issue area, or both. *Leaders* are those legislators who mentioned the issue area as a policy priority *and* devoted a relatively high proportion of their bills (greater than the state median) to the issue area. Leaders are a subset of active legislators.

* Sex differences for these values are statistically significant ($p \leq .05$).

In addition, a smaller subset of activists are designated as "leaders" within each policy arena. Leaders are those who both cited the issue area as a priority *and* devoted a considerable proportion of their bills to it.

Among the Arizona legislators, activity and leadership in almost all issue areas examined here could be designated as either female- or male-dominated. With the exception of environmental issues, so-called women's issues truly were the bailiwick of women in the Arizona legislature. On issues dealing with women, children and families, and education, approximately three-quarters of the female lawmakers were actively involved, as compared to only 31 percent, 44 percent, and 59 percent of their male colleagues, respectively.[10] The Arizona women also were somewhat more likely than the Arizona men to be active in health and public safety issues, and in poverty- or welfare-related issues.

Policy *leadership* (as defined here) in women's issues in the Arizona legislature was even more sex segregated. Leadership in women-specific, familial, educational, and welfare-related policymaking was, in fact, almost exclusively female. Both women and men assumed leadership roles on health and public safety matters, but the women were a bit more likely to do so than the men were. That environmental issues captured the attention of many Arizona legislators, male and female alike, is understandable, given (a) the ambiguity of popular expectations regarding gender and leadership in such matters (as evidenced in the research cited above) and (b) the long-standing, vital importance of such issues for the state.

Presenting a mirror image of female-dominated activity in women's issues, activity in issue areas traditionally associated with men was, in fact, dominated by men in the Arizona legislature. Two-thirds of these men were actively concerned about economic development, finance, and the regulation of business and labor (commerce issues), as compared to only 39 percent of the Arizona female legislators. Twice as many men as women could be considered leaders in this area (22 percent compared to 11 percent). The Arizona men dominated fiscal policymaking just as much as the Arizona women dominated policymaking regarding women. The vast majority of men (84 percent) were actively involved in such budget- and tax-related matters, compared to only 39 percent of the women. Three times as many men as women could be considered leaders in this issue area (37 percent compared to 11 percent). On agricultural issues, the Arizona men were much more involved than the women, although few of either sex could be considered agricultural leaders.[11]

In contrast to the Arizona legislature, California legislative activity in all but one of the women's issues was *not* sex segregated. The California men and women were equally involved in issues of children and families, education, health and public safety, poverty, and the environment. Nor was activity on men's issues dominated by one sex or the other—although California male legislators were more active in the commerce arena. It was on issues dealing specifically and directly with women that California legislative activity was most sexually differentiated; and on those issues, the women were more active than the men (64 percent of women, compared to 35 percent of men).

When it came to policy *leadership*, however, the female and male California officials did part ways, to some extent. Most notable is the fact that while a substantial proportion of the California female lawmakers (29 percent) took the lead on women-specific issues, none of their male colleagues did. California women also were three times as likely as their male colleagues to assume a leadership role on issues involving children and families (36 percent compared to 12 percent); twice as likely to be leaders on poverty issues (14 percent compared to 6 percent) and almost twice as likely to take the lead on health and public safety matters (43 percent compared to 23 percent). California men, meanwhile, were a bit more likely to be leaders in commerce (23 percent compared to 14 percent of the women); and they were the only ones who could be considered leaders on fiscal issues (12 percent of the men, none of the women). While sex differences in policy leadership among California legislators did not extend to educational, environmental, or agricultural issues, and the sex difference in leadership on women issues is the only one large enough to be statistically significant, there was a fairly consistent, albeit muted, pattern of sex differences in policy leadership in the California legislature.

These patterns of sex segregation in policy activity and leadership are summarized by the average scores on the policy leadership indices, displayed in Table 6.2. These indices combine all three measures of policy priorities—self-reported policy goals, bills introduced, and committee assignments—into a leadership scale for each of the nine issue areas. Each legislator received one point for mentioning an issue area as one of their policy priorities; one point for devoting a relatively large percentage (greater than the state median) of their bills to that issue area; and half a point for being a member of at least one issue-relevant standing committee. Thus, legislators who were completely inactive in a policy area scored a zero on the corresponding leadership index. Leaders in a given policy area (as defined above) who sat on at least one relevant standing committee received the highest score of 2.5.

As Table 6.2 shows, Arizona female lawmakers scored significantly higher than their male colleagues on the leadership indices for three of the six women's issues (women, children and families, and education) and somewhat higher on two others (health and public safety, and poverty). There was no difference between Arizona women's and men's leadership

## Table 6.2 Policy Leadership Index

| Issue Area | Arizona Legislators | | California Legislators | |
| --- | --- | --- | --- | --- |
| | Men | Women | Men | Women |
| Sample Size (N) | | | | |
| All | 32 | 18 | 17 | 14 |
| Democrats | 13 | 9 | 10 | 9 |
| Republicans | 19 | 9 | 7 | 5 |
| "Women's Issues" | | | | |
| Women | | | | |
| All | .55* | 1.17* | .47* | 1.14* |
| Democrats | .42* | 1.00* | .40* | 1.33* |
| Republicans | .63* | 1.33* | .57 | .80 |
| Average sex difference | | | | |
| (women−men) | | .64† | | .66† |
| Average party difference | | | | |
| (Republicans−Democrats) | | .25 | | −.14 |
| Children and Families | | | | |
| All | .75* | 1.33* | .79 | 1.11 |
| Democrats | .88 | 1.28 | .90 | 1.00 |
| Republicans | .66* | 1.39* | .64 | 1.30 |
| Average sex difference | | .57† | | .31 |
| Average party difference | | −.10 | | −.01 |
| Education | | | | |
| All | .77* | 1.56* | .88 | 1.18 |
| Democrats | 1.04* | 1.94* | 1.10 | 1.11 |
| Republicans | .58 | 1.17 | .57 | 1.30 |
| Average sex difference | | .74† | | .28 |
| Average party difference | | −.58† | | −.21 |
| Health and Public Safety | | | | |
| All | .95 | 1.33 | .97 | 1.29 |
| Democrats | .69* | 1.61* | .70 | 1.11 |
| Republicans | 1.13 | 1.06 | 1.36 | 1.60 |
| Average sex difference | | .39 | | .35 |
| Average party difference | | .07 | | .58† |
| Poverty | | | | |
| All | .70 | 1.03 | .62 | .82 |
| Democrats | .88 | 1.22 | .55 | .94 |
| Republicans | .58 | .83 | .71 | .60 |
| Average sex difference | | .29 | | .20 |
| Average party difference | | −.34† | | −.06 |
| Environment | | | | |
| All | .98 | 1.06 | 1.03 | 1.21 |
| Democrats | 1.00 | 1.17 | .90 | 1.17 |
| Republicans | .97 | .94 | 1.21 | 1.30 |
| Average sex difference | | .06 | | .20 |
| Average party difference | | −.10 | | .23 |

**Table 6.2** (*continued*)

| Issue Area | Arizona Legislators | | California Legislators | |
|---|---|---|---|---|
| | Men | Women | Men | Women |
| **"Men's Issues"** | | | | |
| Commerce | | | | |
| All | 1.20* | .75* | 1.23 | .82 |
| Democrats | 1.23 | .83 | 1.35 | 1.17 |
| Republicans | 1.18 | .67 | 1.07* | .20* |
| Average sex difference | −.46† | | −.45 | |
| Average party difference | −.09 | | −.58† | |
| Fiscal | | | | |
| All | 1.47* | .64* | .76 | .71 |
| Democrats | 1.35* | .39* | .40 | .61 |
| Republicans | 1.55* | .89* | 1.29 | .90 |
| Average sex difference | −.80† | | −.02 | |
| Average party difference | .31 | | .62† | |
| Agriculture | | | | |
| All | .91* | .53* | .65 | .54 |
| Democrats | .81 | .50 | .60 | .61 |
| Republicans | .97 | .56 | .71 | .40 |
| Average sex difference | −.37 | | −.13 | |
| Average party difference | .12 | | −.03 | |

NOTE: Leadership index scores range from 0 to 2.5. Legislators received one point if they mentioned the issue area as a policy priority, one point if they devoted a relatively high proportion of their bills to the issue area (greater than the state median), and half a point if they served on at least one standing committee relevant to the issue area. Average sex differences across parties and average party differences across sexes were calculated by regressing the leadership indices on sex and party, which are both dichotomous variables. Average sex differences are the OLS regression coefficients for sex; average party differences are the regression coefficients for party.
* Sex differences for these values are statistically significant ($p \leq .05$).
† These average differences are statistically significant ($p \leq .05$).

scores on environmental issues. The Arizona men scored significantly higher than the women on the leadership indices of all three men's issues. Among the California legislators, only one issue area witnessed truly significant sex differences in leadership index scores: on the women leadership index, the women's average score was considerably higher than the men's. On all other women's issues, the California women's leadership scores were only slightly higher than those of their male colleagues. California men did score higher than the women on the commerce leadership index, but their leadership scores on the other two men's issues were practically identical.

Using the leadership indices, Table 6.2 also shows the degree to which partisanship influenced legislators' policy priorities. There were some issues that tended to attract more attention from members of one party than another. In Arizona, Democrats were significantly more active than Republicans on issues of education and poverty, but somewhat less active on fiscal issues. In California, Republicans were more active on health and public safety issues as well as fiscal matters, and Democrats were more active in the area of commerce. In comparison to the overwhelming influence of partisanship on legislators' policy *preferences*, however, the impact of partisanship on policy *priorities* was minor.

Moreover, the patterns of sex differences in policy priorities were, with only a few exceptions, the same within each party. In Arizona, female legislators were more active in all women's issues except environmental ones, and male legislators were more active in men's issues—regardless of party. The only notable exception to this rule occurred in the area of health and public safety: among the Arizona Democrats, women were much more active than the men; among the Arizona Republicans, however, women and men were equally active. In California, the general rule was that, regardless of party, male legislators were either as active or slightly less active on women's issues and female legislators were either as active or slightly less active on men's issues. There were only a few notable exceptions to this rule. Among California Republicans, men were considerably less active than women on issues dealing with children, families, and education, and women were *much* less active than men on issues of commerce. In addition, the sex difference in activism on women issues was much greater among California Democrats than among Republicans.

### Sex Discrimination?

The prevalence of sex-segregated activity, such as that observed here, raises important questions about the underlying causes. Was it a result of sex discrimination, "legislative typecasting" (Cohen 1991), "ghettoizing" (De Hart 1995: 237), and women's marginality in state legislatures (Githens and Prestage 1977, 1978)? Or was it a true reflection of women's (and men's) own interests and goals?

Some of the early research on women in public office interpreted sex differences in policy activity in the more foreboding light of sex discrimination. Dismayed by the disjuncture between the wide array of female officials' policy interests and the narrow range of bills they introduced, Marianne Githens and Jewel Prestage, for instance, concluded that women's integration into state legislatures was incomplete. "[P]ressures of some sort," they noted, "obviously encourage women to sponsor most legislation in the area of health, education, and welfare, in spite of their more diverse areas of interests and committee assignments" (1978: 269). More recent studies of legislative behavior tend to view women's concentration on women's issues more favorably. Sue Thomas and Susan Welch, for example, expected that the female legislators they studied in 1988 would be "more attentive to women's issues" because, unlike their predecessors, they no longer "feared being labelled as too 'narrow' or 'only' interested in women's issues" (1991: 446). Placing a high priority on women's issues was, Thomas and Welch assumed, what the female lawmakers really *wanted* to do.

Through which lens should one interpret the sex differences in policy activity revealed in this study? As Githens and Prestage suggest, one way of investigating the degree to which sexual division of legislative activity is voluntary is to look closely at the intersections between legislators' self-reported priorities or goals, their committee assignments, and the bills they introduce. Assuming that legislators' stated priorities and goals are the best indicator of legislators' true desires—what they want to do rather than what they have to do—one can see whether or not legislators' committee work and legislative proposals actually correspond. At issue here is whether female legislators' committee assignments and bills were any less congruent with their own stated preferences than male legislators' assignments and bills were. For example, were women who served on health-related committees less likely than their male counterparts to cite such issues as a personal priority? Were women who devoted a relatively high proportion of their bills to health issues less likely than their male counterparts to cite such issues as personal priorities?

As Tables 6.3 and 6.4 demonstrate, there is little evidence that these women were any less interested in their "women's issue" committee work or bills than the men were. In both states, female legislators who served on "women's issue" committees were no less likely than their male counterparts to cite such issues as their personal priorities (see Table 6.3). If anything, women on such committees were *more* likely than the men to claim corresponding women's issues as personal priorities—although the differences tend to be fairly small (and statistically insignificant). For example, while 75 percent of the Arizona women on education committees mentioned education as a policy priority, only 60 percent of the Arizona men on the same committees did so. While two-thirds of the California women in health-related committees cited health issues as priorities, only 40 percent of their male counterparts did the same. Similar sex differences can be found among almost all "women's issue"–oriented committee members in both states.

Among the Arizona legislators, there also is some indication that the women were less interested in their "men's issue"–oriented committee assignments than were the men. Arizona women on commerce and agriculture committees were slightly less likely than their male counterparts to mention the corresponding issues as one of their policy priorities. Differ-

**Table 6.3  Policy Priorities among Legislative Committee Members**

| | Percentage Who Claim Committee's Issue Area as a Personal Priority | | | |
| | Arizona Committee Members | | California Committee Members | |
| Issue Area | Men | Women | Men | Women |
|---|---|---|---|---|
| **"Women's Issues"** | | | | |
| Women | 0 | 10 | 0* | 50* |
| | (N = 15) | (N = 10) | (N = 4) | (N = 6) |
| Children and Families | 19 | 30 | 33 | 60 |
| | (N = 16) | (N = 10) | (N = 3) | (N = 5) |
| Education | 60 | 75 | 100 | 80 |
| | (N = 5) | (N = 6) | (N = 2) | (N = 5) |
| Health and Public Safety | 36 | 50 | 40 | 67 |
| | (N = 11) | (N = 10) | (N = 5) | (N = 6) |
| Poverty | 14 | 29 | 0 | 20 |
| | (N = 7) | (N = 7) | (N = 3) | (N = 5) |
| Environment | 29 | 50 | 57 | 37 |
| | (N = 17) | (N = 10) | (N = 7) | (N = 8) |
| | | | | |
| **"Men's Issues"** | | | | |
| Commerce | 43 | 22 | 33 | 29 |
| | (N = 21) | (N = 9) | (N = 12) | (N = 7) |
| Fiscal | 69* | 20* | 25 | 0 |
| | (N = 16) | (N = 5) | (N = 4) | (N = 6) |
| Agriculture | 25 | 14 | 17 | 33 |
| | (N = 12) | (N = 7) | (N = 6) | (N = 3) |

NOTE: Entries are the percentage of members of relevant committees who mentioned the issue area as one of their personal policy priorities or goals. See Appendix C, Table C.3 for a list of relevant standing committees for each issue area in each legislative chamber.
* Sex differences for these values are statistically significant ($p \leq .05$).

ences are most striking among the members of Arizona's fiscal committees: while only 20 percent of the female members cited such issues as priorities, almost 70 percent of the male members did.

In both states, then, female members of "women's issue" committees were, if anything, *more* interested in their work than male members were. If Arizona female officials were any less enthusiastic about their committee work, it was about their work on *"men's"* committees, not their work on "women's" committees. California female officials were, according to the figures in Table 6.3, just as interested in being on "men's" committees as their male colleagues were.

Nor is there any evidence to suggest that women in either legislature

Table 6.4  Policy Priorities among Bill Sponsors

| | Percentage Who Mentioned Issue Area as a Policy Priority | | | |
| | Arizona Bill Sponsors | | California Bill Sponsors | |
| Issue Area | Men | Women | Men | Women |
| --- | --- | --- | --- | --- |
| **"Women's Issues"** | | | | |
| Women | 0 | 14 | 0* | 50* |
| | ($N = 10$) | ($N = 14$) | ($N = 5$) | ($N = 8$) |
| Children and Families | 15* | 50* | 29 | 62 |
| | ($N = 13$) | ($N = 12$) | ($N = 7$) | ($N = 8$) |
| Education | 25* | 83* | 67 | 56 |
| | ($N = 12$) | ($N = 12$) | ($N = 6$) | ($N = 9$) |
| Health and Public Safety | 40 | 70 | 50 | 86 |
| | ($N = 15$) | ($N = 10$) | ($N = 8$) | ($N = 7$) |
| Poverty | 7 | 27 | 12 | 29 |
| | ($N = 14$) | ($N = 11$) | ($N = 8$) | ($N = 7$) |
| Environment | 31 | 56 | 67 | 44 |
| | ($N = 16$) | ($N = 9$) | ($N = 6$) | ($N = 9$) |
| **"Men's Issues"** | | | | |
| Commerce | 37 | 33 | 44 | 40 |
| | ($N = 19$) | ($N = 6$) | ($N = 9$) | ($N = 5$) |
| Fiscal | 60 | 40 | 25 | 0 |
| | ($N = 20$) | ($N = 5$) | ($N = 8$) | ($N = 7$) |
| Agriculture | 16 | 20 | 40 | 20 |
| | ($N = 19$) | ($N = 5$) | ($N = 5$) | ($N = 5$) |

NOTE: Bill sponsors in each issue area are those legislators who devoted a relatively high proportion of the bills they introduced to that issue area (greater than the state median).
* Sex differences for these values are statistically significant ($p \leq .05$).

were introducing "women's issue" bills against their will, or with little enthusiasm. Table 6.4 shows the percentage of legislators who devoted a considerable proportion of their bills to each issue area, who also mentioned such issues as one of their own policy priorities or goals. For example, 25 percent of the Arizona men whose bills tended to focus on education issues actually mentioned education as a policy priority. The patterns of sex differences in Table 6.4 are, in fact, quite similar to those found in Table 6.3. Women introducing "women's issue" bills were either as likely or *more* likely than men introducing "women's issue" bills to cite such issues as their own priorities. Arizona and California women introducing fiscal bills were slightly less likely than their male counterparts to place a high priority on such issues.

**Table 6.5  Relevant Committee Assignments among Policy Activists**

| Issue Area | Percentage Who Served on At Least One Issue-related Legislative Committee | | | |
| --- | --- | --- | --- | --- |
| | Arizona Policy Activists | | California Policy Activists | |
| | Men | Women | Men | Women |
| **"Women's Issues"** | | | | |
| Women | 20* | 64* | 17* | 67* |
| | (N = 10) | (N = 14) | (N = 6) | (N = 9) |
| Children and Families | 57 | 54 | 20 | 50 |
| | (N = 14) | (N = 13) | (N = 10) | (N = 8) |
| Education | 16 | 43 | 20 | 44 |
| | (N = 19) | (N = 14) | (N = 10) | (N = 9) |
| Health and Public Safety | 37 | 50 | 40 | 44 |
| | (N = 19) | (N = 12) | (N = 10) | (N = 9) |
| Poverty | 28 | 33 | 37 | 57 |
| | (N = 18) | (N = 12) | (N = 8) | (N = 7) |
| Environment | 61 | 78 | 50 | 78 |
| | (N = 18) | (N = 9) | (N = 10) | (N = 9) |
| **"Men's Issues"** | | | | |
| Commerce | 71 | 71 | 73 | 50 |
| | (N = 21) | (N = 7) | (N = 11) | (N = 16) |
| Fiscal | 48* | 14* | 22 | 43 |
| | (N = 27) | (N = 7) | (N = 9) | (N = 7) |
| Agriculture | 55 | 60 | 33 | 40 |
| | (N = 20) | (N = 5) | (N = 6) | (N = 5) |

NOTE: Policy activists are legislators who either mentioned the issue area as a policy priority, or devoted a relatively high proportion of their bills to the issue area (greater than the state median), or both.
* Sex differences for these values are statistically significant ($p \leq .05$).

All told, the evidence suggests that whatever sex segregation in policy activity there was in these two legislatures was voluntary. When female lawmakers were more active in "women's issues," it most likely was because they wanted to be. When female lawmakers were less active in "men's issues," it most likely was their choice as well; at the very least, they seem to have had as much choice in the matter as their male colleagues did.

Finally, one other manifestation of sex discrimination also can be ruled out: these female lawmakers were not prevented from serving on committees that dealt with their issue concerns and priorities—at least, not any more so than their male colleagues were. Table 6.5 shows the percentage of legislators active in each issue area who were members of issue-relevant committees. In almost every issue area women activists in both states were either as likely or *more* likely than their male counterparts to have a relevant committee assignment. There is only one exception to this rule in each state. In Arizona, female legislators active in fiscal policy were considerably less likely than their male counterparts to serve on a fiscal committee (14 percent compared to 48 percent). In California, female activists in commerce policymaking were slightly less likely than their male counterparts to serve on one of the (many) commerce-related committees.

## Feminist Political Activity

Feminist political activity, as I have defined it here, requires not only involvement in a particular set of issues, but also support for a certain, feminist policy *direction* within those issue areas. The issues or subjects designated as potentially feminist encompass all those that were included in the "women" issue category (anything having to do with women, pregnancy, abortion, violence against women, etc.) plus a few that were included in the "children and families" category: namely, (1) family law regarding divorce, child custody, etc.; (2) child care and parental leave; and (3) anything else having to do with parents or parenthood. Feminist policy activists are those legislators who (1) mentioned in the interview one or more of these issues as their own personal policy priority and/or introduced at least one bill dealing with one of these issues *and* (2) cast more liberal than conservative votes on women's rights legislation (included in Chapter 5's analysis of roll call voting).[12]

Using these criteria, it is clear that female legislators in both states were much more likely than their male colleagues to be feminist policy activists. Approximately two-thirds of these female lawmakers (67 percent of the Arizona women, 64 percent of the California women) could be considered feminist activists, as compared to only about a third of the male lawmakers (31 percent of the Arizona men, 35 percent of the California men).[13] Because feminist activism, as defined here, required support for women's rights legislation, Democratic legislators were much more likely to take part than their Republican colleagues were. Feminist activism in each state, therefore, was strongest among Democratic women and weakest among Republican men (although the differences between Republican men and women were slight). In the Arizona legislature, all of the female Democrats were, according to the criteria used here, feminist activists, compared to only 38 percent of the male Democrats, a third of the female Republicans, and 26 percent of the male Republicans. Almost all of the California Democratic women (89 percent) were feminist activists, but only one (20 percent) of the Republican women was. A majority of California Democratic men (60 percent) could be considered feminist activists, but none of the Republican men could.

In examining the prevalence of feminist policy activism, it is important to recognize that such activism in no way precludes activism in other policy areas. In fact, many of the bills and policy priorities included in the feminist issue category also involved matters of education, health, welfare, and commerce. A few also dealt with the environmental and fiscal matters. There were no bills introduced in 1990 or policy priorities mentioned in the interviews conducted that same year that involved both feminist and agricultural issues. But there is no a priori reason why a feminist agenda could not be applied to some agricultural matters. Theoretically, a feminist agenda can be pursued within any policy area.

Such a theoretical possibility begs numerous empirical questions. To what extent did these Arizona and California state legislators apply a feminist agenda to their various policy concerns and activities? Were female legislators more likely than male legislators to bring feminist concerns to the table? Were some policy arenas more or less conducive to feminist activism? Answers to these questions can be found in Table 6.6, which shows the percentage of activists in each of the nine issue areas (six "women's issues" and three "men's issues") who could also be considered feminist activists.

The extent to which legislators brought a feminist agenda to their policy activities depended upon several factors, as Table 6.6 shows. First, it depended upon the sex of the legislator. In both states and in each issue area, female activists were either as likely as or (more often) more likely than male activists to be feminist policy activists as well. Second, it depended upon the state. In almost all issue areas, California female policy activists were more likely to bring feminist concerns to the table than were their Arizona counterparts. California male activists were either as likely as or somewhat more likely than their Arizona counterparts to do so. Third, it depended upon the issue area. For each of the four groups of legislators (Arizona men and women, California men and women), the percentage of feminist policy activists decreases as one goes down the list of issue areas listed in Table 6.6. Feminist activism was most prevalent in the first two women's issues—those dealing with women specifically, and those dealing with children and families. With the exception of the California women, feminist policy activism was usually low and often nonexistent among legislators active in all other issue areas.

The exceptional behavior of the California female lawmakers warrants further notice. A substantial proportion—almost always more than half—of the California female activists brought a feminist agenda to their work in each of the nine policy arenas. Unlike their California (male) and Arizona

**Table 6.6  Feminist Policy Activity among Policy Activists**

| | Percentage Who Engaged in Feminist Policy Activities[a] | | | |
| | Arizona Policy Activists | | California Policy Activists | |
| Issue Area | Men | Women | Men | Women |
|---|---|---|---|---|
| **"Women's Issues"** | | | | |
| Women | 60 | 64 | 50 | 89 |
| Children and Families | 29* | 69* | 50 | 75 |
| Education | 0* | 43* | 30 | 56 |
| Health and Public Safety | 21 | 25 | 20 | 44 |
| Poverty | 11 | 17 | 12* | 57* |
| Environment | 0 | 22 | 0* | 56* |
| **"Men's Issues"** | | | | |
| Commerce | 9 | 43 | 18 | 50 |
| Fiscal | 0 | 0 | 11* | 57* |
| Agriculture | 0 | 20 | 0* | 80* |

[a] Activists were counted as engaging in feminist policy activities if they (1) mentioned at least one issue affecting women directly and disproportionately as a policy priority, or introduced at least one bill dealing with such an issue, or both; and if they (2) cast more liberal than conservative votes on women's rights legislation. The number of activists in each issue area is the same as in Table 6.5.
* Sex differences for these values are statistically significant ($p \leq .05$).

(male and female) colleagues, these women applied feminism to *all* their policy activities, not just to women's issues. Or, looking at the data from a different angle, the California female feminists were evenly distributed across a wide range of policy activities. Unlike their California and Arizona colleagues, they were not concentrated primarily in women's issue arenas. This broadly applied feminism of the California women recalls the argument, briefly considered in Chapter 1, that women, as individuals and as a group, have a stake in every policy issue, not just in women's issues.

In sum, feminist activism was alive and well in the 1990 Arizona and California legislatures. It was much stronger among female members than among male, and among Democrats than among Republicans; and it tended to be concentrated in the "women" and "children and families" issue areas. California female lawmakers, however, applied their feminist activism across the issue spectrum. Two extremely important qualifications to these conclusions must be noted, though.

First, while feminist activism tended to be more prevalent among "women's issue" activists than among "men's issue" activists, feminism was not a prerequisite for activism in women's issues—not even for women issues such as abortion, and violence against women. There were, for example, almost as many Arizona women issue activists introducing "pro-life" abortion bills (8) as there were introducing pro-choice bills (10). The single abortion bill sponsored by California legislators participating in this study was introduced by one of the most conservative men in the California Assembly. Four of the fifteen California women issue activists, including one woman, cast either all or almost all conservative votes on women's rights bills.

A second, related point is that—except among California female legislators—feminist activists rarely constituted a majority of activists in any particular issue area. Among Arizona male legislators, feminists were in the majority only on women issues—and it was not an overwhelming majority. Among Arizona female legislators, feminists held a fairly slim majority among "women" activists and among "children and family" activists. Outside these two issue areas, few Arizona legislators were actively concerned about setting or implementing a feminist agenda. Among California male legislators, feminist activists never constituted a majority of policy activists; the closest they came was to claim half of the activists in the "women" and "children and families" arenas. Outside these two issue areas, the California men—and, thus, most of the legislature as a whole—seemed fairly unconcerned about feminist policymaking.

## Conclusions

To varying degrees, there was a sexual division of policymaking labor within the 1990 Arizona and California state legislatures. "Women's issues" often captured more attention from female lawmakers and "men's issues" often captured more attention from male lawmakers, especially in Arizona. Regardless of whether "women's issues" are defined broadly or narrowly, according to traditional gender roles or feminist agendas, Arizona women were more likely than their male colleagues to give them high priority and act upon them. On only one women's issue, the environment, were Arizona women and men equally active. While feminist activism among Arizona legislators was concentrated in only a couple of women's issue areas, it was the female legislators (especially the Democrats among them) who most often led the way. Meanwhile, in all three "men's issue" areas explored here, the Arizona men were more active than their female colleagues.

Only when "women's issues" are defined narrowly and in feminist terms were the California female lawmakers significantly more committed than their male colleagues. In issue areas of traditional concern to women—namely, those dealing with family law, children, education, health, welfare, and the environment—California male lawmakers were either as active as or only slightly less active than their female colleagues. Nonetheless, when it came to issues dealing specifically and exclusively with women, the California women were front and center. And when it came to feminist activism, the California women were in the forefront within every policy arena.

Karen Tamerius (1995) and Shelah Leader (1977) were right, then. If you want to find sex differences among legislators—if you want to see how women are "making a difference" in public policymaking—this is the place to look. Recalling from the previous chapter, legislators' policy preferences, especially in the form of roll call votes, were highly constrained both by the narrow range of choices and by very strong partisan pressures (Schiller 1995; Tamerius 1995). When setting their own policy priorities, however, legislators were much less constrained by such factors. Partisanship did not dictate policy priorities the way it did roll call votes, even in California. Moreover, this chapter provides no evidence to suggest that coercive forms of sex discrimination were channeling female and male legislators into gender-"appropriate" activities. Thus relatively free of partisan demands and discriminatory coercion, these legislators, especially those of Arizona, seem to have taken sex, gender, and the representation of women into account when choosing to focus their policy activity in certain areas.

CHAPTER SEVEN

# The Rules of the Game

There are at least three ways in which a legislator can "act for" women in the policymaking arena. As discussed in Chapter 6, legislators can act as agenda-setters, expanding the set of questions and problems addressed by their colleagues to include those of concern to women. Subsequently, lawmakers may participate in debates about the content of legislation, helping to steer legislative solutions in directions most beneficial to women. This stage of the policymaking process is where legislators' policy preferences and roll call votes come into play, as seen in Chapter 5. Third, legislators can affect the policy process itself, altering the very ways in which they and their colleagues advocate and consider various policy proposals. This chapter explores these more procedural aspects of legislative life, the policy process rather than policy inputs and outputs. Specifically, I examine legislators' self-conscious strategies for getting bills passed, how they described their own legislative power, and their orientations toward hardball politics within their legislatures. At issue is whether the women and men of the 1990 Arizona and California state legislatures employed different methods to obtain their policy goals or preferred different models of the legislative process. Did female and male officials exert — or, at least, think about — power, influence, and leadership differently? Were the women introducing and advocating an alternative legislative style, a new way of doing politics?

Over two decades ago, Jeane Kirkpatrick (1974: 112–13) posed a very similar set of questions:

What is effective performance? More specifically, what constitutes effective performance in the view of these women legislators? What do they believe to be the requirements for success? Are there special rules for women? Do they have an outsider's perspective on the life of the legislature? Is there a "feminine" perception of a legislature? Do they see the "rules of game" as male legislators see them? Are these "male" rules, devised by and for men, and uncomfortable for women?

The subsequent, anecdotal response seems quite clear. Women in public office do often see themselves as offering and practicing a different and equally (if not more) effective set of game rules.

Former congresswoman and vice presidential candidate Geraldine Ferraro claims that women in politics do speak "in a different voice," just as Carol Gilligan has suggested.

> Women political leaders bring a different perspective to solving the problems that face us as a global society. . . . Instead of engaging in confrontation, women are more apt to negotiate. Instead of dealing in win-lose terms, women are more apt to see the gray area in between. Instead of thinking only of today, women are more apt to think in terms of the needs of generations to come. (Ferraro 1992: 288)

"I believe in consensus building," said Jeanne Shaheen, the first woman to be governor of New Hampshire, in a recent interview. "I think women tend to view decision-making in that way. So that's certainly been a focus for me. I think most people would agree I'm less confrontational than some of my predecessors have been" (Goldberg 1997). Indeed, her immediate predecessor, Stephen Merrill, agrees: "She says, 'I'm the Governor, they're the Legislature; we're working together for your best interest.' When I was Governor, I said, 'I'm Steve Merrill, I fight these people every day for you' " (Goldberg 1997). Vera Katz, who in 1985 became the first woman to be speaker of the Oregon House of Representatives, also believes that "there are some important differences in the way that women approach leadership and policymaking in state legislatures. . . . [W]omen legislators are more apt than men to seek to resolve disputes through consensus building and collaboration, rather than confrontations" (Katz 1987: 213).

In one of the pioneering studies of sex differences among public officials in the United States, the Center for the American Woman and Politics (CAWP), found that many of the women surveyed believed that, as women, they possessed superior interpersonal skills which enabled them to be more understanding of others, more patient, and more skilled at effecting compromise. Many of the male officeholders surveyed by CAWP offered the same observations (Johnson and Carroll 1978: 40A–43A). Santa Clara County officials interviewed by Janet Flammang (1985: 108) echoed many of these same sentiments. Some female officials noted "a distinctive female understanding of power." One described women's power as "less authoritarian and more supportive, collaborative and respectful of intuition." Another stated, "Male power means force and domination. Women use consensus, validation, cooperation, in a win-win direction."

A large proportion of the female state legislative leaders interviewed by Malcolm Jewell and Marcia Whicker (1994: 180) noticed differences in the leadership styles of their male and female colleagues. "The women are most often described as being more consensus oriented and participatory, more likely to seek input into decision making from a larger number of legislators." Indicative of this sentiment are the observations of Nancy Kopp, president pro tem of the Maryland House of Representatives and a political scientist:

> I have read the literature, and I think there is something to the idea that women's style of leadership is different from that of men. I think that a consensus style works in these difficult times. While this is not unique to women by any means, they feel more comfortable with it. They prefer to work with and through other people. And women tend to be more impatient with some things that men do, such as the rituals of standoffs. Women often think we could just sit down and work it out.

Female state legislators in Sue Thomas's (1994) study had not yet succeeded in reforming the legislative process, but they certainly had the desire and the will to do so. These women wanted to make policymaking in their own image; they wanted it to be more cooperative and less competitive, a "less zero-sum, less ad hoc, less a fly-by-the-seat-of-the-pants process, less a game of winners and losers, and more a process by which everyone can participate and as many people as possible can emerge with something to praise" (1994: 110).

Companion to these observations about women are certain assumptions about how male officials go about their business and have thus defined the norms of political behavior. Legislative leaders in Jewell and Whicker's (1994: 146) study often described their male colleagues as "more assertive and more manipulative, more likely to use rewards and punishments, more concerned with asserting themselves, more likely to be risk-takers." Having dominated politics for so long, men have been able to define the standard operating procedures, the norms of behavior, what is and what is not considered "traditional" (Duerst-Lahti and Kelly 1995a). "Traditionally," Vera Katz (1987: 213) asserts,

> "leadership" has been a word that is often associated with assertive, if not aggressive behavior. How many of us know of male legislators whose intimidating, manipulative and retaliatory behaviors have

been put in a positive light by a reference to their "strong leadership qualities"? All too often, behavior that works to encourage conflict and magnify differences is characterized as the vigorous exercise of "leadership."

In her historical analysis of ERA battles within state legislatures, Jane Sherron De Hart (1995: 221–22) identifies hardball politics as the way the game of politics was played. "A male-defined style, . . . [hardball politics] was perfected in a male ethos of wheeling and dealing, where ambition, aggressiveness, toughness, and even ruthlessness were privileged over the qualities of connectedness, nurturance, and selflessness traditionally associated with women." (See also C. Matthews 1988.)

These gendered expectations and assumptions about *political* leadership styles are echoed and amplified by a recent flood of "how-to" advice for and research about women in the corporate world of business administration and management. Judy Rosener (1990), for example, contrasts women's transformational, interactive leadership style with the more traditional, male-oriented, transactional, "command-and-control" style.[1] The men in her study of business leaders were more likely than the women to

> view job performance as a series of transactions with subordinates — exchanging rewards for services rendered or punishment for inadequate performance. The men are also more likely to use power that comes from their organizational position and formal authority.
>
> The women respondents, on the other hand, described themselves in ways that characterize "transformational" leadership — getting subordinates to transform their own self-interest into the interest of the group through concern for a broader goal. Moreover, they ascribe their power to personal characteristics like charisma, interpersonal skills, hard work, or personal contacts rather than to organizational stature. . . . [T]hese women actively work to make their interactions with subordinates positive for everyone involved. More specifically, the women encourage participation, share power and information, enhance other people's self-worth, and get others excited about their work. All these things reflect their belief that allowing employees to contribute and to feel powerful and important is a win-win situation — good for the employees and the organization. (Rosener 1990: 120)

Marilyn Loden's "masculine" and "feminine" leadership models (Loden 1985) provide a very similar set of alternatives, as do Faith Popcorn and Lys Marigold's "OldThink" and "FemaleThink" mind-sets (Popcorn and Marigold 1996).[2]

Businesswomen and the experts who advise and study them are becoming more and more wary of traditional, masculine corporate culture. Unlike the first generation of female executives, reports Rosener, "a second wave of women is making its way into top management, not by adopting the style and habits that have proved successful for men, but by drawing on the skills and attitudes they have developed from their shared experience as women" (Rosener 1990: 119). They also argue that these alternative management styles are the cutting-edge solution to recent changes in the American workforce and global economy; what's good for women is good for business (Cantor and Bernay 1992; Helgesen 1990; Loden 1985; Popcorn and Marigold 1996; Rudolph 1990).

Much of the literature on women's leadership styles suggests that these alternative approaches are reflections of gendered socialization and experience within both the home and the workplace. It is indeed easy to see how these expectations and observations of sex differences in leadership, management, and the exertion of power and influence are extrapolated from the traditional gender roles of women and men. Women, as mothers, wives, community volunteers, and pink-collar workers, are assumed to be more experienced, skilled, and comfortable using the more nurturing and cooperative methods. The female county supervisors in Flammang's study, for example, attributed their distinctive approaches or styles to domestically honed diplomatic skills: "an insistence upon mutual respect, consensus decision-making, validation of the feelings of others, and non-competitive power" (1985: 111). Men, as fathers, husbands, athletes, soldiers, and workers, are apparently better versed in the ways of domination, hierarchical control, and competition. Yet, as was the case with expectations about legislators' policy preferences and priorities, feminism also plays a role in shaping expectations for how women and men operate within legislative organizations.

Feminists involved in movement organizing, consciousness-raising groups, women's centers, rape crisis centers, feminist bookstores, and so forth have a long tradition of theorizing and practicing a certain style of organization. Kathy Ferguson (1984: 189–90) associates this organizational style with radical feminism in particular:

> As the early manifestos of the radical feminists make clear, they are committed to an internal style of organization that is deliberately anti-bureaucratic: the groups are decentralized; they rely on personal, face-to-face relations rather than formal rules; they are egalitarian rather than hierarchical; and they see skills and information as resources to be shared, not hoarded. They are frequently more concerned with process than with outcome, operating with a view of power that stresses the ability to empower the members to do col-

lectively that which they could not do alone. Debates among radical feminists over the role of leadership and formal structure, while often heated, take place within a context in which all assume that hierarchy should be minimized in favor of equality.

(See also Echols 1989; H. Eisenstein 1996; Iannello 1992.) Feminist theorists also address the issue of power, some asserting that women tend to define and exercise power differently from men (Ferguson 1984; Flammang 1983; Hartsock 1983; Mansbridge 1990; Miller 1982, 1986).[3] Feminists, according to Flammang (1983: 71), "recognize that women have been denied power, but insist that women do not want power if what that means is business as usual." Feminist scholars thus offer a critique of traditional, masculinist conceptions of "power over" and often advocate alternative, feminist conceptions of "power to."[4] "Power over" shares the same characteristics as the masculine leadership styles described above: dominance, control, and coercion; formal, hierarchical authority; win-lose, zero-sum competition and conflict; aggressiveness. "Power to," like the feminine leadership styles, is associated with empowering, egalitarian, mutually beneficial, reciprocal relationships; compromise, consensus-building, and cooperation; and interpersonal skills that emphasize honesty, openness, respect, and integrity.

There is, then, widespread belief among public officials, business executives, business management researchers, feminist activists, and feminist theorists that women and men tend to think about and practice leadership and power differently—and that such differences reflect gendered norms, roles, identities, and experiences. The political science research that compares the policymaking and administrative styles of men and women, however, paints a different picture.

Quite a few studies have found significant, gender-related differences in political behavior. Sue Tolleson Rinehart's study of big-city mayors (Rinehart 1991) reveals familiar sex differences in leadership styles: the women adopted a more "hands-on" approach with an emphasis on collegiality and cooperation, while the men incorporated more of a "command" approach involving hierarchical, authoritative relationships. In their study of cabinet-level appointees in Connecticut, Catherine Havens and Lynne Healy (1991) discovered that the women, who were more open and responsive to the input of those working below them, exhibited less hierarchical, more consensual leadership strategies than did their male counterparts. Lyn Kathlene's innovative analysis of conversational dynamics in committee hearings of the Colorado state legislature reveals an interesting contrast in the ways female and male committee chairs conducted themselves. While "women were more likely to act as a facilitator of the hearing . . . [m]en used their position of power to control hearings in ways that we commonly associate with the notion of positional power and leadership" (Kathlene 1994: 572). Finally, Jewell and Whicker (1994) confirm the suspicions of the state legislative leaders they interviewed: female leaders were, in fact, much more likely than male leaders to adopt "consensus" leadership styles. While the alternative, "command" leadership style seemed to be going out of style, Jewell and Whicker found that the few legislators who still clung to it were almost exclusively men.

But there also are numerous studies that have *not* uncovered sex differences. Comparing the female state legislators she studied to the male legislators of previous studies, Kirkpatrick (1974: 110) concluded: "There is no sex based difference in reports about how to 'make it' in a legislature. The comments of these women make it abundantly clear that they see the task very much as previous studies report it is seen by males." Nor did Kirkpatrick find any evidence that women "bring into the legislature a distinctive orientation to interpersonal relations" (134).

Researchers involved in CAWP's more recent survey of state legislators investigated legislative leadership styles (with respect to committee meetings), fully expecting to uncover significant sex differences. They "expected women to prefer a more inclusive and consensual style of leadership" and "anticipated that men might prefer a hierarchical, pragmatic leadership style" (Dodson and Carroll 1991: 83). What the CAWP investigators found was that large majorities of *both* female and male state legislators chose the more "feminine" leadership style. These women and men surveyed by CAWP also were in agreement on the importance of the following "feminine" leadership qualities: a sense of mission, a concern with providing leadership opportunities for others, the ability to convince people to do something they initially might not be inclined to do, a concern with encouraging everyone involved in a decision to express their views, a willingness to share recognition for accomplishments, and a concern with how those affected by a decision feel about the decision. Majorities of both sexes felt all six traits were very important (Dodson and Carroll 1991: 83).[5]

Two other recent studies have found a preponderance of similarities and only a few differences between women's and men's attitudes toward power and leadership. When asked if they thought there were particular personality traits, skills, or abilities a legislator needs in order to be powerful, the men and women of the Arkansas and Texas legislatures interviewed by Diane Blair and Jeanie Stanley (1991: 497) gave almost identical answers: "popularity, issue expertise, knowledge of rules and process, hard work and dedication, credibility, sensitivity to others' political base, the ability to compromise and to forge coalitions."[6] Interestingly, the only set of traits mentioned more frequently by women than by men were those dealing with the projection of strength, force, assertiveness, and aggressiveness—traits commonly associated with masculine leadership styles. Blair and Stanley attribute these women's aggressive stance to their very small numbers in both legislatures and their consequent vulnerability.

In their study of management styles among state public administrators, Georgia Duerst-Lahti and Cathy Marie Johnson (1990, 1992) also uncover very few sex differences. Describing their own management traits and those of hypothetical "good" administrators and colleagues, these women and men exhibited very similar preferences. The traits they valued the most (e.g., being conscientious, reliable, and efficient) were gender neutral. Feminine traits (e.g., being appreciative, helpful, and understanding) and masculine traits (e.g., being independent, assertive, and competitive) were equally valued by male and female bureaucrats. Whatever sex differences did occur found women placing more emphasis on masculine traits (such as being analytical and aggressive). Similar to Blair and Stanley's rationale, Duerst-Lahti and Johnson's reasoning suggests that these women have learned, perhaps from past experience, that blatant deviations from traditionally valued masculine traits will be punished.

This study of Arizona and California state legislators also reveals a remarkable degree of similarity in women's and men's legislative strategies, conceptions of power, and attitudes toward hardball politicking. In the remainder of this chapter, I examine the contours of these similarities in detail. I also use the legislators' responses to explore a possible explanation for the divergent findings and conclusions presented by political scientists thus far.

There is one factor that distinguishes the studies that have not found sex differences from those that have: the presence of strong institutional norms of behavior. The state legislators surveyed by Kirkpatrick, CAWP, Blair and Stanley, and myself were subject to certain norms common to legislative institutions, while the public administrators surveyed by Duerst-Lahti and Johnson most likely were subject to their own set of bureaucratic norms. In contrast to the mayors in Rinehart's study and the executive-level state appointees in Havens and Healy's study, these legislators and bureaucrats were members of a large institution in which accepted and valued patterns of behavior were, perhaps, well established. In contrast to the legislative leaders in Kathlene's and Jewell and Whicker's studies, rank-and-file lawmakers in other studies were in no position to either ignore the norms or create new ones of their own. In short, this contrast in the research findings suggests that certain institutional norms have, under certain conditions, the ability to overrule or negate gender-specific assumptions, expectations, or inclinations regarding leadership and power.

The potential significance of institutional norms raises several very interesting questions for the study of gender, power, and leadership, which I address in this chapter.

1. What *are* these institutional norms? Are they related to the gendered models of leadership and constructs of power?
2. How powerful are these institutional norms? To what degree are institution members aware of such norms? To what degree do members adhere to such norms? Do institutional norms, in fact, have the power to override gender norms?
3. Is the power of institutional norms conditional? Does it vary across institutions, even institutions of the same type? Does it vary among individual members of the same institution?

### Strategies for Legislative Success

Each legislator participating in this study was asked to imagine addressing a group of newly elected legislators in an orientation session. The question posed was: "What would be your advice to them on how to be successful?" If necessary, the legislator was asked to give specific advice on how to get bills passed and how to influence his or her colleagues.[7] From these responses, one can cull a set of legislative strategies—the how-tos and skills legislators consider important and helpful not only for new colleagues but also for themselves. Although a few legislators (10 percent)—all of them men, most of them conservative—claimed that enacting legislation was not important to them, all but one of the participants in this study had specific advice to offer. This is a strong indication that legislators do, indeed, have legislative strategies, that their efforts are deliberate and intentional rather than haphazard and unconscious. Nevertheless, different legislators may play the policymaking game differently. Do female and male legislators compose different playbooks for winning the legislative game? More generally, to what extent are legislative strategies gendered, exhibiting either masculine "power over" or feminine "power to" characteristics?

### "Power Over" Strategies

Table 7.1 lists and compares the strategies most frequently recommended by male and female members of the Arizona and California state legislatures.[8] As the figures imply, "power over" strategies were mentioned quite infrequently. Only 30 percent of the legislators interviewed endorsed any such strategies, and only one legislator endorsed more than one. On average, legislators devoted a minuscule proportion (8 percent) of their advice to "power over" strategies.

**Table 7.1 Recommended Legislative Strategies**

| | Percentage Who Recommended Strategy | | | | |
| | Arizona Legislators | | California Legislators | | Total |
| Types of Legislative Strategies | Women (*N* = 18) | Men (*N* = 32) | Women (*N* = 14) | Men (*N* = 17) | Sample (*N* = 81) |
|---|---|---|---|---|---|
| **"Power over"** | | | | | |
| Target influential, powerful colleagues | 17 | 16 | 7 | 18 | 15 |
| Stand firm; be aggressive | 0* | 16* | 14 | 12 | 11 |
| Make deals, trade votes | 17* | 0* | 0 | 6 | 5 |
| **"Power to"** | | | | | |
| Do *not* make deals, trade | 22 | 22 | 0 | 6 | 15 |
| Do *not* use force, intimidation, etc. | 11 | 12 | 0 | 6 | 9 |
| Integrity; honesty | 44 | 31 | 57 | 65 | 46 |
| Lobby colleagues personally | 33 | 44 | 57 | 47 | 44 |
| Build personal relationships with colleagues | 50 | 41 | 36 | 59 | 46 |
| Compromise | 50 | 50 | 50 | 35 | 47 |
| Work with constituents | 6 | 6 | 7 | 23 | 10 |
| Let others get credit | 17 | 12 | 7 | 0 | 10 |
| **Neutral/mixed** | | | | | |
| Hard work; knowledge | 67 | 44 | 43 | 53 | 51 |
| Write a good proposal | 17 | 25 | 21 | 6 | 18 |
| Specialize; be selective | 17 | 22 | 29 | 6 | 18 |
| Work with lobbyists and interest groups | 6 | 3 | 7* | 47* | 14 |
| Nuts and bolts | 28 | 22 | 14 | 29 | 23 |

* Sex differences for these values are statistically significant ($p \leq .05$).

The most authoritarian or coercive command-and-control tactics were either not mentioned or rejected. A small percentage (11 percent) did believe legislative success was achieved (at least, in part) by avoiding compromise, standing firm, and/or being aggressive—"Fight the fight, win or lose, . . . stick to your guns," as an Arizona man put it. But while these legislators placed a premium on being strong and assertive, they in no way advocated the use of force, threat, coercion, or intimidation; nor did any other legislators. In fact, several Arizona legislators and one California legislator explicitly *rejected* the use of such tactics. An Arizona woman, for example, described herself as a "real team player."

I work *with* the [Democratic legislative] Caucus and *with* the other members . . . as opposed to being demanding. We have some members of our caucus who, for example, are not going to vote for the tax package unless they get this and this and this and this.

Arizona legislators in particular were concerned about such demands and quite a few were aware of the fine line between trading votes and coercion. Making deals and trading votes may be construed in such a way as to connote "power over," but this strategy also was rejected more often than it was endorsed. Most of those who did recommend "making deals" and trading votes as a way to gather support for one's legislation couched such behavior in positive terms: "I'll vote for your bill if you'll vote for mine." In this way, such negotiations are more akin to compromise than coercion. There was only one Arizona legislator who both endorsed and described such bargaining in any sort of threatening way: "We won't guarantee it if you can't guarantee this." Many of the Arizona legislators who *objected* to such deals, however, did perceive them as bargains with the devil or, at the very least, morally wrong. Said one Arizona man:

> I have not done what I'm sure many other people do: you know, you can barter. . . . "I have supported your legislation; now is the time to cash in." I have almost never done that because I just think that's wrong.

The role that hierarchy and position power played in these legislators' strategies was either passive or indirect. Many legislators in both states and in both political parties acknowledged the built-in advantages of majority party status, but, of course, no one went so far as to suggest seriously that one should switch parties to get one's bills passed. With the exception of one Arizona male legislator, positions of leadership, seniority, and electoral security were not explicitly recognized as personal assets one could use to gather support for legislation or to influence colleagues. Some legislators (15 percent) did, however, recommend targeting or working with *other* legislators in such powerful and influential positions.

### "Power To" Strategies

While legislators tended to ignore—sometimes even shun—"power over" strategies, they put a great deal of faith in "power to" strategies. Almost every legislator interviewed (95 percent) mentioned at least one "power to" strategy. On average, each legislator mentioned two such strategies. Moreover, "power to" strategies constituted well over half (59 percent) of all the strategies mentioned by the average legislator in this study.

One of the most frequently mentioned and strongly emphasized "power to" strategies was some variant of "Keep your word." One California man, for example, offered this piece of advice "for people in their work here in the Capitol":

> [Y]ou've got to be above-board in all your dealings. You've got to be forthright with people. If you give your word to somebody on how you're going to vote on something, you do it that way—or, at least, you don't change without letting them know ahead of time that something's happened. Because, you know, your effectiveness here really depends upon how people view you, whether they trust you.

Ironically and sadly enough, personal integrity and honesty loomed large in the minds of at least 46 percent of these state legislators, some of whom (in California) were watching as a colleague was being convicted of accepting bribes and some of whom (in Arizona) would learn a year later that a number of their colleagues were in the process of accepting bribes. "Be fair and honest," an Arizona man advised, "because the only thing we all have coming into this system, whether you're rich or poor, is your word."

Equally, if not more important to these legislators was making contact —*personal* contact—with colleagues. "This is a people business," stated a California woman. The purpose of such "one-on-one" contact was either to lobby and discuss legislation in particular (mentioned by 44 percent of the legislators) or simply to get to know each other in a more personal, friendly sort of way (mentioned by 46 percent). Legislators' lobbying strategies were, as one Arizona man put it, straight out of the textbook: full information, conviction, and understanding count for a lot more than one-sided arguments and threats. He was referring, no doubt, to political science textbooks (e.g., Ornstein and Elder 1978; Schlozman and Tierney 1986), but he could have just as well been referring to the "feminine leadership" textbooks (e.g., Loden 1985). Establishing mutual interests was often the key. Colleagues, according to a California female legislator, "have to know where you're coming from. They have to know this is of great interest to you and not only your constituency, but theirs too. . . . You have to make it *their* issue as well as yours."

While such lobbying among colleagues was thought to be most effective when done in an amiable and nonantagonistic way, being friendly and getting to know one's colleagues personally often were regarded as valuable strategies in and of themselves. At the risk of sounding "really devious or dishonest," an Arizona female representative explained how being "nice and friendly" wins not only friends but also votes: "[I]f they don't care for it [your bill] very much, but they like you, then they might vote for it. Or if they don't care one way or the other and they like you, then they might vote for it." A California assemblywoman would tell newly elected members to "remember the personal side of this business," adding,

Which doesn't mean you have to go to the bar with people or anything like that, but be professional, kind, and considerate. Remember that these are coworkers and not adversaries. Too many people, I
think, come here with sort of a pugnacious attitude, and the process
is really served by developing personal relationships. Remember the
phone company's ad: the best relationships are personal; reach out
and touch someone. I think there is something to be said for taking
the time to ask people how they are.

Along with integrity and personal contact, compromise and coalition-
building were among the most frequently mentioned and strongly recommended legislative strategies. Politics according to these legislators (47 percent) is, indeed, the art of compromise. Warned an Arizona woman,

Don't think that any situation in politics is black and white. You may
have the highest ideals in the world and maybe you feel they are pure
and there is no alternative to any of those things that you are sure
about. If you think that, you're likely to be very ineffective, because
this is a give-and-take proposition.

A California assemblyman explained in detail just how this give-and-take
process works, and why: He approaches "Senator Smith" and says,

"I need your help on this bill." Well, Senator Smith looks at it and
goes, "Well, I understand what you're doing, but you know, I don't
really like this part and this part and this part." And I look at him and
I may learn something from that. I may not have even bothered with
that particular concern. So I say, "Well, Senator, how 'bout if I amend
that portion out and change that portion to your liking? Would you—
do you think you could consider it?" . . . What I'm telling him is, "I
need you to help me work on this bill. I need your support on it and
I'm gonna get your input on how it's put together. Can you handle
the concept of the bill? Okay, we agree on the concept of the bill.
You don't like the particulars? I can change the particulars to get your
vote." . . .*That* is the most effective way to get things done around here.
It's such a consensus process. A lot of people say, "No, never compromise!" Well that's crap! This is a legislative body. I've somehow got to
find common ground with the majority of the legislators that represent the majority of the people out there. I've got to find that common
ground and pass a law that will apply to all the people of California.

Touching upon the open, egalitarian, collaborative, and empowering aspects of the "power to" leadership style, a small percentage (10 percent)
of the legislators advised newly elected members to work with and pay at-

tention to constituents in order to succeed in the legislative arena. These legislators did not see a trade-off between constituency-related activities and legislative activities. Like the female Arizona legislator who claimed that she got some of her best ideas for her bills from her constituents, these legislators thought constituency work enhanced rather than detracted from their legislative work.

The following legislative strategy, suggested by a female Arizona legislator, is perhaps the most extreme example of "power to" empowerment:

> Sometimes you give it to someone else, and it will make them a star. . . . You give them every piece of information, you go through everything. You just walk them through it. You write the bill, you take it in to them and you ask them to prime-sponsor it. So they can be a hero. . . . If you're willing to put your ego aside to help somebody else, to give them more than they can give themselves, then you will get what you want. . . . [Y]ou've got your bill; you just didn't get it with your name on the front.

While this woman was more altruistic than most, there were a few other legislators (10 percent) who felt legislative success was at least partly contingent on helping others and not being selfish, even to the point of letting someone else get the credit for their proposals.


### Other Strategies

There were other, very important legislative strategies mentioned by the Arizona and California legislators that do not fit clearly in either the "power over" or the "power to" construct. These "neutral" or "mixed" strategies constitute, on average, a third of the strategies for success legislators discussed. All but 20 percent of the legislators offered at least one neutral strategy.

Included in these neutral strategies was the most frequently offered (by 51 percent of the legislators) piece of advice: work hard and do your homework.[9] The purpose of such efforts is twofold, according to these lawmakers. First, one gains intricate and accurate knowledge of one's legislation (and the consequences thereof) and can therefore address any and all questions and misgivings of others. In addition, the commitment of time and effort speaks for itself. "There's a natural tendency," explained an Arizona man, "to give sway to someone else who's very actively involved and who has a deep, abiding concern—maybe not to pass their bill, but at least pay attention."

The legislators also suggested some more practical, more procedural strategies. About one-fifth (18 percent), for example, recommended limiting and focusing one's efforts by either specializing in a certain policy area or simply being selective and refraining from sponsoring too many bills at a time. Another 18 percent stressed the importance of writing a good proposal, one that is reasonable (i.e., not too extreme) or, ideally, one that offers something that no reasonable person could refuse or oppose. Some legislators (14 percent) relied heavily on lobbyists and interest groups for information and ideas, as well as some of the legwork. Finally, quite a few legislators in both states (23 percent) stressed the importance of being familiar with and taking advantage of parliamentary procedures and the "nuts and bolts" of the policy process.

### Sex Differences

As Table 7.1 shows, the legislative strategies suggested by female and male legislators within each state were very similar. Among the Arizona legislators, men and women were equally likely to stress the importance of personal integrity and honesty, lobbying colleagues, building personal relationships with colleagues, and compromise. They also were equally likely to warn against making deals and trading votes, to reject the use of force or intimidation to get what they wanted, and to recommend the alternative of helping others succeed. Working with constituents and working with lobbyists and interest groups were two strategies barely mentioned by either female or male Arizona officials. Equal proportions of these men and women mentioned more practical considerations, such as writing a good proposal, specializing, and becoming experts at negotiating the nuts and bolts of the formal policymaking procedures. Overall, there are no significant sex differences in either the number or proportion of "power over" or "power to" strategies recommended by these legislators.

Nonetheless, there are a few notable sex differences in the Arizona legislators' strategies. First, Arizona female officials (67 percent) were more likely than their male colleagues (44 percent) to mention the value of hard work and knowledge. While this difference does not necessarily correspond to the "power over" versus "power to" dichotomy and is not quite statistically significant ($p$ = .061), it does hint at the possibility that fewer Arizona women than men felt they had the latitude or ability to be successful without working extremely hard. This, in turn, confirms the popular notion that women have to work harder than men to be equally successful and respected.

Some sex differences among Arizona officials also arose with regard to "power over" types of recommendations. While only a small percentage of the men (16 percent) thought it was important to stand one's ground and be assertive, none of the Arizona women offered such advice. Lest one conclude from this that the Arizona men were more likely to recommend "power over" strategies, one should note that the gender tables were turned when it came to making deals and trading votes. Some of the Arizona female officials (17 percent), but none of their male colleagues, recommended such strategies. Thus, there is no consistent evidence to suggest that Arizona male legislators were any more enamored with "power over" strategies than were their female colleagues. Nor is there any reason to suspect that the Arizona female officials valued "power to" strategies any more than their male colleagues.[10]

The story is much the same among the California legislators: very few significant sex differences. The California women and men were equally *un*likely to recommend any "power over" strategies; 79 percent of the women and 65 percent of the men did not mention any such strategies. On average, "power over" strategies constituted only 6 percent of both the women's and the men's responses. Both male and female California legislators, like their Arizona counterparts, were much more likely to cite "power to"-type strategies. On average, 62 percent of the women's strategies and 60 percent of the men's strategies were "power to" ones.

All but a few specific strategies received the same amount of attention from California female and male officials (see Table 7.1). The most glaring and only statistically significant difference within the California delegation concerns working with lobbyists and interest groups, which cannot be considered either a "power over" or a "power to" strategy. Only one woman offered such a strategy, compared to almost half the men. The women, on the other hand, were somewhat more likely to stress the importance of two other neutral strategies: specialization and writing good proposals. Contrary to widespread expectations, two "power to" strategies received slightly more attention from the California *men* than from the women: working with constituents and building personal relationships with their colleagues.[11]

In neither state, then, is there any consistent pattern of sex differences in legislators' recommended strategies for legislative success. There is almost no evidence to support the notion that female legislators endorse "power to" strategies more frequently than male legislators or that male legislators endorse "power over" strategies more frequently than female legislators. Furthermore, the strategies most frequently endorsed by *both* female and male legislators closely correspond to feminine and feminist conceptions of shared power and cooperative leadership. Being honest and straightforward, working hard, lobbying colleagues, getting to know colleagues personally, and being open to compromise are all characteristics of leaders who want to agree upon mutually beneficial outcomes, not leaders who impose their will on others.

## Sources of Personal Power

Legislative success is in many ways a reflection of power. Power, according to Robert Dahl's well-known definition, is the ability to cause someone to do something he or she would not otherwise do (Dahl 1957). This is the essence of what legislators do when they gather support for their proposals. Yet, "power" may mean many different things to different legislators, and legislative effectiveness may be just one of those meanings. Even Dahl's definition is broad and ambiguous enough to elicit multiple interpretations; there are many very different ways in which one can affect another's behavior, and legislators may not regard every method as equally powerful. Moreover, legislators' ideas about what does and does not constitute "power" may very well reflect the gender-related concepts of "power over" and "power to." Perhaps, then, a more direct approach to studying conceptions of power among state legislators would confirm popular expectations of sex differences.

Arizona and California officials interviewed for this study were asked several questions specifically about power. This somewhat lengthy discussion was prefaced with the notion that "everyone has different ideas about what power is." Legislators were then asked what they thought power meant within their legislature: "How does a(n) (Arizona/California) (representative/assemblymember/senator) accumulate power? What are the sources of power in the (House/Assembly/Senate)?" [12] Finally, they were asked to describe their own power: "What are the sources of *your* power?" Responses to this question about personal sources of power are summarized in Table 7.2.

The patterns of responses in Table 7.2 are very similar to those in Table 7.1. As was the case with legislative strategies, discussions of power included many more references to elements of the "power to" construct than to those of the "power over" idea. References to the ability to persuade, integrity, respect of colleagues, fairness, willingness to compromise, interpersonal skills, giving or receiving support to or from other legislators, and the strength or support of constituents far outnumbered references to positions of authority and privilege or connections to those who were in such positions. [13] Overall, "power to" sources constituted an average of 59 percent of all sources mentioned by the legislators in this study; "power over" sources constituted an average of only 14 percent.

While the vast majority of legislators (87 percent) mentioned at least one "power to" source, two-thirds of the legislators mentioned no "power over" sources at all. Moreover, the "power over" sources discussed were quite limited in terms of both variety and force. A quarter of the legislators saw their positions of leadership, rank, and/or seniority as a source of

**Table 7.2 Sources of Personal Power**

| Types of Power Sources | Percentage Who Mentioned Source | | | | |
|---|---|---|---|---|---|
| | Arizona Legislators | | California Legislators | | Total Sample |
| | Women (*N* = 18) | Men (*N* = 30) | Women (*N* = 14) | Men (*N* = 17) | (*N* = 79) |
| **"Power over"** | | | | | |
| Position | 22 | 23 | 14* | 41* | 25 |
| Connections within legislature; ties to leadership | 11 | 3 | 7 | 0 | 5 |
| One's vote; strategic use of vote | 11 | 7 | 14 | 6 | 9 |
| **"Power to"** | | | | | |
| *Not* force, intimidation, coercion, etc. | 22 | 27 | 29 | 6 | 21 |
| *Not* leadership positions or ties to | 6 | 7 | 21 | 12 | 10 |
| Does not want/like "power" | 28 | 20 | 7 | 12 | 18 |
| Being fair, reasonable; willing to compromise, build consensus | 6* | 23* | 7 | 6 | 13 |
| Honesty; integrity; trust and/or respect of colleagues | 11 | 27 | 36 | 23 | 24 |
| Interpersonal skills; getting along with colleagues | 17 | 7 | 7* | 35* | 15 |
| Persuasiveness | 28 | 27 | 7 | 18 | 21 |
| Helping other legislators | 6 | 10 | 0 | 0 | 5 |
| Help/support from other legislators (coalition) | 17 | 7 | 7 | 6 | 9 |
| Constituency support; ability to serve constituents | 6 | 3 | 7 | 23 | 9 |
| **Neutral/mixed** | | | | | |
| Policy expertise, effectiveness | 33* | 7* | 57 | 35 | 28 |
| Willingness to work hard, be persistent | 11 | 0 | 21 | 6 | 8 |
| General knowledge and experience; intelligence | 28 | 13 | 7 | 18 | 16 |
| Connections outside legislature | 11 | 7 | 0* | 18* | 9 |

* Sex differences for these values are statistically significant ($p \leq .05$).

power, but they did not regard such power as granting them carte blanche; instead, they tended to qualify the power inherent in their positions as limited in scope and ephemeral at best. As one Arizona male committee chair reflected:

> I think my power is within my sphere of influence as a committee chairman. So I have some limited power with [various interests that deal with the committee]. The power is not so much scaring them. I

think the power comes from—as long as I'm in the legislature, they've got to deal with me. And I've got to deal with them. And so, of course, they want to keep on my good side as much as possible because I'm an instrument for them to use. . . . Now if I'm defeated or I decide not to run, hell, I probably won't get a Christmas card from any of them. . . . Your power is only in the title that you have.

A few legislators (5 percent) cited their connections within the legislature, which is only an indirect "power over" source of power. Although some legislators recommended aggressiveness as a legislative strategy (see Table 7.1), no one mentioned such traits as a source of his or her personal power. A few legislators (8 percent) did refer to their persistence and willingness to work hard as a source of power, but such references did not carry clear tones of "power over." The only other "power over"-type source of power mentioned by the legislators (9 percent) was the strategic use of one's vote. "There are a number of ways to utilize the voting power that one has," explained an Arizona male official. "You can withhold it, or you can give it for something else. [It gives you the] power to trade, bargain, negotiate." This type of power, then, is directly tied to the legislative strategy of making deals and trading votes mentioned previously.

Once again, many Arizona and California legislators explicitly rejected elements of the "power over" construct. Twenty-one percent stated that their power was *not* based on the use of force, intimidation, and the like. A California female official, for example, observed that some of her colleagues

> will use intimidation as a way of [gaining] power, and that is not "power" to me. I think power is respect; people will follow your lead because they feel that you have the information, that you have an understanding of the issue. That's far more significant to me than somebody who can, say, manipulate a vote simply by intimidating, by virtue of "Well, wait and see what I'll do"—you know, that sort of thing, that kind of vindictive action. That may be *a* form of power, but that's not a form of power that I respect.

Another 10 percent claimed that they did not rely on leadership positions or close ties to those in such positions. Finally, some of the legislators (18 percent) rejected the term "power" altogether, largely because they associated with it only ideas of "power over." For example, a California male legislator said he did not want to have anything to do with "power":

> I don't think a legislator should look at his or her self as having "power." Power rests with the constituents, with the voters. I look at myself more as a servant than someone with power. . . . A lot of politicians covet power—they like power—and I've never been that way.

Responses to questions about power resemble those to questions about legislative strategies, not only in the preponderance of "power to" references but also in the lack of any clear patterns of sex differences among the legislators (see Table 7.2). The few sex differences that did arise among the Arizona legislators give no support to the idea that female officials think in "power to" terms while male officials think in "power over" terms. In fact, the *men* were more likely than the women to mention such "feminine" or feminist notions of power as fairness and ability to compromise and build consensus, or trust and respect of colleagues. Moreover, "power to" sources constitute, on average, a significantly greater proportion of the Arizona men's responses (71 percent) than of the women's (50 percent).[14] The average *number* of "power to" sources mentioned by Arizona lawmakers did not differ according to sex, however. Nor did the number or percentage of "power over" responses.

Significant sex differences in the California legislators' conceptions of personal power also were few and far between. And, once again, they do not reveal any consistent evidence that the male legislators relied predominantly on "masculine," hierarchical sources of power or that only female legislators relied predominantly on "feminine," egalitarian sources of power. On the one hand, the California men were more likely than the women to mention their position or status within the legislature as a source of power. Plus, the California women were slightly more likely to reject outright intimidation, coercion, and ties to leadership. On the other hand, these male legislators were much more likely than the female legislators to talk about power arising from their interpersonal skills or their ability to get along with and understand their colleagues. Overall, there were no sex differences in either the number or percentage of "power over" or "power to" sources cited by the California legislators.[15]

### Beyond Norms: Hardball Politics

Clearly, a very powerful set of norms was at work in the Arizona and California state legislatures. Judging from the legislators' self-styled legislative strategies and their conceptions of personal power, these norms stressed the importance of honesty, compromise, and consensus-building and placed sanctions, or at least strict limits, on manipulation, coercion, and intimidation. Legislators were much more likely to present themselves in "power to" terms than in "power over" terms.

As Kirkpatrick noted in her study, this is nothing new or novel; these rules of the game are "those already familiar from previous studies of legislative behavior" (1974: 115). "The social world they describe is that described in Wahlke, Eulau, et al., Sorauf, Epstein, Patterson, Barber, Keefe,

Jewell, Ogul and other students of legislative behavior whose evidence was based chiefly on males" (1974: 134). Indeed, the classic texts on American legislative politics, which have not been particularly interested in gender dynamics, attest to the widespread adherence (or at least, lip-service paid) to ideals of professional courtesy, collegiality, and reciprocity among legislators, especially in more institutionalized or professional legislatures (Jewell and Patterson 1986; D. R. Matthews 1960; Polsby 1968; Rosenthal 1981; Wahlke, Eulau, Buchanan, and Ferguson 1962).[16]

While this somewhat idyllic image of legislative life may conflict with both media and scholarly images of the rough-and-tumble world of self-interested, credit-seeking politicians (Mayhew 1974), it is no less important or real. According to Gregory Caldeira, John Clark, and Samuel Patterson (1993: 3), it also is no less true today than it was in previous years.

> The legislature is a highly interactive collectivity. Its institutional life gravitates around two poles: one the nexus of the representative and the represented and the other the networks of affect and respect among legislators themselves. The internal ecology of the legislature may be noted for its conflict and cleavage, but coalitions are built not only from calculations of self-interest but also on the bases of trust, affection, and respect. Indeed, social networks and interpersonal bonds constitute crucial elements in the firm foundation of purposive action in legislatures.

These sorts of "social networks and interpersonal bonds" are "crucial elements" of the leadership styles most frequently endorsed not only in this study but in all other studies of female and male state legislators cited earlier (Blair and Stanley 1991; Dodson and Carroll 1991; Jewell and Whicker 1994; Kirkpatrick 1974).

But norms, like any other rules, are made to be broken, as the saying goes. The question is, who is more or less likely to break them? If norms of legislative behavior really are more akin to feminine than to masculine gender roles and socialization, then one would expect female legislators to be less willing to make exceptions. What happens, then, when legislators go beyond the realm of normative behavior?

In between the discussion of legislative strategies and the discussion of sources of power, legislators participating in this study were asked a series of questions about hardball politics. First, they were asked if there were ever conflicts among their colleagues that they would describe as "hardball" or "cutthroat." Every legislator interviewed agreed that there were indeed such instances, and most saw them as infrequent yet notable exceptions to the normal, everyday course of events.[17]

Of course, the terms "hardball" and "cutthroat" could mean something different to each legislator. Legislators, therefore, were asked to describe the types of conflicts they would label as such: "What about those conflicts makes them 'hardball'?"[18] Their responses fell into three main categories, each reflecting some aspect of the "power over" construct, or at least some sort of deviation from the normative "power to" type of relationships.

The following description of hardball politics offered by an Arizona woman illustrates well the most frequently cited type of hardball politics. It also reveals the exceptionalism often associated with such conflicts.

> Well, it just comes down to the point of what is someone willing to do in order to get a bill passed. You just can't be [sweet all the time]. You have to sometimes withhold your vote on things. There *are* threats that are given to people. They certainly play hardball. . . . You often-times—however collegial it may be—you oftentimes make enemies for a short time. You have to step on toes. You have to say, "Well, I'm sorry; I'm not down here to be liked. I'm down here to represent the folks." . . . Oftentimes the leadership takes you in and says, "Your committee chairmanship: you may not be a committee chairman next year if you don't vote for this bill."

This sort of hardball politics invokes both the command-and-control leadership style and the darker, more manipulative side of making deals and trading votes. Intimidation, threats, force, and coercion were the main themes of this version of hardball politics, as described by 73 percent of the legislators interviewed.

Another type of hardball politics mentioned by 22 percent of the legislators involves the refusal to cooperate, compromise, or budge in any way —very much the opposite of consensus-building. The third major type of hardball politics described by 23 percent of the legislators focuses on personal, as opposed to policy-oriented, conflicts. Such "ego conflicts" often entail personal attacks on the integrity of another legislator, holding personal grudges, and vindictive behavior in general.

After conjuring up these images of hardball politics, the legislators were asked how they felt about such behavior: "Do you think this is how disagreements in the (House/Assembly/Senate) should be resolved? Do you, or would you, have any qualms about engaging in 'hardball' politics yourself?" Table 7.3 summarizes the legislators' attitudes toward whichever type of hardball politics they had just described.

The Arizona and California legislators, female and male alike, expressed a wide range of attitudes toward hardball politics. Personal, vindictive attacks (Type C) were the only type of hardball summarily rejected by almost all the legislators who mentioned it; there was no tolerance for such behav-

**Table 7.3 Attitudes toward Hardball Politics**

| | Percentage Expressing Attitude | | | |
|---|---|---|---|---|
| | Arizona Legislators | | California Legislators | |
| Types of Hardball Politics | Women | Men | Women | Men |
| **Type A: "Command-and-control"** | (N = 11) | (N = 27) | (N = 9) | (N = 7) |
| 1. no problem | 36 | 33 | 11 | 14 |
| 2. reluctant participant | 45 | 18 | 22 | 0 |
| 3. refuses to participate | 18 | 48 | 67 | 86 |
| Mean score | 1.82 | 2.15 | 2.56 | 2.71 |
| **Type B: No compromise** | (N = 4) | (N = 3) | (N = 5) | (N = 4) |
| 1. no problem | 50 | 67 | 40 | 0 |
| 2. reluctant participant | 25 | 33 | 60 | 50 |
| 3. refuses to participate | 25 | 0 | 0 | 50 |
| Mean score | 1.75 | 1.33 | 1.60* | 2.50* |
| **Type C: Personal attacks** | (N = 6) | (N = 2) | (N = 4) | (N = 5) |
| 1. no problem | 0 | 0 | 0 | 0 |
| 2. reluctant participant | 0 | 0 | 25 | 20 |
| 3. refuses to participate | 100 | 100 | 75 | 80 |
| Mean score | 3.00 | 3.00 | 2.75 | 2.80 |
| **Any Type**[a] | (N = 17) | (N = 30) | (N = 13) | (N = 14) |
| 1. no problem | 18 | 37 | 8 | 7 |
| 2. reluctant participant | 29 | 13 | 23 | 21 |
| 3. refuses to participate | 53 | 50 | 69 | 74 |
| Mean score | 2.35 | 2.13 | 2.61 | 2.64 |

[a] Entries are based on the highest score, or strongest objection, made by each legislator, regardless of the particular type of hardball politics mentioned.

* Sex differences for these values are statistically significant ($p \leq .05$).

ior. Some legislators refused to engage in or tolerate the other types of hardball politicking as well. One Arizona male representative, for example, believed that any legislator who holds up the budget or tax package for his or her own "going-home" bill (Type A hardball politics) "should be removed from office."

At the other end of the spectrum, some legislators had no qualms at all about engaging in what they described as hardball politics. "I can play 'hardball' with the best of them, you know, and be real tough, and real demanding, and very uncompromising," said an Arizona female official. "I can play *that* game just as good as the next guy!" she insisted. A few legislators wished hardball politics occurred more often, for in their eyes such tactics were conducive to efficient and effective decision-making. "The 'hardball,' the stand-firm line is what encourages and brings about the negotiations and the debate," explained a California female legislator. "If you didn't have that, there'd be no reason to negotiate. So we do that, and I believe in it."

In between those who applauded hardball tactics and those who despised them were those legislators who saw such behavior as a necessary evil. They would do it, but only because they felt they had to, because that was the way the game was played. "The legislative process is not pretty," a California male legislator pointed out. "If we could always come to a nice, simple compromise, that'd be nice," an Arizona man admitted.

> But I'm not gonna sit here and tell you that will ever happen—*ever!* I don't think it's ever happened in all humankind. . . . In the world of politics, where the rules are set up [so] that we have maximum amounts of leverage if we want them, we're always going to use them. So I just consider it a fact of political life.

These legislators saw hardball politics as a norm in and of itself—a norm that conflicted with other, more collegial "power to" norms. This would explain their ambivalence toward playing hardball. Indeed, some legislators, like the California woman quoted below, were truly torn between their principles or preferences and what they saw as the unavoidable side of politics.

> I don't really like playing hardball politics. I'm more of a diplomat. I see myself as a stateswoman and not a politician. . . .

> [Q: Are you able to avoid playing the hardball politics?]

> Yeah, but sometimes you have to. I've had occasions where I've had to do it. I've had to threaten to hold people's legislation in committee. If you want to be effective, you've got to play within the rules. You can't be naive. I come from an education background, you know, you *teach.* But sometimes you have to resort to hard-ball. I hate it! I hate the political aspect of the political arena. I like the diplomacy. I like coming to an agreement.

As the figures in Table 7.3 illustrate, there are very few significant sex differences in the legislators' attitudes toward hardball politics. While there were many legislators who were willing to cross the boundaries of normative cooperative behavior and engage in hardball politics, the male legislators were in no way more willing to do so than were the female legislators.[19] What sex differences do arise run contrary to the expectation that the women would be more wary of such behavior than the men. Among the Arizona officials who described the command-and-control type of hardball politics (Type A), the men were more likely than the women to refuse to play such games. The same can be said for the (relatively few) California officials who cited the uncompromising type of hardball politics (Type B): the men's attitudes were more negative than the women's.

Perhaps, as other researchers have suggested (Blair and Stanley 1991; Duerst-Lahti and Johnson 1990, 1992), the women's minority status in both state legislatures made them a bit *less,* rather than more, likely than their male colleagues to eschew masculine hardball tactics. But if that were the case, then one should find that the California women, who constituted a much smaller minority than the Arizona women, were even less likely to reject hardball or "power over" tactics. As Table 7.3 shows, however, the California women were either as likely or *more* likely than their female Arizona counterparts to refuse to participate in hardball politics. Plus, the California and Arizona women were equally unlikely to advocate "power over" legislative strategies or to claim "power over" sources of power; and they were equally likely to cite "power to" strategies and power sources. In any case, these few instances of sex difference should not detract from the main finding of this chapter: male and female legislative styles rarely differed.

## Conclusions

Traditionally, or stereotypically, speaking, women are not supposed to want power, much less power over others. Men are expected to covet and monopolize power, especially the sort of power with which some dominate others. Nevertheless, women nowadays are redefining and reclaiming power and leadership in ways that recognize and appreciate their particular personalities, experiences, and skills as women. None of this "received wisdom," however, proves applicable to the women and men of the Arizona and California state legislatures. In discussing their own sources of power and their own legislative strategies for success, these women and men did not seem to think about or to use power differently. This is not simply because the women had assimilated into the rough-and-tumble, male-dominated world of state legislative politics. Nor is it the case that these female officeholders failed in their mission to redefine the policy process by making it more honest, less antagonistic, and more consensual (Thomas 1994). The men seem to have already defined it as such. Thus, these male and female officials were equally critical of "power over," coercive, and manipulative methods of achieving policy goals. They also were equally likely to gush over various "power to" ideas about the value and effectiveness of compromise, consensus-building, getting along with colleagues, being nice, fair, etc.

As was the case in Chapter 3's analysis of representational priorities, the power of long-standing legislative norms offers a plausible and interesting explanation for this lack of sex-based differentiation. Political scientists have long been aware of the normative and structural incentives for legislators to at least appear to be collegial, courteous, and cooperative. The rational-actor legislator who wants to succeed in the legislative arena is, according to the textbooks, well aware of the dangers of ruffling feathers, stepping on toes, and burning bridges. Male and female legislators, according to this study, are equally likely to recognize and pay homage to these imperatives.

Additional evidence that legislative norms were at work is revealed when the Arizona legislators' attitudes about hardball politics are compared to those of the California legislators (see Table 7.3). The California delegation was less likely to participate willingly in hardball politics and more likely to refuse to engage in such behavior altogether. This pattern confirms Nelson Polsby's assertion that behavioral norms are more powerful in more "institutionalized" legislative bodies (Polsby 1968). Clearly, the more professional California state legislature—with its relatively low turnover rates, competitive open-seat elections, ominous responsibilities, impressive productivity, and elaborate staff support—was more institutionalized than was the Arizona "citizens" legislature (Squire 1992).

When public officials are interviewed by inquisitive political scientists, they no doubt will try to present themselves in the best possible light—in the light of widely held expectations for proper behavior. All one can gather from talking to politicians is what they *say* they do or would do, not what they actually do. The cynic would point out that politicians may very well say one thing and do another. If one were to observe closely the actual behavior of these legislators, one may very well find a much less pleasant, less collegial, less cooperative, and less respectful scenario. Nonetheless, this study of legislators' claims about themselves is quite revealing and informative, regardless of the behavioral manifestations of such claims (or lack thereof). Talking to lawmakers about their legislative strategies, sources of personal power, and attitudes toward hardball politics provides rich information about institutional norms, information that addresses the very questions with which this chapter began.

What are these norms? They are the same modes of leadership and power most often associated with women, not men. How powerful are these norms? So powerful that they were readily endorsed by the vast majority of both female and male politicians, but not so powerful that they were never violated. And not so powerful that they never took a backseat to other, competing norms. This study did attempt to lead legislators outside the comforting, protective cover of normative politics and into the harsher realities of hardball politics. When push came to shove, were the men more willing than the women to push and shove? Apparently not. In neither state delegation did the female legislators appear any less willing than their male colleagues to enter the fray. The power of these institutional norms *was* conditional. Some legislators apparently were more willing than others to ignore the norms of collegiality, or at least to put them aside temporarily. Their willingness, however, had more to do with the nature of the institution than with the sex of its members.

# PART IV

# Conclusions, Explanations, and Implications

## CHAPTER EIGHT

# When Women Do Not Make a Difference

The banner headline of this study is not "Women Legislators Make a Difference!" Many who look to female public officials to effect certain changes as women, for women, may, in fact, be disappointed with the findings presented here (see Table 8.1). The women of the 1990 Arizona and California state legislatures did not pay more attention to their constituents than did their male colleagues; nor did they try to adhere more steadfastly to their constituents' wishes. Their policy preferences, even on gender gap and women's rights issues, were not much different from those of their male counterparts. And their legislative styles in no way deviated from the well-honed path laid by their male contemporaries and predecessors.

This is not to say that these female legislators *never* distinguished themselves from their male colleagues. On the contrary, there were several instances in which women and their political interests seemed better served by female representatives than by male representatives. Compared to their male colleagues, female officials of both states, but especially those of California, perceived stronger support from their female constituents and were more likely to identify themselves as representatives of women or women's issues. Many of these women agreed that, as women, they tended to be better able or at least more willing to represent women's policy concerns. Their policy priorities confirmed these perceptions, to some degree. Arizona female lawmakers were more actively involved in a variety of traditional and feminist women's issues than were their male counterparts. While sex differences in policy activity were not so striking among the California legislators, the women were noticeably more active in a more narrowly defined set of women's issues: those dealing with women per se and those congruent with mainstream feminist agendas.

**Table 8.1  Summary of Sex Differences in Legislative Behavior**

| | | Confirmation by Data [b] | |
|---|---|---|---|
| Dimensions of Legislative Behavior | Expectations [a] | Arizona | California |
| **I. Constituent responsiveness** | W > M | | |
| A. Time spent working on constituent casework and meeting with constituents | | | |
| B. Importance of helping people in the district who have personal problems with government | | | |
| C. Importance of making sure the district gets its fair share of government funds and projects | | | |
| D. Importance of keeping in touch with constituents about what the government is doing | | | |
| E. Frequency of consulting constituents when preparing and gathering support for legislation | | ✓ | |
| F. Adoption of delegate rather than trustee role | | | |
| **II. Legislative activities** | W < M | | |
| A. Time spent working on legislation | | | |
| B. Time spent meeting with lobbyists | | | |
| C. Importance of working on legislation | | | |
| D. Number of bills introduced | | | |
| **III. Ties to female constituents** | W > M | | |
| A. Electoral support from female constituents | | ✓ | ✓+ |
| B. Recognition of "women's issues" | | | |
| C. Relatively willing and able to represent "women's issues" | | ✓ | ✓+ |
| D. Identifies oneself as a representative of women, women's issues, or women's groups | | ✓ | ✓+ |
| **IV. Liberal/pro-women policy preferences** | W > M | | |
| A. Survey responses | | | |
|     1. All issues | | | |
|     2. Gender gap issues | | | |
|     3. Women's (feminist) issues | | | |
| B. Roll call votes | | | |
|     1. All issues | | | ✓– (Sen Reps only) |
|     2. Gender gap issues | | ✓– (House only; weak) | ✓– (Sen Reps only) |
|     3. Women's (feminist) issues | | ✓– (excl. House Dems; weak) | |

**Table 8.1** (*continued*)

| Dimensions of Legislative Behavior | Expec-tations[a] | Confirmation by Data[b] | |
| --- | --- | --- | --- |
| | | Arizona | California |
| **V. Policy priorities/leadership** | | | |
| A. "Women's issues" | W > M | | |
|    1. Women | | ✓ | ✓ |
|    2. Children and families | | ✓ | ✓– (weak) |
|    3. Education | | ✓ | ✓– (weak) |
|    4. Health and public safety | | ✓– (Dems only) | ✓– (weak) |
|    5. Poverty | | ✓– (weak) | ✓– (weak) |
|    6. Environment | | | |
| B. Feminist issues | W > M | ✓ | ✓ |
| C. "Men's issues" | W < M | | |
|    1. Commerce | | ✓ | ✓– (Reps only) |
|    2. Fiscal | | ✓ | |
|    3. Agriculture | | ✓ | |
| **VI. "Power to" legislative style** | W > M | | |
| A. Strategies for success | | | |
| B. Conception of (personal) power | | | |
| C. Attitudes toward hardball politics | | | |

[a] Female legislators were expected to exhibit the attitudes and behaviors listed either more than (W > M) or less than (W < M) their male colleagues.

[b] Key to entries:

  ✓ means the expectation was confirmed.

  ✓+ means the expectation was confirmed and that the sex differences were particularly strong (in California relative to Arizona).

  ✓– means that the expectation was only partially or weakly confirmed; sex differences were weak and/or limited to only a subgroup of legislators in the state.

A blank cell means the expectation was not confirmed.

These instances of sex differences are extremely important and should not be discounted. But they make the many similarities between these same female and male lawmakers quite puzzling. The similarities should not be discounted any more than the differences should. Especially in light of the many differences reported in other recent studies of sex, gender, and political behavior, the similarities discovered here warrant explanation.

In evaluating various explanations for the sex similarities that arose in this study, I turn to two recurring themes that ran through many of the preceding chapters: the interaction of sex, gender, and institutional forces; and the nature, or definition, of women's political representation. These thematic lenses shed light on why the women in this study "made a differ-ence" in some instances but not in others. They also give reason to believe that *not* "making a difference" does not necessarily translate into a failure to "act for" women. The similarities between female and male legislators, in other words, are not necessarily indicative of women's *lack* of substantive political representation.

### Explanation 1: Selecting Out

In many instances, we expect women and men in public office to think and behave differently because we assume they have been socialized in gender-specific ways, that they adhere to gender-related norms, and that they pos-sess certain gender-differentiated experiences. Ruth Mandel and Debra Dodson of the Center for the American Woman and Politics, for example, argue: "Understanding that women come to public office with life experi-ences very different from those of their male colleagues is key to under-standing why the priorities and attitudes of women in public office often differ from those of men" (1992: 154). Conversely, if the priorities and atti-tudes of women in public office do *not* differ from those of men—as was often the case among the Arizona and California legislators in this study—perhaps the reason is that their life experiences do not differ either.

As Kent Jennings and Norman Thomas cautioned three decades ago, the political selection process may see to it that women who exemplify tradi-tionally feminine characteristics and common female experiences do not get very far.

> [W]e are, indeed, dealing with a relatively rarefied political group. The general norms operative in society do not necessarily hold there. Consider first the tremendous amount of self-selection which takes place in becoming a politico. Since conventionally politics has been deemed more appropriate for men than women, the self-selection fac-tors are probably especially crucial for women. High motivation and deviance from conventional norms would seem to characterize these members of the fairer sex. Consider also the anticipatory and post-entry socialization of elites. Such processes may well produce a homo-geneous band of individuals, or at least one where sex-typing is a minor concern. (Jennings and Thomas 1968: 474–75)

Recruitment to public office is, even at the state legislative level, a highly selective process which may somehow weed out the women who do not fit the typical—male—profile of an elected official (Kirkpatrick 1974: 141). Women who conform to feminine gender norms, who work in female-dominated professions, who fulfill traditional nurturing roles, or who promote feminist agendas—in effect, the very women believed most likely to "act for" women may never have the opportunity to do so. They may be discouraged from running for public office altogether. If such women do run, they may very well find (or believe) it necessary to discard or at least cover up such women-centered goals and proclivities in order to avoid being defeated at the polls (Carroll 1984, 1994; Perkins and Fowlkes 1980; Witt, Paget, and Matthews 1994).

In this scenario, the precious few women who manage to enter the "man's world" of legislative politics are, for whatever reason, no different from the men who already inhabit it. Being female is of little or no consequence to them, at least when it comes to their legislative and representational duties and activities. Such women, we would assume, have little or no desire to "act for" women in particular. Such a scenario, moreover, would be more likely to occur in a state like California, where the selection process is extremely competitive and the political elite so male-dominated, than in a state like Arizona, whose "citizens'" legislature has historically been more open to men and women alike.

A quick comparison of the social and political status of the men and women of the 1990 Arizona and California legislatures lends some credence to this scenario. As revealed in Chapter 2, these women were somewhat unusual for their generation. They were just as highly educated and they had just as much experience in the business world and in public office as did their male colleagues. Plus, there is some indication that the California women were even more like their male colleagues than the Arizona women were. While many of the Arizona female politicians had experience in female-dominated occupations—and several identified themselves as homemakers—considerably fewer of their California counterparts possessed such gender-differentiated backgrounds. None of the California female lawmakers identified herself as a homemaker.

On the other hand, the idea that the women who "made it" into these two state legislatures, especially those who made it into the California legislature, attributed no significance to their being female and had no desire to "act for" or even *as* women is belied by the findings presented in Chapter 4. Many of these women believed that they and their female colleagues, as women, did have something to offer women. They relied on women as their most supportive constituency group. They felt that, as women, they were either uniquely qualified or at least extra-motivated to represent women's political concerns. Quite a few identified themselves as representatives of women, women's groups, or women's issues. And in each case, it was the California women, not the Arizona women, who were more apt to do so.[1]

### Explanation 2: Institutional Constraints

If we accept the notion that many members of this "rarefied" group of women who obtained elective office did manage to hang on to their connections to women, then we must look elsewhere for explanations for the frequent lack of differentiation between their behavior and that of their male colleagues. If the problem is not the women themselves, then it must lie in outside forces, forces beyond the women's immediate control. Denise Antolini (1984: 34) comes to a similar conclusion in her review of the extant research on women in local office: "Though local female politicians seem to exhibit gender-distinctive political attitudes, it is crucial to inquire about the institutional forces that operate for and against women's ability to implement these political goals before reaching any conclusions about women's impact on policy." Likewise, historian Jane Sherron De Hart (1995: 241–42) warns, "Individual consciousness is inevitably transmuted as elected officials interact with institutional circumstances and oppositional forces. . . . [F]emale officeholders will continue to have to answer to the same constituencies that men do if they want to stay in power."

Those constituencies, moreover, are made up of equal proportions men and women. This is, indeed, the most basic of institutional constraints. The electoral system, based on geographically drawn districts, is simply not set up to facilitate the representation of women, or men, in particular. All elected officials are accountable to men and women alike, in roughly equal proportions. Yet, again, the sex differences in legislators' ties to their female constituents, revealed in Chapter 4, suggest that this institutional constraint is rather weak. Raw numbers do not tell the entire story. Elected officials do not simply count their constituents; they make very important distinctions between those they consider more or less supportive. In this more subjective assessment of constituencies, female lawmakers in Arizona and California were more likely than their male counterparts to give women more weight.

Nonetheless, there are other institutional constraints to consider. "The behavior patterns exhibited by women in local politics," Antolini (1984: 34) suggests, "may be 'unnaturally' suppressed by three interrelated institutional pressures—realpolitik, tokenism, and institutional sexism." Realpolitik is the realization that there are multiple, competing demands placed on public officials. "Female officeholders," Antolini explains, "do not operate in a vacuum, and they cannot focus on their particular interests to the exclusion of the demands of a wide variety of pressing issues any more than can men" (1984: 34). Other, more recent studies of local officials have drawn similar conclusions, each suggesting that electoral and/or institutional structures, norms, demands, and constraints offer women little maneuvering room in which they can "make a difference" (Beck 1991; Fox and Schuhmann 1996).

Such pressures may be greater at the local level, but state legislatures certainly have their share of constraints. Paying more attention to constituents may be difficult when legislative work is more highly valued than constituency work, as I argued in Chapter 3. Political parties and the necessity of majority coalitions certainly influence legislators' roll call votes, as was illustrated in Chapter 5. Very strong norms govern the legislative process and the interpersonal relations within it, according to Chapter 7.

Yet, as Antolini and others suggest, there is more to it than that. Realpolitik presumably constrains men's behavior just as much as women's. Other institutional forces, namely "tokenism and institutional sexism," are not so gender-neutral. Women in public office, according to this more foreboding argument, are like strangers in a strange (yet familiar) land; they are women in "a man's world." They are outsiders, intruders, anomalies in an androcentric world created and organized by men for men (Duerst-Lahti and Kelly 1995a; N. Norton 1994). In this world, there is a price to pay for making a difference for women. The fewer the women and the more androcentric the institution, one can assume, the higher the price (Kanter 1977).

Sue Thomas's interviews with female state legislators, for instance, reveal "that women officeholders feel their status as collective outsiders to the political world . . . sets them apart from the norm in a negative fashion" (Thomas 1997: 31). As a result, there is an assumed risk involved in any gender-differentiated behavior, and that risk is even further marginalization. "In other words," Thomas explains, "rather than being perceived in either a positive or neutral way, these differences are often interpreted as being problematic or as tendencies to be overcome" (31). Women in one southern state, she notes, were particularly fearful of "doing anything 'radical' [read: feminist] . . . and much was made of a couple of legislators who pushed a women's agenda and were sanctioned" (36). But even those female legislators in other, less androcentric states who actively pursued a feminist agenda recognized the consequences for doing so: "all else being equal, being considered marginal at best and disruptive to the central agenda at worst" (38).

Other researchers have documented similar fears among female politicians outside the United States. Hege Skjeie reports that female members of the Norwegian Parliament "from several parties told about the heavy costs they perceived as attached to involvement in women-specific activities." Said one Labor party delegate:

There is still a bias in the distribution of power. It is men who distribute the various positions. This is a closed system. You need to be strong indeed to push women's policies. Those who do see that it doesn't pay off. Then they stop. You do not get real influence, or important positions. You're placed in a corner. (Skjeie 1991: 249)

Australian female parliamentarians interviewed by Rosemary Whip (1991) also were quite wary of being marginalized. "Although many of the women in this study were concerned about women and recognized the need for someone to take up their interests, they were very conscious of the fact that concentration on women's interests might lead to their being perceived as single issue members and might consequently be detrimental to their political careers" (Whip 1991: 14–15). "I do care about women," said one parliamentarian, "but I also care about my career and I suspect that allowing myself to get boxed into the sort of easy label, 'female parliamentarian-women's issues' is not where I want to be" (16).

This more sinister portrayal of institutional forces suggests the following:

1. Institutional norms, priorities, and standard operating procedures are not gender-neutral; they discourage or simply prevent any activity associated with women and women's political interests.
2. As a result, very few politicians will engage in behavior commonly associated with women or thought to be representative of women.
3. The ones who resist and do "act for" or as women will be punished. They will be denied the perquisites of institutional prestige and power such as party leadership positions, committee chairs, and choice committee assignments. Stripped of such institutional leverage and shunned by colleagues, they also will be less effective in getting their own legislation passed.

If true, these propositions would go a long way toward explaining why the women and men of the Arizona and California legislatures so often behaved so similarly—despite the fact that the women felt stronger ties to their female constituents than the men did. Gendered institutional forces may also explain why sex differences in legislative behavior (e.g., policy activity) were even rarer in the California legislature. Institutional norms should have been even more androcentric in California, given the long absence of women from positions of political power and the only recently diminished masculine political culture of the state. Punishment for nonconformity to such norms should have been even harsher in California where there was no woman, such as Jane Hull, Speaker of the Arizona House, who had control over the disbursement of institutional rewards and sanctions.

But there is little evidence that things actually worked that way. Some of the most powerful institutional norms observed in this study were those governing the legislative process and the legislative styles of individual participants (Chapter 7). While these norms were fashioned by men, they were decidedly *not* masculine in nature. The emphasis legislators placed on compromise and consensus building, mutually beneficial and personable relationships, honesty and integrity sounded much more like feminine-style leadership models than a masculine "command-and-control" approach. These norms were widely recognized and endorsed—by male and female lawmakers alike. While many legislators admitted to occasional violations of such norms, and some even advocated the practice of hardball politics, such behavior was almost always viewed as exceptional. Thus, rather than discouraging behavior associated with women, these norms promoted it.

The institutions of partisan and ideological factions operated in a similar fashion (Chapter 5). Instead of thwarting any attempts at "making a difference" for women, they organized and mobilized coalitions (oftentimes majority coalitions) in support of women's presumed interests in gender gap and women's rights legislation. Most of the liberal gender gap and women's rights bills examined in Chapter 5's analysis of roll call voting passed, thanks in large part to the Democratic party in California and to the coalition of moderate Republicans and Democrats in Arizona. Moreover, the influence of such coalitions is one of the most likely explanations for why male legislators in both states tended to be just as supportive of such legislation as their female colleagues were.

In both these cases of institutional force, the "problem" standing in the way of sex differences in legislative behavior was not that too few women were brave enough to resist institutional forces to "make a difference." The "problem," such as it were, was that institutional forces provided large percentages of *both* women and men incentives to engage in activities or behaviors associated with women. Women's presumed interests, therefore, did not go unattended.

This same argument, however, does not provide an adequate explanation for the lack of sex differences in constituent responsiveness (Chapter 3). Here the institutional norms and demands were such that "making a difference" by paying more attention to constituents *was* discouraged. As I argued in Chapter 3, institutional prestige and power were associated with legislative acumen and independent decision-making, not with constituency service or responsiveness. Too much attention to constituents, some have suggested, reduces the amount of respect legislators receive from their colleagues (Hibbing and Thomas 1990). Thus, while most of the officials in this study believed that constituent service was an extremely important aspect of their role as representatives, they did not devote large percentages of their time to such activities. Far fewer legislators rated other constituent-related activities as extremely important. Nor did many of them regularly consult their constituents on legislative matters. Finally, very few legislators assumed a delegate role, that is, being willing to sublimate their own preferences to those of their constituents. The possibility remains, therefore, that institutional pressures did discourage legislators from engaging in this type of behavior and thus suppressed any attempts of women to "make a difference" in this realm of representation.

The third proposition outlined above suggests that resistance to such institutional pressure or violation of such institutional norms should result in systematic loss of institutional prestige and power. The data presented in Table 8.2 test this proposition, not only with respect to constituent responsiveness but also with regard to all the other activities associated with the substantive representation of women (as outlined in previous chapters). For this analysis, institutional status is measured in three ways: (1) a formal position of leadership, either as a party leader or as a committee chair; (2) appointment to the most prestigious and powerful committees — those dealing with state budget and taxes, as well as the Rules Committees, with their gatekeeping role; and (3) legislative effectiveness, defined here as the percentage of bills a legislator introduces that manage to pass the originating house (D. R. Matthews 1960).[2]

That the distribution of such rewards and accomplishments is profoundly affected by party membership is taken as a given. Party leaders in both states were elected by party members. In turn, party leaders (sometimes in cooperation with the Rules Committee) appointed committee chairs. In both states, committee chairs almost invariably went to members of the majority party. Members of the majority party, according to previous research, are almost always more capable of getting their bills passed than are members of the minority party, for obvious reasons (Box-Steffensmeier and Sinclair 1996; Ellickson 1992; Frantzich 1979; Moore and Thomas 1991; see also Meyer 1980; but see Hamm, Harmel, and Thompson 1983).[3] For all these reasons, Table 8.2 examines the relationship between institutional status and behavior deemed representative of women for each party separately.

The first thing apparent from the figures in Table 8.2 is that attitudes and activities thought to be representative of women are rarely associated with any significant, systematic loss of institutional status. Of the twenty-two different attitudes and activities listed in Table 8.2 and among the four party caucuses—thus, out of eighty-eight possibilities—there are only eighteen instances in which representing women (as defined) resulted in a significant loss of one or more types of status. There are as many instances (nineteen) in which representing women was associated with significant *gains* in power, prestige, or effectiveness. A few attitudes and activities carried,

**Table 8.2  Institutional Status of Legislators Who "Act for" Women**

| | Arizona Legislators | | California Legislators | |
| | Majority Party (R) | Minority Party (D) | Majority Party (D) | Minority Party (R) |
|---|---|---|---|---|
| Total sample | (N = 28) | (N = 22) | (N = 19) | (N = 12) |
| % leadership position | 57 | 14 | 58 | 25 |
| % prestige committee | 50 | 50 | 47 | 50 |
| % bills passed | 46 | 39 | 75 | 61 |
| **Subgroup (by attitude or behavior)** | Deviation from Total Sample Average[a] | | | |

**Constituent Responsiveness**

| | | | | |
|---|---|---|---|---|
| Helping people in district, extremely important[b] | (N = 16) | (N = 8) | (N = 10) | (N = 9) |
| % leadership position | −3 | +5 | −6 | 0 |
| % prestige committee | −7 | +19* | −3 | 0 |
| % bills passed | 0 | −1 | −1 | 0 |
| Ensuring district's fair share, extremely important[b] | (N = 5) | (N = 4) | (N = 6) | (N = 6) |
| % leadership position | −12 | −7 | +10 | +11 |
| % prestige committee | −23 | +5 | +6 | +5 |
| % bills passed | +5 | +2 | −2 | −2 |
| Keeping in touch with district, extremely important[b] | (N = 5) | (N = 5) | (N = 3) | (N = 5) |
| % leadership position | −13 | −7 | −55* | −2 |
| % prestige committee | −43* | +4 | −36 | +15 |
| % bills passed | +5 | +4 | −5 | +6 |
| Consult constituents, great deal or fair amount[b] | (N = 9) | (N = 2) | (N = 7) | (N = 5) |
| % leadership position | −8 | −7 | −14 | −22 |
| % prestige committee | −8 | −15 | +1 | −4 |
| % bills passed | −4 | +2 | −3 | −6* |
| Time devoted to constituency, greater than 20%[b] | (N = 9) | (N = 6) | (N = 5) | (N = 5) |
| % leadership position | −20 | +10 | −10 | −2 |
| % prestige committee | +4 | +17 | −7 | −4 |
| % bills passed | +2 | +6 | −3 | +1 |
| Delegate role | (N = 8) | (N = 5) | (N = 3) | (N = 3) |
| % leadership position | −7 | −14* | +9 | −25* |
| % prestige committee | −13 | +10 | −14 | +50* |
| % bills passed | +1 | +13* | −10 | +10 |

**Ties to Female Constituents**

| | | | | |
|---|---|---|---|---|
| Support from women, strong[b] | (N = 7) | (N = 5) | (N = 6) | (N = 1)[c] |
| % leadership position | −14 | −7 | +29* | no |
| % prestige committee | −35* | +31* | +7 | no |
| % bills passed | +2 | +5 | +1 | −15 |

Table 8.2 (*continued*)

| Subgroup | Arizona Legislators | | California Legislators | |
|---|---|---|---|---|
| | Majority Party (R) | Minority Party (D) | Majority Party (D) | Minority Party (R) |
| Believes women have particular policy concerns | (N = 10) | (N = 19) | (N = 18) | (N = 8) |
| % leadership position | −10 | −5 | −2 | +12* |
| % prestige committee | −5 | +2 | −3 | −25* |
| % bills passed | −2 | +1 | +1 | −4 |
| Relatively willing and able to represent women's concerns | (N = 6) | (N = 9) | (N = 14) | (N = 8) |
| % leadership position | −10 | +1 | +6 | −8 |
| % prestige committee | −28* | +22 | −4 | −17 |
| % bills passed | −2 | +6 | 0 | −3 |
| Self-identified representative of women | (N = 3) | (N = 5) | (N = 7) | (N = 1)[c] |
| % leadership position | −24 | −14* | +28* | yes |
| % prestige committee | −17 | −30 | −18 | yes |
| % bills passed | −8 | −8 | +4 | +17 |
| **Policy Preferences** | | | | |
| Liberal votes on gender gap bills, above party average[d] | (N = 19) | (N = 15) | (N = 25) | (N = 17) |
| % leadership position | +13 | +5 | +3 | −3 |
| % prestige committee | +11 | +8 | −10* | +29* |
| | (N = 10) | (N = 9) | (N = 6) | (N = 3) |
| % bills passed | +2 | −3 | +6 | +8 |
| Liberal votes on women's rights bills, above party average[d] | (N = 20) | (N = 14) | (N = 62) | (N = 15) |
| % leadership position | +4 | +14 | +3 | +6 |
| % prestige committee | +2 | +20* | −2 | +27* |
| | (N = 13) | (N = 7) | (N = 16) | (N = 5) |
| % bills passed | +3 | 0 | +1 | −4 |
| **Policy Priorities** | | | | |
| Women issues, active | (N = 16) | (N = 8) | (N = 10) | (N = 5) |
| % leadership position | −7 | +11 | +2 | +15 |
| % prestige committee | −19* | −13 | +13 | −30* |
| % bills passed | −3 | −7 | 0 | −8* |
| Women issues, leader | (N = 1)[c] | (N = 1)[c] | (N = 3) | N = 1)[c] |
| % leadership position | no | no | +9 | yes |
| % prestige committee | no | yes | +20 | yes |
| % bills passed | −4 | +15 | +9 | +17 |
| Children and family issues, active | (N = 15) | (N = 12) | (N = 11) | (N = 7) |
| % leadership position | −4 | −6 | −13 | +18* |
| % prestige committee | −10 | 0 | +17* | +7 |
| % bills passed | −7* | +3 | −3 | +1 |

Table 8.2 (*continued*)

| | Arizona Legislators | | California Legislators | |
| --- | --- | --- | --- | --- |
| Subgroup | Majority Party (R) | Minority Party (D) | Majority Party (D) | Minority Party (R) |
| Children and family issues, leader | (*N* = 4) | (*N* = 4) | (*N* = 5) | (*N* = 2) |
| % leadership position | −57* | +11 | +2 | −25 |
| % prestige committee | −50* | −25 | +33* | +50 |
| % bills passed | −9 | −2 | −1 | +7 |
| Education issues, active | (*N* = 15) | (*N* = 18) | (*N* = 11) | (*N* = 8) |
| % leadership position | −24* | −3 | −3 | 0 |
| % prestige committee | +10 | −6 | −2 | +12 |
| % bills passed | +2 | +2 | −2 | +5* |
| Education issues, leader | (*N* = 3) | (*N* = 10) | (*N* = 7) | (*N* = 2) |
| % leadership position | −24 | −4 | −1 | +25 |
| % prestige committee | +17 | −10 | −18 | 0 |
| % bills passed | −8 | +3 | −2 | +11 |
| Health issues, active | (*N* = 18) | (*N* = 13) | (*N* = 9) | (*N* = 10) |
| % leadership position | −1 | +9* | +9 | −5 |
| % prestige committee | +6 | −4 | −3 | +10 |
| % bills passed | +3 | −2 | −3 | +3 |
| Health issues, leader | (*N* = 7) | (*N* = 6) | (*N* = 5) | (*N* = 5) |
| % leadership position | −14 | +3 | +42* | −25* |
| % prestige committee | +7 | −17 | −7 | +10 |
| % bills passed | +8* | −2 | +4 | 0 |
| Poverty issues, active | (*N* = 14) | (*N* = 16) | (*N* = 9) | (*N* = 6) |
| % leadership position | +14 | −2 | −2 | −8 |
| % prestige committee | −7 | +12* | +9 | 0 |
| % bills passed | −1 | 0 | −3 | −4 |
| Poverty issues, leader | (*N* = 1)[c] | (*N* = 3) | (*N* = 3) | (*N* = 0) |
| % leadership position | yes | +19 | +9 | — |
| % prestige committee | no | +17 | +20 | — |
| % bills passed | −8 | −4 | −2 | — |
| Environmental issues, active | (*N* = 14) | (*N* = 13) | (*N* = 11) | (*N* = 8) |
| % leadership position | +7 | +1 | −3 | −13 |
| % prestige committee | 0 | +11 | −11 | +12 |
| % bills passed | +2 | +5 | +5* | +3 |
| Environmental issues, leader | (*N* = 5) | (*N* = 5) | (*N* = 5) | (*N* = 3) |
| % leadership position | +3 | −14* | +2 | −25* |
| % prestige committee | −10 | −10 | −7 | −17 |
| % bills passed | −2 | +7 | +12* | +2 |
| Feminist policy activist | (*N* = 8) | (*N* = 14) | (*N* = 14) | (*N* = 1)[c] |
| % leadership position | +5 | 0 | −1 | yes |
| % prestige committee | 0 | −7 | +10 | yes |
| % bills passed | +5 | −1 | −2 | +17 |

**Table 8.2** (*continued*)

| Subgroup | Arizona Legislators | | California Legislators | |
|---|---|---|---|---|
| | Majority Party (R) | Minority Party (D) | Majority Party (D) | Minority Party (R) |
| **Legislative Styles** | | | | |
| "Power to" legislative strategies, strong emphasis (≥70%) | (N = 7) | (N = 6) | (N = 6) | (N = 3) |
|   % leadership position | 0 | +36* | −8 | +8 |
|   % prestige committee | +7 | −17 | −14 | +17 |
|   % bills passed | +3 | +2 | −3 | +7 |
| "Power to" sources of personal power (≥70%) | (N = 13) | (N = 8) | (N = 4) | (N = 3) |
|   % leadership position | +4 | +11 | −8 | +8 |
|   % prestige committee | −12 | +12 | +28 | +17 |
|   % bills passed | +1 | −3 | +9 | +6 |
| Refuses to engage in at least one type of hardball politics | (N = 14) | (N = 10) | (N = 12) | (N = 7) |
|   % leadership position | +7 | +7 | −8 | −11 |
|   % prestige committee | +7 | −10 | −5 | +7 |
|   % bills passed | +1 | −7* | +1 | +3 |
| Refuses to engage in any type of hardball politics | (N = 10) | (N = 5) | (N = 7) | (N = 5) |
|   % leadership position | +13 | +6 | −15 | −5 |
|   % prestige committee | +10 | +10 | −4 | +10 |
|   % bills passed | +4 | −1 | −3 | +2 |

[a] Entries in this section of the table are the percentage-point deviations from the state party averages shown in the first three rows of the table. For example, Arizona Republicans (majority party) who believed helping people in the district was extremely important held 3 percent fewer leadership positions than did Arizona Republicans as a whole.

[b] The state party averages calculated for these items are based on the subsample of legislators who completed follow-up written questionnaires.

[c] "Yes" and "no" indicate whether this single legislator held a leadership position or a prestige committee assignment.

[d] "Above party average" is (roughly) the top 40 percent.

* Deviation is statistically significant ($p \leq .05$).

within one party or another, simultaneous losses in one status marker and gains in another.

In almost no case was there a consistent pattern of status loss or gain. Rarely was a single attitude or activity associated with significant losses (or even a pattern of near-significant losses) in all three status markers, even within a given party. No single dimension of behavior—paying attention to constituents, paying attention to female constituents, roll call voting, policy leadership, or legislative style—was associated with a preponderance of below-average status. In both states, Republicans who "acted for" women were more likely than Democrats who did the same to possess significantly below-average status on one or more indicator; but even among the Republicans, there are only six out of twenty-two instances of such low status.

Further analysis (not shown in Table 8.2) uncovers no evidence to suggest that female legislators who "acted for" or as women were punished any more than male legislators who did the same—except in the case of Arizona Republicans. Arizona Republican women witnessed significant loss in one or more types of status (with no countervailing gain in status) in eight instances: when they believed that ensuring the district's "fair share" was extremely important; when they assumed a delegate role; when they became a leader on children and family issues, health issues, or environmental issues; when they became feminist policy activists; when they placed strong emphasis on "power to" legislative strategies; and when they refused to engage in any type of hardball politics. Arizona Republican men experienced comparable losses in only three instances: when they believed that helping constituents was extremely important; when they became active in children and family issues; and when they placed strong emphasis on "power to" sources of personal power.

It is doubtful, however, that these eight instances of significant status loss constituted any systematic form of punishment or were enough to deter women from engaging in behavior that was (or might have been) feminized. The idea that it was only Arizona Republican women who were so punished runs contrary to what one would expect, given the assumptions of how institutional sexism works (outlined above). Of all the women in this study, the Arizona Republicans should have been the *least* likely either to have received such punishment or to have been deterred by such punishment. Given the high percentage of women in the Arizona legislature, and in Arizona politics more generally, one would expect institutional norms to have been less gender-biased in Arizona than in California. Punishment for violating such norms, therefore, should have been less frequent in Arizona, especially among the Republicans, whose top leader was female.

Furthermore, there is no discernible pattern to the status losses incurred by the Arizona Republican women. Some aspects of constituent responsiveness, for example, were associated with lower status; others were not.[4] Leadership on some women's issues was related to lower status, while leadership on others (namely, education) was related to *higher* status. Leadership in children and family issues was associated with lower status, but this was one arena in which Arizona Republican women were most, not least, different from their male counterparts (see Table 6.2). Overall, then, there is little reason to believe that legislative behavior associated with women was systematically punished, even among the Arizona Republican women—or that Arizona Republican women were any more likely than others to be deterred by such sanctions.

In sum, the theory that tokenism and institutional sexism "unnaturally" suppressed women's behavior in public office finds little support here. Contrary to the three propositions suggested by this theory: (1) many institutional norms *en*couraged or simply *allowed* activity associated with women and women's political representation; (2) as a result, *many* legislators, male and female, engaged in such behavior; and (3) those who did were not systematically denied institutional power, prestige, or effectiveness.

### Explanation 3: The Meaning of Representing Women

The rejection of Explanation 1 and the institutional sexism version of Explanation 2 presents a puzzle that has been only partially resolved. Female politicians of both states were more likely than their male colleagues to be predisposed to the idea of representing women. They perceived stronger support from their female constituents; they believed that, in general, female lawmakers are better able or more willing to represent women's policy concerns—and they were more likely to believe that than the men were to refute it; and, perhaps most telling of all, they were much more likely to identify themselves as representatives of women, women's groups, or women's issues. Why, then, were these same female lawmakers only occasionally more likely than their male counterparts to actually do or advocate the very things that are believed to be representative of women?

The answer, according to my conducive norms version of Explanation 2, is that their male counterparts had other reasons, or incentives, to engage in the very same behavior. Institutional norms of professional courtesy, collegiality, and reciprocity encouraged male (and female) legislators to endorse legislative styles that embody various notions of "power to" approaches and to reject those that reflect "power over" approaches. Partisan and/or ideological beliefs often led just as many men as women to liberal positions on gender gap and women's rights issues.

While institutional incentives may explain a great deal, yet another explanation is worth considering. Thus far, for argument's sake, I have defined certain attitudes and activities as representative of women. On the basis of both popular expectations and previous research on women in public office, I have assumed that the substantive representation of women entails the following: increased responsiveness to constituents; stronger ties to female constituents in particular; liberal positions on gender gap and women's rights issues; policy activism in both traditionally defined and feminist-oriented women's issues; and, finally, more cooperative, egalitarian, and empowering legislative styles. The possibility remains, however, that the Arizona and California state legislators studied here did not share this particular definition of women's political representation, at least not in its entirety. Thus, while women in each state legislature may have been more predisposed to the *idea* of representing women, they may not have shared this particular definition—or any common definition—of what that idea means or entails. The idea of women's substantive political representation is, after all, a social construct much like the construct of gender. Its meaning, therefore, is not necessarily uniform across time and place, or individuals.

To explore this possibility, I return to the discovery in Chapter 3 that some legislators, when asked if they represented certain groups of people, identified themselves (in one way or another) as representatives of women. What did representing women mean to these legislators? Why did these legislators associate themselves with the representation of women, while others did not? What did they do or think that set them apart from the others? To what extent did they share the attitudes and engage in the activities I and others have designated as representative of women? To answer these questions, Table 8.3 provides a detailed behavioral profile of the legislators in each state who identified themselves as representatives of women. For each dimension of women's political representation, as defined in Chapters 3–7, the attitudes and activities of the self-identified representatives are compared to those of their colleagues. As a shorthand, I refer to the self-identified representatives of women as "identifiers" or, simply, "representatives."

To begin, there are two distinguishing characteristics of these self-designated representatives of women, which provide a baseline of comparison. First, the vast majority of them were female. Six of the eight Arizona representatives of women were women; eight of the nine California representatives were. Second, most—but not all—were Democrats. In the Republican-dominated Arizona delegation, five of the eight women's representatives were Democrats; in California, all but one of the nine were. Thus, while being female and Democratic was neither necessary nor sufficient for such self-identification, it certainly made it more likely. According to the many comparisons made in Table 8.3, however, there is not much beyond these two characteristics that truly distinguishes the self-designated representatives of women from other legislators.

In neither state were self-identified representatives of women any more responsive to constituents (in general) than were their colleagues. In fact, the California identifiers tended to be somewhat *less* responsive. They spent significantly less time on constituent activities, rated the various types of constituent activities listed in Table 8.3 slightly lower in importance, and consulted constituents less frequently than did other California legislators.

**Table 8.3  Behavioral Profile of Self-Identified Representatives of Women**

| Characteristic (attitude or behavior) | Arizona Legislators | | California Legislators | |
|---|---|---|---|---|
| | Self-ID Reps | All Others | Self-ID Reps | All Others |
| **Constituent Responsiveness**[a] | (N = 7) | (N = 26) | (N = 4) | (N = 15) |
| Percentage of time spent on constituent work | | | | |
|   0–10% | 14% | 15% | 50% | 27% |
|   11–20% | 71 | 33 | 50 | 6 |
|   21–30% | 0 | 41 | 0 | 48 |
|   > 30% | 14 | 11 | 0 | 19 |
|     Mean (%) | 18 | 21 | 10 | 22* |
| Helping people in district | | | | |
|   Extremely important (5) | 57% | 78% | 75% | 100% |
|   (4) | 14 | 18 | 0 | 0 |
|   (2–3) | 28 | 4 | 25 | 0 |
|     Mean (1–5) | 4.14 | 4.74 | 4.50 | 5.00 |
| Ensuring district's fair share | | | | |
|   Extremely important (5) | 29% | 27% | 50% | 61% |
|   (4) | 14 | 26 | 0 | 26 |
|   (3) | 29 | 29 | 50 | 13 |
|   (1–2) | 29 | 18 | 0 | 0 |
|     Mean (1–5) | 3.14 | 3.53 | 4.00 | 4.48 |
| Keeping in touch | | | | |
|   Extremely important (5) | 29% | 32% | 25% | 45% |
|   (4) | 43 | 45 | 50 | 55 |
|   (3) | 29 | 22 | 25 | 0 |
|     Mean (1–5) | 4.00 | 4.10 | 4.00 | 4.45 |
| Consult constituents | | | | |
|   Great deal or fair amount (4–5) | 57% | 31% | 25% | 67% |
|   Sometimes (3) | 43 | 51 | 50 | 26 |
|   Hardly ever (2) | 0 | 18 | 25 | 7 |
|     Mean (1–5) | 3.71 | 3.19 | 3.00 | 3.67 |
| Representational role | (N = 8) | (N = 42) | (N = 9) | (N = 22) |
|   Trustee | 50% | 45% | 78% | 59% |
|   Politico | 37 | 26 | 11 | 18 |
|   Delegate | 12 | 29 | 11 | 23 |

| | Arizona Legislators | | | California Legislators | | |
|---|---|---|---|---|---|---|
| | Self-ID Reps | All Others | Other Women | Self-ID Reps | All Others | Other Women |
| **Relationship to Female Constituents**[b] | | | | | | |
| Support from female constituents | (N = 7) | (N = 25) | (N = 7) | (N = 4) | (N = 14) | (N = 4) |
|   Strong (5) | 43% | 35% | 38% | 75% | 23% | 55% |
|   Moderate (4) | 57 | 54 | 51 | 25 | 55 | 45 |

**Table 8.3** (*continued*)

| Characteristic | Arizona Legislators | | | California Legislators | | |
|---|---|---|---|---|---|---|
| | Self-ID Reps | All Others | Other Women | Self-ID Reps | All Others | Other Women |
| Little or no (3) | 0 | 11 | 11 | 0 | 21 | 0 |
| Mean (1–5) | 4.43 | 4.23 | 4.27 | 4.75 | 4.02* | 4.55 |
| Identified issues of concern to women in particular | (N = 8) | (N = 32) | (N = 11) | (N = 9) | (N = 22) | (N = 6) |
| | 87% | 69% | 73% | 100% | 77%* | 67% |
| Female legislators "make a difference" on such issues (responses of women only) | (N = 6) | | (N = 10) | (N = 8) | | (N = 6) |
| Yes, effective | 67% | — | 40% | 100% | — | 67% |
| No | 17 | — | 10 | 0 | — | 0 |
| Ambivalent | 0 | — | 20 | 0 | — | 0 |
| No such issues | 17 | — | 30 | 0 | — | 33 |

| | Arizona Legislators | | | California Legislators | | |
|---|---|---|---|---|---|---|
| | Self-ID Reps | All Others | Other Demo-crats | Self-ID Reps | All Others | Other Demo-crats |
| **Policy Preferences** | | | | | | |
| Index of liberal opinion on gender gap and women's rights issues[c] | (N = 7) | (N = 25) | (N = 9) | (N = 4) | (N = 15) | (N = 7) |
| Mean score (10–40) | 36 | 30* | 33* | 35 | 30* | 33 |
| Liberal votes cast on gender gap issues[d] | (N = 8) | (N = 42) | (N = 17) | (N = 9) | (N = 22) | (N = 11) |
| Mean (%) | 78 | 55* | 80 | 93 | 52* | 87* |
| Feminist votes cast on women's rights issues | | | | | | |
| Mean (%) | 69 | 62 | 73 | 96 | 51* | 91* |

| | Arizona Legislators | | | California Legislators | | |
|---|---|---|---|---|---|---|
| | Self-ID Reps | All Others | Other Women | Self-ID Reps | All Others | Other Women |
| **Policy Priorities**[e] | (N = 8) | (N = 42) | (N = 12) | (N = 9) | (N = 22) | (N = 6) |
| Women | | | | | | |
| % active | 62 | 45 | 83 | 67 | 41 | 50 |
| % leader | 12 | 2 | 8 | 33 | 4 | 17 |
| Mean index score (0–2.5) | 1.00 | .73 | 1.21 | 1.22 | .59* | .83 |

Table 8.3 (*continued*)

| Characteristic | Arizona Legislators | | | California Legislators | | |
|---|---|---|---|---|---|---|
| | Self-ID Reps | All Others | Other Women | Self-ID Reps | All Others | Other Women |
| Children and Families | | | | | | |
| % active | 62 | 52 | 75 | 67 | 55 | 50 |
| % leader | 25 | 14 | 42 | 33 | 18 | 33 |
| Mean index score (0–2.5) | 1.12 | .93 | 1.50 | 1.17 | .84 | 1.00 |
| Education | | | | | | |
| % active | 75 | 64 | 75 | 56 | 64 | 67 |
| % leader | 37 | 24 | 58 | 44 | 23 | 17 |
| Mean index score (0–2.5) | 1.25 | 1.01 | 1.58 | 1.22 | .93 | .92 |
| Health and Public Safety | | | | | | |
| % active | 62 | 62 | 67 | 56 | 64 | 67 |
| % leader | 50 | 21* | 25 | 44 | 27 | 33 |
| Mean index score (0–2.5) | 1.31 | 1.05 | 1.25 | 1.22 | 1.07 | 1.17 |
| Poverty | | | | | | |
| % active | 87 | 55* | 58 | 67 | 41 | 33 |
| % leader | 0 | 9* | 25* | 22 | 5 | 0 |
| Mean index score (0–2.5) | 1.00 | .79 | 1.08 | 1.11 | .55* | .42 |
| Environment | | | | | | |
| % active | 62 | 52 | 42 | 56 | 64 | 83 |
| % leader | 62 | 12* | 8* | 33 | 23 | 33 |
| Mean index score (0–2.5) | 1.56 | .90 | .71* | 1.17 | 1.09 | 1.42 |
| Feminist | | | | | | |
| % active | 75 | 38* | 67 | 89 | 32* | 33* |

| | Arizona Legislators | | California Legislators | |
|---|---|---|---|---|
| | Self-ID Reps | All Others | Self-ID Reps | All Others |
| **Legislative Style** | | | | |
| Strategies recommended*f* | (*N* = 8) | (*N* = 42) | (*N* = 9) | (*N* = 22) |
| No "power over" | 75% | 69% | 89% | 64% |
| Mean % "power over" | 5 | 11 | 4 | 7 |
| Mean # "power to" | 2.12 | 2.26 | 2.56 | 2.18 |
| Mean % "power to" | 59 | 57 | 65 | 59 |
| Sources of personal power*g* | (*N* = 8) | (*N* = 40) | (*N* = 9) | (*N* = 22) |
| No "power over" | 50% | 75% | 89% | 50%* |
| Mean % "power over" | 20 | 12 | 7 | 18 |
| Mean # "power to" | 1.62 | 1.50 | 1.56 | 1.27 |
| Mean % "power to" | 40 | 68* | 63 | 47 |
| Most negative attitude toward hardball politics*h* | (*N* = 7) | (*N* = 40) | (*N* = 8) | (*N* = 19) |
| No problem (1) | 14% | 32% | 0% | 10% |
| Reluctant (2) | 29 | 17 | 37 | 16 |

**Table 8.3** (*continued*)

| Characteristic | Arizona Legislators | | California Legislators | |
|---|---|---|---|---|
| | Self-ID Reps | All Others | Self-ID Reps | All Others |
| Refuses (3) | 57 | 50 | 62 | 74 |
| Mean (1–3) | 2.43 | 2.17 | 2.62 | 2.63 |
| Most positive attitude toward hardball politics | | | | |
| No problem (1) | 43% | 42% | 0% | 32% |
| Reluctant (2) | 43 | 22 | 75 | 16 |
| Refuses (3) | 14 | 35 | 25 | 53 |
| Mean (1–3) | 1.71 | 1.92 | 2.25 | 2.21 |

[a] See Table 3.1 for more information on response categories and calculation of means.
[b] See Tables 4.1–4.3 for more information on response categories.
[c] See Table 5.1 for more information on the items used to construct this index.
[d] See Table 5.2 and Appendix B for more information on the roll call votes used.
[e] See Table 6.1 for definitions of "active" and "leader." See Table 6.2 for more information on the policy leadership index.
[f] See Table 7.1 for more information.
[g] See Table 7.2 for more information.
[h] See Table 7.3 for more information.
* Statistically significant difference ($p \leq .05$) from the state's self-identified representatives of women.

The Arizona identifiers simply did not differ from their colleagues in this respect, at least not in any consistent fashion. It is doubtful, therefore, that paying more attention to constituents was associated with representing women in these legislators' minds.

There is some evidence presented in Table 8.3 to suggest that representing women (according to the behavior of these legislators) may have entailed a closer relationship to *female* constituents in particular. For example, the California legislators who thought of themselves as representatives of women perceived much stronger support from female constituents than did their colleagues—although not much more than their female colleagues did. Every single one of the California identifiers believed their female constituents had particular policy concerns and that they, as women or men, had a legitimate and effective role to play in representing such concerns; the women felt they, as women, were more effective in doing so, while the one man who identified himself as a representative of women felt equally capable of doing so. Most, but not all, of the other female California lawmakers (67 percent) felt the same; and only 44 percent of the other male legislators agreed with this one male identifier.

The Arizona officials who readily identified themselves as representatives of women did not perceive any stronger support from their female constituents than did their colleagues, male or female. The Arizona identifiers did, however, rate female constituents as much more supportive than any other constituency group listed in the questionnaire. But so did the other female Arizona legislators. The Arizona identifiers were somewhat more likely than even their female colleagues to believe that they, as women or men, had a productive role to play in representing their female constituents' policy concerns. Two-thirds of the female identifiers believed that female legislators in general did or should "make a difference" in such matters, as compared to only 40 percent of their female colleagues. While 71 percent of the Arizona male legislators who did not identify themselves as representatives of women either denied that female constituents had particular policy concerns or admitted that their female colleagues were better able to represent such concerns, the two male identifiers were split; both recognized "women's issues" (in this sense), but one agreed that women were more effective at representing such concerns, while the other did not. Among legislators of both states, then, forging a closer relationship to female constituents had more to do with simply being female than with thinking of oneself as a representative of women, but such identification did seem to add an extra incentive.

The legislative styles of the self-identified representatives of women were much like their colleagues' as well. Most legislators, regardless of whether or not they saw themselves as representatives of women, studiously avoided "power over" strategies and sources of influence in favor of the more consensual "power to" approach. The willingness to participate in hardball politics, again, had more to do with the state and the strength of the institutional norms affecting a legislator than with the legislator's predisposition toward representing women. The figures in Table 8.3 give some indication that the Arizona self-identified representatives of women were a bit *less* wary of "power over" sources of personal influence and *less* likely to emphasize "power to" sources than were their colleagues. But neither their legislative strategies nor their opinion of hardball politics strayed from the norm. There also is some indication that the California identifiers were *more* wary of "power over" sources and strategies than their colleagues were, but such "power over" notions never captured much support from any California officials. Those who did endorse "power over" strategies or sources never mentioned more than one, and such references rarely constituted more than a third of any California official's responses. All told, there is little to suggest that "power to" or "feminine" leadership styles were any more popular among the self-designated representatives of women than among other legislators. Thus, it is unlikely that such stylistic or procedural preferences were associated with the idea of representing women.

The patterns of policy activism and leadership displayed in Table 8.3 also provide little evidence to suggest that self-identified representatives of women placed a higher priority on women's issues than other legislators did. The identifiers were quite active in women's issues, but so were their colleagues—especially their female colleagues. Compared to their male and female colleagues, the Arizona identifiers were only marginally more active in issues pertaining to women, children and families, education, health and public safety, and poverty. Arizona identifiers were considerably more active than their male colleagues in feminist policymaking, but not any more active than their female colleagues were. Compared to their female colleagues only, the Arizona identifiers were marginally *less* active in policy dealing with women, children and families, and education. Only on environmental issues were the Arizona identifiers significantly more likely to take the lead than were their male or female colleagues. On average, the Arizona identifiers were active in four of the (first) six issue areas listed in Table 8.3, but so were their female colleagues; 75 percent of the identifiers (all but two) were leaders in at least one of the issue areas, but so were 92 percent of their female colleagues (all but one).

The California self-designated representatives of women were much more active in the "women" policymaking arena than were their male colleagues but only slightly more active than their female colleagues were. They were only marginally more active than either their male or female colleagues in issues dealing with children and families, education, and health. There were only two policy areas in which the California identifiers were significantly more active than both their male and female colleagues: poverty issues and feminist issues. On average, the California identifiers were active in 3.67 out of six "women's issue" areas, but their male and female colleagues were not far behind, with averages of 2.83 and 3.50, respectively. All of the California identifiers were leaders in at least one issue area, as were all but one of their female colleagues (83 percent) and most of their male colleagues (61 percent).

Like forging closer ties to female constituents, placing a high priority on women's issues in both states had more to do with being female than with identifying oneself as a representative of women. That the California identifiers were more active in feminist issues than even their female colleagues, moreover, may have as much to do with their partisanship as with their predisposition toward representing women. The nine identifiers, eight of whom were Democrats, were only slightly more active in feminist policymaking than were their Democratic colleagues as a whole, 64 percent of whom were feminist policy activists. Plus, both of the California female Democrats who did not identify themselves as representatives of women were active in feminist issues.

The Democratic, liberal, and feminist proclivities of the self-identified representatives of women, from both states, are more clearly reflected in

their policy preferences. As the figures in Table 8.3 demonstrate, the identifiers were more liberal and feminist on gender gap and women's rights
issues than were their in-state colleagues—although, it must be noted, the
Arizona identifiers did not cast any more feminist votes on women's rights
bills than their colleagues did. At the same time, however, it must also be
noted that the identifiers were not much more liberal or feminist than were
their *Democratic* colleagues who did not readily consider themselves representatives of women. Nevertheless, the Democratic identifiers were often a
bit more steadfast in their liberalism than the other Democratic legislators.
Moreover, the few Republican identifiers were, as a group, much more liberal than other Republican legislators. Two of the three Arizona Republican
identifiers were among that state's most liberal Republican legislators, as
was the single California Republican identifier. Only one Republican identifier from Arizona could be considered relatively conservative.

The centrality of partisanship and ideology in these legislators' conceptions of women's political representation is further reflected in the *other*
types of issues, causes, and groups they perceived themselves as representing. In addition to representing women, women's groups, or women's issues, they often saw themselves as representing liberal interests often associated with the Democratic party. Labor, disadvantaged minorities, and
environmentalists, as well as women, figured prominently in their lists.
Three Arizona Democrats, for example, identified themselves with the following groups:

- women, environmentalists, the lesbian and gay community, nurses, and
  labor
- "Women's groups, environmental groups, teachers' groups. All the good
  guys"
- "a friend of lawyers" (especially trial lawyers), environmental groups,
  women's rights advocates, consumer groups, campaign finance reformers, the disabled

California Democrats' lists were similar:

- minorities, women, consumers
- organized labor, environmentalists, women
- educators, social workers, the working class, women, and ethnic minorities
- "so-called disadvantaged groups," such as "the deaf and blind communities," senior citizens, welfare recipients, children, women, and "minority
  groups"
- educators, "health care groups," and "several underrepresented groups,"
  including women, blacks, liberals, and Catholics

One California Democrat said she worked a lot with "women's groups" and nurses "with the objective of equalizing things." She concluded, "I guess I have sort of the basic Democratic instincts."

Republicans who identified themselves as representatives of women also included certain liberal causes in their lists of groups they represented. One Arizona Republican cited "environmental, prison [reform], and day care sectors." Another cited "the pro-choice constituency," reproductive health issues in general, and "the AIDS activist community." The California Republican began, "I think you start with your basic beliefs. And I believe very strongly that we have got to give people who have not been served—minorities and women—tremendous opportunities." Even the very conservative Arizona Republican pointed out that she was not as "narrow" in her thinking as people (especially the media) often thought. Her "special feeling for . . . single women, unmarried . . . who are having a terrible time trying to get their child support" not only led her to become "very vocal on child support issues" but also helped her "to be well-rounded."

If the characteristics and behavior of self-designated representatives of women are any indication, then the concept of women's substantive political representation was rather narrowly defined by the Arizona and California legislators in this study. Actively representing women, as inferred from the attitudes, perceptions, and behavior of these legislators, had little or nothing to do with constituent responsiveness, legislative styles, or even policy priorities. It did entail a somewhat closer relationship with female constituents, at least in terms of perceived support and the belief (among women) that female legislators had a distinctive role to play in representing their policy concerns (or, among men, that male legislators were just as capable of representing such concerns). Most clearly, though, representing women was associated with being female, Democratic, and more liberal than most. These three characteristics were neither necessary nor sufficient criteria (individually or collectively) for legislators to identify themselves as representatives of women. Not all such identifiers were female, Democratic, and/or liberal; and there were plenty of other female, Democratic, and/or liberal legislators who did not identify themselves as representatives of women. Nonetheless, these characteristics come closest to suggesting what representing women might have meant to the women and men of the 1990 Arizona and California state legislatures.

## Conclusions

There is no single, catch-all explanation for why sex differences in legislative behavior were not more prevalent or pronounced in this study of Arizona and California officials. There are, however, some that seem more plausible than others. And part of what makes some more plausible than others is the recognition that the lack of sex-based differentiation is not always attributable to female legislators falling short of expectations for lawmakers to "make a difference" or "act for" women. Rather, some similarities can be attributed to *male* legislators living up to such expectations (unexpectedly).

Thus, the lack of sex differences in policy preferences, roll call voting, and legislative styles cannot be attributed to either androcentric selection processes or a set of androcentric institutional norms, rules, or pressures. Far from discouraging activity believed to be representative of women, some institutional forces—such as partisan and ideological coalitions, as well as norms of interpersonal behavior—*promoted* or, at least, enabled such activity. Furthermore, there is very little evidence presented in this chapter to support the notion that behavior associated with the representation of women was systematically discouraged by the imposition of negative sanctions.

Not all institutional norms were so benign, however. Those that privileged legislative activities and accomplishments over constituent service and relations and that valued independently informed decision-making over strict adherence to constituent (or public) opinion may have discouraged legislators from being more responsive to their constituents. With such powerful norms in place, female officials who wanted to "make a difference" in this way may have had second thoughts, fearing that such behavior would make them appear less serious, less ambitious, less worthy to their colleagues. Such fears may have been enough to deter them from paying "too much" attention to their constituents, regardless of the absence of any visible, systematic forms of punishment for doing so.

Explanation 3, however, challenges the assumption that female (or male) lawmakers who wanted to "make a difference" for women or as women—who thought of themselves as representatives of women—included constituent responsiveness as part of the package. The abstract notions of representing women, women's political interests, or gender-differentiated political behavior were not alien to these politicians (as I argued in Chapter 4). The attitudes and activities of those who readily identified themselves as representatives of women do suggest, however, that such concepts were rather narrowly defined in terms of issues or policy positions that liberal Democrats tend to support. If there were a conscientious, agreed-upon agenda for "making a difference" for women or as women in these state legislatures, it most likely did not extend to all aspects of legislative behavior examined here, and it most certainly did not extend to constituent responsiveness.

I am not suggesting that we as citizens, activists, or students of American politics should revise our own conceptions of what it means to represent women. Instead, I wish merely to reinforce the notion that such conceptions are by no means universally shared. "Acting for" women may not have included such goals as improving constituent relations or reforming the legislative process in the 1990 Arizona and California state legislatures. But it may have done so in other places and/or in other times. Conversely, it is also important to recognize that lawmakers need not acknowledge certain activities or goals as representative of women in order to pursue them. Many Arizona and California legislators, for example, took exception to hardball politics, supported liberal proposals on gender gap and women's rights issues, and introduced legislation dealing with women, children, education, health, welfare, and the environment without simultaneously thinking of themselves as representing women in particular. Similarly, many of the legislators in this study engaged in behavior we often associate with women and women's political interests, without being women.

## CHAPTER NINE

# The Difference It Makes

Discussions about women in public office almost always confront the "so what" question: What difference does it make? Why should we care how many women run for and win elective office? What does it matter what they do once they occupy those offices? Feminists (and others) have argued that one of the most important reasons for electing more women to public office is that such women "make a difference" for women, as women. Joining in the discussions, female politicians themselves have pointed to various ways in which they will (or do) act for or as women. They will pay more attention to and be more responsive to their constituents, especially their female constituents. They will vote for and otherwise support women's positions on various gender gap and women's rights issues. They will prioritize various women's issues, placing them on the agenda and serving as their primary, most vigorous advocates. They will alter the policymaking process, rejecting its more competitive and coercive tendencies and emphasizing its more cooperative and collegial potential.

Embedded in these hopes and expectations are certain assumptions about sex, gender, and women's political representation. The first is that women's descriptive representation (the presence of women in government) ensures or at least promotes women's substantive representation. The second is that there is a clear and mutually agreed-upon definition of what that substantive representation entails, and that that definition includes the various predispositions and activities listed above. Also part and parcel of this second assumption is the notion that, among both the represented and the representing, women's political interests, concerns, priorities, and preferences differ substantially from those of men. Finally, the third assumption posits that gender is so powerful and so monolithic a force that it shapes and differentiates the behavior of women and men in public office no matter what the context or situation.

As an argument for electing women to public office, then, this is a strategy that revolves around notions of gender difference translated into sex difference. Emphasizing women's differences from men and offering them as solutions to current social and political maladies is a familiar, time-tested strategy for asserting women's right to equally meaningful and effective opportunities for political participation, as noted in Chapter 1. It has been invoked at least since the Revolutionary era, in the form of republican motherhood, and continues to carry a lot of weight in contemporary discussions of gender gaps and women's roles in public office. As a means of mobilizing and enhancing women's collective power in politics, this strategy seems to have withstood the test of time.

Nonetheless, this study of Arizona and California state legislators suggests that the strategy of difference is one in need of a reality check. The "reality" portrayed here is a sobering one, indeed. While the women of these state legislatures did seem better connected to their female constituents and more willing to take the lead on some women's issues, they were no different from their male counterparts in several other respects. In both states, male legislators paid just as much attention and were just as responsive to their constituents as were female legislators. Sex differences in these lawmakers' policy preferences and roll call votes were few and far between, and rarely consequential. Most of these men and women endorsed the more cooperative aspects of the legislative process, claiming as their own the types of legislative strategies and sources of influence most congruent with such a "feminine" approach. Quite a few were willing to make exceptions to these rules prescribing collegial, honest, and mutually beneficial relations, but the men were no more likely to do so than were the women.

These findings and the most likely explanations behind them also challenge the various assumptions underlying the strategy of difference. In neither state legislature was being female (descriptive representation) a guarantee of attitudes and activities associated with women (substantive representation). For each dimension of representational activity examined here, there always were at least a few women who did not "act for" women or act as women are so often expected to act. In some cases—namely, ties to female constituents and policy activity on some women's issues—descriptive representation did at least increase the likelihood of substantive representation, but in other cases it did not even do that. Moreover, there always were more than a few male legislators willing and able to provide substantive representation for women, as defined. In this sense, then, descriptive representation was, as a criterion for substantive representation, neither absolutely necessary nor always sufficient.

In trying to explain why the behavior of women and men of the 1990 Arizona and California state legislatures was so similar in so many ways, I have also cast aspersions on the assumption that women's and men's political interests are so clearly and easily distinguished. In Chapter 5, for example, I suggested that sex differences in constituents' policy preferences were rarely large enough to be translated into sex differences in elected representatives' roll call votes. Referring to California public opinion data, I argued that majorities of men and women are rarely found on opposite sides of an issue. Thus, even if all or most female lawmakers were willing and able to use their roll call votes to give voice to their female constituents' wishes, they would end up casting votes no different from those of their mostly male colleagues who were not so motivated.

Paradoxically, the profile of those legislators who identified themselves as representatives of women (presented in Chapter 8) suggests that, within the 1990 Arizona and California legislatures, it was precisely this dimension of legislative behavior—policy preferences—that was most readily associated with the idea of representing women. Perhaps because of the widespread media portrayal of the gender gap as favoring Democratic politicians and policies (Bonk 1988; Wirls 1985), these legislators tended to associate women with other generally liberal and/or Democratic constituencies and causes. Thus, the Democratic legislators who thought of themselves as representatives of women tended to be a bit more liberal than their Democratic peers, and the (few) Republican self-designated representatives of women were, as a group, much more liberal than their partisan counterparts. The other attitudes and activities of these self-identified representatives of women further suggested that the meaning of women's substantive representation did not, in these two legislatures, extend much beyond the realm of partisanship and ideology. Most clearly, it did not include the dimensions of constituent responsiveness or legislative style.

To further explain the apparent lack of sexual differentiation in legislative behavior, I have suggested that the dictates, pressures, and constraints of gender norms are sometimes outweighed and sometimes subsumed by the dictates, pressures, constraints, and norms of electoral and legislative institutions. For example, degrees of constituent responsiveness seem to have been limited by a clear set of institutional norms that associated prestige, power, and leadership with legislative prowess and independent decision-making. Thus, if there were any gender-related propensity for female officials to be more connected to their constituents, it was counteracted by these more powerful norms. Similarly, the institutional requirements of majority coalitions and the partisan structure of both electoral and legislative processes may have rendered gender irrelevant as far as legislators' policy preferences and roll call votes were concerned. Thus, if there were any gender-related propensity for female legislators to support certain positions on gender gap or women's rights issues, it was matched by the partisan and/or ideological motivations of their male colleagues—not to mention their own partisan and ideological concerns.

Occasionally, gender norms did prevail. The fact that every legislative district contained roughly equal proportions of men and women did not preclude many of the Arizona and California officials in this study from forging close representational ties to their female constituents in particular. Nor did it mean that male and female legislators were equally likely to forge such ties. As revealed in Chapter 4, female legislators in both states were more likely than their male colleagues to "see" women as a particularly supportive and important constituency group, to think of themselves as representatives of women, and to feel relatively capable and responsible for representing women's political concerns. The analysis of policy priorities in Chapter 6 also revealed that female lawmakers in both states were, indeed, more likely to take the lead on various types of women's issues. In effect, the electoral constraints of district demographics did not negate all incentives for legislators, especially female legislators, to pay particular attention to their female constituents.

This is not to say that institutional norms associated with electoral and legislative processes were uniformly woman-friendly or even gender-neutral. The norms that limited constituent responsiveness no doubt placed a premium on certain characteristics associated with masculinity (independence, rationality) and male-dominated activities (the law) at the expense of certain characteristics associated with femininity (connectedness, empathy) and female-dominated activities (relationships). Other scholars have warned of the stifling and mutually reinforcing effects of tokenism and institutional sexism (Antolini 1984; Dahlerup 1988; Kanter 1977). As women enter political office, they enter an institution that is profoundly male-centered, not only with respect to its membership but also in terms of what is considered "normal," acceptable, and praiseworthy. There is only so much a few women can accomplish for women, as women, in such a setting—so the argument goes. "Making a difference," especially in a legislative setting, quite often depends on having access to majority coalitions and majority control of institutional rules and regulations, rewards, and sanctions. Until women constitute a majority or even a substantial minority of legislators in any given assembly, their ability to "make a difference" will be severely constrained.

On the one hand, this study of the Arizona and California state legislatures suggests that such pessimism may be somewhat exaggerated. As I argued in previous chapters, institutional norms, pressures, and demands are not uniformly sexist; they do not always or necessarily privilege behavior, preferences, or priorities generally associated with men; and they do not always run counter to the representation or realization of women's political interests. The interpersonal norms of behavior that governed the legislative process in both states clearly valued and reinforced a wide array of feminine attributes while denigrating a number of masculine attributes, thus promoting behavior thought to be representative of women.

On the other, more pessimistic hand, other aspects of this study cast doubt on the promise that growing numbers of women in public office will solidify the links between women's descriptive and substantive representation. The comparison of Arizona legislators, 30 percent of whom were women, and California legislators, only 16 percent of whom were women, provided an opportunity to test the proposition that electing more women to public office means more women will have the freedom and ability to "make a difference" for women, as women. According to this proposition, the women of the Arizona legislature should have been more likely than those of the California legislature to engage in the behavior and exhibit the traits thought to be representative of women. Indeed, the Arizona women had not only numbers but also institutional status in their favor.

Yet the women of the Arizona legislature were no more likely to "act for" women than were their California counterparts. They did not pay any more attention to their constituents; they did not seem any more connected to their female constituents; they were no more supportive of gender gap or women's right legislation, no more active in women's issues, no more enamored with cooperative, consensual legislative styles, and no more reluctant to engage in hardball politics. If there were any differences between these two sets of female lawmakers, it was the *California* women who were more likely to "act for" women. The California women were the ones who could claim stronger support from their female constituents; who were more likely to believe that they and their female colleagues could make a difference on issues of concern to women; who were more likely to identify themselves as representatives of women; whose feminist policy activism extended beyond issues of women and children; and who were more likely to refuse to participate in hardball politics. And it was the California female lawmakers who generated enough solidarity amongst themselves to organize and maintain an effective women's legislative caucus. In contrast, the Arizona case suggests that increasing the number of female lawmakers may only increase the diversity among them, thereby making such solidarity more and more difficult. Moreover, the long history of substantial female presence in both the Arizona state legislature and Arizona state politics may have made being a woman seem less notable and representing women seem less salient or less pressing to that state's political elite.

Does all this mean that we should no longer be concerned about electing more women to public office, or about the still too few women who have managed to gain public office? Hardly. Thus far, I have used the conclusions of this study to highlight the ways in which the expected links between women's descriptive and substantive representation are often weak, misguided, and fraught with complications. I have highlighted the ways in which the women of the 1990 Arizona and California legislatures did *not* "make a difference" for women, as women. And I have cast doubt on hopes for a more promising future in which a greater number or critical mass of female officials will *really* "make a difference." But the conclusions of this study should not be taken to the extreme. They do not rule out *any* possible links between women's descriptive and substantive representation. They do not mean that women *never* "make a difference"—or that they never did or never will. And most importantly, they say nothing about the other very important benefits of electing (more) women to public office.

## The Difference It Does Make

First and foremost, the women of the Arizona and California state legislatures did "make a difference" in two respects. Compared to their male colleagues, they were in several ways more closely connected to their female constituents, and they were more active in various women's issues, including those identified as feminist women's issues. These two dimensions of substantive representation are extremely important, especially in the context of women's political representation. If, as I have argued, the very meaning of women's political interests and representation is often debatable and uncertain, then ties to female constituents and the formative stages of public policymaking become all the more important. These are the arenas in which women's substantive political representation can be defined. Moreover, of all the dimensions of women's substantive representation examined in this study, these are two that arguably demand the most concerted leadership and the most vigorous advocacy. Allies who *support* women's priorities and preferences—in roll call voting, for instance—are easier to come by than are self-motivated leaders.

Second, it is important to remember that this is a study of only two state legislatures at one point in time. If, as I have argued, the degree to which female officials (or male officials) "act for" women depends upon the institutional and political context, then what went on in the Arizona and California state legislatures may not have gone on elsewhere; and what went on in 1990 may not have gone on in previous years, and may not continue on into future years. Indeed, I have cited throughout the numerous studies of other public officials in other places and in other times whose findings differ from those reported here. Just because the women in the 1990 Arizona and

California legislatures did not "make a difference" (in some ways) does not mean there were not other women in public office who did, other women in public office who do, and other women in public office who will. This study may focus on the various reasons why such links between women's descriptive and substantive representation are often weak and/or conditional—and thus less frequent than many assume—but it does not rule out any possibility that such links occur or may occur.

Third, the presence of women in public office makes a difference, and a very important difference, even if it is no guarantee of greater substantive representation for women. Women's descriptive representation has value above and beyond whatever substantive group interests are at stake. This value is symbolic but no less meaningful, no less "real," no less consequential.[1] The symbolic benefits of women's descriptive representation are widely recognized, but in the face of limited substantive benefits, they deserve more emphasis and appreciation.

The symbolic value or effect of women in public office is premised on the recognition that women are a historically disadvantaged and subordinated group, one that has been systematically excluded from formal political participation. It also is premised on the determination to challenge and rectify the continuing legacy of women's political exclusion. The politics of presence, which Anne Phillips (1995: 39–40) so eloquently defends, "is one of the many avenues for challenging existing hierarchies of power."

> Including those previously excluded matters *even if* it proves to have no discernible consequences for the policies that may be adopted. Part of the purpose, that is, is simply to achieve that necessary inclusion: to reverse previous histories of exclusion and the way these constituted certain kinds of people as less suited to govern than the rest. (Phillips 1995: 40, emphasis in original)

Within the historical context of women's political, social, and economic subordination, the very small number of women in public office carries very distinct messages. It challenges, first of all, the democratic legitimacy of our electoral processes and our governing bodies by suggesting that all is not fair, open, and equitable and that certain people and certain voices are still silenced, ignored, or at least discounted. More specifically, it reinforces the notion that politics is, indeed, a "man's world," a "male domain" (Sapiro 1981: 712) in which women are out of place. It implies that women are second-class citizens unable or unfit to rule (Mansbridge 1996: 21), unworthy of meaningful participation in political life (Carroll 1994: 13).

Conversely, then, the presence of women in public office in larger and larger numbers would say a great deal about the legitimacy of our political system, the relationship between that political system and gender, and what it means to be a woman in American society (Mansbridge 1996). To many an observer, "female representatives are standard-bearers for the entire movement seeking greater involvement of women in the spheres of power" (Antolini 1984: 38). The growing proportions of female politicians signal the end of women as political outsiders and anomalies and the establishment of women as political leaders, movers and shakers. If women were fully included in politics from the highest ranks on down, the idea that politics is a man's world would seem incongruous at best.

Instead of discouraging women's political participation, the "brave new world" of more women visibly in positions of political power would "help to stimulate greater political interest and participation among female citizens" (Carroll 1994: 14). Women in public office would demonstrate to all, but particularly to other women and girls, that politics is not just the art of the possible, but the realm of the possible. "We are not talking about quotas, bean-counting or special treatment," writes Anna Quindlen (1993), "although sometimes it seems like special treatment for women and minorities to get equal treatment. We are talking about the sense of universal possibility that should be inherent in democracy, the sense a little girl gets now when she sees the official portrait of the Supreme Court and realizes that girls can be justices, too." An even greater sense of possibility opens up, I would add, when that little girl looks at both Sandra Day O'Connor and Ruth Bader Ginsburg and realizes that it is not just the top girl or just *some* girls who can be justices.

Perhaps most importantly, the presence of women in public office makes women's political self-determination possible. In this sense, there is an extremely important difference between men legislating on behalf of women and women legislating on behalf of women—even if the substantive outcome is the same, even if the policymaking process from beginning to end is the same. In a society in which gender remains a signifier for unequal power relations and in which men still possess the vast majority of positions of social, economic, and political power, men making choices and decisions for women seems paternalistic. As Phillips (1995: 43–44) puts it, "there is something distinctly odd about a democracy that accepts a responsibility for redressing disadvantage, but never sees the disadvantaged as the appropriate people to carry this through."

This picture may seem especially "odd" when issues of women's health are concerned, as recent developments in Congress illustrate. Observers note that congressmen are becoming more and more involved in such issues, but that their involvement has been greeted with a degree of wariness and skepticism from many women. "[C]urrent and former female members of Congress," reports the *New York Times* (Stolberg 1997), "complain that a sense of paternalism still prevails in Congress, a sentiment they say becomes evident when women's health matters, especially those involving reproduction, are discussed." Republican representative Constance Morella notes that while many of her male colleagues seem eager to initiate debate on abortion, "They don't want to intervene in the bodily functions of men." Former Democratic congresswoman Patricia Schroeder adds:

> It seems to all go back to our reproductive organs. You know why? We're just not smart enough to deal with this by ourselves. We need Congress's help. Now, if we did this on their health, they would be nuts.

Similarly, when pro-choice advocates ask "Who Decides?" they are questioning not simply the government's role in what (they believe) should be private decisions, but the *male-dominated* government's role in what should be *women's* decisions.

It is both the skewed proportions and the historical context of inequality that fuel this ambivalence toward men "acting for" women.

> When those charged with making the political decisions are predominantly drawn from one of the two sexes or one of what may be numerous ethnic groups, this puts the others in the category of political minors. They remain like children, to be cared for by those who know best. However public-spirited their mentors may be, this infantilization of large segments of the citizenry is hardly compatible with modern-day democracy, and it becomes particularly burdensome when associated with popular ideologies that have presumed the inferiority of the excluded groups. (Phillips 1995: 39)

The problem is not that men cannot speak for women or that only women can speak for women. Rather, the problem is that women should be able to speak for themselves. Anna Jónasdóttir (1988) goes even further to argue that women must have control over the conditions under which they speak. Children speak only when they are spoken to. Women must be able to speak —and be heard—whenever, wherever, and on whatever they please. Thus, women, according to Jónasdóttir, must not simply be present and heard in public affairs and political decision-making; they must have a *controlling* presence.

Phillips, Jónasdóttir, and Jane Mansbridge further contend that women's controlling or self-determinative presence is all the more crucial when women's interests are contested or, as Mansbridge (1996) puts it, "uncrystallized." If women's interests, needs, preferences, and priorities were readily apparent and easily discernible, then anyone could effectively understand, convey, and act upon them. Mansbridge (1996) argues that when a group's interests are uncrystallized and therefore unanticipated, group members are the most likely to keep a vigilant lookout for when such interests do or can arise. Phillips (1991) notes that when issues evoke strong yet complex and conflicting reactions among women, as do many women's issues (not just those of reproductive rights), women's experiences should be even more central to the deliberations. Jónasdóttir asserts that women "must be visible politically as women, and be empowered to act in that capacity" precisely because the content of women's needs and desires is an "open question"—because "there is the continual possibility (not necessity) that they may have needs and attitudes on vital issues which differ from those of men" (1988: 41, 53).

Under this logic, the conclusions of this study render women's increased presence in public office—and, thus, women's descriptive representation—more, not less, important. Women's political interests and the meaning of women's substantive political representation are oftentimes uncrystallized, as demonstrated in Chapters 1, 5 and 8. But they also remain a distinct possibility. By forging closer ties to their female constituents and by assuming active roles in a wide range of policymaking arenas, the women of the Arizona and California legislatures did indeed put themselves in positions where they could discern, understand, contemplate, and voice women's political concerns, needs, desires, interests, and perspectives.

## On Sexual Dimorphism

If the conclusions and implications of this study seem ambiguous, complicated, and conditional, it is by design. My intentions were, in fact, to avoid the simplicity of unambiguous, uncomplicated, unconditional assertions about representing women. All too often such seemingly straightforward claims reflect, reinforce, and/or lead to a dichotomous portrayal of gender politics, which I believe is misleading and which I fear is ultimately counterproductive. The "oppositional model" I wish to avoid (Deaux and Major 1990: 89) not only takes "sexual dimorphism as a starting point" but frames the entire inquiry in either/or terms: women and men are either different or the same. In this framework, the questions, and hence the answers, are presented in terms of an either/or choice between similarity and difference, between women acting just like men and women rejecting and changing the male-defined status quo altogether.

In recent years, this sameness vs. difference framework has come under attack from numerous feminist scholars. The points of contention are many. To begin, such a framework views women in terms of men and male norms (Z. Eisenstein 1988; Silverberg 1990). As both an analytic and a political tool, its binary choices are much too limiting. Focusing on one or the other, similarities or differences, does justice neither to reality (current or historic) nor to feminist visions of progress. Several scholars have noted that, in theory and in practice, feminism in the United States has always rested on a paradoxical embrace of *both* similarity and difference. Deborah Rhode (1990: 1–2), for example, has called on feminists to "become more attentive to an enduring paradox in feminist traditions."

> In an important sense, the women's movement rests on the differ-ences it seeks to challenge. From its beginning, the feminist campaign has sought to prevent sex-related differences from limiting individu-als' aspirations and achievements. Yet by definition the movement also presupposes some recognition of women's common interests and concerns. In that respect, feminism assumes a shared experience it seeks in large measure to challenge.

Complicating matters even further, she adds, is the diversity of experience and outlook among women, which the women's movement is now strug-gling to recognize. (See also Cott 1987: 3–10.)

In a recent volume of essays entitled *Beyond Equality and Difference*, Carole Pateman argues that "the history of women's struggle for citizenship" can-not be interpreted only in terms of equality. "From at least 1792, when Mary Wollstonecraft's *A Vindication of the Rights of Women* was published," she in-structs, "women have demanded both equal civil and political rights, and that their difference from men should be acknowledged in their citizen-ship" (1992: 17–18). In the same volume, Karen Offen (1992) contends that if feminists use either an "individualistic" approach (ones that focuses on similarities between the sexes and on principles of equality) or a "relational" approach (one that focuses on gender difference) *to the exclusion of the other,* their efforts will backfire.

These writers and others (e.g., Epstein 1988) have called for change in how feminist scholars approach our research. Joan Scott (1986: 1065), I be-lieve, captures many of these sentiments in the following directive:

> We need a refusal of the fixed and permanent quality of the binary opposition, a genuine historicization and deconstruction of the terms of sexual difference. We must become more self-conscious about dis-tinguishing between our analytic vocabulary and the material we want to analyze. We must find ways (however imperfect) to continu-ally subject our categories to criticism, our analyses to self-criticism.

Closer to home, Anne Phillips concludes that "the case for gender parity among our political representatives inevitably operates in a framework of probabilities rather than certainties" (1995: 82).

This study is an empirical response to these exhortations. It portrays female and male politicians as neither entirely different nor entirely similar.

It deconstructs various assumptions about sexual difference, gender, and women's political representation by approaching such ready-made categories as "women's issues" with a mixture of skepticism and openness and by putting such assumptions to the empirical test. Most importantly, the 1990 Arizona and California state legislators vividly demonstrate the uncertain, probabilistic framework in which women's political representation can occur.

# Research Design

## Data Collection

A great deal of the information needed for this study came from the legislators themselves in the form of subjective assessments of attitudes and behavior. There are several ways a researcher can elicit information from her/his subjects, and two methods were especially appropriate for this study: face-to-face interviews and self-administered written questionnaires.

Many of the questions I wanted to ask the legislators were rather straightforward and lent themselves to basic "yes/no" or "agree/disagree" answers. Neither the questions nor the answers needed any explanation, elaboration, or discussion. Such questions are best suited for self-administered written questionnaires, for there is no reason for the researcher to be present. In general, such questionnaires often are preferable research tools because they require relatively little time and effort from everyone involved. A significant portion of the self-reported information I needed from the legislators, however, was more complicated and nuanced, involving questions that were not quite so easy to answer and which often required detailed explanations and elaboration. Such questions were almost always open-ended (i.e., response options such as a simple "yes" or "no" are not provided) and, thus, were better suited for face-to-face, in-depth interviews.

On the assumption that relatively uncommon requests for personal interviews would be more difficult for legislators to refuse than more common requests for filling out questionnaires, I sent letters to targeted legislators requesting the former. In these letters, I described my primary research interest as the study of representation as actually practiced and perceived by representatives themselves. In addition, I wrote that I was particularly interested in comparing legislators from the two states and comparing female and male legislators. Finally, I requested anywhere from 30 minutes to an hour of time for an interview.[1] It was not until the interview was completed that I asked the legislators to fill out and mail back the written questionnaires. Thus, only legislators who granted interviews were asked to fill out questionnaires.

In the interviews legislators were asked to discuss their general goals in office, their policy priorities and districts' concerns, their attitudes about trustee vs. delegate representation and about representing certain groups of people, and their advice to newly elected representatives about how to be successful. They also were asked to describe and evaluate the legislative process within their own institutions with regard to the committee process, patterns of conflict, and power dynamics. Finally, the legislators were asked several questions about women in politics—both women in the general public and their female colleagues in the state legislature. Time permitting, each legislator was asked the same set of questions in the interviews, although occasionally the order of the questions was altered. Table A.1 provides a complete list of the interview questions asked of the Arizona legislators and the general order in which they were asked. The same schedule was followed in interviewing the California legislators.[2]

Table A.1   Sample Interview Schedule

I.  **Goals and priorities**

A. I imagine that becoming an AZ legislator involves making a very big commitment. So, I'm curious: what convinced you to make that commitment, to go ahead and run for the House that first time?

[If necessary:] Were you recruited/supported by the party?

B. Do you have any general or specific goals you want to achieve before you leave office?

C. [If answers to I.A–B. are not policy-specific] What issues are at the top of your agenda? Which issues do you care about the most?

[If answers to I.A–B. are policy-specific] Are these the issues that are at the top of your agenda; are they the ones you care about the most?

[If time permits:] Why are these issues so important to you?

Are these the issues you end up spending most of your time on?

[If no] What issues do you spend most of your time on?

Why do you spend so much time on these issues?

II.  **District**

A. What are the major issues and concerns in your district?

III.  **Representation**

A. Has there ever been an issue in which you felt strongly one way and a majority of your constituents felt strongly another way?

[If yes] What is the most recent instance you can recall?

What did you end up doing? How did you handle it? Was it a difficult decision for you to make?

[If no] Do you see any possibility of an issue such as this arising in the future?

[If yes] What issue is that? What will you do if that issue comes up in the House or in a campaign?

What about when you're faced with significant, or vocal, minority opposition. How do you handle that situation?

B. Do you see yourself as representing certain constituency groups (kinds of people, or groups of people—within or outside your own district)?

[If yes] Who are they?

Do you find it easier to represent these people's concerns? Why/Why not?

Do you feel you are better able than most other legislators to represent these people's concerns?

[If no] Are there any groups you find easier to represent than others? Any you identify with or feel you understand better? Who? Why?

[If yes] Do you feel you are better able to represent their concerns than most other legislators?

## IV. Strategies for success

A. If you were asked to address a group of newly elected state legislators, what would be the first piece of advice you would offer on how to be a successful legislator? [If having trouble, ask what is the first thing that pops into R's head.]

Do you have any specific advice on:

1. Developing and gathering support for legislation; getting your bills passed.

2. [If necessary:] How to influence your colleagues

3. Would you encourage them to seek leadership positions (both party and committee positions)?

[If yes] How would you recommend they go about doing this?

[If no] Why not?

4. [If time permits:] How to go about representing your constituents

B. Are there any types of occupational or political experiences you think might help a new member of the House succeed?

Are there any that might put one at a disadvantage?

## V. The legislative process

A. If you were chairing a committee, how would you want that committee to operate? Would you have any specific goals or rules about how you want things run?

[If necessary:] Do you have any ideas about:

1. How to get bills out: Would you be concerned with building consensus and/or avoiding partisan splits?

2. Testimony: placing limits on the number of witnesses or the amount of time they're allowed to speak? Would you enforce the five-minute limit?

3. Would you try to work out most problems concerning the bills before or during the committee meetings?

4. Would you try to do something about members' attendance?

[NOTE: If R is a committee chair, or was at one time, change conditional tense to present or past.]

## VI. Fitting in

A. Looking at the institution as a whole, would you say that the House is a very collegial place? Why/Why not?

1. When disagreements and conflicts [do] occur, what are they usually about/over?

2. [If necessary:] Are the disagreements mostly personal or ideological in nature?

3. Still looking at the conflicts as a whole (rather than just the ones you're involved in personally) . . . When these conflicts are resolved, is it usually the case that both parties are satisfied—or is it more often the case that one person is left dissatisfied or disgruntled, feeling like (s)he's been left with the short end of the stick?

4. Do people think in terms of winners and losers?

5. Are these the kind of conflicts most people would describe as hardball or cutthroat—or do you think they're better described as negotiation, friendly debate, bargaining, etc.?

[If hardball] What about them makes them hardball?

6. This kind of conflict you've just described . . . do you think this is how disagreements in the House should be resolved? How House business should be conducted?

[If no] How would you like to have disagreements resolved?

7. What about the conflicts and disagreements you find yourself involved in? How would you describe them? Are they any different from what you see going on around you?

[If necessary:] Personal or ideological? Both parties happy? Hardball?

8. Would you say you're involved in a fair amount of conflict (as you've described), or do you prefer (or are you able) to avoid it?

B. Everyone has different ideas about what power is. What is your definition of power in the House? How does an AZ Representative accumulate power? What are the sources of power in the House?

[If necessary:] What is the most effective form/source of power?

Do you think power in the House should be based on [sources mentioned by R]? Is this sort of power beneficial or detrimental for the House as a whole?

[If no, or detrimental] What would you like to see power based upon?

How would you describe your own power? Do you have a lot of power? What are the sources of your power?

[If time permits and if necessary:] Comparing yourself to a hypothetical Representative who is very "powerful" according to your general definition of power. . . . Can you tell me, how do you and he go about getting what you want?

C. Do you socialize much with other legislators?

[If yes] About how often? A few times a year/session? Every month? Every week? Every day?

How informal is this socializing? Is it business-related, or completely social?

[If no] Why not?

[If necessary:] Has there ever been a time when you felt you were being excluded from a social gathering (or a series of gatherings, caucuses, etc.)?

[If yes] Why do you think you were being excluded?

Has this hurt you in any way?

For a legislator trying to get a bill passed, is this kind of socializing very important? Is it necessary?

[If time permits or if important and/or necessary:] Is it important because you discuss particular legislative issues in these get-togethers? Why is it so important?

How about for a legislator trying to get a leadership position? Important? Necessary?

## VII. Women in politics

A. As you know, the Arizona Legislature has an unusually high percentage of women members. Do you think that having so many women in the House makes a difference in the legislative decisions that are made?

Are there any issues that would not be dealt with otherwise, if there were no women?

What about the legislative process and the atmosphere in general?

B. Do you feel that women as a group have particular concerns which the government should address?

[If no] Why not? [GO TO QUESTION C]

[If yes] What are some of those concerns?

Do you feel that [you and] your female colleagues are better able than your male colleagues to represent such concerns?

[If yes] Why?

Do [you and] your female colleagues seem to be more willing than your male colleagues to represent such concerns?

[If necessary:] Have you personally done any work on any of these issues?

[If yes] What is the most recent issue you've worked on? What did you do?

[If no] Why not?

C. [If time permits:] I asked you earlier about advice you would give to newly elected legislators. Would you have any additional advice to offer if you were addressing a group of newly elected women legislators?

[If no] Why not?

[If yes] What would that advice be?

[If R has advice for women:] How about male legislators, do you have any particular advice for them?

[If no] Why not?

[If yes] What would that advice be?

[If necessary:] Would you want to offer any advice to men on how to deal with women legislators?

D. [If necessary:] Do the women legislators in the House have any advantages or disadvantages in influencing decisions?

   [If yes] What are they?

E. [If time permits] Do you think there is a need for a formal Women's Caucus in the Legislature? Why/Why not?

## VIII. Wrap-up [If time permits]

A. Of all the things you do in this job, what do you enjoy doing the most?

   What do you find most difficult?

The follow-up written questionnaires began by asking the legislators to indicate the degree of support they had received in their last election from various organized interest groups and unorganized constituency groups. Next, legislators were asked to rank the importance they placed and the amount of time they spent on various representational duties, such as working on legislation and meeting with constituents. A few questions were devoted to legislative strategies: whom they consulted when preparing and gathering support for their legislative proposals, plus personal skills and traits they considered either assets or liabilities. A significant portion of the questionnaire was devoted to opinions on a wide range of current social, economic, and political issues, including, but not limited to, issues of women's rights and sex roles. Finally, the questionnaire elicited some background information that could not be obtained easily from other, outside sources: occupational background, organizational activities, previously held elective and appointed offices, desire to obtain another public office, and number and age of children. The written questionnaire is reproduced in Table A.2.

### Table A.2 Sample Written Questionnaire

Thank you very much for the time you have already devoted to the interview portion of this study. This questionnaire is an important follow-up component to my study. It is brief and should not take more than 15 minutes to complete. Please take this extra time to answer the questions below. Like the interview, all this information will be treated confidentially and anonymously.

### Section I. Bases of support

A. This question concerns the groups—organized and unorganized—that constitute your base of support (financial or otherwise). For each group listed below, please indicate how strongly they supported you in your last campaign. (Do not worry if some of these groups overlap.)

| | Strong Support | Moderate Support | Little or No Support | Moderate Opposition | Strong Opposition |
|---|---|---|---|---|---|
| **Organized Groups:** | | | | | |
| 1. Homeowner and neighborhood groups | — | — | — | — | — |
| 2. Service clubs (for example: Kiwanis, Rotary, Lions) | — | — | — | — | — |
| 3. Business and professional associations (for example: Chamber of Commerce, (Jaycees, Business and Prof. Women) | — | — | — | — | — |
| 4. Political party organizations | — | — | — | — | — |
| 5. School related groups | — | — | — | — | — |
| 6. Women's groups | — | — | — | — | — |
| 7. Ethnic group organizations | — | — | — | — | — |
| 8. Church related groups | — | — | — | — | — |
| 9. Labor unions | — | — | — | — | — |
| 10. Environmental groups | — | — | — | — | — |
| 11. Other (Please specify.) | — | — | — | — | — |
| **Unorganized Groups:** | | | | | |
| 1. Elderly; retired persons | — | — | — | — | — |
| 2. Ethnic minorities (Please specify.) | | | | | |
| (a) _____ | — | — | — | — | — |
| (b) _____ | — | — | — | — | — |
| 3. Blue collar workers | — | — | — | — | — |
| 4. Professionals | — | — | — | — | — |
| 5. Poor people | — | — | — | — | — |
| 6. Women | — | — | — | — | — |
| 7. Environmentalists | — | — | — | — | — |
| 8. Business people | — | — | — | — | — |
| 9. Farmers | — | — | — | — | — |
| 10. Other (Please specify.) | — | — | — | — | — |

## Section II. Representation: activities, duties, priorities

A. Below is a list of things people often think of as duties of a representative. Please rate the importance of each item on a scale of 1 (not at all important) to 5 (extremely important) by *circling* the corresponding number.

| | Not at all Important | | | | Extremely Important |
|---|---|---|---|---|---|
| 1. Helping people in the district who have personal problems with government | 1 | 2 | 3 | 4 | 5 |
| 2. Making sure the district gets its fair share of government funds and projects | 1 | 2 | 3 | 4 | 5 |
| 3. Keeping track of the way government agencies are carrying out laws passed by the legislature | 1 | 2 | 3 | 4 | 5 |
| 4. Keeping in touch with the people about what the government is doing | 1 | 2 | 3 | 4 | 5 |

| | | | | | |
|---|---|---|---|---|---|
| 5. Working on legislation | 1 | 2 | 3 | 4 | 5 |
| 6. Representing the program of one's political party | 1 | 2 | 3 | 4 | 5 |
| 7. Smoothing out conflicts and effecting compromise with other representatives | 1 | 2 | 3 | 4 | 5 |

Are there any other activities you feel are important duties of a representative?

_____

_____

Which activity do you think is *most* important? _____

Which activity do you think is *least* important? _____

B. Please estimate the number of hours per week you spend on matters related to your office, both while the legislature is in session and when it is not.

When legislature is in session _____

When legislature is not in session _____

C. When your legislature is in session, about what percentage of your time do you spend on the following activities? (Again, some of these categories may overlap. Thus, your answers do not necessarily have to add up to 100%.)

| | 0–5% | 6–10% | 11–20% | 21–30% | 31–50% | over 50% |
|---|---|---|---|---|---|---|
| 1. Working on legislation, including committee work and time on the floor | — | — | — | — | — | — |
| 2. Working on constituent casework and meeting with constituents | — | — | — | — | — | — |
| 3. Raising money for your next campaign | — | — | — | — | — | — |
| 4. Meeting with lobbyists and interest groups | — | — | — | — | — | — |
| 5. Meeting with other legislators outside of committee meetings and floor sessions | — | — | — | — | — | — |
| 6. Meeting with the press/media | — | — | — | — | — | — |

D. When preparing and gathering support for your legislative proposals, to what extent do you consult the following groups of people? Do you consult them a great deal, a fair amount, sometimes, hardly ever, or never?

| | Great Deal | Fair Amount | Some-times | Hardly Ever | Never |
|---|---|---|---|---|---|
| 1. Committee staff | — | — | — | — | — |
| 2. Majority staff | — | — | — | — | — |
| 3. Minority staff | — | — | — | — | — |
| 4. Colleagues in your party | — | — | — | — | — |
| 5. Colleagues *not* in your party | — | — | — | — | — |
| 6. Lobbyists, interest groups, organized constituent groups | — | — | — | — | — |
| 7. Unorganized constituent groups, constituents | — | — | — | — | — |
| 8. Executive agency personnel | — | — | — | — | — |
| 9. Other (Please specify.) | — | — | — | — | — |

E. In terms of getting your bills passed by the House of Representatives, would you say that you are very successful, somewhat successful, or not very successful?

Very successful _____ Somewhat successful _____ Not very successful _____

F. Below is a list of skills and traits often attributed to successful legislators. Please indicate with a "+" the attributes you consider to be your own personal strengths and, with a "–" the attributes you consider personal weaknesses. (If you consider an attribute neither a strength nor a weakness, leave the space blank.)

___ 1. Valuable past training and experience

___ 2. Financial and economic background
___ 3. Getting along with colleagues
___ 4. Willingness to work hard
___ 5. Influence and prestige with colleagues in leadership positions
___ 6. Imagination, creativity
___ 7. Understanding people's behavior and motivations
___ 8. Interest in public service

___ 9. Ability to raise money and mobilize votes
___ 10. Ability to get media attention
___ 11. Responsiveness to constituents
___ 12. Independence
___ 13. Honesty

___ 14. Ability to argue persuasively
___ 15. Interest in social problems

___ 16. General knowledge and intelligence

Of these skills, which do you think help(s) you the most when influencing other legislators?

_____

G. On a scale of 1 to 5 (1 being very low and 5 being very high), how strongly do you support your political party?

Very low      Average      Very high
  1     2     3     4     5

## Section III. Opinion on current issues

A. Below is a list of some of the issues you and other legislators around the country often deal with. Some people think government should devote more time, energy and resources to these issues, while others think government is doing enough already. Still others think the government should become less involved than it is now, and some believe the government should not get involved in these issues at all. For each issue below, please indicate what *you* feel the government's role should be by circling the corresponding letter.

a = Government should do more.
b = Government is doing enough.
c = Government should do less.
d = Government should not do anything.

| | | | | |
|---|---|---|---|---|
| 1. Controlling air and water pollution | a | b | c | d |
| 2. Improving the availability and quality of medical care | a | b | c | d |
| 3. Preventing inflation | a | b | c | d |
| 4. Assuring full employment | a | b | c | d |
| 5. Assuring equal rights for women | a | b | c | d |

| | | | | |
|---|---|---|---|---|
| 6. Assuring equal rights for minorities | a | b | c | d |
| 7. Protecting the consumer against poor services or products and unreasonable prices | a | b | c | d |
| 8. Encouraging industry and commercial development | a | b | c | d |
| 9. Providing child care services for parents | a | b | c | d |
| 10. Improving the quality of public education | a | b | c | d |

Would you face any significant disagreement from within your district on any of these issues?
Yes ___ No ___
(If yes) Please specify which issues. _____

B. There has been much discussion about abortion in recent months. Of the opinions listed below, which one best agrees with your view?

___ 1. Abortion should never be permitted.
___ 2. Abortion should be permitted only if the life of the woman is in danger, or in cases of rape or incest.
___ 3. Abortion is morally wrong, but the decision to have an abortion should be left up to the woman and her doctor.
___ 4. Abortion should never be forbidden.

C. The death penalty should be an option as a punishment for those who commit murder. Do you agree strongly, agree somewhat, disagree somewhat, or disagree strongly with this statement?

___ Agree strongly
___ Agree somewhat
___ Disagree somewhat
___ Disagree strongly

D. Some people think that certain groups have too much influence in American life and politics, while other people feel that certain groups don't have as much influence as they deserve. Please indicate whether you think the following groups have too much influence, too little influence, or just about the right amount of influence.

| | Too much | Too little | About right |
|---|---|---|---|
| 1. Business and industry | ___ | ___ | ___ |
| 2. Labor unions | ___ | ___ | ___ |
| 3. Hispanics | ___ | ___ | ___ |
| 4. Women | ___ | ___ | ___ |
| 5. Poor people | ___ | ___ | ___ |
| 6. Rich people | ___ | ___ | ___ |
| 7. Middle class people | ___ | ___ | ___ |
| 8. Native Americans | ___ | ___ | ___ |
| 9. Older, retired people | ___ | ___ | ___ |
| 10. Blacks | ___ | ___ | ___ |
| 11. Feminists | ___ | ___ | ___ |

E. Overall, do you think that women's efforts to achieve equality have improved the status of women in society, damaged it, or not affected it much?

Improved ___   Damaged ___   Not affected ___

Have such efforts improved the status of *men* in society, damaged it, or not affected it much?

Improved ___   Damaged ___   Not affected ___

Have the efforts of women to achieve equality helped *you* personally, hurt you, or have they not affected you much?

Helped ___   Hurt ___   Have not affected ___

F. Beside each statement below, please indicate the letter that comes closest to your own opinion:

(a) Strongly agree       (c) Moderately disagree       (e) Unable to decide
(b) Moderately agree     (d) Strongly disagree

___ 1. Most women no longer face job discrimination; in fact they are favored in many training and job programs.
___ 2. Men have more of the best jobs because they usually have more drive and ambition than women do.
___ 3. It is not enough for a woman to be successful herself; women must join together to change laws and customs that are unfair to all women.
___ 4. Women should work outside the home only if it is financially necessary.
___ 5. Mothers and fathers should be equally responsible for raising children and keeping household affairs in order.
___ 6. Women have just as much opportunity as men to become political leaders.
___ 7. Women in office generally devote more time to the job than do men in office.
___ 8. Women in office usually are better at the "human relations" aspects of the job.
___ 9. In general, women in office are not as politically astute as men.
___ 10. The qualifications and training of women in public office are usually not as good as those of men in office.

### Section IV. Background information

A. In addition to holding office, are you now employed?   Yes ___   No ___
   (If yes) Are you employed full time or part time?
      Full time ___   Part time ___
   What is your main occupation? _____
   (If no) Were you employed before you took office?   Yes ___   No ___
      (If yes) What was your main occupation? _____

B. Indicate below the *main* positions you held or groups you were *most* active in before becoming a Representative. (Categories may overlap.)

___ 1. Appointive board(s) or commission(s). Please specify. _____
_____
___ 2. Elective position(s). Please specify. _____
_____

___ 3. Women's group(s). Please specify. _____

___ 4. Homeowners and neighborhood group(s).
___ 5. Service club(s) (for example: Kiwanis, Rotary, Lions).
___ 6. Business and professional association(s) (for example: Chamber of Commerce, Jaycees, Business and Professional Women).
___ 7. Political party organizations.
___ 8. School related groups.
___ 9. Ethnic group organizations.
___ 10. Other. Please specify. _____

C. How likely is it that you will seek another office in the future?

Very likely ___  Somewhat likely ___  Not very likely ___  Not at all likely ___
(If very or somewhat likely) What office(s) will you seek? _____

D. Do you have any children?  Yes ___  No ___
(If yes) How many? ___
What are their ages? ___
Do they live with you?  Yes ___  No ___

E. Do you have primary responsibility for maintaining your household's affairs?
Yes ___  No ___

### Section V. Additional comments
If you have any additional comments regarding any aspect of the interview or questionnaire, please include them here or attach an additional sheet.

Documented sources of information regarding legislators' backgrounds, electoral status, legislative activities, and districts were numerous and varied. Official "histories" of legislation compiled by each state legislature provided detailed information on the sponsor(s), life cycle, votes for and against, and final outcome of each piece of legislation proposed during the 1989 and 1990 regular and special sessions. This information was used to determine (1) the number of bills introduced by each legislator (see Chapter 3), (2) legislators' votes on key bills and motions (see Chapter 5), and (3) legislative success rates for each legislator (see Chapter 8).

Information about the subject matter of bills introduced in the Arizona legislature was obtained from the *Arizona Capitol Times,* a weekly newspaper that covers all aspects of the state government—legislative, executive, and judicial. For each legislative session, the editors of this newspaper not only compile short summaries of all legislation introduced; they also track the progress of each bill and report all close votes. Reported in a timely and accurate fashion, this information was immensely helpful. Unfortunately, no comparable source of information on the California legislature was available to the general public. Instead, private firms were set up to summarize and track California legislation for clients who paid substantially more than the price of a newspaper subscription. One of those firms, Legi-Tech, generously provided (for a greatly discounted fee) the summaries used in this study to code the subject matter of legislation introduced in the 1990 session of the California legislature.

The *Arizona Capitol Times* also provided some biographical data, such as the legislators' ages, occupations, educational backgrounds, tenures in office, and committee assignments. Comparable information for California legislators was found in the seventh edition of the *Almanac of California Government and Politics,* published by the *California Journal,* one of two monthly newsmagazines devoted entirely to California politics. Written biographical sketches, which were collected from legislators interviewed for this study, were also used to supplement and corroborate the information obtained from other sources.

Voter registration and electoral returns reported by each state's secretary of state were used for two purposes: to estimate each legislator's electoral security, and to estimate the partisan and ideological leanings of each legislator's district. Both states kept records of the partisan affiliations of registered voters. The margins by which legislators defeated their recent opponents and by which their party claimed the allegiance of their constituents were used to gauge their electoral security. Constituents' registered partisanship and 1988 vote for president were used as indicators of district-level political preferences.

## Sampling Procedure and Response Rates

The goal in selecting the sample of legislators was to interview all the female legislators of each state's upper and lower houses, plus an equal number of male legislators. For example, I wanted to interview all fourteen of the California assemblywomen and all five of the female California senators, plus at least fourteen assemblymen and five male senators. Thus, letters requesting interviews were sent to all female members and to a randomly selected sample of male members of each state's upper and lower houses. To make up for a potentially lower response rate among the men, letters were sent to approximately twice an many men as women. The Arizona House of Representatives provides the exception to this sampling procedure. There were twenty-two women in the Arizona House during the 1989–90 term. If one were to add to that twice as many men, one would get sixty-six representatives altogether. However, the House has a total of only sixty representatives. Thus, letters were sent to every male and female Arizona representative.

**Table A.3  Response Rates**

| Respondent Category | Interviews Conducted | | Written Questionnaires Completed | | |
| --- | --- | --- | --- | --- | --- |
| | Number | % of Total Requests | Number | % of Interviewees | % of Total Requests |
| **Total sample** | 81 | 63 | 53 | 65 | 41 |
| Women | 32 | 70 | 20 | 62 | 44 |
| Men | 49 | 59 | 33 | 67 | 40 |
| **Arizona** | 50 | 67 | 34 | 68 | 45 |
| Women | 18 | 67 | 13 | 72 | 48 |
| Republican Women | 9 | 56 | 7 | 78 | 45 |
| Democratic Women | 9 | 82 | 6 | 67 | 54 |
| Men | 32 | 67 | 21 | 66 | 44 |
| Republican Men | 19 | 70 | 12 | 63 | 44 |
| Democratic Men | 13 | 62 | 9 | 69 | 43 |
| **California** | 31 | 57 | 19 | 61 | 35 |
| Women | 14 | 74 | 7 | 50 | 37 |
| Republican Women | 5 | 55 | 4 | 80 | 44 |
| Democratic Women | 9 | 90 | 3 | 33 | 30 |
| Men | 17 | 49 | 12 | 71 | 34 |
| Republican Men | 7 | 41 | 5 | 71 | 29 |
| Democratic Men | 10 | 55 | 7 | 70 | 39 |

Table A.3 provides the response rates of male and female legislators in both states, in terms of both the interviews and the written questionnaires. Interviews were conducted with a total of eighty-one legislators, producing an overall response rate of 63 percent.[3] Most of the California legislators were interviewed between late February and early April of 1990.[4] All the Arizona legislators were interviewed between mid-April and late June of 1990. Questionnaires were received from fifty-three (65 percent) of the interviewees.

Because the men responded at a higher rate than expected (59 percent, as compared to 70 percent of the women), the sample is not evenly divided by sex, as was originally intended. Of those interviewed, 32 were women (39 percent) and 49 (61 percent) were men; of those who completed questionnaires, twenty were women (38 percent) and thirty-three (62 percent) were men. The California male legislators, however, stand out as being particularly reluctant to grant interviews; only half granted requests for interviews—as compared to nearly three-quarters of the California female legislators, and two-thirds of both female and male Arizona legislators. Among the legislators interviewed, the California women stand out as particularly reluctant to complete the written questionnaire; only half of them returned the questionnaires, as compared to 71 percent of the California men interviewed, 72 percent of the Arizona women interviewed, and 66 percent of the Arizona men interviewed.

For the purposes of this study, these disparities in response rates of the four groups of legislators do not pose a problem. My objective was to collect four representative samples of male and female state legislators in Arizona and California, rather than two representative samples of each state legislature as a whole. Throughout the analysis presented here, I separate and compare these four groups. My only concern, therefore, is that each of these four subsamples is representative of its respective subgroup—that the sample of Arizona female legislators is representative of all Arizona female legislators holding office in 1990, that the sample of California male legislators is representative of all California male legislators in 1990, and so on.

To examine the degree to which these samples are representative, Tables A.4 and A.5 compare, respectively, the background characteristics and the legislative status of the interview and questionnaire samples to those of the sample populations. The figures in these tables show that the subsamples are, for the most part, quite representative.

**Table A.4  Personal Background Characteristics of Arizona and California State Legislators**

| Personal Background Characteristic | Percentage of Sample Population | | | | Percentage of Interview Sample | | | | Percentage of Questionnaire Sample | | | |
|---|---|---|---|---|---|---|---|---|---|---|---|---|
| | Arizona | | California | | Arizona | | California | | Arizona | | California | |
| | Women ($N=27$) | Men ($N=63$) | Women ($N=19$) | Men ($N=97$) | Women ($N=18$) | Men ($N=32$) | Women ($N=14$) | Men ($N=17$) | Women ($N=11$) | Men ($N=21$) | Women ($N=8$) | Men ($N=12$) |
| **Party** | | | | | | | | | | | | |
| Democratic | 41 | 44 | 53 | 61 | 50 | 41 | 64 | 59 | 41 | 43 | 52 | 58 |
| Republican | 59 | 56 | 47 | 38 | 50 | 59 | 36 | 41 | 59 | 57 | 48 | 42 |
| Independent | 0 | 0 | 0 | 1 | 0 | 0 | 0 | 0 | 0 | 0 | 0 | 0 |
| **Race/Ethnicity** | | | | | | | | | | | | |
| White/Anglo | 89 | 78 | 79 | 89 | 94 | 84 | 79 | 88 | 100 | 90 | 100 | 92 |
| African American | 7 | 2 | 16 | 5 | 6 | 0 | 14 | 6 | 0 | 0 | 0 | 0 |
| Hispanic | 4 | 16 | 5 | 6 | 0 | 12 | 7 | 6 | 0 | 5 | 0 | 8 |
| Native American | 0 | 5 | 0 | 0 | 0 | 3 | 0 | 0 | 0 | 5 | 0 | 0 |
| **Age** | | | | | | | | | | | | |
| < 40 | 19 | 17 | 11 | 16 | 22 | 16 | 15 | 23 | 15 | 14 | 29 | 25 |
| 40–49 | 46 | 32 | 33 | 29 | 56 | 37 | 31 | 18 | 63 | 33 | 17 | 17 |
| 50–64 | 27 | 40 | 50 | 36 | 17 | 34 | 46 | 41 | 15 | 33 | 53 | 42 |
| ≥ 65 | 8 | 12 | 6 | 19 | 6 | 12 | 8 | 18 | 7 | 19 | 0 | 17 |
| Average age (years) | 49 | 51 | 53 | 52 | 48 | 51 | 54 | 52 | 49 | 52 | 52 | 51 |
| **Age When First Elected** | | | | | | | | | | | | |
| < 35 | 19 | 27 | 0 | 32 | 28 | 31 | 0 | 29 | 14 | 24 | 0 | 33 |
| 35–44 | 46 | 30 | 50 | 32 | 44 | 25 | 46 | 23 | 57 | 29 | 47 | 25 |
| 45–54 | 27 | 27 | 39 | 20 | 22 | 22 | 38 | 29 | 22 | 24 | 41 | 25 |
| ≥ 55 | 8 | 17 | 11 | 16 | 6 | 22 | 15 | 18 | 9 | 24 | 12 | 17 |
| Average age (years) | 42 | 43 | 45 | 42 | 40 | 43 | 46 | 43 | 42 | 44 | 45 | 42 |

| | | | | | | | | | | | | |
|---|---|---|---|---|---|---|---|---|---|---|---|---|
| **Education** | | | | | | | | | | | | |
| Unspecified | 26 | 23 | 10 | 6 | 11 | 3 | 7 | 6 | 15 | 5 | 0 | 8 |
| Some college | 33 | 22 | 16 | 14 | 39 | 19 | 21 | 23 | 30 | 19 | 29 | 25 |
| B.A. (or equiv.) | 18 | 29 | 42 | 35 | 22 | 44 | 36 | 35 | 22 | 43 | 24 | 25 |
| M.A. (or equiv.) | 15 | 9 | 10 | 12 | 17 | 16 | 14 | 6 | 17 | 19 | 29 | 8 |
| M.B.A. | 4 | 2 | 5 | 2 | 6 | 3 | 0 | 0 | 8 | 0 | 0 | 0 |
| J.D. | 4 | 8 | 5 | 27 | 6 | 9 | 7 | 24 | 7 | 9 | 17 | 25 |
| Ph.D. or M.D. | 0 | 8 | 10 | 3 | 0 | 6 | 14 | 6 | 0 | 5 | 0 | 8 |
| **Education Score (excluding "unspecified")** | | | | | | | | | | | | |
| 1. Some college | 45 | 30 | 18 | 15 | 44 | 19 | 23 | 25 | 36 | 20 | 29 | 27 |
| 2. B.A. | 25 | 36 | 47 | 37 | 25 | 45 | 38 | 37 | 26 | 45 | 24 | 27 |
| 3. Graduate degree | 30 | 34 | 35 | 47 | 31 | 35 | 38 | 37 | 37 | 35 | 47 | 45 |
| Average score (1-3) | 1.85 | 2.04 | 2.18 | 2.32 | 1.87 | 2.16 | 2.15 | 2.12 | 2.02 | 2.15 | 2.17 | 2.18 |
| **Selected Occupations** | | | | | | | | | | | | |
| Homemaker | 18* | 0* | 0 | 0 | 17* | 0* | 0 | 0 | 25* | 0* | 0 | 0 |
| Education | 30 | 17 | 32* | 11* | 33 | 25 | 43* | 12* | 37 | 24 | 41 | 8 |
| Female-dominated[a] | 59* | 19* | 32* | 7* | 56* | 22* | 43* | 0* | 63* | 14* | 36* | 0* |
| Business[b] | 48 | 56 | 58* | 29* | 44 | 47 | 64 | 59 | 32 | 52 | 71 | 50 |
| Lobbyist | 11 | 2 | 10 | 4 | 17* | 0* | 14 | 6 | 22 | 0 | 8 | 0 |
| Government Employee | 15 | 16 | 32 | 28 | 17 | 9 | 21 | 18 | 17 | 14 | 17 | 17 |
| Aide to public official | 4 | 3 | 23 | 23 | 6 | 3 | 21 | 12 | 8 | 5 | 17 | 8 |
| Lawyer | 4 | 8 | 5* | 27* | 6 | 9 | 7 | 23 | 7 | 9 | 17 | 25 |

[a]Includes social worker, homemaker, primary and/or secondary school teacher, health professional (other than an M.D. or dentist), service employee, clerical worker, nonprofit director or employee.

[b]Includes accounting, banking, financial investments (stocks), real estate investment and development, real estate sales, property management, insurance, small business owner (retail, manufacturing, and service), advertising, marketing, public relations, private sector management and administration, tourism, hotel and restaurant, sales, and any general references to business (e.g., "businesswoman").

* Sex differences for these values are statistically significant ($p \le .05$).

Table A.5 Legislative Status of Arizona and California State Legislators

| | Percentage of Sample Population | | | | Percentage of Interview Sample | | | | Percentage of Questionnaire Sample | | | |
| | Arizona | | California | | Arizona | | California | | Arizona | | California | |
| Legislative Status | Women (N=27) | Men (N=63) | Women (N=19) | Men (N=97) | Women (N=18) | Men (N=32) | Women (N=14) | Men (N=17) | Women (N=11) | Men (N=21) | Women (N=8) | Men (N=12) |
|---|---|---|---|---|---|---|---|---|---|---|---|---|
| Senators | 18* | 40* | 26 | 34 | 11 | 19 | 29 | 29 | 8 | 23 | 29 | 25 |
| Majority Party | 59 | 56 | 53 | 61 | 50 | 59 | 64 | 59 | 59 | 57 | 52 | 58 |
| Leadership Position | 11 | 16 | 10 | 14 | 11 | 16 | 7 | 18 | 0* | 19* | 17 | 17 |
| Committee Chair | 30 | 27 | 37 | 41 | 22 | 28 | 50* | 18* | 25 | 24 | 47* | 8* |
| Years in Office | | | | | | | | | | | | |
| 0–3 (1 term) | 30 | 24 | 21 | 8 | 39 | 31 | 21 | 18 | 46 | 33 | 12 | 8 |
| 4–7 (2–3 terms) | 30 | 21 | 26 | 10 | 22 | 12 | 21 | 29 | 24 | 9 | 47 | 42 |
| 8–11 (4–5 terms) | 22 | 22 | 21 | 42 | 22 | 25 | 21 | 18 | 24 | 24 | 24 | 8 |
| ≥12 (≥ 6 terms) | 18 | 33 | 32 | 39 | 17 | 31 | 36 | 35 | 7 | 33 | 17 | 42 |
| Average (years) | 7.3 | 8.7 | 7.6* | 10.4* | 7.4 | 8.0 | 7.9 | 8.8 | 7.0 | 8.4 | 6.9 | 9.2 |
| Party Margin in District Voter Registration, 1990[a] | | | | | | | | | | | | |
| -19--1% | 18 | 5 | 16 | 9 | 28 | 6 | 7 | 12 | 34 | 5 | 0 | 17 |
| 0-15 | 30 | 24 | 21 | 28 | 33 | 22 | 14 | 23 | 34 | 33 | 29 | 17 |
| 16-30 | 41 | 49 | 26 | 39 | 33 | 59 | 36 | 41 | 32 | 57 | 53 | 42 |
| 31-76 | 11 | 22 | 37 | 24 | 6 | 12 | 43 | 23 | 0 | 4 | 17 | 25 |
| Average margin (%) | 15* | 22* | 26 | 20 | 11* | 19* | 30 | 19 | 8* | 17* | 19 | 17 |
| Last Margin of Victory[b] | | | | | | | | | | | | |
| 0-9% | 26 | 16 | 5 | 10 | 33 | 16 | 7 | 18 | 44 | 19 | 0 | 17 |
| 10-19% | 18 | 21 | 5 | 8 | 28 | 28 | 7 | 18 | 22 | 38 | 12 | 25 |

| | | | | | | | | | | | | |
|---|---|---|---|---|---|---|---|---|---|---|---|
| 20–39% | 33 | 29 | 42 | 36 | 22 | 34 | 29 | 18 | 34 | 33 | 29 | 25 |
| 40–100% | 22 | 34 | 47 | 45 | 17 | 22 | 57 | 47 | 0 | 9 | 59 | 33 |
| Average margin (%) | 28* | 44* | 46* | 36* | 21* | 36* | 47 | 33 | 13* | 26* | 49 | 29 |
| 1990 Primary Margin | | | | | | | | | | | | |
| –14–50% | 37 | 29 | 21 | 11 | 33 | 37 | 29 | 12 | 25 | 29 | 36 | 17 |
| 52–98% | 7 | 2 | 10 | 6 | 0 | 0 | 7 | 0 | 0 | 0 | 0 | 0 |
| 100% | 52 | 56 | 47 | 67 | 61 | 56 | 43 | 71 | 66 | 67 | 35 | 75 |
| Did not run[c] | 4 | 13 | 21 | 16 | 6 | 6 | 21 | 18 | 8 | 5 | 29 | 8 |
| Average margin (%) (excluding did-not-runs) | 72 | 72 | 73 | 88 | 75 | 68 | 65 | 88 | 81 | 73 | 55 | 85 |
| 1990 General Election Margin | | | | | | | | | | | | |
| –20–15% | 48 | 38 | 10 | 20 | 61 | 55 | 14 | 18 | 68 | 67 | 12 | 25 |
| 16–30% | 22 | 21 | 21 | 33 | 17 | 17 | 14 | 35 | 15 | 17 | 12 | 50 |
| 31–100% | 26 | 28 | 47 | 32 | 17 | 21 | 50 | 29 | 8 | 11 | 47 | 17 |
| Did not run[d] | 4 | 14 | 21 | 16 | 6 | 7 | 21 | 18 | 8 | 6 | 8 | 29 |
| Average margin (%) (excluding did-not-runs) | 34 | 34 | 48* | 29* | 26 | 28 | 52 | 29 | 17 | 16 | 56 | 24 |

[a] For Democratic legislators, figures were calculated by subtracting the percentage of registered Republicans from the percentage of registered Democrats within the legislator's district; for Republican legislators, figures were calculated by subtracting the percentage of registered Democrats from the percentage of registered Republicans.

[b] The years for this statistic are 1988 for all Arizona state legislators, all California assembly members, and half of California senators; and 1986 for the other half of California senators.

[c] Includes legislators who retired or ran for another office, California senators not up for reelection, and one Independent.

[d] Includes legislators who retired or ran for another office and California senators not up for reelection. Legislators who lost primaries are excluded.

* Sex differences for these values are statistically significant ($p = .05$).

The questionnaire samples of female legislators (in these tables and throughout the analysis presented in the text) have been weighted to make them more representative of the partisan composition of the total populations of Arizona and California female legislators. Thus, the partisan breakdowns of the questionnaire samples are exactly the same as the partisan breakdowns of the sample populations. If the female questionnaire samples were not weighted, the figures would be as shown in Table A.6.

Table A.6    Party Affiliations in Unweighted Questionnaire Sample

|  | Arizona | | | California | |
| --- | --- | --- | --- | --- | --- |
| Party<br>Affiliation | Women<br>(N = 13)<br>(%) | Men<br>(N = 21)<br>(%) | | Women<br>(N = 7)<br>(%) | Men<br>(N = 12)<br>(%) |
| Democrat | 46 | 43 | | 43 | 58 |
| Republican | 54 | 57 | | 57 | 42 |

While there are no statistically significant sex differences in partisanship in either state, there are potentially serious disparities between the partisanship of the women who returned the questionnaires and the partisanship of all the women who served in the Arizona and California state legislatures. The unweighted Arizona female sample is a little too Democratic, and the unweighted California female sample is too Republican. The fact that Republicans rather than Democrats constitute a majority of the unweighted California female sample presented the strongest argument for introducing weights.

## A Note on Statistical Significance

No matter how large and how randomly selected, a sample can never be a perfect facsimile of the population from which it came. Samples can only be approximations of their respective populations. Thus, a sample of legislators can only approximate the entire legislative body from which they were selected. The sample of California female legislators drawn for this study, for example, can only approximate the entire population of female members of the 1990 California state legislature. Some amount of error is always present whenever one examines the characteristics of a sample. This sampling error is not only unavoidable but also unbiased. Its distortions are random, not going in any particular direction nor favoring any particular result.

The concept of sampling error may be becoming more familiar as a growing number of news media polls are reporting routinely their margins of error (Mann and Orren 1992). An election poll, for example, may report that 45 percent of registered voters who were surveyed plan to vote for Candidate Smith, give or take 3 percentage points. This means that one can be confident that between 42 percent and 48 percent of *all* registered voters (in the relevant population) plan to vote for Candidate Smith. The larger the sampling error is, the wider that range of confidence will be; in other words, one's estimation of the preferences of all registered voters will be less accurate, the greater the sampling error.

Most of the data analysis presented in this study compares samples of female and male state legislators to determine whether or not they differ. But the women and men in this study are not carbon copies of each other; they always differ to some degree. The question, then, is, when are their differences really significant? One way to start answering this question is to figure out whether the sex differences observed in the sample are statistically significant, that is, not simply attributable to sampling error. Say, for example, one observes that 40 percent of the female legislators sampled voted in favor of a particular bill, while only 35 percent of the male legislators sampled did the same. Suppose, also, that the margin of error for these estimates were plus-or-minus 3 percentage points. Thus, one estimates that between 37 percent and 43 percent of all female legislators voted in favor of the bill, as did 32 percent to 38 percent of all male legislators. Note that there is a very good chance that 37 percent or 38 percent of both female and male legislators voted in favor of the bill—that there really is no difference in how female and male legislators voted.

Tests of statistical significance gauge the probability that what one observes in the sample is not, in fact, true for the entire population from which the sample was chosen. In the case of sex differences observed in a sample, a test of statistical significance determines the chances that there really are no sex differences in the sample population. Most often, social scientists report the results of these tests of statistical significance in terms of $p = .xx$, where .xx is the probability that whatever difference or relationship one finds in the sample is due to sampling error and therefore is not present in the sample population. Thus, $p$ can range between zero and one; due to the inevitability of at least some amount of sampling error, however, $p$ can never be absolutely zero or completely one. Conventionally, social scientists declare a difference or relationship to be statistically significant if $p$ is less than or equal to .05, meaning there is no more than a 5 percent chance that there really is no difference or no relationship in the sample population.

Tests of statistical significance can be one-tailed or two-tailed, depending on one's hypotheses, or expectations, about the differences or relationships at hand. One-tailed tests are used if hypotheses are unidirectional; two-tailed tests are used if hypotheses do not specify a direction for the expected differences or relationships. In this study, all hypotheses regarding sex differences are unidirectional. Female and male legislators are expected to differ in a particular way; one sex is expected to be more likely than the other to do, believe, or say some specific thing. A two-tailed hypothesis would not specify which of the two sexes is supposed to be more likely to do, believe, or say that thing. The interpretation of $p$ is slightly different depending on whether the test of statistical significance is one-tailed or two-tailed. The interpretation offered above ($p$ is the chance that there really is no difference in the sample population) is applicable for two-tailed tests, for all one is concerned about in that case is whether or not there is a difference—any difference, in either direction. For a one-tailed test, $p$ is the chance that the particular sort of difference hypothesized and/or observed in the sample is not actually present in the sample population. Given the same sample observation, a one-tailed $p$ will be exactly half the two-tailed $p$.

As stated above, gauging statistical significance is only one way of evaluating the substantive significance of, say, a sex difference observed in a sample of state legislators. It is, in fact, often dangerous to equate statistical significance with substantive significance. One can be confident that an observed difference is probably not due to sampling error, but that does not necessarily mean that the difference is truly significant. One of the main reasons for the discrepancy between statistical and substantive significance is that the former is very much dependent upon sample size, as is sampling error. The larger the sample size (or the number of cases, elements, or observations in a sample), the smaller the sampling error and thus the lower the probability that the difference observed in the sample is due only to sampling error. Hence, a seemingly small percentage difference between male and female legislators—say, a 5 percent difference—may be statistically significant if the sample is very large (and the sampling error thus very small). On the other hand, a relatively large percentage difference—say, a 10 percent difference—may not be statistically significant if the sample is small (and the sampling error thus relatively large).

For this reason, I consider other factors in addition to statistical significance when drawing conclusions about the substantive significance of sex differences observed in this study. First, I examine the sheer magnitude of the sex difference. A 20 percentage point difference seems, on its face, much more significant than a 2 point difference. There is an important common-sense component to these evaluations. Second, I often explore the potential "real life" ramifications of the sex differences. For example, when investigating sex differences in legislators' roll call votes, I ask: Did the women provide the winning margin of victory (or the losing margin of defeat)? Would the bill have passed (or failed) if only women had voted, or if the women had not voted? Third, I look at patterns of sex differences across multiple indicators of the same general type of attitude or behavior. Consistent patterns of sex differences are considered more significant than inconsistent, sporadic ones. In the end, assessing the significance of sex differences cannot be an entirely objective process. It is very much a matter of judgment, argumentation, and persuasion.

# Roll Call Votes

Tables B.1 and B.2 list all roll call votes recorded and analyzed in this study for, respectively, the Arizona and California legislatures (see Chapter 5). Short descriptions of each proposed bill and motion are included. "Yes" votes are liberal votes unless indicated otherwise. Bills or votes marked (GG) were included in the index of support for women's (modal) positions on gender gap issues, issues on which women and men in public opinion polls tend to differ; those marked (W) were included in the index of support for women's rights, as reported in Table 5.2.

Table B.1   Arizona Roll Call Votes, 1990

| Bill | Chamber | Date | Vote (Yes–No) | Description |
|------|---------|------|---------------|-------------|
| H2002 | Senate | 6/28 | 16–12 | Kindergarten: appropriate $1.4 million to operate full-day kindergarten programs in low-income areas (GG) |
| H2057 | Senate | 6/18 | 14–15 | Firearms: bar law agencies from destroying a seized firearm unless it has been altered or is an automatic weapon ("yes" = conservative) (GG) |
| H2067 | Senate | 5/8 | 17–12 | Day Care Credits: provide income tax credits to employers who provide day care services to employees (W) |
| H2127 | House | 6/20 | 22–36 | Auto Insurance: require state approval of auto insurance rate hike exceeding 3.5% and create rate advocate office |
| H2154 | Senate | 5/1 | 19–10 | Lake Fund: exempt money in the state Lake Improvement Fund from annual legislative appropriation (GG) |

| Bill | Chamber | Date | Vote (Yes–No) | Description |
|------|---------|------|---------------|-------------|
| H2173 | Senate | 6/14 | 16–12 | AIDS Testing: protect confidentiality of persons testing positive for AIDS; prohibit testing without consent (GG) |
| H2177 | Senate | 6/14 | 16–12 | Homeless: appropriate $705,000 for homeless shelters this year and set up permanent homeless trust fund (GG) |
| H2197 | Senate | 6/11 | 19–7 | Traffic Arrests: allows police to stop a person for "actual or suspected" violation of any traffic law ("yes" = conservative) |
| H2219 | House | 2/22 | 32–20 | Superfund: fund state water quality Superfund with a variety of taxes on potential polluters (GG) |
| H2240 | House | 6/28 | 31–25 | Pool Fences: require new swimming pools to be enclosed by an inner fence with a self-latching gate (GG) |
|  | Senate | 6/28 | 16–11 |  |
| H2256 | House | 2/22 | 26–26 | Tuition Freeze: floor motion on H2256 to freeze tuition rates paid by Arizona residents at the three state universities (GG) |
| H2268 | House | 4/18 | 37–17 | AHCCCS Services: allow outpatient surgical centers to provide nonabortion family planning services through AHCCCS (W) |
| H2354 | House | 3/22 | 31–29 | Sex Shops: change obscenity standard to make prosecution easier and impose various restrictions on sex shops ("yes" = conservative) (GG,W) |
| H2361 | House | 3/22 | 34–26 | AIDS Education: require Arizona public schools to offer AIDS-education programs at all grade levels (GG) |
| H2384 | House | 6/4 | 21–29 | Animal Release: make it a felony to release laboratory animals without consent of owner or custodian ("yes" = conservative) |
|  | Senate | 5/24 | 19–9 | Lab Animal Tests: motion on H2384 to instruct conference committee to prohibit use of live animals for cosmetic experimentation |
| H2433 | House | 4/2 | 41–17 | Drunk Driving: allow DUI suspects to undergo blood-alcohol testing up to two hours after arrest ("yes" = conservative) (GG) |
| H2506 | House | 4/5 | 34–24 | Health Insurance: allow small businesses to offer scaled-back health insurance benefits to employees ("yes" = conservative) (GG) |

| Bill | Chamber | Date | Vote (Yes–No) | Description |
|------|---------|------|---------------|-------------|
| H2507 | House | 3/27 | 35–25 | Privatization: state agencies must maintain lists of private entities seeking to provide public goods and services ("yes" = conservative) |
|  | Senate | 6/8 | 16–12 | Privatization: sets up procedure by which private businesses may bid to take over government functions ("yes" = conservative) |
| H2524 | Senate | 6/28 | 16–10 | Welfare Aid: increase minimum welfare assistance payments to dependent children (GG) |
| H2562 | House | 5/8 | 36–20 | State Superfund: tax household chemical products, city water use, landfills, etc. to finance state water quality Superfund (GG) |
| H2565 | Senate | 6/15 | 17–12 | Preschool Project: appropriate $600,000 for pilot project to help children in low-income areas avoid poor start in school (GG) |
| H2583 | House | 5/10 | 35–23 | State Comp Fund: make State Compensation Fund operate more like a private business by severing some of its state ties ("yes" = conservative) |
| H2592 | Senate | 6/28 | 16–12 | Unemployment Aid: increase the maximum weekly unemployment benefit to $165 from $155 (GG) |
| H2630 | Senate | 5/1 | 17–12 | Youth Suicide: begin suicide prevention pilot projects in one rural school district and one urban school district (GG) |
| H2675 | Senate | 5/1 | 18–11 | Earth Schooling: require all school districts to offer environmental education as part of the general curriculum (GG) |
| (Special Session) | | | | |
| H2026 | House | 6/28 | 31–26 | Tax Increases: boost taxes on personal and corporate income, cigarettes, Palo Verde plant, etc. to raise $250 million |
|  | Senate | 6/27 | 16–12 | |
| (Special Session) | | | | |
| H2027 | House | 6/28 | 31–26 | Gasoline Tax: increase the per-gallon gasoline tax to 17 cents from 16 cents beginning Sept. 30 to raise $20.8 million |
|  | Senate | 6/27 | 16–12 | |
| S1004 | House | 5/3 | 38–21 | Concealed Guns: allow residents to be licensed to carry concealed weapons upon completion of firearms safety course ("yes" = conservative) (GG) |

| Bill | Chamber | Date | Vote (Yes–No) | Description |
|------|---------|------|---------------|-------------|
| S1044 | Senate | 2/26 | 17–11 | AIDS: insurance policy discrimination against people with HIV infection or AIDS would be illegal (GG) |
| S1060 | Senate | 2/19 | 17–11 | Homeless: school district governing boards must admit nonresident children without paying tuition in certain cases (GG) |
| S1082 | House | 6/21 | 34–12 | Air Pollution: allow state DEQ to seek civil penalty of up to $10,000 a day against air-pollution violators (GG) |
| S1099 | House | 4/30 | 23–29 | Worker Politics: motion on S1099 to reject amendment allowing state government workers to participate in political campaigns ("yes" = conservative) |
| S1140 | House | 6/22 | 32–22 | Med-Mal Coverage: provide $205,000 |
|       | Senate | 6/25 | 16–9 | obstetrical malpractice insurance subsidy mainly to clinics that serve working poor (W) |
| S1195 | House | 6/18 | 34–23 | Hardwood Ban: motion on S1195 to have conference committee reinsert provision barring tropical hardwoods in state buildings (GG) |
| S1205 | Senate | 5/21 | 16–12 | Child Care: allow the Department of Economic Security to establish a child care resource and referral system (W) |
| S1207 | Senate | 3/19 | 18–12 | Midwives: expands Health Services Department authority and regulation of midwives, including licensing, fees, penalties (W) |
| S1250 | House | 5/15 | 35–23 | Seat Belts: require front passenger use of seat |
|       | Senate | 5/22 | 16–13 | belts and call on insurers to "reflect" accident savings in rates (GG) |
| S1286 | House | 4/12 | 33–22 | Inmate Leave: restrict compassionate leave of prison inmates to cases of family emergency, death, or grave illness ("yes" = conservative) (GG) |
| S1525 | Senate | 4/10 | 16–12 | Privatization: establish a nine-member Commission on Efficiency in State Government and Privatization ("yes" = conservative) |

(Special Session)

| Bill | Chamber | Date | Vote (Yes–No) | Description |
|------|---------|------|---------------|-------------|
| S1001 | House | 5/16 | 35–25 | King Day: cancel King/Columbus Day |
|       | Senate | 5/15 | 16–14 | referendum; reestablish paid King Day; keep paid Columbus Day (GG) |

| Bill | Chamber | Date | Vote (Yes–No) | Description |
|------|---------|------|---------------|-------------|
| SCM1003 | Senate | 3/15 | 15–10 | Federal Budget: asks Congress to propose a constitutional change limiting federal spending to a percentage of the GNP ("yes" = conservative) |

Source: *Arizona Capitol Times*, February 21–July 4, 1990.

Table B.2   California Roll Call Votes, 1989–1990

| Bill | Chamber | Date | Vote (Yes–No) | Description |
|------|---------|------|---------------|-------------|
| AB11 | Assembly | 9/14/89 | 50–28 | AIDS Education: require AIDS prevention instruction for grades 7–12, providing notice and permission slips to parents (GG) |
|      | Senate | 9/12/89 | 23–6 | |
| AB25 | Assembly | 8/30/90 | 44–26 | AIDS Education (watered-down version of AB11, which was vetoed by governor) (GG) |
|      | Senate | 8/29/90 | 24–7 | |
| AB65 | Assembly | 9/13/89 | 45–31 | AIDS Discrimination: regarding employment and housing (GG) |
|      | Senate | 9/11/89 | 25–6 | |
| AB77 | Assembly | 8/31/90 | 45–25 | Family Rights Act: guarantee four months per year unpaid family leave; prohibit related employment discrimination (W) |
|      | Senate | 8/30/90 | 23–14 | |
| AB80 | Assembly | 6/8/89 | 55–19 | Solid Waste Recycling Act: require local governments to prepare, adopt and implement waste reduction and recycling plans (GG) |
| AB357 | Assembly | 5/18/89 | 41–35 | Firearms: increase criminal penalties for manufacture, possession, and/or use of assault weapons (GG) |
|       | Senate | 5/18/89 | 27–11 | |
| AB360 | Assembly | 9/14/89 | 60–16 | Mental Health Insurance Reform Act: require provision of a specified level of mental health services (GG) |
| AB390 | Assembly | 6/30/89 | 42–27 | Old-growth Timber Stands: prohibit clear-cutting of any virgin old-growth timber; commission study of economic impact (GG) |
| AB497 | Assembly | 2/15/90 | 46–26 | Firearms: extend regulations and restrictions on concealable weapons to all firearms (GG) |
|       | Senate | 2/8/90 | 23–10 | |
| AB510 | Assembly | 8/27/90 | 42–29 | Higher Education: employer-employee relations |
|       | Senate | 5/10/90 | 25–8 | |

| Bill | Chamber | Date | Vote (Yes–No) | Description |
|---|---|---|---|---|
| AB795 | Assembly | 7/1/89 | 56–14 | Homeless Persons: creation of state Homeless Coordinated Intake System Program for delivery of services, data collection, and individual case management (GG) |
| AB870 | Assembly | 9/13/89 | 45–27 | Child Care Facilities, Public Buildings: extend requirement to all public buildings, not just new or newly renovated ones (W) |
| | Senate | 9/11/89 | 25–7 | |
| AB939 | Assembly | 9/15/89 | 43–28 | California Integrated Solid Waste Management Act: create state Waste Management and Recycling Board; make counties and cities liable (GG) |
| | Senate | 9/15/89 | 22–15 | |
| AB1223 | Assembly | 7/1/89 | 50–20 | In-home Support Services for Aged, Blind, and Disabled: increase oversight and services (GG) |
| | Senate | 9/14/89 | 21–15 | |
| AB1377 | Assembly | 7/10/89 | 43–31 | Recycling: mandate increased use of recycled products by public entities and tax breaks for private users (GG) |
| AB1494 | Assembly | 6/26/89 | 45–27 | County Welfare Departments, Procedural Rules: ease application requirements for AFDC (GG) |
| | Senate | 9/5/89 | 11–12 | |
| AB1680 | Assembly | 4/16/90 | 42–31 | Firearms, Sale and Transfer: require and establish basic firearms safety course and certification (GG) |
| | Senate | 4/26/90 | 21–16 | |
| AB1718 | Assembly | 7/5/89 | 43–25 | Greenhouse Gas Reduction and Ozone Protection Act (GG) |
| AB1719 | Assembly | 9/13/89 | 42–32 | AIDS Information to Employees: require provision by public and private employers of 25+ full-time employees (GG) |
| | Senate | 9/11/89 | 21–17 | |
| AB2549 | Assembly | 6/7/90 | 43–29 | Air Pollution: increase regulation of hazardous waste facilities (GG) |
| | Senate | 8/29/90 | 22–8 | |
| AB2677 | Assembly | 6/11/90 | 42–30 | State Boards and Commissions: establish new guidelines re gender composition (W) |
| AB3050 | Assembly | 6/14/90 | 42–24 | Beverage Containers, Recycling: define "beverage" for purposes of the California Beverage Container Recycling and Litter Reduction Act; exclude wine (GG) |
| AB3580 | Assembly | 8/30/90 | 46–29 | Local taxes, Graffiti: authorize cities and counties to levy taxes on aerosol paint and felt-tip markers, to be used for removal and prevention of graffiti (GG) |
| | Senate | 8/29/90 | 29–3 | |

| Bill | Chamber | Date | Vote (Yes–No) | Description |
|------|---------|------|---------------|-------------|
| AB3642 | Assembly | 5/21/90 | 46–22 | Auto Insurance, Assigned-Risk Plan: establish state advisory committee to administer and operate plan (rather than private insurers) |
|  | Senate | 8/31/90 | 29–1 |  |
| AB3779 | Assembly | 6/7/90 | 44–28 | Acutely Hazardous Materials Management: increase regulations regarding public information; require public hearings (GG) |
|  | Senate | 8/29/90 | 21–4 |  |
| AB4006 | Assembly | 5/7/90 | 47–22 | Occupational Safety and Health: increase by 50% the amount of civil penalties (GG) |
|  | Senate | 8/9/90 | 27–9 |  |
| AJR69 | Assembly | 8/20/90 | 44–31 | Federal Labor Laws: call on Congress to further protect employee rights regarding union activity, collective bargaining |
|  | Senate | 8/16/90 | 22–10 |  |
| AJR97 | Assembly | 6/14/90 | 51–16 | Flag Desecration: call for constitutional amendment ("yes" = conservative) |
| ACR84 | Senate | 3/22/90 | 19–14 | STRS & PERS, international investments |
| SR42 | Senate | 3/15/90 | 22–12 | Senate Commission on Property Tax Equity and Revenue, Creation: to address disparities in property taxes due to Proposition 13 |
| SJR62 | Assembly | 8/22/90 | 43–27 | Civil Rights: support federal Civil Rights Act of 1990 (W) |
|  | Senate | 5/24/90 | 22–5 |  |
| SB2 | Senate | 5/26/89 | 29–6 | Capital Punishment Act: specify additional conduct subject to death penalty ("yes" = conservative) (GG) |
| SB991 | Senate | 9/14/89 | 23–10 | Aid to Families with Dependent Children: ease residency requirements; expedite immediate assistance (GG) |
| SB1770 | Assembly | 8/31/90 | 44–27 | Air Pollution: create San Joaquin Valley Air Quality Management District (GG) |
|  | Senate | 8/31/90 | 22–9 |  |
| SB1781 | Assembly | 8/29/90 | 43–31 | Natural Disaster Relief: include assistance for temporary shelter (GG) |
|  | Senate | 6/14/90 | 29–3 |  |
| SB1787 | Assembly | 8/29/90 | 42–32 | Coastal Resources, Enforcement: establish civil liability for violations of the California Coastal Act (GG) |
|  | Senate | 8/31/90 | 21–13 |  |
| SB2078 | Assembly | 8/22/90 | 46–29 | Commission on Pay Equity, Creation; with representation of California Commission on the Status of Women (W) |
|  | Senate | 6/12/90 | 25–13 |  |
| SB2154 | Assembly | 8/22/90 | 57–18 | Adolescent Health Programs: appropriate funds from leftover federal maternal and child health funds (GG) |
|  | Senate | 6/14/90 | 24–8 |  |

| Bill | Chamber | Date | Vote (Yes–No) | Description |
|------|---------|------|---------------|-------------|
| SB2217 | Assembly | 8/22/90 | 43–3 | Labor Disputes, Liability: limit liability to |
| | Senate | 5/24/90 | 23–13 | only those who knowingly participate, authorize or ratify unlawful acts |
| SB2868 | Senate | 6/14/90 | 27–9 | Health Insurance: ensure affordable access to health care for all California residents (GG) |

Source: *California Journal,* March 1991, Vol. 22, no. 3.

# Legislative Subject Codes and Corresponding Standing Committees

Table C.1 lists the legislative subject codes used in the analysis of legislators' policy priorities (see Chapter 6). Table C.2 groups the legislative subject codes into nine more general issue areas. Table C.3 indicates the relevant standing committees for each issue area in the legislative chambers of the two states.

**Table C.1 Legislative Subject Codes**

**Social Welfare, Social Services**

001. General social services
005. Family law: divorce, surrogate parenting, adoption, child custody, family care leave, child support, foster care
007. Day care, child care, parental leave
020. Education (K–12): school districts, buildings, finance; teacher credentials and training
       021. Education: primary/early (elementary school) only
       022. Education: secondary (middle and high school) only
       024. Education: postsecondary (colleges, universities, vocational) only
030. Aged/elderly, Social Security
       031. Widows and widowers
035. Disabled: handicapped access, discrimination, health care
040. Health care: public health, in-home support services, nursing homes, long-term care
       041. Mental health only
       044. Biomedical ethics
       045. Abortion, fetal rights/protection
       046. AIDS
047. Sex education

---

NOTE: These codes were used to categorize legislators' policy priorities, general goals, and bills introduced.

050. Public safety: earthquake protection/preparedness/relief, auto and motorcycle (traffic) safety, emergency services (including medical), fire codes, building safety standards, flood control
   051. Safety in the workplace, occupational safety and health
070. Welfare, Workfare, antipoverty, measures: aid for economically disadvantaged
071. Housing: providing housing for the poor/homeless
080. Community service, volunteer programs, charitable organizations
090. Religion, religious organizations

## Agriculture

100. Farm economics: agriculture, food and livestock, food quality/safety control
   105. Rodeos and agricultural fairs
110. Rural concerns (general)
115. Fish and game, hunting
120. Animal rights, protection, health (not including endangered species)

## Environment, Natural Resources, Planning and Development

150. Conservation/preservation of natural resources: protecting the environment/endangered species, energy conservation, oil spill prevention and response, clean air/water
160. Waste management: hazardous/toxic/radioactive and non-; dumps, landfills
   165. Regulation and handling of toxic substances (including cleanup)
170. Development and management of natural resources/energy sources: regulation of state water resources, administration of water districts, development of solar energy, mining
175. Quality of life, open space, parks and recreation (development and maintenance), urban beautification (litter and graffiti abatement), noise pollution, amusements and sports
180. Development: local and regional planning, redevelopment, land use, eminent domain, zoning
185. Transportation: development, planning, maintenance, administration, etc.; congestion, commuting problems

## Groups

200. Children, juveniles, minors
210. Women
   215. Women and infants, pregnant women
216. Parents
220. Ethnic and racial minorities (including Native Americans)
240. General disadvantaged, "at-risk," underrepresented

## Civil Rights and Crime

300. Civil rights and civil liberties, human rights
301. Equality, injustice (general goals only)
   305. Antidiscrimination
   310. Affirmative action

320. Civil procedures only (without reference to specific areas such as insurance, corporate law, real estate law, etc.), tort law, regulation of arbitrators/arbitration and mediators/mediation
330. Drugs
    331. Drugs: supply-side only, criminal sanctions for sale and manufacture
    332. Drugs (and alcohol): demand-side only, education, detoxification, criminal sanctions for use, drug testing, use surveys
333. Gangs
340. Crime: criminal law, law enforcement, sentencing, testimony, parole, criminal investigations
    341. Crime: victims only
    342. Sex offenses, domestic violence (including shelters and other victim support services)
    343. Harassment
    344. Gun control, regulation of manufacture and sale of firearms; use of guns in criminal acts
    346. Pornography, obscenity
    350. Driving under the influence of alcohol or drugs
    360. Child abuse and neglect (including sex offenses against children)
370. Corrections: prison maintenance, prison education, rehabilitation, prisoner health and well-being, general probation regulations

## Economics, Business, Finance, Insurance, etc.

400. Taxes and revenues (nonprogrammatic): sales, property, income taxes; regulation of bonds; fees (including motor vehicle fines, registration fees, park fees, etc., but not criminal fines); public financing and investments; administration of Franchise Tax Board (in California)
425. Banking, finance, etc.: securities and commodities; surety bonds; mortgages; management of institutional funds, trusts, etc.; creditors
430. Wills, real estate, probate, escrow, property (not specifically related to property taxes)
432. Owner-tenant relations
450. Professions and occupations: licensing, educational requirements, certification (not including teachers, peace officers, and other public employees)
475. Insurance: auto, home, health, malpractice, etc.; auto liability enforcement; availability
500. Public utilities: administration, rates, procurement
525. Consumer/buyer protection: product safety, consumer privacy, fraud, false advertising, unfair or deceptive business practices related to individual consumers (or potential consumers), product labeling and information
526. Small claims
550. Labor: wages, unions, employee contracts, benefits, unemployment compensation, workers' compensation, hiring and firing, employment/job training (not including public employees/employment: see 825)
570. Small business
575. Commerce: economic development, commercial fishing, contracting, shipping, corporations, trade secrets, promotion/protection of state industries, antitrust and commercial law
    576. "Sin" commerce: gambling, tobacco, alcohol, adult entertainment
    580. Tourism

## Foreign Affairs, Veteran Affairs

700. International relations (general)
710. Relations with Soviet Union and Eastern Europe
720. Relations with Central and South America
725. Relations with Canada
730. Relations with South Africa: sanctions, antiapartheid
735. Relations with the Middle East
740. Relations with Japan
741. Relations with other Asian countries
750. Veterans: recognition, benefits
755. Current military personnel: recognition, honors, benefits, etc.
760. Immigration, resident aliens, refugees
765. Border relations, international/border trade
770. Defense/military: spending, industries, bases

## Government Operations, Elections, Bureaucracy

800. Local Government: administration of counties, municipalities, service districts (not including school, community college or water districts); state-local relations
815. Ethics in government: honoraria, lobbying, revolving door, term limits, open meetings, notification of public meetings
820. Campaign finance and expenditures, campaign advertising and communication
825. Public employees and officials: wages and salary, retirement systems
828. Prevent bad legislation (general goal only)
829. Limited, efficient government (general goal only)
830. Agency administration: government efficiency, oversight, procurement and government contracting, administration of state land and buildings, maintenance of public records and archives ("agency" includes commissions and boards)
831. Miscellaneous motor vehicle regulations (not directly related to traffic safety or auto insurance): licensing, registration, towing
835. Judicial administration: court facilities, judicial appointments, jurisdictions, court employees
840. Budget and budget reform
845. Preventative spending (general goal only): rearrange state spending priorities away from prisons and crime toward early intervention in health and education
850. Elections: voter records, redistricting, initiatives and referenda
860. Procedural rules of the legislative body, administration of the legislature, reform of the legislative system, leadership

## Miscellaneous

900. Miscellaneous (e.g., California Poppy Day, decorative heirloom marriage certificates, geographic and historic names board, state holidays—not including Martin Luther King Day)
910. Personal advancement, higher office (general goal only)
920. Partisan concerns (general goals only)
925. District: promotion, individual problems, district-specific problems, constituent honors
951. Increase state powers; federalism; state-federal relations (general goal only)
975. Purely technical (usually used in Arizona as a carrier for a "strike everything" amendment)

## Table C.2 Issue Areas and Legislative Subject Codes

| Issue Area | Legislative Subject Codes |
|---|---|
| **"Women's Issues"** | |
| Women | 045. Abortion |
| | 210. Women |
| | 215. Women and infants, pregnant women |
| | 342. Sex offenses, domestic violence |
| Children and Families | 005. Family law: divorce, child support/custody, etc. |
| | 007. Day/child care, parental leave |
| | 200. Children |
| | 216. Parents |
| | 360. Child abuse and neglect |
| Education | 020. Education (general) |
| | 021. Primary/early education only |
| | 022. Secondary education only |
| | 024. Higher education only |
| Health and Public Safety | 030. Aged/elderly |
| | 035. Disabled |
| | 040. Health care (general) |
| | 041. Mental health only |
| | 044. Biomedical ethics |
| | 046. AIDS |
| | 050. Public safety |
| | 051. Occupational safety |
| Poverty | 070. Welfare/workfare/antipoverty |
| | 071. Housing, homeless |
| | 240. Poor, disadvantaged, "at risk," underrepresented |
| Environment | 150. Conservation/preservation of natural resources |
| | 160. Waste management |
| | 165. Toxic substances: clean-up, disposal, etc. |
| | 170. Development and management of natural/energy resources |
| **"Men's Issues"** | |
| Commerce | 425. Banking, finance |
| | 430. Wills and estates, real estate |
| | 432. Owner-tenant relations |
| | 450. Professions and occupations |
| | 475. Insurance |
| | 500. Public utilities |
| | 550. Labor |
| | 575. Commerce, economic development |
| | 576. "Sin" commerce only (gambling, alcohol, etc.) |
| | 580. Tourism |

| Fiscal | 400. Taxes and revenues (nonprogrammatic) |
| | 829. Government efficiency |
| | 840. Budget and budget reform |
| Agriculture | 100. Agriculture, farming and ranching |
| | 105. Rodeos and agricultural fairs |
| | 110. Rural concerns (general) |
| | 115. Fish and game |

**Table C.3   Issue Area Committees in the Arizona and California State Legislatures**

| | Relevant Legislative Committees | | | |
| | Arizona | | California | |
| Issue Area | House | Senate | Assembly | Senate |
|---|---|---|---|---|
| Women | Health Judiciary | Judiciary | Health Public Safety | Health and Human Services |
| Children and Families | Human Resources and Aging Judiciary | Health, Welfare, Aging and Environment Judiciary | Human Services Judiciary | Health and Human Services Judiciary |
| Education | Education | Education | Education | Education |
| Health and Public Safety | Health Human Resources and Aging | Health, Welfare, Aging and Environment | Aging and Long Term Care Earthquake Preparedness and Natural Disaster Health | Health and Human Services |
| Poverty | Human Resources and Aging | Health, Welfare, Aging and Environment | Housing and Community Development Human Services | Health and Human Services Housing and Urban Affairs |
| Environment | Environment Natural Resources and Agriculture Public Institutions and Rural Development | Health, Welfare, Aging and Environment Natural Resources and Agriculture | Environmental Safety and Toxic Materials Natural Resources Water, Parks, and Wildlife | Agriculture and Water Resources Energy and Public Utilities Natural Resources and Wildlife Toxics and Public Safety Management |

| | Relevant Legislative Committees | | | |
| | Arizona | | California | |
| Issue Area | House | Senate | Assembly | Senate |
| --- | --- | --- | --- | --- |
| Commerce | Banking and Insurance Commerce Tourism, Professions, and Occupations | Commerce, Labor, Insurance, and Banking | Economic Development and New Technology Finance and Insurance Government Organization Labor and Employment Utilities and Commerce | Banking and Commerce Business and Professions Energy and Public Utilities Government Organization Industrial Relations Insurance, Claims, and Corporations |
| Fiscal | Appropriations Ways and Means | Appropriations Finance | Revenue and Taxation Ways and Means | Appropriations Bonded Indebtedness and Methods of Financing Budget and Fiscal Review Revenue and Taxation |
| Agriculture | Natural Resources and Agriculture Public Institutions and Rural Development | Natural Resources and Agriculture | Agriculture Water, Parks and Wildlife | Agriculture and Water Resources Natural Resources and Wildlife |

# Notes

## Introduction

1. Information obtained from the National Information Bank on Women in Public Office, Center for the American Woman and Politics (CAWP), Eagleton Institute of Politics, Rutgers University.

2. For good summaries of this research, see Carroll (1991); Kelly, Saint-Germain, and Horn (1991); Mandel and Dodson (1992); Mezey (1994). A great deal of this research has been conducted by or under the auspices of CAWP.

3. These conclusions are drawn from analyses of both roll call votes and survey responses.

4. This preoccupation with sex differences and the concomitant neglect of similarities is not limited to political science. Epstein (1988: 39) notes a general failure in social science gender research to report adequately "similarities between males and females because it is the differences that are regarded as 'findings' " and "a tendency for isolated positive findings to sweep through the literature, while findings of no difference . . . are ignored." See also Thorne's (1990) analysis of sex difference research in psychology.

5. This focus on male domination as the primary explanation for similarity among male and female officeholders is more characteristic of the research literature on U.S. officials than of that on public officials in other democratic nations. Studies of sex differences among Australian legislators, for example, have stressed the equalizing role of strong party government as an explanation for similarity (Considine and Deutchman 1994; McAllister and Studlar 1992). See also Skjeie (1991) on parliamentarians in Norway.

6. Berkman and O'Connor (1993) provide some interesting evidence that women do manage to "make a difference" on abortion policy even when they are few in number. Yet the ways in which these women affect policy are much more subtle and defensive than the more obvious routes of policy initiation and leadership and, therefore, are more difficult to capture empirically.

7. Other scholars who have expressed similar doubts about Kanter's numerically oriented theory include Considine and Deutchman (1996), Dahlerup (1988), Skjeie (1991), and Yoder (1991).

Chapter One

1. These results are reported in Sapiro (1983: 145).

2. According to Alexander and Andersen (1993: 534), a great deal of the research about gender-differentiated public perceptions of political candidates' skills and traits has been commissioned by NWPC. Indeed, most of the references to such polls in the popular press cite NWPC.

3. Only 14 percent of those polled thought male candidates were more likely to bring about change.

4. See Costello and Krimgold (1996) for the latest statistics. Amott and Matthaei (1996) provide an excellent overview of how these trends in labor force participation of women vary across racial-ethnic lines.

5. See Herz and Wooton (1996) for exact figures on gender composition of various occupations.

6. Gilligan's work has elicited quite a bit of critical commentary, including journal-sponsored symposia (*Signs* 1986, vol. 11, no. 2; *Social Research* 1983, vol. 50, no. 3). Much of this criticism focuses on methodological and inferential flaws in Gilligan's empirical research, which, critics claim, led her to draw unsubstantiated, oversimplified, and exaggerated conclusions about gender differences.

7. Chodorow's work also has been subject to a substantial amount of criticism (e.g., Spelman 1988), including a journal-sponsored symposium (*Signs* 1981, vol. 6, no. 3).

8. The work of Jean Baker Miller (1986) has also been quite influential in this respect.

9. Grant (1993) classifies the work of Gilligan and Chodorow, along with that of Alice Walker, Sara Ruddick, Adrienne Rich, and Jean Bethke Elshtain, as "mothering theory," which is a subset of the substantively broader and historically older tradition of "feminine feminism." The latter posits some form of universal womanhood that is based on "female experience," broadly defined and not necessarily tied to motherhood. Dietz (1989) identifies a very similar subset of feminist theory, which she labels "maternalism" or "maternal feminism."

10. For a summary of these themes from the revolutionary years to the passage of woman suffrage, Paula Baker's 1984 analysis is particularly informative. Sara Evans's 1989 text also provides a very useful and comprehensive overview of the history of women in the United States with an eye to these themes of gender-differentiated political roles.

11. See also Conway (1971–72), Ryan (1983), and Skocpol (1992).

12. In an early statement of this philosophy, Henry Ward Beecher wrote in his 1860 treatise *Woman's Influence in Politics* that "the easiest, the most natural and proper method of introducing reformation into public affairs, is to give woman a co-ordinate influence there" (quoted in Hogeland 1976).

13. See also "The Life and Times of Rosie the Riveter," a film documentary produced and directed by Connie Field (Franklin Lakes, N.J.: Clarity Educational Productions, 1984).

14. At times the similarities between the rhetoric of contemporary activists and their foremothers is uncanny. Reminiscent of Frances Willard's "enlarged housekeeping" ideas, Ann Stone, founder of Republicans for Choice, offered her own "housekeeping theory of government" for the 1990s: "men make the mess, and we clean it up" (Salholz 1992: 25).

15. Pitkin (1967) distinguishes descriptive representation from symbolic representation as two ways in which public officials can "stand for" others. In this study, these terms—descriptive and symbolic representation—are used interchangeably. Both refer to ways in which women in public office represent women at large simply because they are women, not because they actually *do* anything on behalf of women.

16. These questions address the issue of representing women on an individual level. In comparing the behavior of individual female and male legislators, this study examines the relationship between sex and legislative behavior congruent with women's substantive interests. Yet, one could also address the issue of representing women on an aggregate, or institutional, level. Is the percentage of women occupying positions in a governing body positively related to that body's commitment to the substantive representation of women? Although this study compares the behavior of Arizona state legislators (30 percent of whom were women) to that of California state legislators (16 percent of whom were women), it cannot draw any general conclusions about the behavior of state legislatures as a whole on the basis of only two cases.

17. Phillips's rejection of the shared-experience/shared-beliefs nexus is also premised on its inability to take into account "a multiplicity of identities and experiences" (1995: 53). This issue of women's individual and collective diversity is addressed below.

18. The work of both Gilligan and Chodorow has been widely criticized along these lines.

19. On the reluctance of white middle-class leaders to forge meaningful alliances with working-class and African American women in the struggle for the ERA, see Giddings (1984: 343–44).

20. Clarence Thomas's recent remarks to the African American National Bar Association provide a particularly stark illustration of such accusations. Thomas accused his critics of portraying him as less "black" because of his conservative beliefs and decisions. "Despite some of the nonsense that has been said about me," he asserted, "I am a black man, I am an American" (Lewis 1998: A14). Cynthia Tucker, a fairly liberal African American editor of the *Atlanta Constitution*, wrote in response that this was one point on which she and Thomas agreed: "The notion that all blacks should think alike is ridiculous, stereotypical and demeaning" (2 August 1998, E5).

21. Much of the current research in gender psychology casts doubts on such binary or dichotomous expectations for sex differences in individuals' attitudes and behaviors. Some of this research, for example, suggests that people have considerably more trouble stereotyping themselves than they do stereotyping others. Traditional sex role stereotypes, or conceptions of femininity and masculinity, often are *not* consistently internalized (Bem 1974, 1975; Bernard 1980; Spence, Helmreich, and Stapp 1975). Inventories of research on sex differences in personality traits that people actually exhibit also provide evidence that often does not conform to conventional stereotypes. In their landmark study, Maccoby and Jacklin (1974) found incontrovertible evidence for only a few gender-related personality traits and behavioral patterns. Reviewing this literature, Epstein (1988) argues that psychological differences between women and men have been vastly overblown and misrepresented among the general public and the academy alike. She concludes: "Like assumptions about the attributes of blacks (that they are more sexually or musically proficient than whites) or Jews (that they are overly ambitious, avaricious, cunning, or smart) or women (that they are less sexual, more emotional, more practical, less

creative than men), what 'everyone' believes, or even observes, may not be so at all" (1988: 72).

Chapter Two

1. After the November 1990 elections, Arizona had the highest percentage of female state legislators of all the states. The percentage of women in the California legislature remained unchanged (information provided by CAWP's National Information Bank on Women in Public Office).

2. Each Arizona state legislative district elects two representatives and one senator for two-year terms.

3. Standing committees of the Arizona legislature did have a few full-time legislative analysts, plus an intern or two. While these analysts worked closely with the committee chairs, the extent to which their services were available to other legislators is unclear.

4. My definition and use of the concept of institutionalization are based loosely on the work of Polsby (1968), Squire (1992), and Weber (1947).

5. Elazar notes that there is often a local bias to this sort of communitarianism. The moralistic commitment to government intervention, then, does not necessarily extend to "outside governments" (1972: 98), and federal intervention is not always welcome.

6. In the ten years between 1978 and 1988, campaign spending on all 120 California legislative seats rose from a little more than $20 million to $68 million. In 1990, Pete Wilson spent about $24 million to win the governor's office, compared to the $4.6 million spent by Jerry Brown in 1978. Spending on ballot propositions topped them all, totaling $129 million in 1988 and $91 million in 1990 (Syer and Culver 1992: 168).

7. Erikson, Wright, and McIver (1993: 69) find no correlation between Elazar's classifications and their own public opinion–based measures of state partisanship and ideology. They also argue, quite convincingly, that Elazar's political subcultures tell us more about the process of representation—the linkages between state opinion and policy or those between citizens and elected officials—than about the direction of either state opinion or policy (1993: 151-55).

8. Labor unions in Arizona, like the Democratic Party, are also considered weak and relatively conservative. Mason (1987: 27-28) argues that "labor has been 'in bed' with business" when it comes to issues of economic growth such as nuclear energy development, water projects, and gasoline taxes for highway construction. See also Martínez (1987), Peirce and Hagstrom (1983), and Rosenblum (1995).

9. The data presented by Erikson, Wright, and McIver (1993) also show that Nevada's Democrats were more liberal than California's. However, the authors have serious reservations about the validity of their Nevada data. Following their example, I exclude the Nevada case when comparing California and Arizona to other states.

10. For a detailed synopsis of the 1981–82 reapportionment battles, see Syer and Culver (1992: 176–77) and Richardson (1996: 275–93).

11. Clucas's research also reveals that Assembly Democrats' roll call votes are not affected by the amount of financial support they receive from the Speaker: "There is no direct quid pro quo of campaign assistance for roll-call support" (1994: 425).

12. This is, in fact, exactly what happened at the end of the 1990 session. The final budget and tax packages were passed by a coalition of moderate Republicans and Democrats.

13. While there is no documentation (that I know of) of the number of female lobbyists in California at the time, I suspect that female lobbyists were practically nonexistent in Unruh's and Burton's day.

14. Maxine Waters is the notable exception. She has been adjudged the "one woman in the Legislature . . . who has the position, experience and perhaps the temperament to be a major player" (Zeiger and Jeffe 1988: 9; see also Walters 1988: 6).

15. The survey (Kelly, Burgess, and Kaufmanis 1987) apparently did not query legislators about gender biases within the legislature, as opposed to the electoral process. Thus, the researchers do not discuss women's access to leadership within the institution. In contrast to the literature on California politics, the literature I examined on Arizona included no discussions on the operation of gender biases *within* the Arizona legislature.

16. In both states, proponents of woman suffrage were closely aligned with the temperance movement. Thus, the difference in the margins by which each state passed woman suffrage could be a reflection of the relative power of those who opposed Prohibition within each state, rather than (or in addition to) the degree to which voters accepted women's political participation and equality.

17. In a *Ms.* cover story titled "The Belles of Recall," Claudia Dreifus argues that "the fall of Evan Mecham had been punctuated by the rise of Arizona women as a political force" largely because women were "the active undoers of Mecham" (1988: 44). The article profiles four such women: Rose Mofford; Donna Carlson, the primary whistle-blower and the one who received the death threat at issue in Mecham's obstruction of justice conviction; Carolyn Warner, the 1986 Democratic gubernatorial candidate who narrowly lost to Mecham and who was the top-seeded candidate slated to run against him in the recall election (which never took place); and Naomi Harward, co-coordinator of the recall petition drive.

18. Feminists pointed out that Mecham did not ban *all* women from serving in his administration, just those whose roles, policies, or life circumstances clashed with his extremely conservative views on gender. For example, Betsey Bayless, whom Babbitt had appointed head of the Department of Administration, was transferred after Mecham "reportedly said she 'needs to go home, get married, and have babies'" (Dreifus 1988: 46).

19. There were a couple of issues, however—divorce and child support laws—on which the women did take a more feminist stance than the men.

20. Margaret Hance's career as mayor of Phoenix (1975–83) is remarkably similar to Carlson's. According to Sheridan (1995: 320–21), it was Hance's election that marked the end of the Phoenix white-male establishment's monopoly of political power. She herself recognized that she did not get their endorsement because she was "a woman, and therefore couldn't win." She won numerous elections without their endorsement and was one of the first women in the country to lead such a large city. She also was a very conservative Republican. Faced with Reagan administration cuts in federal social and urban spending, Hance's response was to maintain basic services such as police and firefighters by cutting programs to aid the poor. "The poor are a federal, not a local responsibility," she argued. "If Washington cannot afford those programs, we certainly can't. Local people do not feel that welfare programs should be financed by local taxes" (Peirce and Hagstrom 1983: 739).

21. For a historical perspective on the conservatism of Arizona women, see Berman (1992).

22. Many of the statistics on the status of legislators presented here can be found in Appendix A, Tables A.2 and A.3.

23. Other studies of state legislators (Carroll and Strimling 1983; Diamond 1977; Thomas 1994) have revealed similar sex-related patterns in political experience, at least in terms of quantity. Throughout the 1970s and 1980s, female legislators were either as likely as or more likely than their male colleagues to have held elected office previously. In the 1970s, women were more likely to have served on school boards, but according to Thomas (1994: 46), by the 1980s, the types of offices previously held were no longer sex-segregated.

24. The average tenure of the Arizona female legislators given here (5.4 years) excludes one outlier case: a woman who had been in the legislature for 40 years, which is at least 20 years more than any other legislator (in either state). When this individual is included in the calculation, the average tenure of the Arizona women rises to 7.3 years.

25. There were a few exceptions, none of which indicate a clear pattern of gender bias. In both chambers of the Arizona legislature, women were less likely than the men to serve on revenue and tax committees but more likely to be on the appropriations committees. In the House, women were slightly less likely than men to be on the Rules Committee; but the situation in the Senate was quite the opposite—four of the five women were members of the Rules Committee. In the California Assembly, there were no women on the Revenue and Taxation Committee; but women were well represented (numerically speaking) on the Ways and Means, Judiciary, and Rules Committees. In the California Senate, there were no women on the Rules Committee, but women were well represented on the Revenue and Taxation, Appropriations, and Judiciary Committees—and overrepresented on the Budget and Fiscal Review Committee.

26. A couple of the Arizona female officials had somewhat similar complaints. Their female colleagues, they thought, were rather weak-kneed, too willing to compromise, not competitive enough, and/or unwilling to play hardball when necessary. One California woman also expressed disappointment with some of her female colleagues who were not willing to "fight" like (or with) the men to get what they wanted.


Chapter Three

1. I have made two basic alterations to Wahlke, Eulau, Buchanan, and Ferguson's (1962) original conception of representational style. First, Wahlke and colleagues did not limit the "focus" of this stylistic decision to that of constituents. The dilemma they pose is one of choosing between the instructions or mandate of others and one's own judgment. Such instructions could come from interest groups, political parties, the chief executive, or any other group or individual who seeks to influence legislative decision making. Yet many other scholars have framed their inquiry as narrowly as I have, applying the term "delegate" to those who follow constituents' instructions (Jewell 1982: 96). Second, I took the advice of Kirkpatrick (1974) and Jewell (1982) and did not assume in my interviews with state legislators that the conflict that gives rise to the delegate-trustee choice occurs often. As Jewell (1982: 99) argues: "Most legislators believe that they share the general attitudes and

viewpoints of the majority of their constituents. This is one important reason why conflict between these roles of trustee and delegate is more apparent than real." Kirkpatrick (1974: 157) claims that to most of the female state legislators she interviewed "the dichotomy between their district's opinion and their personal opinion is unreal." Moreover, there are many issues, especially in state politics, about which constituents have little or no interest or opinion, thus making the trustee-delegate decision moot (Jewell 1970: 489). Thus, legislators in this study were asked first to recall or (if necessary) anticipate an instance in which they believed they disagreed with a majority of their constituents; then they were asked to state what they would do in such cases. I further agree with Jewell that these roles are not meant to be stereotypes, characterizing legislators' every decision, with no exceptions. Instead, they are most useful for understanding legislators' general outlook on representation and the "emphasis they give to constituent demands" (Jewell 1982: 104).

2. Both these studies (Richardson and Freeman 1995; Thomas 1992) are based on survey responses, that is, self-reported figures on the number of constituent casework requests received or the amount of time devoted to constituent activities. Thus, neither is completely objective; but neither asked female officials directly to compare themselves to other (male) colleagues.

3. In absolute terms, male and female legislators in each state reported spending roughly equivalent amounts of time on all matters related to their office while in session. The Arizona women, on average, worked 53 hours a week; the Arizona men, 56 hours. California legislators worked significantly longer hours than their Arizona counterparts, but the average workweek for men (66 hours) was only slightly shorter than that for women (70 hours). Thus, these women and men devoted not only the same proportion of their time to constituents, but also roughly the same absolute number of hours.

4. This survey question was part of a series of questions about whom legislators consulted "when preparing and gathering support for [their] legislative proposals." Other groups included committee staff, personal staff (California only), in-party colleagues, out-party colleagues, lobbyists and interest groups, and executive agency personnel.

5. This analysis is based solely on the bills that legislators introduced as primary sponsors, not as coauthors. The Arizona legislature allows for multiple "primary sponsors" (and coauthors); the California legislature permits only one primary sponsor for each bill. Table 3.2 presents the average number of bills introduced in 1989 *and* 1990 because the California legislature convenes for two-year sessions. This means that bills introduced in the California legislature in 1989 can still be active in 1990. Thus, the number of bills a California legislator introduces in the second year of the legislative session most likely is dependent on the number of bills she or he introduced during the first year of the session that remain active. Indeed, California legislators (female and male) introduced an average of ten more bills in 1989 than in 1990. Separate analyses of 1989 and 1990 bill introduction show no sex differences in either state in either year. There also is no indication of sex differences in the scope or difficulty of bills introduced. Men were no more or less likely to introduce symbolic resolutions. Women's bills were no more or less likely to pass with unanimous consent. Female and male sponsors had, on average, roughly equal numbers of coauthors.

6. The relationship between education and representational style was particularly strong among Arizona legislators, male and female. Among California legisla-

tors (female and male), a status occupation in business or the law was also associated with a preference for the trustee role over the delegate role. Among Arizona legislators, however, the opposite was the case: for both men and women, a background in business or (less frequently) law was associated with a greater preference for the delegate role, not the trustee role.

7. After knowledge and leadership, the most common theme in the interviews with trustees and politicos was principled conviction: the imperative, even obligation, to adhere to one's principles, to have the integrity to do what one thinks is right. Trustees of this sort applied this dictum to every important decision. Politicos, by and large, distinguished between moral, or "gut level," issues—such as abortion or (in Arizona) the Martin Luther King Jr. holiday—and other, more technical or pragmatic issues. On the moral issues, they insisted on sticking to their own beliefs; on the other issues, they were willing to abide by or at least negotiate with others. Once again, female and male legislators cited this rationale at roughly equal rates.

8. Hanna Pitkin (1967) makes the same argument, that the delegate role in its extreme negates the very act of representation. So too, she maintains, does the extreme version of the trustee role; when one does not ever consider the demands of one's constituents, one cannot be said to represent.

9. These questions asked about power as generally perceived or recognized in the legislatures. Chapter 7 examines legislators' perceptions of their own power and the sources thereof.

10. The second most frequently cited source of power was formal positions of leadership, including speaker, majority/minority leader, committee chair, membership on powerful committees, etc.

## Chapter Four

1. The equation of feminism with representing women and "women's issues" in this passage is indicative of much of the research literature Githens reviews. I believe this is an unfortunate conceptual error. Thus, I have been careful in my own research not to stipulate or assume that the substantive representation of women or women's issues is necessarily feminist.

2. Hedlund (1988) and Skjeie (1991) report similar trends among Swedish and Norwegian politicians, respectively.

3. Specifically, legislators were asked, "Do you think women *as a group* have particular concerns that government should address, or is addressing?" If necessary, I tried to make it clear that the question referred to women in the electorate, not (necessarily) to their female colleagues within the legislature. Note that this is not the same as asking whether women as a group *agree* with each other and disagree with men on the direction such policies should take. Abortion is a good illustration of this distinction. Public opinion polls show that while women are more concerned about abortion policy than are men, they do not take positions on the issue that are any different from the positions men take. (A good example of this can be found in the July 1989 California Poll. Male and female respondents were equally likely to approve of abortion during the first trimester, but 20 percent more women than men felt it was very important that a candidate have the same position on the issue.) Policy agreement among group members and policy disagreement between group members and nonmembers is certainly a valid indicator of a group's political sig-

nificance. And in this case, it presents a more difficult test of group cohesion than do measures of policy concern.

4. However, district demographics can*not* explain why California female legislators reported significantly lower levels of support from ethnic minorities than did their male colleagues. These California men and women served districts with roughly equal proportions of minority residents, according to 1980 census data provided by the California Assembly Committee on Elections, Reapportionment, and Constitutional Amendments. Precise data on other demographic characteristics of 1990 Arizona and California state legislative districts (e.g., percentage elderly, percentage blue-collar) are unavailable. Thus, I can only speculate that at least some of the sex differences in reported support from the elderly (observed in both states) and blue-collar workers (in California) may be attributed to differences in district composition. It is also possible that these sex differences are gender-related, namely that female legislators assumed that older constituents and/or blue-collar workers were not very supportive of women in politically powerful positions. Unfortunately, I have no data with which to test this hypothesis.

5. Due to time constraints, ten of the Arizona legislators interviewed (one woman, nine men) were not asked this question; nor did they provide an adequate answer in response to other questions in the interview. Thus, these percentages are based on the responses of a total of seventeen female and twenty-three male legislators.

6. This interview was one of the few that were not recorded. Thus, this is not an exact quotation.

7. Occasionally, legislators' responses to other, more general questions about the impact of women in the legislature were used to supplement answers to these questions.

8. Even the two California women who disputed the existence of women's issues per se nevertheless believed that they and their female colleagues offered a uniquely female point of view on legislative matters.

9. This figure (47 percent) includes the six men who said women were not more effective plus the two men who believed women offered a unique perspective on issues but denied that women were more effective (more capable or more active) on women's issues. It does not, however, include the three men whose responses were coded as ambivalent.

10. The exact question was (usually) "Do you see yourself as representing certain constituency groups—kinds of people, or groups of people—within or outside your own district?" This question was asked long before any questions referring specifically to women in politics or women in the legislatures. Thus, I tried to prevent any priming with regard to sex and gender issues. In fact, all questions explicitly concerning women were saved for the very end of the interview so as to avoid, as much as possible, such priming on all other questions.

11. These figures include one California female legislator who named the civil rights community as a constituency she felt she represented. In explaining why, she says she sees herself as "being a minority person who answers several underrepresented groups," one of which is women. Also included is an Arizona female legislator who stated, "I'm considered one of the people that represents the pro-choice constituency," since abortion is one of the most frequently recognized women's issues.

12. Gertzog (1995: 162) sees the Congresswomen's Caucus as having served the same purpose in the U.S. Congress and having had the same effects on its members.

In its early days especially, he reports, the Caucus served "as a magnet for female representatives interested in issues directly affecting women . . . [and was] a source of positive reinforcement for those who wanted to politicize incipient women's concerns."

## Chapter Five

1. There are, of course, a few exceptions: Gehlen 1977; Mueller 1987b; Tamerius 1995; Thomas 1989.

2. Throughout this chapter, the categories of "gender gap" and women's rights issues are considered to be mutually exclusive. As explained in Chapter 1, there is little or no evidence of significant sex differences in public opinion on women's rights issues.

3. The exact question reads as follows: "Below is a list of some of the issues you and other legislators around the country often deal with. Some people think government should devote more time, energy, and resources to these issues, while others think government is doing enough already. Still others think the government should become less involved than it is now, and some believe the government should not get involved in these issues at all. For each issue below, please indicate what you feel the government's role should be."

4. The exact wording of the survey questions are as follows. On the death penalty: "The death penalty should be an option as a punishment for those who commit murder. Do you agree strongly, agree somewhat, disagree somewhat, or disagree strongly with this statement?" On abortion: "There has been much discussion about abortion in recent months. Of the options listed below, which one best agrees with your view? (1) Abortion should never be permitted. (2) Abortion should be permitted only if the life of the woman is in danger, or in cases of rape or incest. (3) Abortion is morally wrong, but the decision to have an abortion should be left up to the woman and her doctor. (4) Abortion should never be forbidden." Among those who chose option (3) are four legislators (two Arizona men, one Arizona woman, and one California man) who did not agree with (and crossed out) the phrase "Abortion is morally wrong." Also included in this category is one Arizona male legislator who restricted his position to cases of first-trimester abortions only.

5. Note that while the average scores of male and female legislators are almost identical on these issues, the Arizona women were more polarized than the Arizona men on the issue of women's rights and the California women were more polarized than the California men on the issue of abortion.

6. The actual range of index scores was from 19 to 40.

7. Two criteria were used to select the sample roll call votes for this analysis. First, only relatively close votes were recorded. In most cases, this meant that no more than two-thirds of the votes cast were in any given direction (yea or nay). Second, the contending positions had to be readily identifiable as either liberal or conservative. The process of finding and selecting votes that met these criteria was a bit different in each state. The editors of the weekly *Arizona Capitol Times* published all roll call votes in which fewer than two-thirds of the Arizona House or Senate voted on one side or the other. From a total of 114 "close votes" recorded in 1990, I chose 49 that seemed most clearly associated with ideological choices (liberal vs. conservative). Unfortunately, there was no comparable resource available for the

California legislature. After combing all the *Daily Journals* of the California Assembly and Senate for the 1990 legislative session, I recorded hundreds of close votes. Faced with such an overwhelming number of votes to choose from, I turned to the *California Journal*'s biennial survey of legislative voting records (March 1991, vol. 22, no. 3). The 40 bills selected by the *Journal*'s editors for the 1989–90 survey were chosen because they represented clear ideological divisions within the legislature. Consultation with legislative staff members formed the basis of this evaluation. This sample of bills not only covers a wide variety of issues, but also does a good job of covering the most important and most controversial issues facing the state. For all these reasons, I limited my own California roll call vote analysis to the 40 bills used in the *Journal*'s survey.

8. One Arizona House roll call vote was classified as both a gender gap issue and a women's rights issue: the vote on H2354, which proposed changing obscenity standards to make prosecution easier and imposing various restrictions on "sex shops." A vote in favor of this measure was considered supportive of women in both cases.

9. These frequencies are based on the total number of votes cast by each legislator. Abstentions were not counted. For each legislator, the number of liberal votes cast was divided by the total number of votes (liberal and conservative) cast. There were no significant sex differences in the total number of votes cast; female legislators were no more or less likely to abstain than were male legislators.

10. Nor did they tend to represent more liberal districts (measured in terms of percentage vote for George Bush in 1988) than men did. Female officials in both state legislatures did, however, tend to represent less rural and more urban districts than did their male counterparts. Controlling for these differences in district (or constituency) characteristics in multivariate analysis (not presented here) does not alter the findings presented in Table 5.2. Thus, these differences cannot account for any of the gender gaps uncovered in the roll call vote analysis.

11. These data, originally collected by the Field Research Corporation, were provided by the University of California, Berkeley Data Archive. The Archive is not responsible for the analysis and interpretation of the data presented here.

12. See Reingold (1992) for a similar analysis of gender gaps in the 1988 American National Election Study. See also Clark and Clark 1993, 1996; Frankovic 1982; Gilens 1988; *Public Opinion* 1982; Poole and Zeigler 1985; Shapiro and Mahajan 1986; Smith 1984.

13. This scenario also relies on the rather questionable assumption that state legislators have such accurate information about the policy preferences of their female and male constituents.

Chapter Six

1. I asked the legislators if they had any goals, specific or general, that they wanted to achieve while in office. If the response to this question was policy related, I then asked if these were the policies at the top of the legislator's agenda, the ones he or she cared about the most. If the response to the question on goals was not policy oriented, I asked the legislator to name the issues that were at the top of her or his agenda and that she or he cared about the most.

2. In the California legislature, only one legislator could be the designated primary sponsor (or, using their terminology, "primary author") for any given bill. The Arizona legislature, however, allowed any number of legislators to be primary spon-

sors; plus, it did not rank multiple primary sponsors in any order of importance or responsibility.

3. Only assignments on permanent standing committees were recorded. Membership on "special" or "select" committees was not.

4. Carroll and Taylor (1989) did not find, however, that women were forced onto committees dealing with traditionally or stereotypically female concerns such as health and welfare or education—at least, not any more often than men were. Most of the women (and men) on such committees were, according to their analysis, happy to be there. Rather, Carroll and Taylor report: "The committees that show the greatest differences in dissatisfaction between women and men are finance and revenue committees and appropriation and budget committees in state senates. . . . Clearly, some women do not want to serve on the so-called "prestige" committees but are assigned to them anyway" (15). In conclusion, the authors argue that women's greater dissatisfaction with their committee assignments may have more to do with tokenism than with gender stereotyping.

5. The exceptions are as follows. Gehlen's 1977 study of the men and women of the 88th Congress (1963–64) found that while women's bills were more likely than men's to fall into the broad category of "traditionally feminine areas of interest," women's bills were no more likely to be referred to committees such as Education and Labor than to committees such as Veteran's Affairs. Gehlen also found that all of the women (and almost all of the men) she interviewed rejected the idea that "there is an area of legislative specialization unique to women, or at least in which women are predominantly interested" (1977: 315). Mezey's (1978b) study of Hawaiian politicians found that women and men were equally concerned about such issues as day care and education. Thomas's study of members of twelve state legislatures found that while women were more likely than men to rank issues regarding children and family as high priorities, they were no more likely to make education, health, or welfare their personal priority (Thomas 1994; Thomas and Welch 1991; Welch and Thomas 1991). Finally, neither the 1977 CAWP study of public officials (Johnson and Carroll 1978) nor Fox and Schuhmann's recent study of city managers (1996) found any significant sex differences in levels of concern for a number of such women's issues.

6. To determine more systematically which standing committees were most relevant to each of the nine issue areas, I examined the frequency with which bills in each category were assigned to various committees.

7. Operationally, activists in each policy area are defined as those who (a) cited the policy area as one of their policy goals or priorities, or (b) devoted a relatively large proportion of the bills they introduced to the issue area (more than the median percentage within each state), or (c) both.

8. This includes goals and bills that deal with abortion, violence against women, family law, parenting, and child care (subject codes 005, 007, 045, 210, 215, 216, and 342).

9. All activists in the women policy area automatically fulfill this criterion.

10. The threshold for being considered "active" on women issues was, in both states, quite low. Since the median number of women bills introduced in each state was zero, all a legislator had to do in order to be classified as active in this area was to introduce at least one such bill.

11. Agricultural issues simply did not capture much attention from any legisla-

tors—male or female, Arizona or California. Very few legislators mentioned such issues as their own policy priorities (12 percent of Arizona men, 6 percent of Arizona women, 18 percent of California men, and 7 percent of California women interviewed). The median number of agricultural bills introduced was zero in both legislatures. Thus, all one had to do in order to be classified as active in agricultural issues was to introduce at least one bill in that area.

12. The Arizona House bill on the regulation of "sex shops" was excluded from this analysis because of its ideological ambiguity. From a civil libertarian viewpoint, it is a conservative measure; and for such reasons, many feminists would oppose it as ultimately harmful to women. Many other feminists, however, would see such an antipornography measure as in the best interest of women and would therefore support it. The issue of pornography has long been one of the most divisive *among* feminists in the United States.

13. The sex difference in feminist policy activism among Arizona legislators is statistically significant ($p = .008$); among California legislators, it is almost statistically significant ($p = .058$).

## Chapter Seven

1. The concepts of transformational and transactional leadership were originally developed by James McGregor Burns (1978).

2. See also Helgesen (1990) and Rudolph (1990). For a summary of this literature, see Kelly, Hale, and Burgess (1991). Washington and Scott (1999) also examine gender dynamics in corporate leadership, but unlike the other writers cited here, they do not offer a strictly dichotomous view of male and female leadership styles.

3. Much of this literature (as well as the political and business literature cited above) is inspired by other feminist scholars, such as Gilligan (1982), Ruddick (1989), and Chodorow (1974, 1978), who emphasize gender difference and revalue women's traditional, nurturing roles and identities (see Chapter 1). For a review and critique of feminist theory on power, see Deutchman (1991, 1996). Collins (1991) and hooks (1984) contrast dominant forms of power to those practiced by African American women in particular.

4. Jane Mansbridge (1990: 133) attributes this "power over" vs. "power to" distinction and terminology to Mary Parker Follett in her 1940 text *Dynamic Administration* (New York: Harper & Brothers).

5. Among CAWP respondents who actually held legislative leadership positions, however, sex differences did occur with regard to some leadership traits. In each case, the female leaders were more likely than the male leaders to consider the trait "very important" (Dodson and Carroll 1991: 84).

6. Note that many of these traits are those commonly associated with feminine leadership styles, while none of them seem related to stereotypically male leadership styles.

7. Legislators also were encouraged to think about and recommend strategies for long-term success, rather than success during the first term only.

8. A few other strategies were mentioned but are not included in Table 7.1 because they were cited by only a very few legislators. These included the following: be patient; "sell" your bill like a salesperson sells a product; listen carefully to others; and avoid or don't trust lobbyists and/or organized interest groups.

9. Although hard work is identified as a component of "feminine" or "interactive" leadership and power in the business management literature (e.g., Loden 1985; Rosener 1990), I classify it as mixed, or neutral, in both this analysis of legislative strategies and the following analysis of power. First, hard work has not been associated with women, femininity, or feminism in the political science literature. Second, in coding the legislators' responses to interview questions, it was difficult to distinguish hard work from knowledge and expertise (in the case of legislative strategies) or from persistence (in the case of legislators' assessments of their own power).

10. The male and female Arizona legislators did not differ significantly in terms of political party affiliation, the number of party leadership positions or committee chairs, previous political experience, or education (see Chapter 2). Thus, any sex differences in their legislative strategies cannot be attributed to these factors. Arizona female legislators did, on average, have less seniority and less electoral security than their male colleagues; they were also slightly more likely to have been a lobbyist before getting elected to public office. Controlling for these factors (using logistic or ordinary least squares regression wherever appropriate), however, does not alter the general conclusions presented thus far.

11. The female and male California officials in this sample were very similar with respect to almost every variable that might influence the type of legislative strategies they would recommend: party affiliation, party leadership positions, seniority, electoral security, previous political experience (including lobbying), and education. The female legislators, however, were significantly more likely to chair a committee. As with the Arizona sample, controlling for this sex difference has no effect on the conclusions reached in this section.

12. Responses to this question are discussed briefly in Chapter 3.

13. As was the case for legislative strategies listed in Table 7.1, the conceptions of personal power listed in Table 7.2 and discussed here were suggested entirely by the legislators themselves. I did not code responses to these open-ended interview questions with any preconceived categories in mind. Thus, if other conceptions of power are not mentioned here, it is simply because none of the legislators mentioned them in their interviews.

14. This gender gap disappears, however, when sex differences in seniority, electoral security, and previous experience in lobbying are controlled for. These controls do not affect any other findings or conclusions about Arizona legislators presented in this section.

15. Controlling for the fact that the California female legislators in this sample were more likely to chair a committee does not alter any of the general conclusions of this section.

16. Along the same lines, Neustadt (1990) has argued that presidential power, with respect to members of Congress and the executive branch, is based on (or at least is more effective when based on) the ability to persuade rather than the ability to coerce.

17. Quite a few legislators insisted that *any* serious conflict or disagreement among their colleagues was unusual. Most bills, they pointed out, attract little or no opposition.

18. Up to two responses or definitions were coded.

19. Controlling for sex differences in seniority, electoral security, and experience

with lobbying (among Arizona legislators) and in committee chairs (among California legislators) does not alter any of the results reported in this section.

## Chapter Eight

1. It is also worth noting that 71 percent of the female legislators (of both states) who completed the written questionnaire reported being active in at least one women's group before entering the legislature. Such women's groups included a wide variety of organizations: Republican women's clubs, the League of Women Voters, Business and Professional Women, the American Association of University Women, the National Organization for Women, the National Women's Political Caucus, Mothers Against Drunk Driving, and Planned Parenthood. Only one male legislator (in California) listed any such organizational activity.

2. If "acting for" women were punished, legislative effectiveness most likely would be affected immediately. One's leadership position or appointment to a powerful committee might not be affected immediately. To take into account the possibility of delayed effects, I replicated the analysis of leadership positions and powerful committee assignments for the subsequent year, 1991. My findings for 1991 only reinforce those for 1990, presented below. Legislators who acted for women in 1990 experienced very few significant losses—or gains—in institutional status in 1991; among the few changes that did occur, there were more gains than losses.

3. This was certainly the case in California, where Democrats managed to get, on average, 14 percent more bills passed (in the originating house) than did Republicans. Among the Arizona legislators, there was only a 7 percent difference between majority and minority passage rates, no doubt because the factionalism in the Republican party enabled Democrats to gain more allies than they might otherwise expect and made it more difficult for Republicans to muster their own majorities.

4. Keeping in touch with constituents was associated with a *loss* of prestigious committee assignments but a *gain* in legislative effectiveness.

## Chapter Nine

1. I agree with Mansbridge (1996: 24) that political symbols and symbolic benefits suffer from widespread derision "in this empirical age." But rather than avoid the terminology or framework of symbolic politics, I wish to defend it by using it and challenging outright its devaluation.

## Appendix A

1. Only a few of the interviews lasted less than 30 minutes. Quite a few lasted more than an hour. Most were between 30 minutes and an hour. The average interview lasted approximately 45 minutes to an hour.

2. At the beginning of each interview, I gave a quick synopsis of my research interests to refresh their memories about who I was and why I was there. I then explained that I would guarantee their anonymity; that I might quote them, but that I would not identify them in any way. Finally, I asked permission to make an audiotape of the interview. Only one legislator refused to be taped. Two other interviews were not tape-recorded due to technical difficulties.

3. One interview in California had to be conducted with the legislator's chief staff assistant. The aide had worked with the representative throughout his lengthy legislative career and assured me that she could speak for him accurately and honestly.

4. One California legislator was interviewed in August of 1990; two were interviewed in February 1991. Scheduling difficulties were the primary reason for these delays.

# References

Abramovitz, Mimi. 1996. *Regulating the Lives of Women: Social Welfare Policy from Colonial Times to the Present.* Rev. ed. Boston: South End Press.

Abzug, Bella. 1984. "Women Candidates." *Ms.* 12 (March): 93.

Abzug, Bella, with Mim Kelber. 1984. *Gender Gap: Bella Abzug's Guide to Political Power for American Women.* Boston: Houghton Mifflin.

Albritton, Robert. 1990. "Social Services: Welfare and Health." In *Politics in the American States: A Comparative Analysis,* 5th ed., edited by Virginia Gray, Herbert Jacob, and Robert B. Albritton. Glenview, Ill.: Scott, Foresman.

Alexander, Deborah, and Kristi Andersen. 1993. "Gender as a Factor in the Attribution of Leadership Traits." *Political Research Quarterly* 46(3): 527–45.

Alozie, Nicholas O. 1995. "Political Tolerance Hypotheses and White Opposition to a Martin Luther King Holiday in Arizona." *Social Science Journal* 32(1): 1–16.

Amott, Teresa L., and Julie A. Matthaei. 1996. *Race, Gender, and Work: A Multicultural Economic History of Women in the United States.* Rev. ed. Boston: South End Press.

Antolini, Denise. 1984. "Women in Local Government: An Overview." In *Political Women: Current Roles in State and Local Government,* edited by Janet A. Flammang. Beverly Hills, Calif.: Sage.

Bachrach, Peter. 1967. *The Theory of Democratic Elitism: A Critique.* Boston: Little, Brown.

Bachrach, Peter, and Morton S. Baratz. 1962. "The Two Faces of Power." *American Political Science Review* 56: 947–52.

Baker, Paula. 1984. "The Domestication of Politics: Women and American Political Society, 1780–1920." *American Historical Review* 89 (June): 620–47.

Barnes, James A. 1990. "Losing the Initiative." *National Journal* 22(35): 2046–53.

Barrett, Edith J. 1995. "The Policy Priorities of African American Women in State Legislatures." *Legislative Studies Quarterly* 20(2): 223–47.

Bayes, Jane. 1989. "Women in the California Executive Branch of Government." In *Gender, Bureaucracy, and Democracy: Careers and Equal Opportunity in the Public Sector,* edited by Mary M. Hale and Rita Mae Kelly. New York: Greenwood.

Beck, Susan Abrams. 1991. "Rethinking Municipal Governance: Gender Distinctions on Local Councils." In *Gender and Policymaking: Studies of Women in Office,* edited by Debra L. Dodson. New Brunswick, N.J.: Center for the American Woman and Politics, Eagleton Institute, Rutgers University.

Bell, Charles G. 1984. "California." In *The Political Life of the American States*, edited by Alan Rosenthal and Maureen Moakley. New York: Praeger.

Bem, Sandra L. 1974. "The Measurement of Psychological Androgyny." *Journal of Consulting and Clinical Psychology* 42: 155–62.

———. 1975. "Sex Role Adaptability: One Consequence of Psychological Androgyny." *Journal of Personality and Social Psychology* 31: 634–43.

———. 1994. "In a Male-Centered World, Female Differences Are Transformed into Female Disadvantages." *Chronicle of Higher Education* (17 August): B1–B3.

Berk, Sarah F., ed. 1980. *Women and Household Labor*. Beverly Hills, Calif.: Sage.

Berke, Richard L. 1993. "Year of Woman Falters in 2 State Races for Governor." *New York Times* (1 November): B9.

———. 1994. "In '94, 'Vote for Woman' Does Not Play So Well." *New York Times* (3 October): A1, A8.

Berkman, Michael B., and Robert E. O'Connor. 1993. "Do Women Legislators Matter? Female Legislators and State Abortion Policy." *American Politics Quarterly* 21(1): 102–24.

Berman, David R. 1992. *Reformers, Corporations, and the Electorate: An Analysis of Arizona's Age of Reform*. Niwot, Colo.: University Press of Colorado.

Berman, David R., and Janalee Jordan-Meldrum. 1993. "Arizona's Priorities: Public Spending." In *Politics and Public Policy in Arizona*, edited by Zachary A. Smith. Westport, Conn.: Praeger.

Bernard, Larry Craig. 1980. "Multivariate Analysis of New Sex Role Formulations and Personality." *Journal of Personality and Social Psychology* 38: 323–36.

Bers, Trudy Haffron. 1978. "Local Political Elites: Men and Women on Boards of Education." *Western Political Quarterly* 31: 381–91.

Biemesderfer, Susan. 1990. "Political Women Give Even Cowboys the Blues." *State Legislatures* 16(9): 21–23.

Biersack, Robert, and Paul S. Herrnson. 1994. "Political Parties and the Year of the Woman." In *The Year of the Woman: Myths and Realities*, edited by Elizabeth Adell Cook, Sue Thomas, and Clyde Wilcox. Boulder, Colo.: Westview.

Black, Naomi. 1989. *Social Feminism*. Ithaca, N.Y.: Cornell University Press.

Blair, Diane D., and Jeanie R. Stanley. 1991. "Personal Relationships and Legislative Power: Male and Female Perceptions." *Legislative Studies Quarterly* 16: 495–507.

Boles, Janet K. 1991. "Local Elected Women and Policymaking: Movement Delegates or Feminist Trustees?" Paper presented at the annual meeting of the American Political Science Association, Washington, D.C.

Bonfante, Jordan. 1990. "Charm Is Only Half Her Story." *Time* 135 (18 June): 24–26.

Bonk, Kathy. 1988. "The Selling of the 'Gender Gap': The Role of Organized Feminism." In *The Politics of the Gender Gap: The Social Construction of Political Influence*, edited by Carol M. Mueller. Beverly Hills, Calif.: Sage.

Box-Steffensmeier, Janet M., and Valeria N. Sinclair. 1996. "Legislative Effectiveness in the U.S. House of Representatives: Struggle, Strategy, and Success." Paper presented at the annual meeting of the Midwest Political Science Association, Chicago.

Bradshaw, Ted K., and Charles G. Bell, eds. 1987. *The Capacity to Respond: California Political Institutions Face Change*. Berkeley: Institute of Governmental Studies, University of California.

Brady, David W., and Kent L. Tedin. 1976. "Ladies in Pink: Religion and Political Ideology in the Anti-ERA Movement." *Social Science Quarterly* 56: 564–75.

Brown, Clyde, Neil R. Heighberger, and Peter A. Shocket. 1993. "Gender-Based Differences in Perceptions of Male and Female City Council Candidates." *Women and Politics* 13(1): 1–17.

Brown, Douglas A. 1993. "The Arizona Legislature." In *Politics and Public Policy in Arizona,* edited by Zachary A. Smith. Westport, Conn.: Praeger.

Browning, Rufus P., Dale R. Marshall, and David H. Tabb. 1984. *Protest Is Not Enough: The Struggle of Blacks and Hispanics for Equality in Urban Politics.* Berkeley: University of California Press.

Brownmiller, Susan. 1975. *Against Our Will: Men, Women, and Rape.* New York: Simon and Schuster.

Burns, James MacGregor. 1978. *Leadership.* New York: Harper and Row.

Burrell, Barbara C. 1994. *A Woman's Place Is in the House: Campaigning for Congress in the Feminist Era.* Ann Arbor: University of Michigan Press.

Caldeira, Gregory A., John A. Clark, and Samuel C. Patterson. 1993. "Political Respect in the Legislature." *Legislative Studies Quarterly* 18(1): 3–28.

Caldeira, Gregory A., and Samuel C. Patterson. 1988. "Contours of Friendship and Respect in the Legislature." *American Politics Quarterly* 16: 466–85.

California Journal. 1989. *Almanac of California Government and Politics,* 7th ed. Sacramento: California Journal Press.

Cantor, Dorothy W., and Toni Bernay (with Jean Stoess). 1992. *Women in Power: The Secrets of Leadership.* Boston: Houghton Mifflin.

Capell, Elizabeth A. 1989. "Patterns of Committee Membership and Leadership in the California Legislature: 1967–1988." Paper presented at the annual meeting of the Western Political Science Association, Salt Lake City.

———. 1991. "The Rules of the Lobbying Game: A California Perspective." Paper presented at the annual meeting of the Western Political Science Association, Seattle.

Carlson, Margaret. 1990. "It's Our Turn." *Time* 136 (Fall, Special Issue): 16–18.

Carney, Eliza Newlin. 1992. "Weighing In." *National Journal* (13 June): 1399–1403.

Carroll, Susan J. 1984. "Woman Candidates and Support for Feminist Concerns: The Closet Feminist Syndrome." *Western Political Quarterly* 37 (June): 307–23.

———. 1991. "Taking the Lead." *Journal of State Government* 64(2): 43–47.

———. 1994. *Women as Candidates in American Politics.* 2d ed. Bloomington: Indiana University Press.

Carroll, Susan J., and Wendy S. Strimling. 1983. *Women's Routes to Elective Office: A Comparison with Men's.* New Brunswick, N.J.: Center for the American Woman and Politics, Eagleton Institute, Rutgers University.

Carroll, Susan J., and Ella Taylor. 1989. "Gender Differences in the Committee Assignments of State Legislators: Preferences or Discrimination?" Paper presented at the annual meeting of the Midwest Political Science Association, Chicago.

Carroll, Susan J., and Linda M. G. Zerilli. 1993. "Feminist Challenges to Political Science." In *Political Science: The State of the Discipline II,* edited by Ada W. Finifter. Washington, D.C.: American Political Science Association.

Cart, Julie. 1998. "When It Comes to Arizona Officeholders, It's a Woman's World." *Los Angeles Times* (17 December): A-5.

Center for the American Woman and Politics (CAWP). 1996. *Women Elected Officials:*

*A Fifty State Resource*. New Brunswick, N.J.: Eagleton Institute, Rutgers University.

Chisholm, Shirley. 1970. "A Visiting Feminine Eye." *McCall's* (August): 6.

Chodorow, Nancy. 1974. "Family Structure and Feminine Personality." In *Woman, Culture, and Society*, edited by Michelle Zimbalist Rosaldo and Louise Lamphere. Stanford, Calif.: Stanford University Press.

———. 1978. *The Reproduction of Mothering: Psychoanalysis and the Sociology of Gender*. Berkeley: University of California Press.

Clark, Cal, and Janet Clark. 1993. "The Gender Gap 1988: Compassion, Pacifism, and Indirect Feminism." In *Women in Politics: Outsiders or Insiders?* edited by Lois Lovelace Duke. Englewood Cliffs, N.J.: Prentice Hall.

———. 1996. "Whither the Gender Gap? Converging and Conflicting Attitudes among Women." In *Women in Politics: Outsiders or Insiders?* 2d ed., edited by Lois Lovelace Duke. Upper Saddle River, N.J.: Prentice Hall.

Clift, Eleanor. 1990. "Battle of the Sexes." *Newsweek* 115 (30 April): 20–22.

Clucas, Richard A. 1992. "Legislative Leadership and Campaign Support in California." *Legislative Studies Quarterly* 17(2): 265–83.

———. 1994. "The Effect of Campaign Contributions on the Power of the California Assembly Speaker." *Legislative Studies Quarterly* 19(3): 417–28.

Cobb, Roger W., and Charles D. Elder. 1983. *Participation in American Politics: The Dynamics of Agenda-Building*. 2d ed. Baltimore, Md.: Johns Hopkins University Press.

Cohen, Naomi K. 1991. "Shaking Off Legislative Typecasting." *Journal of State Government* 64(2): 57–59.

Collie, Melissa P. 1985. "Voting Behavior in Legislatures." In *Handbook of Legislative Research*, edited by Gerhard Loewenberg, Samuel C. Patterson, and Malcolm E. Jewell. Cambridge, Mass.: Harvard University Press.

Collins, Patricia Hill. 1991. *Black Feminist Thought: Knowledge, Consciousness, and the Politics of Empowerment*. New York: Routledge.

Conover, Pamela Johnston. 1981. "Political Cues and the Perception of Candidates." *American Politics Quarterly* 9 (October): 427–48.

———. 1988. "The Role of Social Groups in Political Thinking." *British Journal of Politics* 18: 51–76.

Considine, Mark, and Iva Ellen Deutchman. 1994. "The Gendering of Political Institutions: A Comparison of American and Australian State Legislators." *Social Science Quarterly* 75(4): 854–66.

———. 1996. "Instituting Gender: State Legislators in Australia and the United States." *Women and Politics* 16(4): 1–19.

Conway, Jill. 1971–72. "Women Reformers and American Culture, 1870–1930." *Journal of Social History* 5: 164–77.

Costain, Anne N. 1988. "Women's Claims as a Special Interest." In *The Politics of the Gender Gap: The Social Construction of Political Influence*, edited by Carol M. Mueller. Beverly Hills, Calif.: Sage.

Costello, Cynthia, and Barbara Kivimae Krimgold, eds. 1996. *The American Woman, 1996-97: Women and Work*. New York: W. W. Norton.

Costello, Cynthia, and Anne J. Stone, eds. 1994. *The American Woman, 1994-95: Women and Health*. New York: W. W. Norton.

Cott, Nancy F. 1987. *The Grounding of Modern Feminism*. New Haven, Conn.: Yale University Press.

————. 1990. "Across the Great Divide: Women in Politics Before and After 1920." In *Women, Politics, and Change,* edited by Louise A. Tilly and Patricia Gurin. New York: Sage.

Coverman, Shelley. 1989. "Women's Work Is Never Done: The Division of Domestic Labor." In *Women: A Feminist Perspective,* 4th ed., edited by Jo Freeman. Mountain View, Calif.: Mayfield.

Coverman, Shelley, and Joseph F. Sheley. 1986. "Change in Men's Housework and Child-Care Time, 1965–1975." *Journal of Marriage and the Family* 48 (May): 413–22.

Dahl, Robert A. 1957. "The Concept of Power." *Behavioral Science* 2: 201–15.

Dahlerup, Drude. 1988. "From a Small to a Large Minority: Women in Scandinavian Politics." *Scandinavian Political Studies* 11(4): 275–98.

Dart, Bob. 1994. "From Welfare Mom to Lawmaker." *Atlanta Constitution* (11 February): C1.

Deaux, Kay, and Brenda Major. 1990. "A Social-Psychological Model of Gender." In *Theoretical Perspectives on Sexual Differences,* edited by Deborah L. Rhode. New Haven, Conn.: Yale University Press.

Debenport, Ellen. 1992. "Women Energize Proceedings as Clinton Shares Spotlight." *St. Petersburg* (Fla.) *Times* (15 July): 1A.

De Hart, Jane Sherron. 1995. "Rights and Representation: Women, Politics, and Power in the Contemporary United States." In *U.S. History as Women's History: New Feminist Essays,* edited by Linda K. Kerber, Alice Kessler-Harris, and Kathryn Kish Sklar. Chapel Hill: University of North Carolina Press.

DeMeis, Debra K., and H. Wesley Perkins. 1996. " 'Supermoms' of the Nineties: Homemaker and Employed Mothers' Performance and Perceptions of the Motherhood Role." *Journal of Family Issues* 17(6): 776–92.

Demoruelle, Sandra L., and Joseph R. Thysell Jr. 1993. "Executive Organization in Arizona." In *Politics and Public Policy in Arizona,* edited by Zachary A. Smith. Westport, Conn.: Praeger.

Deutchman, Iva Ellen. 1991. "The Politics of Empowerment." *Women and Politics* 11(2): 1–18.

————. 1996. "Feminist Theory and the Politics of Empowerment." In *Women in Politics: Outsiders or Insiders?* 2d ed., edited by Lois Lovelace Duke. Upper Saddle River, N.J.: Prentice-Hall.

Diamond, Irene. 1977. *Sex Roles in the State House.* New Haven, Conn.: Yale University Press.

Dietz, Mary G. 1989. "Context Is All: Feminism and Theories of Citizenship." In *Learning about Women: Gender, Politics and Power,* edited by Jill K. Conway, Susan C. Bourque, and Joan W. Scott. Ann Arbor: University of Michigan Press.

Doan, Michael, with Patricia Avery. 1985. "New Women Politicians: Tested, Tougher, Wiser." *U.S. News and World Report* 98 (4 March): 76–77.

Dodson, Debra L. 1996. "Representing Women's Interests in the U.S. House of Representatives." Paper prepared for the annual meeting of the Midwest Political Science Association, Chicago.

Dodson, Debra L., and Susan J. Carroll. 1991. *Reshaping the Agenda: Women in State Legislatures.* New Brunswick, N.J.: Center for the American Woman and Politics, Eagleton Institute, Rutgers University.

Dolan, Julie. 1997. "Support for Women's Interests in the 103rd Congress: The Distinct Impact of Congressional Women." *Women and Politics* 18(4): 81–94.

Douthitt, Robin A. 1989. "The Division of Labor within the Home: Have Gender Roles Changed?" *Sex Roles* 20: 693–704.

Dowd, Maureen. 1993. "Growing Sorority in Congress Edges into the Ol' Boys' Club." *New York Times* (5 March): A1, A18.

Dreifus, Claudia. 1988. "The Belles of Recall." *Ms.* 16 (June): 44–51.

DuBois, Ellen Carol. 1978. *Feminism and Suffrage: The Emergence of an Independent Women's Movement in America, 1848–1869.* Ithaca, N.Y.: Cornell University Press.

Duerst-Lahti, Georgia, and Cathy Marie Johnson. 1990. "Gender and Style in Bureaucracy." *Women and Politics* 10(4): 67–120.

———. 1992. "Management Styles, Stereotypes, and Advantages." In *Women and Men of the States: Public Administrators at the State Level,* edited by Mary E. Guy. Armonk, N.Y.: M. E. Sharpe.

Duerst-Lahti, Georgia, and Rita Mae Kelly. 1995a. "On Governance, Leadership, and Gender." In *Gender Power, Leadership, and Governance,* edited by Georgia Duerst-Lahti and Rita Mae Kelly. Ann Arbor: University of Michigan Press.

Duerst-Lahti, Georgia, and Rita Mae Kelly, eds. 1995b. *Gender Power, Leadership, and Governance.* Ann Arbor: University of Michigan Press.

Durst, Samantha L., and Ryan W. Rusek. 1993. "Different Genders, Different Votes? An Examination of Voting Behavior in the U.S. House of Representatives." Paper presented at the annual meeting of the American Political Science Association, Washington, D.C.

Dye, Nancy Schrom. 1975. "Creating a Feminist Alliance: Sisterhood and Class Conflict in the New York Women's Trade Union League, 1903–1914." *Feminist Studies* 2(2/3): 24–38.

Echols, Alice. 1989. *Daring to Be Bad: Radical Feminism in America, 1967–1975.* Minneapolis: University of Minnesota Press.

Eisenstein, Hester. 1983. *Contemporary Feminist Thought.* Boston: G. K. Hall.

———. 1996. *Inside Agitators: Australian Femocrats and the State.* Philadelphia: Temple University Press.

Eisenstein, Zillah. 1988. *The Female Body and the Law.* Berkeley: University of California Press.

Elazar, Daniel J. 1972. *American Federalism: A View from the States.* 2d ed. New York: Thomas Y. Crowell.

Ellickson, Mark C. 1992. "Pathways to Legislative Success: A Path Analytic Study of the Missouri House of Representatives." *Legislative Studies Quarterly* 17(2): 285–302.

Ellis, Virginia. 1991. "Women Gain Clout in Capitol." *Los Angeles Times* (6 November): A1, A14.

Elshtain, Jean Bethke. 1993 [1981]. *Public Man, Private Woman: Women in Social and Political Thought.* 2d ed. Princeton, N.J.: Princeton University Press.

———. 1982. "Antigone's Daughters." *Democracy* 2(2): 46–59.

Epstein, Cynthia Fuchs. 1988. *Deceptive Distinctions: Sex, Gender, and the Social Order.* New Haven, Conn., and New York: Yale University Press and Russell Sage Foundation.

Erikson, Robert S., Gerald C. Wright, and John P. McIver. 1993. *Statehouse Democracy: Public Opinion and Policy in the American States.* New York: Cambridge University Press.

Etulain, Richard W. 1987. "Contours of Culture in Arizona and the Modern West."

In *Arizona at Seventy-Five: The Next Twenty-Five Years,* edited by Beth Luey and Noel J. Stowe. Tempe: Arizona State University Public History Program and the Arizona Historical Society (distributed by University of Arizona Press, Tucson).

Eulau, Heinz. 1994. "Legislative Norms." In *Encyclopedia of the American Legislative System,* edited by Joel H. Silbey. New York: Scribner's/Macmillan.

Eulau, Heinz, and Paul D. Karps. 1977. "The Puzzle of Representation: Specifying Components of Responsiveness." *Legislative Studies Quarterly* 2: 233–54.

Evans, Sara M. 1989. *Born for Liberty: A History of Women in America.* New York: Free Press.

Ezzard, Martha. 1996. "Southern Politics: Where Are the Women?" *Atlanta Journal-Constitution* (4 August): A1.

Feit, Rona F. 1979. "Organizing for Political Power: The National Women's Political Caucus." In *Women Organizing,* edited by Bernice Cummings and Victoria Schuck. Metuchen, N.J.: Scarecrow.

Fenno, Richard F., Jr. 1973. *Congressmen in Committees.* Boston: Little, Brown.

———. 1978. *Home Style: House Members in Their Districts.* HarperCollins.

Ferguson, Kathy E. 1984. *The Feminist Case against Bureaucracy.* Philadelphia: Temple University Press.

Ferraro, Geraldine. 1992. "Afterword." In *Women in Power: The Secrets of Leadership,* by Dorothy W. Cantor and Toni Bernay (with Jean Stoess). Boston: Houghton Mifflin.

Flammang, Janet A. 1983. "Feminist Theory: The Question of Power." *Current Perspectives in Social Theory* 4: 37–83.

———. 1985. "Female Officials in the Feminist Capital: The Case of Santa Clara County." *Western Political Quarterly* 38: 94–118.

———. 1987. "Women Made a Difference: Comparable Worth in San Jose." In *The Women's Movements of the United States and Western Europe: Consciousness, Political Opportunity, and Public Policy,* edited by Mary Fainsod Katzenstein and Carol McClurg Mueller. Philadelphia: Temple University Press.

Fowler, Susanne. 1992. "Women in the News." *Houston Chronicle* (5 January): 4G.

Fox, Richard L., and Robert A. Schuhmann. 1996. "Gender and Policy Agendas of City Managers." Paper presented at the annual meeting of the Southern Political Science Association, Atlanta.

Frankovic, Kathleen A. 1977. "Sex and Voting in the U.S. House of Representatives, 1961–1975." *American Politics Quarterly* 5: 315–30.

———. 1982. "Sex and Politics—New Alignments, Old Issues." *PS* 15: 439–48.

Frantzich, Stephen. 1979. "Who Makes Our Laws? The Legislative Effectiveness of Members of the U.S. Congress." *Legislative Studies Quarterly* 4(3): 409–28.

Freeman, Patricia K., and Lilliard E. Richardson Jr. 1996. "Explaining Variation in Casework among State Legislators." *Legislative Studies Quarterly* 21(1): 41–56.

Galinsky, Ellen, and James T. Bond. 1996. "Work and Family: The Experiences of Mothers and Fathers in the U.S. Labor Force." In *The American Woman, 1996–97,* edited by Cynthia Costello and Barbara Kivimae Krimgold. New York: W. W. Norton.

Gallup Report. 1984. "Many See Women as Less Able to Handle Presidential Duties." In Reports 227/228, 2–14. Princeton, N.J.: Gallup Poll.

Gaventa, John. 1980. *Power and Powerlessness: Quiescence and Rebellion in an Appalachian Valley.* Urbana: University of Illinois Press.

Gehlen, Frieda L. 1977. "Women Members of Congress: A Distinctive Role." In *A Portrait of Marginality: The Political Behavior of the American Woman*, edited by Marianne Githens and Jewel L. Prestage. New York: D. McKay Co.

Gertzog, Irwin N. 1995. *Congressional Women: Their Recruitment, Integration, and Behavior.* 2d ed. Westport, Conn.: Praeger.

Giddings, Paula. 1984. *When and Where I Enter: The Impact of Black Women on Race and Sex in America.* New York: Morrow.

Gilens, Martin. 1988. "Gender and Support for Reagan: A Comprehensive Model of Presidential Approval." *American Journal of Political Science* 32: 19–49.

Gilligan, Carol. 1982. *In a Different Voice: Psychological Theory and Women's Development.* Cambridge, Mass.: Harvard University Press.

Githens, Marianne. 1977. "Spectators, Agitators, or Lawmakers: Women in State Legislatures." In *A Portrait of Marginality: The Political Behavior of the American Woman*, edited by Marianne Githens and Jewel L. Prestage. New York: D. McKay Co.

———. 1984. "Women and State Politics: An Assessment." In *Political Women: Current Roles in State and Local Government*, edited by Janet A. Flammang. Beverly Hills, Calif.: Sage.

———. 1994. "Political Issues." In *Different Roles, Different Voices: Women and Politics in the United States and Europe*, edited by Marianne Githens, Pippa Norris, and Joni Lovenduski. New York: HarperCollins.

Githens, Marianne, and Jewel L. Prestage, eds. 1977. *A Portrait of Marginality: The Political Behavior of the American Woman.* New York: D. McKay Co.

Githens, Marianne, and Jewel L. Prestage. 1978. "Women State Legislators: Styles and Priorities." *Policy Studies Journal* 7 (Winter): 264–70.

Glenn, Evelyn Nakano. 1985. "Racial Ethnic Women's Labor: The Intersection of Race, Gender and Class Oppression." *Review of Radical Political Economics* 17(3): 86–108.

Gluck, Hazel Frank. 1987. "The Difference." *Journal of State Government* 60(5): 223–26.

Goldberg, Carey. 1997. "Women at Helm of New Hampshire Politics." *New York Times* (7 October): A14.

Gordon, Linda. 1976. *Woman's Body, Woman's Right: A Social History of Birth Control in America.* New York: Grossman.

Gordon, Margaret T., and Stephanie Riger. 1989. *The Female Fear.* New York: Free Press.

Grant, Judith. 1993. *Fundamental Feminism: Contesting the Core Concepts of Feminist Theory.* New York: Routledge.

Gray, John. 1992. *Men Are from Mars, Women Are from Venus: A Practical Guide for Improving Communication and Getting What You Want in Your Relationships.* New York: HarperCollins.

Gray, Virginia. 1990. "The Socioeconomic and Political Context." In *Politics in the American States: A Comparative Analysis*, 5th ed., edited by Virginia Gray, Herbert Jacob, and Robert B. Albritton. Glenview, Ill.: Scott, Foresman.

Gruber, Judith E. 1980. "Political Strength and Policy Responsiveness: The Results of Electing Blacks to City Councils." Paper presented at the annual meeting of the Western Political Science Association, San Francisco.

Hale, Mary M., and Rita Mae Kelly. 1989. "Gender, Democracy, and Representative Bureaucracies." In *Gender, Bureaucracy, and Democracy: Careers and Equal Oppor-*

*tunity in the Public Sector,* edited by Mary M. Hale and Rita Mae Kelly. New York: Greenwood.

Hale, Mary, Rita Mae Kelly, Jayne Burgess, and Rhonda Shapiro. 1987. "Women in the Executive Branch of Government." In *Women and the Arizona Political Process,* edited by Rita Mae Kelly. Lanham, Md.: University Press of America.

Hamm, Keith E., Robert Harmel, and Robert Thompson. 1983. "Ethnic and Partisan Minorities in Two Southern State Legislatures." *Legislative Studies Quarterly* 8: 177–89.

Hamm, Keith E., Ronald D. Hedlund, and R. Bruce Anderson. 1994. "Political Parties in State Legislatures." In *Encyclopedia of the American Legislative System,* Vol. 2, edited by Joel H. Silbey. New York: Scribner's/Macmillan.

Hansen, Susan B. 1990. "The Politics of State Taxing and Spending." In *Politics in the American States: A Comparative Analysis,* 5th ed., edited by Virginia Gray, Herbert Jacob, and Robert B. Albritton. Glenview, Ill.: Scott, Foresman.

Hartmann, Heidi. 1976. "Capitalism, Patriarchy and Job Segregation by Sex." *Signs: Journal of Women in Culture and Society* 1 (no. 3, pt. 2): 137–69.

———. 1981. "The Family as the Locus of Gender, Class and Political Struggle: The Example of Housework." *Signs: Journal of Women in Culture and Society* 6: 366–94.

Hartsock, Nancy C. M. 1983. *Money, Sex, and Power: Toward a Feminist Historical Materialism.* New York: Longman.

Havens, Catherine M., and Lynne M. Healy. 1991. "Cabinet-Level Appointees in Connecticut: Women Making a Difference." In *Gender and Policymaking: Studies of Women in Office,* edited by Debra L. Dodson. New Brunswick, N.J.: Center for the American Woman and Politics, Eagleton Institute, Rutgers University.

Hedlund, Gun. 1988. "Women's Interests in Local Politics." In *The Political Interests of Gender: Developing Theory and Research with a Feminist Face,* edited by Kathleen B. Jones and Anna G. Jónasdóttir. London: Sage.

Helgesen, Sally. 1990. *The Female Advantage: Women's Ways of Leadership.* New York: Doubleday Currency.

Hermann, Ria, and Rita Mae Kelly. 1987. "Women in the Judiciary." In *Women and the Arizona Political Process,* edited by Rita Mae Kelly. Lanham, Md.: University Press of America.

Herz, Diane E., and Barbara H. Wooton. 1996. "Women in the Workforce: An Overview." In *The American Woman, 1996-97,* edited by Cynthia Costello and Barbara Kivimae Krimgold. New York: W. W. Norton.

Hewitt, Nancy A. 1985. "Beyond the Search for Sisterhood: American Women's History in the 1980s." *Social History* 10: 299-321. Reprinted in *Unequal Sisters: A Multicultural Reader in U.S. Women's History,* edited by Ellen Carol DuBois and Vicki L. Ruiz, 1-14. New York: Routledge, 1990.

Hibbing, John R., and Sue Thomas. 1990. "The Modern United States Senate: What Is Accorded Respect?" *Journal of Politics* 52(1): 126-45.

Hill, David. 1983. "Women State Legislators and Party Voting on the ERA." *Social Science Quarterly* 64: 318-26.

Hochschild, Arlie, with Anne Machung. 1989. *The Second Shift: Working Parents and the Revolution at Home.* New York: Viking.

Hogan, Dave. 1998. "'90s Prove Good for Women in Congress." *New Orleans (La.) Times-Picayune* (11 October): A1.

Hogeland, Ronald W. 1976. " 'The Female Appendage': Feminine Lifestyles in America, 1820-1860." In *Our American Sisters: Women in American Life and Thought,*

2d ed., edited by Jean E. Friedman and William G. Shade. Boston: Allyn and Bacon.

Holbrook-Provow, Thomas M., and Steven C. Poe. 1987. "Measuring State Political Ideology." *American Politics Quarterly* 15: 399–416.

Honey, Maureen. 1984. *Creating Rosie the Riveter: Class, Gender, and Propaganda during World War II*. Amherst: University of Massachusetts Press.

hooks, bell. 1981. *Ain't I a Woman: Black Women and Feminism*. Boston: South End.

———. 1984. *Feminist Theory from Margin to Center*. Boston: South End.

Hrebenar, Ronald J. 1987. "Interest Group Politics in the American West: A Comparative Perspective." In *Interest Group Politics in the American West*, edited by Ronald J. Hrebenar and Clive S. Thomas. Salt Lake City: University of Utah Press.

Hrebenar, Ronald J., and Clive S. Thomas, eds. 1987. *Interest Group Politics in the American West*. Salt Lake City: University of Utah Press.

Huddy, Leonie, and Nayda Terkildsen. 1993. "Gender Stereotypes and the Perception of Male and Female Candidates." *American Journal of Political Science* 37: 119–47.

Iannello, Kathleen P. 1992. *Decisions Without Hierarchy: Feminist Interventions in Organization Theory and Practice*. New York: Routledge.

Jennings, M. Kent, and Norman Thomas. 1968. "Men and Women in Party Elites: Social Roles and Political Resources." *Midwest Journal of Political Science* 12: 469–92.

Jewell, Malcolm E. 1970. "Attitudinal Determinants of Legislative Behavior: The Utility of Role Analysis." In *Legislatures in Developmental Perspective*, edited by Alan Kornberg and Lloyd D. Musolf. Durham, N.C.: Duke University Press.

———. 1982. *Representation in State Legislatures*. Lexington: University Press of Kentucky.

———. 1985. "Legislators and Constituents in the Representative Process." In *Handbook of Legislative Research*, edited by Gerhard Loewenberg, Samuel C. Patterson, and Malcolm E. Jewell. Cambridge, Mass.: Harvard University Press.

Jewell, Malcolm E., and Samuel C. Patterson. 1986. *The Legislative Process in the United States*. 4th ed. New York: Random House.

Jewell, Malcolm E., and Marcia Lynn Whicker. 1994. *Legislative Leadership in the American States*. Ann Arbor: University of Michigan Press.

Johannes, John R. 1989. "Individual Outputs: Legislators and Constituency Service." In *Congressional Politics*, edited by Christopher J. Deering. Chicago: Dorsey.

Johnson, Marilyn, and Susan Carroll. 1978. "Statistical Report: Profile of Women Holding Office, 1977." In *Women in Public Office: A Biographical Directory and Statistical Analysis*, compiled by Center for the American Woman and Politics, Eagleton Institute, Rutgers University. Metuchen, N.J.: Scarecrow.

Jónasdóttir, Anna G. 1988. "On the Concept of Interest, Women's Interests, and the Limitations of Interest Theory." In *The Political Interests of Gender: Developing Theory and Research with a Feminist Face*, edited by Kathleen B. Jones and Anna G. Jónasdóttir. London: Sage.

Jones, Kathleen B. 1993. *Compassionate Authority: Democracy and the Representation of Women*. New York: Routledge.

Jones, Kathleen B., and Anna G. Jónasdóttir. 1988. "Introduction: Gender as an Analytic Category in Political Theory." In *The Political Interests of Gender: Developing Theory and Research with a Feminist Face*, edited by Kathleen B. Jones and Anna G. Jónasdóttir. London: Sage.

Jones, Rich. 1991. "The State Legislatures." In *The Book of the States: 1990–91 Edition*. Vol. 28. Lexington, Ky.: Council of State Governments.

Kahn, Kim Fridkin. 1993. "Gender Differences in Campaign Messages: The Political Advertisements of Men and Women Candidates for U.S. Senate." *Political Research Quarterly* 46(3): 481–502.

Kanter, Rosabeth Moss. 1977. "Some Effects of Proportions on Group Life: Skewed Sex Ratios and Responses to Token Women." *American Journal of Sociology* 82: 965–90.

Kastenbaum, Robert. 1991. "Racism and the Older Voter? Arizona's Rejection of a Paid Holiday to Honor Martin Luther King." *International Journal of Aging and Human Development* 32(3): 199–209.

Kathlene, Lyn. 1989. "Uncovering the Political Impacts of Gender: An Exploratory Study." *Western Political Quarterly* 42(2): 397–421.

———. 1994. "Power and Influence in State Legislative Policymaking: The Interaction of Gender and Position in Committee Hearing Debates." *American Political Science Review* 88: 560–76.

———. 1995. "Alternative Views of Crime: Legislative Policymaking in Gendered Terms." *Journal of Politics* 57(3): 696–723.

Katz, Vera. 1987. "Women Chart New Legislative Course." *Journal of State Government* 60(5): 213–15.

Kelly, Rita Mae. 1987. "Where Conservatism and Feminism Meet: Gender and Politics in Arizona." In *Women and the Arizona Political Process*, edited by Rita Mae Kelly. Lanham, Md.: University Press of America.

———. 1993. "Women, Politics, and Public Policy." In *Politics and Public Policy in Arizona*, edited by Zachary A. Smith. Westport, Conn.: Praeger.

Kelly, Rita Mae, Jayne Burgess, and Katie Kaufmanis. 1987. "Arizona Women and the Legislature." In *Women and the Arizona Political Process*, edited by Rita Mae Kelly. Lanham, Md.: University Press of America.

Kelly, Rita Mae, Mary M. Hale, and Jayne Burgess. 1991. "Gender and Managerial/Leadership Styles: A Comparison of Arizona Public Administrators." *Women and Politics* 11(2): 19–39.

Kelly, Rita Mae, Michelle A. Saint-Germain, and Jody D. Horn. 1991. "Female Public Officials: A Different Voice?" *Annals of the American Academy of Political and Social Science* 515: 77–87.

Kerber, Linda K. 1980. *Women of the Republic: Intellect and Ideology in Revolutionary America*. Chapel Hill: University of North Carolina Press.

Key, V. O., Jr. 1949. *Southern Politics in State and Nation*. New York: Knopf.

Kingsley, J. Donald. 1944. *Representative Bureaucracy, an Interpretation of the British Civil Service*. Yellow Springs, Ohio: Antioch.

Kirkpatrick, Jeane J. 1974. *Political Woman*. New York: Basic.

Klein, Ethel. 1984. *Gender Politics: From Consciousness to Mass Politics*. Cambridge, Mass.: Harvard University Press.

Klingman, David, and William W. Lammers. 1984. "The 'General Policy Liberalism' Factor in American State Politics." *American Journal of Political Science* 28: 598–610.

Kraditor, Aileen S. 1965. *The Ideas of the Woman Suffrage Movement, 1890–1920*. New York: Columbia University Press.

Leader, Shelah Gilbert. 1977. "The Policy Impact of Elected Women Officials." In

*The Impact of the Electoral Process*, edited by Louis Maisel and Joseph Cooper. Beverly Hills, Calif.: Sage Publications.

Leeper, Mark S. 1991. "The Impact of Prejudice on Female Candidates: An Experimental Look at Voter Inference." *American Politics Quarterly* 19: 248–61.

Lewis, Neil A. 1998. "Justice Thomas Suggests Critics' Views Are Racist." *New York Times* (30 July): A1, A14.

Loden, Marilyn. 1985. *Feminine Leadership or How to Succeed in Business Without Being One of the Boys*. New York: Times Books.

Luey, Beth, and Noel J. Stowe. 1987. "Introduction" to *Arizona at Seventy-Five: The Next Twenty-Five Years*. Tucson: University of Arizona Press.

McAllister, Ian, and Donley T. Studlar. 1992. "Gender and Representation among Legislative Candidates in Australia." *Comparative Political Studies* 25(3): 388–411.

McClain, Paula D. 1988. "Arizona High Noon: The Recall and Impeachment of Evan Mecham." *PS: Political Science and Politics* 21(3): 628–38.

Maccoby, Eleanor E., and Carol N. Jacklin. 1974. *The Psychology of Sex Differences*. Stanford, Calif.: Stanford University Press.

McGlen, Nancy E., and Karen O'Connor. 1995. *Women, Politics, and American Society*. Englewood Cliffs, N.J.: Prentice Hall.

McLanahan, Sara S., Annemette Sørensen, and Dorothy Watson. 1989. "Sex Differences in Poverty, 1950–1980." *Signs: Journal of Women in Culture and Society* 15: 102–22.

Mandel, Ruth B., and Debra L. Dodson. 1992. "Do Women Officeholders Make a Difference?" In *The American Woman, 1992–93: A Status Report*, edited by Paula Ries and Anne J. Stone. New York: W. W. Norton.

Mann, Thomas E., and Gary R. Orren, eds. 1992. *Media Polls in American Politics*. Washington, D.C.: Brookings Institution.

Mansbridge, Jane J. 1985. "Myth and Reality: The ERA and the Gender Gap in the 1980 Election." *Public Opinion Quarterly* 49: 164–78.

———. 1986. *Why We Lost the ERA*. Chicago: University of Chicago Press.

———. 1990. "Feminism and Democracy." *American Prospect* 1 (Spring): 126–39.

———. 1996. "In Defense of 'Descriptive' Representation." Paper presented at the annual meeting of the American Political Science Association, San Francisco.

Margolis, Andrea, and Richard Zeiger. 1987. "Bleeding Hearts, Stone Hearts: A California Journal Survey of Legislative Voting Records." *California Journal* 18: 30–32.

Marshall, Susan E. 1997. *Splintered Sisterhood: Gender and Class in the Campaign against Woman Suffrage*. Madison: University of Wisconsin Press.

Martínez, Oscar J. 1987. "Hispanics in Arizona." In *Arizona at Seventy-Five: The Next Twenty-Five Years*, edited by Beth Luey and Noel J. Stowe. Tucson: University of Arizona Press.

Mason, Bruce B. 1987. "Arizona: Interest Groups in a Changing State." In *Interest Group Politics in the American West*, edited by Ronald J. Hrebenar and Clive S. Thomas. Salt Lake City: University of Utah Press.

Mathews, Donald G., and Jane S. De Hart. 1992. *Sex, Gender, and the Politics of ERA: A State and the Nation*. New York: Oxford University Press.

Matlack, Carol. 1990. "Too Big to Move." *National Journal* 22(35): 2054–60.

Matthews, Christopher. 1988. *Hardball: How Politics Is Played—Told by One Who Knows the Game*. New York: Summit.

Matthews, Donald R. 1960. *U.S. Senators and Their World*. New York: Vintage.

Matthews, Jon. 1989. "Women senators describe subtle sexism in Capitol." *Sacramento Bee* (13 March): A3.

Mayhew, David R. 1974. *Congress: The Electoral Connection.* New Haven, Conn.: Yale University Press.

———. 1986. *Placing Parties in American Politics: Organization, Electoral Setting, and Government Activity in the Twentieth Century.* Princeton, N.J.: Princeton University Press.

Merritt, Sharyne. 1980. "Sex Differences in Role Behavior and Policy Orientations of Suburban Officeholders: The Effect of Women's Employment." In *Women in Local Politics,* edited by Debra Stewart. Metuchen, N.J.: Scarecrow.

Mezey, Susan Gluck. 1978a. "Support for Women's Rights Policy: An Analysis of Local Politicians." *American Politics Quarterly* 6: 485–97.

———. 1978b. "Women and Representation: The Case of Hawaii." *Journal of Politics* 40: 369–85.

———. 1978c. "Does Sex Make a Difference? A Case Study of Women in Politics." *Western Political Quarterly* 31: 492–501.

———. 1980. "Perceptions of Women's Roles on Local Councils in Connecticut." In *Women in Local Politics,* edited by Debra W. Stewart. Metuchen, N.J.: Scarecrow.

———. 1994. "Increasing the Number of Women in Office: Does It Matter?" In *The Year of the Woman: Myths and Realities,* edited by Elizabeth Adell Cook, Sue Thomas, and Clyde Wilcox. Boulder, Colo.: Westview.

Meyer, Katherine. 1980. "Legislative Influence: Toward Theory Development through Causal Analysis." *Legislative Studies Quarterly* 5: 563–85.

Milkman, Ruth. 1982. "Redefining 'Women's Work': The Sexual Division of Labor in the Auto Industry during World War II." *Feminist Studies* 8 (Summer): 337–72.

———. 1987. *Gender at Work: The Dynamics of Job Segregation by Sex During World War II.* Urbana: University of Illinois Press.

Mill, John Stuart. 1972 [1861]. *Considerations on Representative Government.* In *Utilitarianism, On Liberty, and Considerations on Representative Government,* edited by H. B. Acton. London: J. M. Dent and Sons.

Miller, Jean Baker. 1982. "Women and Power." *Work in Progress,* No. 1. Wellesley, Mass.: Stone Center Working Paper Series.

———. 1986. *Toward a New Psychology of Women.* 2d ed. Boston: Beacon Press.

Mills, James R. 1987. *A Disorderly House: The Brown-Unruh Years in Sacramento.* Berkeley: Heyday.

Mills, Kay. 1992. "Looking for an Edge, Candidates are Stressing Their Feminine Traits . . ." *Atlanta Journal-Constitution* (18 October): H2.

Mohanty, Chandra Talpade. 1991. "Under Western Eyes." In *Third World Women and the Politics of Feminism,* edited by Chandra Talpade Mohanty, Ann Russo, and Lourdes Torres. Bloomington: Indiana University Press.

Moore, Michael K., and Sue Thomas. 1991. "Explaining Legislative Success in the U.S. Senate: The Role of the Majority and Minority Parties." *Western Political Quarterly* 44: 959–70.

Mosher, Frederick C. 1968. *Democracy and the Public Service.* New York: Oxford University Press.

Mueller, Carol. 1984. "Women's Organizational Strategies in State Legislatures." In *Political Women,* edited by Janet A. Flammang. Beverly Hills, Calif.: Sage.

———. 1987a. "Collective Consciousness, Identity Transformation, and the Rise of Women in Public Office in the United States." In *The Women's Movements of the United States and Western Europe: Consciousness, Political Opportunity, and Public Policy,* edited by Mary Fainsod Katzenstein and Carol McClurg Mueller. Philadelphia: Temple University Press.

———. 1987b. "Consensus Without Unity." *Journal of State Government* 60: 230–34.

Muncy, Robyn. 1991. *Creating a Female Dominion in American Reform, 1890–1935.* New York: Oxford University Press.

Nagourney, Adam. 1998. "Ferraro Stresses Status as Only Woman in Race." *New York Times* (31 July): B2.

Nash, Gerald D. 1987. "Reshaping Arizona's Economy: A Century of Change." In *Arizona at Seventy-Five: The Next Twenty-Five Years,* edited by Beth Luey and Noel J. Stowe. Tucson: University of Arizona Press.

Nechemias, Carol. 1994. "Democratization and Women's Access to Legislative Seats: The Soviet Case, 1989–1991." *Women and Politics* 14(3): 1–18.

Neustadt, Richard E. 1990. *Presidential Power and the Modern Presidents: The Politics of Leadership from Roosevelt to Reagan.* New York: Free Press.

Norton, Mary Beth. 1980. *Liberty's Daughters: The Revolutionary Experience of American Women, 1750–1800.* Boston: Little, Brown.

Norton, Noelle. 1994. "Women Policymakers." *Policy Sciences* 27: 277–82.

Offen, Karen. 1992. "Defining Feminism: A Comparative Historical Approach." In *Beyond Equality and Difference: Citizenship, Feminist Politics and Female Subjectivity,* edited by Gisela Bock and Susan James. London and New York: Routledge.

Okin, Susan Moller. 1990. "Thinking Like a Woman." In *Theoretical Perspectives on Sexual Differences,* edited by Deborah L. Rhode. New Haven, Conn.: Yale University Press.

O'Neil, Daniel J. 1995. "Arizona: Pro-Choice Success in a Conservative, Republican State." In *Abortion Politics in American States,* edited by Mary C. Segers and Timothy A. Byrnes. Armonk, N.Y.: M. E. Sharpe.

Ornstein, Norman J., and Shirley Elder. 1978. *Interest Groups, Lobbying, and Policy Making.* Washington, D.C.: Congressional Quarterly Press.

Paolino, Phillip. 1995. "Group-Salient Issues and Group Representation: Support for Women Candidates in the 1992 Senate Elections." *American Journal of Political Science* 39: 294–313.

Parker, Glenn R. 1989. "Members of Congress and Their Constituents: The Home-Style Connection." In *Congress Reconsidered,* 4th ed., edited by Lawrence C. Dodd and Bruce I. Oppenheimer. Washington, D.C.: Congressional Quarterly Press.

Pateman, Carole. 1992. "Equality, Difference, Subordination: The Politics of Motherhood and Women's Citizenship." In *Beyond Equality and Difference: Citizenship, Feminist Politics and Female Subjectivity,* edited by Gisela Bock and Susan James. New York: Routledge.

Patterson, Martha Priddy. 1996. "Women's Employment Patterns, Pension Coverage, and Retirement Planning." In *The American Woman, 1996–97,* edited by Cynthia Costello and Barbara Kivimae Krimgold. New York: W. W. Norton.

Pearce, Diana. 1978. "The Feminization of Poverty: Women, Work and Welfare." *Urban and Social Change Review* 24: 28–35.

Peirce, Neal R., and Jerry Hagstrom. 1983. *The Book of America: Inside Fifty States Today.* New York: Norton.

Perkins, Jerry, and Diane L. Fowlkes. 1980. "Opinion Representation versus Social Representation; or, Why Women Can't Run as Women and Win." *American Political Science Review* 74: 92–103.

Peterson, Larry. 1988. "Senator Marian Bergeson: Competent, Respected, Stuck." *California Journal* (April): 179–81.

Phillips, Anne. 1991. *Engendering Democracy.* University Park: Penn State Press.

———. 1995. *The Politics of Presence.* New York: Clarendon/Oxford University Press.

Pitkin, Hanna F. 1967. *The Concept of Representation.* Berkeley: University of California Press.

Pollitt, Katha. 1992. "Are Women Morally Superior to Men?" *Nation* (28 December): 799–807.

Polsby, Nelson W. 1968. "The Institutionalization of the U.S. House of Representatives." *American Political Science Review* 62(1): 144–68.

Poole, Keith T., and L. Harmon Zeigler. 1985. *Women, Public Opinion, and Politics: The Changing Political Attitudes of American Women.* New York: Longman.

Popcorn, Faith, and Lys Marigold. 1996. *Clicking: 16 Trends to Future Fit Your Life, Your Work, and Your Business.* New York: HarperCollins.

*Public Opinion,* [Editors of]. 1982. "Women and Men: Is a Realignment Underway?" (Opinion Roundup feature). *Public Opinion* 5(2): 21–40.

Purdum, Todd S. 1997. "Arizona Governor Convicted of Fraud and Will Step Down." *New York Times* (4 September): A1, A12.

Putnam, Jackson K. 1992. "The Pattern of Modern California Politics." *Pacific Historical Review* 61(1): 23–52.

Pyle, Amy. 1998. "Women to Play Largest Role Ever in Legislature." *Los Angeles Times* (23 November): A3, A11.

Quindlen, Anna. 1993. "Welcome to the Club." *New York Times* (27 January): A23.

Rapoport, Ronald B., Walter J. Stone, and Alan I. Abramowitz. 1990. "Sex and the Caucus Participant: The Gender Gap and Presidential Nominations." *American Journal of Political Science* 34: 725–40.

Reingold, Beth. 1992. "Representing Women: Gender Differences among Arizona and California State Legislators." Ph.D. dissertation, University of California at Berkeley.

Reingold, Beth, and Heather Foust. 1998. "Exploring the Determinants of Feminist Consciousness in the United States." *Women and Politics* 19(3): 19–48.

Rhode, Deborah L. 1990. "Theoretical Perspectives on Sexual Difference." In *Theoretical Perspectives on Sexual Differences,* edited by Deborah L. Rhode. New Haven, Conn.: Yale University Press.

———. 1992. "The Politics of Paradigms: Gender Difference and Gender Disadvantage." In *Beyond Equality and Difference: Citizenship, Feminist Politics and Female Subjectivity,* edited by Gisela Bock and Susan James. New York: Routledge.

Richardson, James. 1996. *Willie Brown: A Biography.* Berkeley: University of California Press.

Richardson, Lilliard E., Jr., and Patricia K. Freeman. 1995. "Gender Differences in Constituency Service among State Legislators." *Political Research Quarterly* 48(1): 169–79.

Ries, Paula, and Anne J. Stone, eds. 1992. *The American Woman, 1992-93: A Status Report.* New York: W. W. Norton.

Riger, Stephanie. 1993. "Gender Dilemmas in Sexual Harassment: Policies and Procedures." In *American Women in the Nineties: Today's Critical Issues,* edited by Sherri Matteo. Boston: Northeastern University Press.

Rinehart, Sue Tolleson. 1991. "Do Women Leaders Make a Difference? Substance, Style, and Perceptions." In *Gender and Policymaking: Studies of Women in Office,* edited by Debra L. Dodson. New Brunswick, N.J.: Center for the American Woman and Politics, Eagleton Institute, Rutgers University.

Ritt, Leonard. 1993. "Parties and Politics in Arizona." In *Politics and Public Policy in Arizona*, edited by Zachary A. Smith. Westport, Conn.: Praeger.

Robinson, John P., Janet Yerby, Margaret Fieweger, and Nancy Somerick. 1977. "Sex-Role Differences in Time Use." *Sex Roles* 2: 443–58.

Rosenblum, Jonathan D. 1995. *Copper Crucible: How the Arizona Miners' Strike of 1983 Recast Labor-Management Relations in America*. Ithaca, N.Y.: ILR Press.

Rosener, Judy B. 1990. "Ways Women Lead." *Harvard Business Review* (November–December): 119–25.

Rosenstone, Steven J. 1983. *Forecasting Presidential Elections*. New Haven, Conn.: Yale University Press.

Rosenthal, Alan. 1981. *Legislative Life: People, Processes, and Performance in the States*. New York: Harper and Row.

Rosenwasser, S. M., R. Rogers, S. Fling, I. Silver-Pickens, and J. Butemeyer. 1987. "Attitudes toward Women and Men in Politics: Perceived Male and Female Candidate Competencies and Participant Personality Characteristics." *Political Psychology* 8: 191–200.

Rosenwasser, Shirley M., and Jana Seale. 1988. "Attitudes Toward a Hypothetical Male and Female Presidential Candidate—A Research Note." *Political Psychology* 9: 591–98.

Rothman, Barbara Katz. 1989. "Women, Health, and Medicine." In *Women: A Feminist Perspective*, 4th ed., edited by Jo Freeman. Mountain View, Calif.: Mayfield.

Rothschild, Mary Aickin, and Pamela Claire Hronek. 1987. "A History of Arizona Women's Politics." In *Women and the Arizona Political Process*, edited by Rita Mae Kelly. Lanham, Md.: University Press of America.

Rothschild, Mary Logan, and Pamela Claire Hronek. 1992. *Doing What the Day Brought: An Oral History of Arizona Women*. Tucson: University of Arizona Press.

Ruddick, Sara. 1989. *Maternal Thinking: Toward a Politics of Peace*. Boston: Beacon.

Rudolph, Deborah. 1990. "Why Can't a Woman Manage More Like . . . a Woman?" *Time* 136 (Fall, Special Issue): 53.

Russell, Diana E. H. 1975. *The Politics of Rape: The Victim's Perspective*. New York: Stein and Day.

Ryan, Mary P. 1983. *Womanhood in America: From Colonial Times to the Present*. 3d ed. New York: F. Watts.

Saint-Germain, Michelle A. 1989. "Does Their Difference Make a Difference? The Impact of Women on Public Policy in the Arizona Legislature." *Social Science Quarterly* 70: 956–68.

Salholz, Eloise. 1992. "Women on the Run." *Newsweek* 119 (4 May): 24–25.

Sapiro, Virginia. 1981. "Research Frontier Essay: When Are Interests Interesting? The Problem of Political Representation of Women." *American Political Science Review* 75: 701–16.

———. 1981–82. "If U.S. Senator Baker Were a Woman: An Experimental Study of Candidate Images." *Political Psychology* 3(1/2): 61–83.

———. 1983. *The Political Integration of Women: Roles, Socialization, and Politics*. Urbana: University of Illinois Press.

———. 1993. "The Political Uses of Symbolic Women: An Essay in Honor of Murray Edelman." *Political Communication* 10: 141–54.

Schattschneider, E. E. 1960. *The Semisovereign People: A Realist's View of Democracy in America*. New York: Holt, Rinehart and Winston.

Schiller, Wendy J. 1995. "Senators as Political Entrepreneurs: Using Bill Sponsorship to Shape Legislative Agendas." *American Journal of Political Science* 39(1): 186–203.

Schlozman, Kay Lehman, and John T. Tierney. 1986. *Organized Interests and American Democracy*. New York: Harper and Row.

Schrag, Peter. 1995. "The Populist Road to Hell." *American Prospect* 24 (Winter): 24–30.

Scott, Hilda. 1984. *Working Your Way to the Bottom: The Feminization of Poverty*. Boston: Pandora.

Scott, Joan W. 1986. "Gender: A Useful Category of Historical Analysis." *American Historical Review* 91(5): 1053–75.

Sears, David O. and Carolyn L. Funk. 1990. "Self-Interest in Americans' Political Opinions." In *Beyond Self-Interest*, edited by Jane J. Mansbridge. Chicago: University of Chicago Press.

Sears, David O., Carl P. Hensler, and Leslie K. Speer. 1979. "Whites' Opposition to Busing: Self-Interest or Symbolic Politics?" *American Political Science Review* 73: 369–84.

Sears, David O., and Leonie Huddy. 1990. "On the Origins of Political Disunity among Women." In *Women, Politics, and Change*, edited by Louise A. Tilly and Patricia Gurin. New York: Sage.

Sears, David O., Richard R. Lau, Tom R. Tyler, and Harris M. Allen Jr. 1980. "Self-Interest versus Symbolic Politics in Policy Attitudes and Presidential Voting." *American Political Science Review* 74: 670–84.

Seltzer, Richard A., Jody Newman, and Melissa Voorhees Leighton. 1997. *Sex as a Political Variable: Women as Candidates and Voters in U.S. Elections*. Boulder: Lynne Rienner.

Shapiro, Robert Y., and Harpreet Mahajan. 1986. "Gender Differences in Policy Preferences: A Summary of Trends from the 1960s to the 1980s." *Public Opinion Quarterly* 50: 42–61.

Sheffield, Carole J. 1989. "Sexual Terrorism." In *Women: A Feminist Perspective*, 4th ed., edited by Jo Freeman. Mountain View, Calif.: Mayfield.

Shepard, Scott. 1992. "'We Embody Change': Angry Voters See Women as Their Salvation." *Atlanta Constitution* (29 April): A12.

Sheridan, Thomas E. 1986. "Anglo Settlement." In *Arizona: The Land and the People*, edited by Tom Miller. Tucson: University of Arizona Press.

———. 1995. *Arizona: A History*. Tucson: University of Arizona Press.

Silverberg, Helene. 1990. "What Happened to the Feminist Revolution in Political Science? A Review Essay." *Western Political Quarterly* 43: 887–903.

Skjeie, Hege. 1991. "The Rhetoric of Difference: On Women's Inclusion into Political Elites." *Politics and Society* 19(2): 233–63.

Skocpol, Theda. 1992. *Protecting Soldiers and Mothers: The Political Origins of Social Policy in the United States*. Cambridge, Mass.: Belknap Press of Harvard University Press.

Smith, Tom W., ed. 1984. "The Polls: Gender and Attitudes toward Violence." *Public Opinion Quarterly* 48: 384–96.

Smolowe, Jill. 1992. "Politics: The Feminist Machine." *Time* 139 (4 May): 34–36.

Snitow, Ann. 1989. "Pages from a Gender Diary: Basic Divisions in Feminism." *Dissent* (Spring): 205-24.

Spelman, Elizabeth V. 1988. *Inessential Woman: Problems of Exclusion in Feminist Thought*. Boston: Beacon.

Spence, Janet T., Robert L. Helmreich, and Joy Stapp. 1975. "Ratings of Self and Peers on Sex Role Attributes and Their Relation to Self Esteem and Conceptions of Masculinity and Femininity." *Journal of Personality and Social Psychology* 32: 29-39.

Squire, Peverill. 1992. "The Theory of Legislative Institutionalization and the California Assembly." *Journal of Politics* 54(4): 1026-54.

Stolberg, Sheryl Gay. 1997. "Many Women Wary of Congress's Newfound Interest in Female Health Issues." *New York Times* (26 May): A9.

Stoper, Emily. 1977. "Wife and Politician: Role Strain Among Women in Public Office." In *A Portrait of Marginality: The Political Behavior of the American Woman*, edited by Marianne Githens and Jewel L. Prestage. New York: D. McKay Co.

———. 1989. "The Gender Gap Concealed and Revealed: 1936-1984." *Journal of Political Science* 17 (1-2): 50-62.

Stoper, Emily, and Roberta Ann Johnson. 1977. "The Weaker Sex and the Better Half: The Idea of Women's Moral Superiority in the American Feminist Movement." *Polity* 10: 192-217.

Syer, John. 1987. "California: Political Giants in a Megastate." In *Interest Group Politics in the American West*, edited by Ronald J. Hrebenar and Clive S. Thomas. Salt Lake City: University of Utah Press.

Syer, John C., and John H. Culver. 1992. *Power and Politics in California*. 4th ed. New York: Macmillan.

Tamerius, Karin L. 1995. "Sex, Gender, and Leadership in the Representation of Women." In *Gender Power, Leadership, and Governance*, edited by Georgia Duerst-Lahti and Rita Mae Kelly. Ann Arbor: University of Michigan Press.

Tannen, Deborah. 1990. *You Just Don't Understand: Women and Men in Conversation*. New York: Morrow.

Terborg-Penn, Rosalyn. 1998. *African-American Women in the Struggle for the Vote, 1850-1920*. Bloomington: Indiana University Press.

Thomas, Sue. 1989. "Voting Patterns in the California Assembly: The Role of Gender." *Women and Politics* 9(4): 43-53.

———. 1991. "The Impact of Women on State Legislative Policies." *Journal of Politics* 53: 958-76.

———. 1992. "The Effects of Race and Gender on Constituency Service." *Western Political Quarterly* 45(1): 169-80.

———. 1994. *How Women Legislate*. New York: Oxford University Press.

———. 1997. "Why Gender Matters: The Perceptions of Women Officeholders." *Women and Politics* 17(1): 27-53.

Thomas, Sue, and Susan Welch. 1991. "The Impact of Gender on Activities and Priorities of State Legislators." *Western Political Quarterly* 44: 445-56.

Thorne, Barrie. 1990. "Children and Gender: Constructions of Difference." In *Theoretical Perspectives on Sexual Differences*, edited by Deborah L. Rhode. New Haven, Conn.: Yale University Press.

Toner, Robin. 1990. "For Women, Better Climate Is Seen." *New York Times* (22 April): A30.

Tucker, Cynthia. 1998. "Ask Clarence Thomas: Not All Blacks Think Alike." *Atlanta Journal-Constitution* (2 August): E5.

Uslaner, Eric M. 1986. "Legislative Behavior: The Study of Representation." In *Annual Review of Political Science*, Vol. 1, edited by Samuel Long. Norwood, N.J.: Ablex.

Vega, Arturo, and Juanita M. Firestone. 1995. "The Effects of Gender on Congressional Behavior and the Substantive Representation of Women." *Legislative Studies Quarterly* 20(2): 213–22.

Verhovek, Sam Howe. 1998. "Democrat or Republican, Woman Will Be Winner." *New York Times* (26 October): A18.

———. 1999. "Record for Women in Washington Legislature." *New York Times* (4 February): A8.

Wahlke, John C., Heinz Eulau, William Buchanan, and Lorna C. Ferguson. 1962. *The Legislative System: Explorations in Legislative Behavior.* New York: John Wiley.

Walker, Jack L. 1969. "The Diffusion of Innovations among the American States." *American Political Science Review* 63: 880–99.

Walters, Dan. 1988. "Women Have Arrived—Finally—in California Politics." *Sacramento Bee* (28 February): Forum 1, 6

Ware, Susan. 1981. *Beyond Suffrage: Women in the New Deal.* Cambridge, Mass.: Harvard University Press.

Warshaw, Robin. 1988. *I Never Called It Rape: The Ms. Report on Recognizing, Fighting, and Surviving Date and Acquaintance Rape.* New York: Harper and Row.

Washington, Paula G., and Diane Scott. 1999. *The Womentor Guide: Leadership for the New Millennium.* Traverse City, Mich.: Sage Creek Press.

Watkins, Ronald J. 1990. *High Crimes and Misdemeanors: The Term and Trials of Former Governor Evan Mecham.* New York: Morrow.

Weber, Max. 1947. *The Theory of Social and Economic Organization.* Glencoe, Ill.: Free Press.

Weberg, Brian, and Beth Bazar. 1988. *Legislative Staff Resources.* Denver: National Conference of State Legislatures.

Welch, Susan. 1985. "Are Women More Liberal than Men in the U.S. Congress?" *Legislative Studies Quarterly* 10: 125–34.

Welch, Susan, and Sue Thomas. 1991. "Do Women in Public Office Make a Difference?" In *Gender and Policymaking: Studies of Women in Office*, edited by Debra L. Dodson. New Brunswick, N.J.: Center for the American Woman and Politics, Eagleton Institute, Rutgers University.

Werner, Emmy E. 1966. "Women in Congress, 1917–1964." *Western Political Quarterly* 19 (March): 16–30.

Whip, Rosemary. 1991. "Representing Women: Australian Female Parliamentarians on the Horns of a Dilemma." *Women and Politics* 11(3): 1–22.

Willey, Keven Ann. 1991. "Arizona: One Dang Thing After Another." *State Legislatures* 17(7): 41–44.

Wirls, Donald. 1985. "Reinterpreting the Gender Gap." *Public Opinion Quarterly* 50: 316–30.

Wirt, Frederick M. 1991. " 'Soft' Concepts and 'Hard' Data: A Research Review of Elazar's Political Culture." *Publius* 21(2): 1–13.

Witt, Linda, Karen M. Paget, and Glenna Matthews. 1994. *Running as a Woman: Gender and Power in American Politics.* New York: Free Press.

Yoachum, Susan. 1990. "Complaints of Gender Politicking." *San Francisco Chronicle* (18 July): A8.

Yoachum, Susan, and Robert B. Gunnison. 1992. "Women Candidates Win Record 71 Nominations." *San Francisco Chronicle* (4 June): A1, A16.

Yoder, Janice D. 1991. "Rethinking Tokenism: Looking Beyond Numbers." *Gender and Society* 5: 178–92.

Young, Cathy. 1992. ". . . But Are They Promoting a New Brand of Sexism?" *Atlanta Journal-Constitution* (18 October): H2.

Zeiger, Richard, and A. G. Block. 1988. "The Decline and Fall of Speaker Willie Brown Jr.?" *California Journal* (April): 152–58.

Zeiger, Richard, and Sherry Bebitch Jeffe. 1988. "Women in Politics." *California Journal* (January): 7–11.

Zinn, Maxine Baca. 1989. "Family, Race, and Poverty in the Eighties." *Signs: Journal of Women in Culture and Society* 14: 856–74.

Zipp, John F., and Eric Plutzer. 1985. "Gender Differences in Voting for Female Candidates: Evidence from the 1982 Election." *Public Opinion Quarterly* 49: 179–97.

# Index

Abortion rights, 2, 16, 23, 39, 40, 73, 80, 120, 124, 138, 139, 140, 143, 144, 149, 152, 153, 156, 157, 166, 182–83, 239, 250, 293 (n. 6), 300 (nn. 3, 7), 301 (n. 11), 302 (nn. 4–5)

Abzug, Bella, 16, 28

Affirmative action, 149, 153–54

African Americans. *See* Blacks

Agriculture, 116–18, 119, 165–66, 170, 171, 174–79, 217, 287, 291, 304–5 (n. 11)

AIDS, 107, 146, 147, 149, 151–52, 154, 239

Alexander, Deborah, 19, 165, 294 (n. 2)

Allocation responsiveness to constituents, 96, 99, 100

*American Federalism* (Elazar), 60–64

Andersen, Kristi, 19, 94 (n. 2), 165

Animal rights, 144

Antolini, Denise, 98, 106, 220, 221, 249

Arizona: history of, as western "frontier" state, 51; agriculture in, 51, 57, 63; business interests in, 51, 63, 66; woman suffrage in, 51, 78, 297 (n. 16); population of, 52, 56, 58; water rights in, 52–53; economic and industrial growth in, 52–53, 56; scandals in, 53–54, 63; ethnic diversity in, 57; political culture of, 61, 63–64; political parties in, 63, 64–65, 68, 72–74; conservatism in, 64–67, 69, 72–74, 80; ideological orientation in, 64–67, 72–74; and Martin Luther King Jr. (MLK) holiday, 66–67, 73, 146, 300 (n. 7); campaign expenditures and fundraising in, 78; labor unions in, 296 (n. 8); state legislative districts in, 296 (n. 2)

Arizona elected officials: women elected in 1998, 1, 43; Mofford as governor, 19; Hull as governor, 43; scandals involving, 53–54, 63. *See also* Arizona state legislators

Arizona state legislators: and election of 1998, 1; sex differences in legislative behavior, 6–9, 112, 147–49, 158, 199–200, 215–41, 243–46; research methodology on, 9–10, 255–77; and

scandals, 53–54; statistics on female legislators, 55, 78–79, 246, 295 (n. 16), 296 (n. 1); and length of legislative sessions, 57, 58; and professionalization and institutionalization of legislature, 57–58; number of constituents per legislator, 58; salaries of, 58; workload of, 58; staff support for, 59, 296 (n. 3); party politics of, 73–74; and sexism, 78, 89, 90; female legislators, 78–92, 298 (n. 24); and lack of legislative women's caucus, 80–81; social status of, 81–83, 219, 299–300 (n. 6); status of women in 1990 legislature, 81–92; political status of, 84–85, 219; and seniority, 85; professional status of, 85–88, 109–10, 298 (n. 25); committee assignments of, 85–88, 163–64, 176–80; and leadership positions in legislature, 85–88, 298 (n. 25); perceptions of women's status in, 88–91; and constituency responsiveness, 99–101, 104, 106–9, 111–12, 216, 220, 223–24, 225, 229, 231–33, 235–36, 240, 244–45, 299 (n. 3), 307 (n. 4); legislative activities of, 102–3, 104, 109–12, 299 (n. 5); institutional context and representational roles of, 103–4; constituency group support for, 115–23; and women's significance as political group, 115–23; and representing women and/or women's policy concerns, 123–33; and "making a difference" by female legislators, 124–27, 133, 146–47, 215–17, 243–48; policy preferences of, 140–60, 226, 233, 237–39, 244; roll call votes of, 144–48, 278–82, 302–3 (nn. 7–9); policy priorities of, 161–84, 226–27, 233–34; issue area committees in, 168, 291–92; and women's issues, 169–84, 216–17, 233–34, 237–39; and men's issues, 170, 171, 174, 176–77, 182, 217; bill sponsorship by, 178, 303–4 (n. 2); as feminist policy activists, 180–83, 217, 227, 229, 234, 305 (n. 13); and "power to" strategies, 190, 195–98, 200–204, 209, 217, 223, 228, 234, 236;

and "power over" strategies, 193–95, 199–204, 206–9, 234–35, 236; and strategies for legislative success, 193–211, 305–6 (nn. 8–9), 306 (n. 10); sources of personal power of, 201–4, 217, 234; and hardball politics, 206–9, 210, 217, 228, 229, 234–35; "selecting out" and female legislators, 218–19, 240; institutional constraints on female legislators, 220–30, 240, 245–46; institutional status of legislators "acting for" women, 224–30, 246, 307 (n. 2); and meaning of representing women, 230–41; personal background characteristics of, 270–73; tenure of female legislators, 298 (n. 24); and bill passage rates, 307 (n. 3)

Arkansas, 191
Asian Americans, 57, 75, 76
Australia, 222, 293 (n. 5)
Auto insurance, 144
"Azscam" scandal, 54

Babbitt, Bruce, 64–65, 67, 79, 297 (n. 18)
Baker, Paula, 294 (n. 10)
Bayless, Betsey, 297 (n. 18)
Beck, Susan Abrams, 105
Bem, Sandra Lipsitz, 44, 45
Berkman, Michael B., 293 (n. 6)
Berman, David, 65
Berry, Rachel, 78
*Beyond Equality and Difference* (Pateman), 252
Bipartisanship: in California, 62, 70
Bird, Rose, 76
Blacks, 22, 34–35, 55, 76, 295 (nn. 20–21), 305 (n. 3)
Blair, Diane, 191–92
Blue-collar workers as constituents, 116–18
Brown, Jerry, 72, 76, 296 (n. 6)
Brown, Willie, 18, 70–72
Buchanan, William, 96, 298 (n. 1)
Bureaucracy: feminist case against, 26–27; representative bureaucracy, 33–34
Burns, James McGregor, 305 (n. 1)
Burrell, Barbara, 158, 162
Burton, Phillip, 72, 75
Bush, George, 119, 303 (n. 10)
Business and commerce issues, 168, 170, 172, 174–80, 181, 217, 288, 290
Business people: as state legislators, 83, 300 (n. 6); as constituents, 116–18; leadership styles of, 188–89
Busing, 156

Caldeira, Gregory, 205
California: history of, as western "frontier" state, 51; agriculture in, 51, 57; business interests in, 51, 69; woman suffrage in, 51, 78, 297 (n. 16); population of, 52, 56, 58; water rights in, 52–53; economic and industrial growth in, 52–53, 56–57; scandals in, 53–54; size and scope of, as nation-state, 56–60; ethnic diversity in, 57; delegation to U.S. House of Representatives, 58; political culture of, 61–64; ballot initiatives in, 62;

lack of party loyalty in, 62; political parties in, 62, 68–72, 74, 131–32; bipartisanship in, 62, 70; campaign expenditures and fundraising in, 62, 70–71, 77, 296 (n. 6); ideological orientation in, 67–70; liberalism in, 67–70; conservatism in, 68, 69, 71–72; reapportionment in, 72

California elected officials: scandals involving, 53–54; political parties of, 68. *See also* California state legislators

California Legislative Women's Caucus, 76, 91, 92, 127–28, 132

California state legislators: and election of 1998, 1; sex differences in legislative behavior, 6–9, 132, 145–56, 158, 171–72, 199–200, 215–41, 243–46; research methodology on, 9–10, 255–77; and scandals, 53–54; statistics on female legislators, 55, 75–76, 246, 295 (n. 1), 296 (n. 1); and length of legislative sessions, 57, 58; salaries of, 57, 58; and professionalization and institutionalization of legislature, 57, 59–60, 210; number of constituents per legislator, 58; workload of, 58; staff support for, 59; and "making a difference" by female legislators, 59–60, 124–27, 147, 215–17, 243–48; and bipartisanship, 62, 70; as liberals, 68; as conservatives, 68, 71–72; party politics of, 70–72, 74; and sexism, 75–77, 89; female legislators in 1960s and 1970s, 75–78; male dominance of legislature in 1960s and 1970s, 75–78; and Legislative Women's Caucus, 76, 91, 92, 127–28, 132; social status of, 81–83, 219, 299–300 (n. 6); female legislators in 1990, 81–92; status of women in 1990 legislature, 81–92; political status of, 84–85, 219; and seniority, 85; and leadership positions in legislature, 85–88; professional status of, 85–88, 110; committee assignments of, 85–88, 163–64, 176–80; perceptions of women's status in, 88–91; and constituency responsiveness, 99–101, 104, 107–9, 111, 216, 220, 223–24, 225, 231–33, 235–36, 240, 244–45, 299 (n. 3), 307 (n. 4); legislative activities of, 102–3, 104, 109–12, 299 (n. 5); institutional context and representational roles of, 103–4; constituency group support for, 115–16, 118–23, 301 (n. 4); and women's significance as political group, 115–23; and representing women and/or women's policy concerns, 123–33; policy preferences of, 140–60, 226, 233, 237–39, 244; roll call votes of, 144–48, 282–85, 303 (n. 7); and California Polls of constituents, 149–56; policy priorities of, 161–84, 226–27, 233–34; issue area committees in, 168, 291–92; and women's issues, 169–84, 216–17, 233–34, 237–29; and men's issues, 170, 172, 174, 182, 217; bill sponsorship by, 178, 303 (n. 2); as feminist policy activists, 180–84, 217, 227, 229, 234, 305 (n. 13); and "power to" strategies, 190, 195–98, 200–204, 209, 217, 223, 228, 234, 236; and "power over" strategies, 193–95, 200–204, 206–9, 234–35, 236; and strategies

and hardball politics, 228; and bill passage rate, 307 (n. 3). *See also* Political parties

Deukmejian, George, 68

Diamond, Irene, 98, 157

Dietz, Mary, 294 (n. 9)

"Difference" feminism, 25–27, 41, 45

Differences between men and women. *See* Gender differences

Divorce, 73, 167, 297 (n. 19)

Dodson, Debra, 218

Dolan, Julie, 157

Domestic labor, 22, 166

Domestic violence, 2, 23, 120, 124–25, 126, 139, 149, 150, 167

Dorr, Rheta Childe, 28–29

Dreifus, Claudia, 297 (n. 17)

Duerst-Lahti, Georgia, 192

DUI (driving under the influence), 146

Echols, Alice, 29

Economic equality, 120

Educational status: and wages, 23; gender differences in, 82, 83; of state legislators, 83, 219; and representational style, 299 (n. 6)

Education issues, 73, 120, 121, 140, 141, 146, 164, 166, 170–73, 175, 177–79, 181, 182, 217, 227, 234, 237, 238, 286, 290

Elazar, Daniel, 56, 60–64, 66, 296 (nn. 5, 7)

Elderly as constituents, 116–18

Elshtain, Jean Bethke, 25, 26, 294 (n. 9)

Employment. *See* Occupational status

Employment issues, 140, 141

"Enlarged housekeeping," 28, 294 (n. 14)

Environmental issues, 40, 69, 116–18, 121, 138, 140, 141, 144, 146, 147, 149, 151, 155, 164, 165, 170, 171, 173, 174, 177–79, 181, 182, 217, 227, 229, 234, 238, 239, 287, 290

Environmentalists as constituents, 116–18, 238

Epstein, Cynthia Fuchs, 155, 293 (n. 4), 295 (n. 21)

Equal Rights Amendment (ERA), 2, 14, 39, 42–43, 65, 80, 139, 156, 157, 188

ERA. *See* Equal Rights Amendment

Erikson, Robert, 69, 296 (nn. 7, 9)

Essentialism, 44–45, 46

Ethnic minorities: as constituents, 116–18, 238, 301 (nn. 4, 11); equal rights for, 140, 141–42, 149, 153–54, 238. *See also* Asian Americans; Blacks; Hispanics

Eulau, Heinz, 96, 103, 298 (n. 1)

Eu, March Fong, 75, 76

Evans, Sara, 29, 294 (n. 10)

Family issues. *See* Children and family issues

Family leave, 138, 139, 144, 147, 180

Family planning, 76

Farmers as constituents, 116–18, 119. *See also* Agriculture

Feinstein, Dianne, 16, 18, 20, 31

Female officeholders/politicians: statistics on, 1, 14–15, 55, 75–76, 78–79, 246, 296 (n. 1); in California generally, 1, 75–76; in Arizona generally, 1, 78–80; and "making a differ-

ence," 2, 3, 6, 7, 8–9, 13–30, 49–50, 54–55, 59–60, 123–27, 133, 137–39, 146–47, 162, 184, 215–18, 242–53, 293 (n. 6); and women's issues, 2, 6, 7, 14–21, 30, 114–15, 120–33, 140–48, 156, 164–84, 216–17, 233–34, 237–39; impact of, on political representation, 2, 9, 36–46; research on impact of generally, 2–3, 8–9; distinctive "feminine" characteristics and values of, 2–3, 18–19, 185–92, 301 (n. 8); avoidance of "women's issues" by, 3, 43, 114, 132–33, 221–22; lack of sex differences in legislative behavior, 3–4, 6–9, 112, 145–60, 191–92, 199–200, 215–41, 243–46; and male domination in politics, 4; diversity among, with increase in number of, 5, 8; and men's issues, 6, 176–80, 182, 217; constituents of, 6–7; and district demographics, 6–7; female constituents of, 6–7, 25, 116–20, 129–31, 216, 219, 220, 225–26, 232–33, 235–36; political advertisements of, 17; public opinion polls on, 17–18, 19, 20; "throw-the-rascals-out" rhetoric of, 19–20; and women's shared experiences, 20–21, 124–25, 130; campaign funds for, 77, 78; conservatism of, 80, 146, 157; political status of, 81, 84–85, 219, 298 (n. 23); professional status of legislators, 81, 85–88, 109–10, 298 (n. 25); social status of, 81–83, 219, 299–300 (n. 6); and constituency responsiveness, 96–101, 104, 105–9, 111–12, 216, 220, 223–24, 225, 231–33, 235–36, 240, 244–45, 299 (n. 3), 307 (n. 4); legislative activities of, 98–99, 101–3, 104, 109–12, 299 (n. 5); constituency group support for, 115–23; and representing women and/or women's policy concerns, 123–33; policy preferences of, 137–60, 226, 233, 237–39, 244; in Democratic party, 139; liberalism of, 139, 143–47, 156, 216; differences among, in policy preferences, 148; policy priorities of, 161–84, 226–27, 233–34; as feminist policy activists, 180–84, 217, 227, 229, 234, 305 (n. 13); leadership style of, 186–92; and "power over" strategies, 190, 193–95, 199–209, 234–35, 236; and "power to" strategies, 190, 195–98, 200–204, 209, 217, 223, 228, 234, 236; and hardball politics, 204–9, 210, 217, 228, 229, 234–35; participation in women's groups by, 218, 307 (n. 1); "selecting out" as explanation for similarities with male officeholders/politicians, 218–19, 240; institutional constraints on, 220–30, 240, 245–46; institutional status of legislators "acting for" women, 224–30, 246, 307 (n. 2); and politics of presence, 248–49. *See also* Arizona state legislators; California state legislators; Women's issues; *and specific women*

Feminine feminism, 25, 294 (n. 9)

Feminism: of female officeholders, 2, 114; as deviant in political culture, 4; "difference" feminism, 25–27, 41, 45; and political representation, 34–35; determinants of feminist consciousness, 37, 38; public opinion polls

Hawaii, 157, 304 (n. 5)
Hazardous waste, 40
Health and public safety, 16, 120, 121, 130, 138,
    140, 141, 144, 146–47, 149, 151–52, 154, 164,
    166, 170–73, 175, 177–79, 181, 182, 217, 227,
    229, 234, 237, 238, 249–50, 286–87, 290
Health insurance, 16, 146
Healy, Lynne, 190, 192
Hedlund, Gun, 300 (n. 2)
Hewitt, Nancy, 42
Hibbing, John, 105
Hill, Anita, 15, 19
Hispanics, 55, 57, 76
Homosexuality. *See* Gays and lesbians
hooks, bell, 305 (n. 3)
Hooley, Darlene, 16
Housekeeping theory of government, 28, 29,
    30, 44, 294 (n. 14)
House of Representatives, U.S. *See* Congress,
    U.S.
Huddy, Leonie, 40
Hull, Jane Dee, 43, 54, 88, 222

Idaho, 64
*In a Different Voice* (Gilligan), 24
Independents in California, 68–69
Individualistic subculture, 60–61, 62, 63, 66
Institutional norms and constraints, 192–93,
    209–11, 220–30, 240, 245–46
Institutional sexism. *See* Sex discrimination
Institutional status of legislators "acting for"
    women, 224–30, 246, 307 (n. 2)
Ireland, Patricia, 15, 33

Jacklin, Carol N., 295 (n. 21)
Jeffe, Sherry Bebitch, 77
Jennings, Kent, 105–6, 218
Jewell, Malcolm, 95, 103, 106, 187, 191, 192,
    298–99 (n. 1)
Johannes, John, 96–97
Johnson, Cathy Marie, 192
Jónasdóttir, Anna, 31, 36, 37, 41, 43–44, 250, 251
Jordan, Barbara, 19
Jordan, Jewel, 79
Jordan-Meldrum, Janalee, 65

Kanter, Rosabeth, 4–5, 55, 293 (n. 7)
Karps, Paul, 96
Kassebaum, Nancy, 15–16, 138
Kathlene, Lyn, 190–91, 192
Katz, Vera, 186–87
Keating, Charles, 53–54
Kelly, Rita Mae, 80
Kerber, Linda, 27
Kirkpatrick, Jeane, 4, 98, 105, 158–59, 185–86,
    191, 192, 204–5, 298–99 (n. 1)
Klein, Ethel, 37
Kopp, Nancy, 187
Kraditor, Aileen, 28

Labor relations, 144
Labor unions, 296 (n. 8)
Latinos. *See* Hispanics

Leader, Shelah, 159–60
Leadership: importance of legislative leader-
    ship, 8, 110, 161–62; positions of, in state
    legislatures, 85–88, 298 (n. 25); sex differ-
    ences in policy leadership, 160, 163–84; in
    · women's issues and men's issues, 170–75,
    226–27, 233–34; sex differences in political
    leadership styles, 186–88, 190–92, 305 (n. 5);
    transformational vs. transactional styles
    of, 188, 305 (n. 1); sex differences in cor-
    porate leadership styles, 188–89; feminist
    perspectives on, 189–90; and "power over"
    strategies, 190, 193–95, 199–209, 234–35, 236;
    and "power to" strategies, 190, 195–98, 200–
    204, 209, 217, 223, 228, 234, 236; and power,
    300 (n. 10)
Legal profession, 83, 300 (n. 6)
Legislative activities: importance of legisla-
    tive skill and accomplishment, 8, 161–62;
    committee assignments, 85–88, 163–64, 176–
    80, 304 (n. 4); and political representation,
    95, 98–99, 101–3; average number of bills
    introduced, 102, 299 (n. 5); time spent on,
    102, 104; of Arizona and California state
    legislators, 102–3, 104, 109–12, 299 (n. 5);
    as source of power, 110, 161–62; and policy
    preferences, 140–60, 226, 233, 237–39, 244;
    roll call voting, 144–48, 159, 161, 162, 278–
    82, 302–3 (nn. 7–9); and policy priorities,
    161–84, 226–27, 233–34; and feminist policy
    activity, 180–84, 227, 229, 234; procedural
    aspects of, 185–211; and "power over" strate-
    gies, 190, 193–95, 199–209, 234–35, 236; and
    "power to" strategies, 190, 195–98, 200–204,
    209, 217, 223, 228, 234, 236; and institu-
    tional norms, 192–93, 209–11, 220–30, 240;
    strategies for legislative success, 193–211,
    305–6 (nn. 8–9; sex differences in legislative
    strategies, 194, 199–211; lobbying among
    legislators, 196–97; "neutral" or "mixed"
    strategies in, 198–99, 202; and sources of
    personal power, 201–4, 217, 234
Legislators. *See* Arizona state legislators;
    California state legislators
Lesbians. *See* Gays and lesbians
Liberalism: women's identification with,
    40, 149; in California, 67–70; of female
    officeholders, 139, 143–47, 156, 216; *National
    Journal*'s liberalism rating, 158
Lobbyists, 76, 102, 104, 109–10, 199, 200, 297
    (n. 13), 306 (n. 10)
Loden, Marilyn, 188

Maccoby, Eleanor E., 295 (n. 21)
McIver, John, 69, 296 (nn. 7, 9)
Madison, James, 33
Major, Brenda, 48, 50, 251
Male officeholders/politicians: lack of sex
    differences in legislative behavior, 3–4, 6–9,
    112, 145–60, 191–92, 199–200, 215–41, 243–
    46; dominance of, 4–5, 75–78, 293 (n. 5);
    and women's issues, 6, 15, 17, 120–33, 140–
    48, 169–84, 216–17, 233–34, 237–39; and

men's issues, 6, 165–66, 171, 172, 174, 182, 217; defeat of Equal Rights Amendment by, 14; and Clarence Thomas's appointment to Supreme Court, 15; political advertisements of, 17; public opinion polls on, 17–18, 19, 20; policy preferences of, 24, 137–60, 226, 233, 237–39; political status of, 81, 84–85, 219, 298 (n. 23); professional status of legislators, 81, 85–88, 109–10; social status of, 81–83, 219, 299–300 (n. 6); and constituency responsiveness, 96–101, 104, 105–9, 111–12, 216, 220, 223–24, 225, 229, 231–33, 235–36, 240, 244–45, 299 (n. 3), 307 (n. 4); legislative activities of, 98–99, 101–3, 104, 109–12, 299 (n. 5); constituency group support for, 115–23; female constituents of, 119, 216, 220, 225–26, 232–33, 235–36, 245; and representing women and/or women's policy concerns, 123–33; policy priorities of, 161–84, 226–27, 233–34; as feminist policy activists, 180–83, 217, 227, 234, 305 (n. 13); leadership style of, 186–88; and hardball politics, 188, 204–9, 210, 217, 228, 234–35; and "power over" strategies, 190, 193–95, 199–209, 234–35, 236; and "power to" strategies, 190, 195–98, 200–204, 209, 217, 223, 228, 234, 236; institutional status of legislators "acting for" women, 224–30, 307 (n. 2); and "acting for" women, 249–50. *See also* Arizona state legislators; California state legislators; Men's issues
Mandel, Ruth, 218
Mann, Judy, 39
Mansbridge, Jane, 43, 248, 249, 250–51, 305 (n. 4), 307 (n. 1)
Marigold, Lys, 188
Martin Luther King Jr. (MLK) holiday, 66–67, 73, 146, 300 (n. 7)
Maryland, 103, 187
Mason, Bruce B., 296 (n. 8)
"Maternal feminism," 294 (n. 9)
Maternal practice. *See* Motherhood
Matthews, Glenna, 13, 46–47, 49
Mayors, 19, 190, 297 (n. 20)
Mecham, Evan, 19, 53, 63, 66–67, 73–74, 79, 80, 297 (nn. 17–18)
Media: on women's issues, 17; on gender gap, 39
Medical care. *See* Health and public safety
Meek, Carrie, 21
Men officeholders/politicians. *See* Male officeholders/politicians
Men's issues: and male legislators, 6, 165–66, 170–72, 174, 217; and female legislators, 6, 170–72, 174, 176–80, 182, 217; lists and description of, 16, 17, 168, 290–91; in political advertisements, 17; public opinion polls on, 17–18; as policy priorities, 165–66, 172, 174; and Arizona state legislators, 170, 171, 174, 217; and California state legislators, 170, 172, 174, 217; leadership of legislators on, 172, 174; committee work on, by legislators, 176–80. *See also* Male officeholders/politicians

Mezey, Susan Gluck, 138, 157, 166–67, 304 (n. 5)
Military policy and spending, 16, 138, 156, 165
Milk, Harvey, 68
Mill, John Stuart, 33
Miller, Jean Baker, 294 (n. 8)
Minorities. *See* Asian Americans; Blacks; Ethnic minorities; Hispanics
Mofford, Rose, 19, 79, 297 (n. 17)
Montoya, Joseph, 54
Moral development, 24, 26
Moralistic subculture, 61
Morella, Constance, 250
Mosher, Frederick, 32, 34
Motherhood, 20, 25–26, 27, 30, 44, 124, 294 (n. 9)
Mueller, Carol, 115
Munds, Frances, 78
Murray, Patty, 21, 43

National Association for the Advancement of Colored People (NAACP), 34–35
National Federation of Business and Professional Women's Clubs, 139
*National Journal*, 158
National Organization for Women (NOW), 14, 15, 39, 139
National Women's Political Caucus (NWPC), 14–15, 31, 139, 158, 294 (n. 2)
Naylor, Robert, 72
Nechemias, Carol, 35
Neustadt, Richard E., 306 (n. 16)
Nevada, 296 (n. 9)
New Hampshire, 98, 186
New Mexico, 61–62
New York, 19, 56, 68
Nineteenth Amendment, 29, 43
Nixon, Richard, 68
Nolan, Patrick, 71
North Carolina, 103
North Dakota, 64
Norton, Mary Beth, 27
Norway, 13, 221–22, 293 (n. 5), 300 (n. 2)
NOW. *See* National Organization for Women
Nuclear power, 40, 149, 155, 156
NWPC. *See* National Women's Political Caucus

Occupational health and safety, 149, 151, 154
Occupational status: gender differences in, 22–23, 81–82; of women during World War II, 29; of state legislators, 82–83, 300 (n. 6); and representational style, 300 (n. 6)
O'Connor, Robert E., 293 (n. 6)
O'Connor, Sandra Day, 249
Offen, Karen, 252
Ohio, 103
Oklahoma, 64
Opinion polls. *See* Public opinion polls
Oregon, 186
Owens, Donna, 19

Pacifism. *See* Peace politics
Paget, Karen M., 13, 46–47, 49

Parliamentary procedures, 199
Pateman, Carole, 252
Patterson, Samuel, 205
Pay equity, 139, 144, 147, 167
Peace politics, 25–26, 40
Peirce, Neal R., 56
Personal-political relationship, 37–38
Personal power. *See* Power
Pflug, Cheryl, 43
Phillips, Anne, 13, 34, 35, 38, 45, 46, 248–52, 295 (n. 17)
Pitkin, Hanna, 30–32, 34, 115–16, 295 (n. 15), 300 (n. 8)
Policymaking: and constituency responsiveness, 96, 99, 100; sex differences in policy preferences, 137–60; preferences of Arizona and California legislators in, 140–60, 233, 237–39, 244; and California Polls, 149–56; priorities of Arizona and California legislators in, 161–84, 226–27, 233–34; measures of policy priorities, 163–64; and committee assignments, 163–64, 176–80, 304 (n. 4); sex differences in policy priorities, 163–84; and women's issues, 164–84, 216–17, 233–34, 236–39; and men's issues, 165–66; feminist policy activists in Arizona and California legislatures, 180–84, 217, 227, 229; procedural aspects of policy process, 185–211; "power over" strategies in, 190, 193–95, 199–209, 234–35, 236; "power to" strategies in, 190, 195–98, 200–204, 209, 217, 223, 228, 234, 236; and institutional norms, 192–93, 209–11, 220–30, 240, 245–46; strategies for legislative success, 193–211, 305–6 (nn. 8–9); sex differences in legislative strategies, 194, 199–211; and lobbying among legislators, 196–97; and hard work and knowledge, 198, 199, 306 (n. 9); limiting and focusing efforts in, 198–99; "neutral" or "mixed" strategies in, 198–99, 202; and parliamentary procedures, 199; and writing good proposals, 199; and sources of personal power, 201–4, 217, 234; and hardball politics, 204–9; and institutional status of legislators "acting for" women, 226–27, 246, 307 (n. 2)
Political advertisements, 17
Political culture: Elazar's typology of, 56, 60–64, 296 (nn. 5, 7); definition of, 60; individualistic subculture, 60–61, 62, 63, 66; of Arizona, 61, 63–64, 68; moralistic subculture, 61; of California, 61–64, 131–32; traditionalistic subculture, 61, 66
Political parties: power of, over legislators, 8; and gender gap among voters, 39, 131, 244; in California, 62, 68–72, 74; in Arizona, 63, 64–65, 68, 72–74; and women's interests, 69, 237–39, 244; of female officeholders, 139; and policy preferences among legislators, 145, 148, 157–59, 175, 226, 237–39, 244; and gender gap among legislators, 157–59, 223; and policy priorities among legislators, 173–75, 226–27; and feminist political activity, 180–81, 227, 229; and institutional status for

legislators "acting for" women, 224–29; and hardball politics, 228, 229; and bill passage rate, 307 (n. 3)
Political representation: questions on, 2, 9; and constituency responsiveness, 21–33, 95–101, 104, 105–9, 111–12, 223–25, 229, 235–36, 240, 244–45, 299 (n. 3), 307 (n. 4); definitions of, 30–32, 95; descriptive vs. substantive representation, 31–36, 46, 49, 295 (n. 15); feminists on, 34–35; of women and/or women's policy concerns, 36–46, 123–33; and gender gap, 38–41, 131; of African Americans and Latinos, 55; and legislative activities, 95, 98–99, 101–3, 104, 109–12, 299 (n. 5); and state-level institutional context, 103–4; meaning of representing women, 230–41
Political status of legislators, 81, 84–85, 219, 298 (n. 23)
Politico relationship with constituents, 96, 100, 105, 107–8, 109, 300 (n. 7)
Politics of presence, 248–49
Pollitt, Katha, 13, 45
Polls. *See* Public opinion polls
Pollution control. *See* Environmental issues
Polsby, Nelson, 210
Poole, Keith, 158
Poor people as constituents, 116–18
Popcorn, Faith, 188
Pornography, 303 (n. 8), 305 (n. 12)
Poverty: feminization of, 23, 166; as policy priority, 170–73, 175, 177–79, 182, 217, 227, 234, 237
Power: and legislative activities, 110, 161–62; and constituency responsiveness, 111; gender differences in, 186–87, 190, 193–210; feminist view of, 190; "power over" strategies, 190, 193–95, 199–209, 234–35, 236; and "power to" strategies, 190, 195–98, 200–204, 209, 217, 223, 228, 234, 236; definition of, 201; sources of personal power, 201–4, 217, 234; and leadership positions in legislature, 300 (n. 10); and African American women, 305 (n. 3); presidential power, 306 (n. 16)
"Power over" strategies, 193–95, 199–209, 234–35, 236
"Power to" strategies, 190, 195–98, 200–204, 209, 217, 223, 228, 234, 236
Presidential power, 306 (n. 16)
Prestage, Jewel, 175, 176
Priest, Ivy Baker, 75
Private and public spheres, 20, 22, 25–28
Privatization, 144, 156, 157
Professionals as constituents, 116–18
Professional status of legislators, 81, 85–88, 109–10, 298 (n. 25)
Progressivism, 51, 62, 63
Public and private spheres, 20, 22, 25–28
Public education. *See* Education issues
Public health. *See* Health and public safety
Public opinion polls: on differences between female and male politicians, 17–18, 19, 20, 294 (n. 3); on women's rights and feminism, 38; gender gaps in, 138; California Polls,

149-56; on men's issues, 165; and National Women's Political Caucus, 294 (n. 2); on abortion, 300 (n. 3)

Quindlen, Anna, 249

Rape. *See* Sexual assault
Raphael, Tamar, 19
Reagan, Ronald, 39–40, 68, 71, 155, 297 (n. 20)
Reapportionment, 72
Reciprocity, 8
Reingold, Beth, 303 (n. 12)
Relational feminism, 25
Religious Right, 73
Representation. *See* Political representation
Representative bureaucracy, 33–34
Reproductive health and rights. *See* Abortion rights
"Republican motherhood," 27, 44
Republican Party: and gender gap among voters, 39; in Arizona, 63, 64–65, 68, 72–74; conservative orientation of, 64; in California, 68, 70–72; and women's interests, 131, 238, 239, 244; and gender gap among legislators, 157–58; and policy priorities among legislators, 173–75, 226–27, 238, 239, 244; and feminist political activity, 180–81, 227, 229; and institutional status of legislators "acting for" women, 224–29; and hardball politics, 228, 229; and bill passage rate, 307 (n. 3). *See also* Political parties
Republicans for Choice, 294 (n. 14)
Retirement, 156, 167
Rhode, Deborah, 45, 252
Richards, Ann, 20
Richardson, Lilliard, 103, 299 (n. 2)
Rinehart, Sue Tolleson, 190, 192
Roberti, David, 71
Roberts, Cokie, 17
Roll call voting, 144–48, 159, 161, 162, 278–82, 302–3 (nn. 7–9)
Rosener, Judy, 188, 189
Rosenthal, Alan, 96
Ruddick, Sara, 25–26, 294 (n. 9), 305 (n. 3)

Salaries. *See* Wages
Sapiro, Virginia, 32–33, 36, 37, 38, 116, 165, 248
Scandals, 53–54, 63
Schlafly, Phyllis, 42–43
Schroeder, Patricia, 16–17, 28, 250
Schuhmann, Robert, 97–98, 99, 304 (n. 5)
Scott, Diane, 305 (n. 2)
Scott, Joan W., 47, 48, 252
Sears, David, 40
"Selecting out" and female legislators, 218–19, 240
Senate, U.S. *See* Congress, U.S.
Seniority in state legislatures, 85
Service responsiveness to constituents, 96, 99, 100, 104
Settlement houses, 28
Sex differences. *See* Gender differences
Sex discrimination: institutional sexism in

politics, 75–77, 78, 89, 90, 220, 221, 229–30, 245; as policy issue, 120, 140, 142, 144, 147, 166
Sex education, 76
Sexual assault, 2, 23–24, 167
Sexual dimorphism, 251–53
Sexual harassment, 15, 23
Sex vs. gender, 46–49
Shaheen, Jeanne, 186
Shepard, Karen, 21
Skjeie, Hege, 13, 221–22, 300 (n. 2)
Smeal, Eleanor, 38–39
Smith, Linda, 43
Social feminism, 25
Social housekeeping, 28, 29, 30, 44, 294 (n. 14)
Social status of legislators, 81–83, 219, 299–300 (n. 6)
Social welfare, 21, 23, 40, 65, 69, 120, 144, 149, 151, 154, 157, 164, 166, 181, 286–87, 297 (n. 20)
Soviet Union, 35, 40
Speier, Jackie, 20
Stanley, Jeanie, 191–92
Stanton, Elizabeth Cady, 42
State legislators. *See* Arizona state legislators; California state legislators
Stereotypes. *See* Gender stereotypes
Stone, Ann, 294 (n. 14)
STOP-ERA, 42
Suffrage movement. *See* Woman suffrage movement
Supreme Court, U.S., 15, 34–35, 63, 249
Sweden, 300 (n. 2)
Symington, Fife, 54

Tamerius, Karin, 159–60, 184
Taxes, 144, 146, 152, 154, 165, 171, 291
Taylor, Ella, 304 (n. 4)
Teen pregnancy, 167
Temperance movement, 28, 29, 297 (n. 16)
Texas, 19, 64, 191
Thomas, Clarence, 15, 19, 34–35, 295 (n. 20)
Thomas, Norman, 105–6, 218
Thomas, Sue, 98–99, 105, 157, 167, 176, 187, 221, 299 (n. 2)
Thorne, Barrie, 293 (n. 4)
Tokenism, 220, 221, 230, 245
"Token" minority, 4–5, 55
Toles, Elsie, 79
Traditionalistic subculture, 61, 66
Trustee relationship with constituents, 96, 100, 101, 105–9, 298–99 (n. 1), 300 (nn. 6–8)
Tucker, Cynthia, 205 (n. 20)

Unruh, Jesse, 57, 75, 76
Utah, 64

Vega, Arturo, 156–57
*Vindication of the Rights of Women* (Wollstonecraft), 252
Violence against women, 2, 23–24, 76, 120, 124–25, 126, 139, 149, 150, 166, 182
Voting rights, 23–29, 33–34
Vuich, Rose Ann, 75, 76

Wages: of black females, 22; gender gap in, 22; and educational attainment, 23; of state legislators, 57, 58
Wahlke, John, 96, 105, 107, 298 (n. 1)
Warner, Carolyn, 297 (n. 17)
Warren, Earl, 62
Washington, Paula G., 305 (n. 2)
Washington (state), 43
Waters, Maxine, 297 (n. 14)
WCTU. *See* Women's Christian Temperance Union
Welch, Susan, 98, 138, 156, 157, 176
Welfare reform. *See* Social welfare
*What Eight Million Women Want* (Dorr), 28–29
Whicker, Marcia, 187, 191, 192
Whip, Rosemary, 222
Whitmire, Kathy, 19
Willard, Frances, 28, 294 (n. 14)
Wilson, Pete, 296 (n. 6)
Witt, Linda, 13, 46–47, 49
Wollstonecraft, Mary, 252
Woman-centered analysis, 25
Woman suffrage movement, 28–29, 42–43, 51, 78, 297 (n. 16)
Women: shared experiences of, 20–21, 36–38, 124–25, 130, 295 (n. 17); as constituency group, 113–33
Women officeholders/politicians. *See* Female officeholders/politicians
Women's Christian Temperance Union (WCTU), 28
Women's groups, 218, 307 (n. 1)
Women's health care, 16, 166, 167, 249–50
Women's interests: objective vs. subjective criteria for, 36–37; points of conflict on, 36–46; representation of, by legislators, 36–46, 123–33; and relationship between personal and political, 37–38; and feminism, 38–39, 120, 300 (n. 1); and gender gap, 38–41, 115, 131; and differences among women, 41–43, 148; and gender polarization, 44; utility of sex and gender distinctions in, 44–45, 46; and gender stereotypes, 45; and liberal and/or Democratic agenda, 69; and California Legislative Women's Caucus, 76, 91, 92, 127–28, 132; institutional status of legislators "acting for" women, 224–30, 246, 307 (n. 2); and meaning of representing women, 230–41; as uncrystallized, 250–51. *See also* Women's issues

Women's issues: and female politicians/office-holders, 2, 6, 7, 14–18, 30, 114–15, 120–33, 140–48, 156, 164–84, 216–17, 233–34, 237–39, 297 (n. 19), 301 (n. 8); avoidance of, by female officeholders, 3, 43, 114, 122, 132–33, 221–22; and male politicians/officeholders, 6, 15, 17, 120–33, 140–48, 176–80, 216–17, 233–34, 237–39; lists and descriptions of, 14, 16–17, 23–24, 120, 290; media portrayal of, 17; in political advertisements, 17; public opinion polls on, 17–18, 138; poverty and welfare as, 23; and feminism, 38–39, 120, 138–39, 166–69, 180–84, 217, 300 (n. 1); definition of, 40–41, 164, 166–67; and liberal and/or Democratic agenda, 69; lack of recognition of, by legislators, 121–22, 301 (n. 8); normative misgivings about, 122, 132–33; policy preferences of legislators on, 140–48, 226, 233, 237–39, 244; as policy priorities of legislators, 164–84, 226–27, 233–34; and Arizona state legislators, 169–84, 216–17, 233–34, 237–39; and California state legislators, 169–84, 216–17, 233–34, 237–39; leadership of legislators on, 170–75; committee work on, by legislators, 176–80; bills sponsored on, 178; and feminist policy activity, 180–84, 217, 227, 229, 234, 305 (n. 13); institutional status of legislators "acting for" women, 224–30, 246, 307 (n. 2); and meaning of representing women, 230–41. *See also* Female officeholders/politicians; Women's interests; *and specific issues*
Women's Political Action Group, 158
*Women's Voting Guide*, 158
Woods, Harriett, 31
Woolsey, Lynn, 21
Workplace. *See* Occupational status
Wright, Gerald, 69, 296 (nn. 7, 9)

Yeakel, Lynn, 19–20
"Year of the Woman" (1992), 13, 16, 45
Young Women's Christian Association (YWCA), 28
YWCA. *See* Young Women's Christian Association

Zeiger, Richard, 77
Zeigler, Harmon, 158
Zerilli, Linda, 40